CHRONICLES OF MAN

ILLUSTRATED HISTORY 1940-1971

ISBN 978-1-907945-98-4

Lily Publications

Published in the Isle of Man by
Lily Publications Ltd.
PO Box 33
Ramsey
Isle of Man
IM99 4LP
www.lilypublications.co.uk

TOWER INSURANCE CO. LTD. 1940 TO 1971

The Grand Opening

DIRECTORS AND COMPANY officials and guests at the opening this week in Athol Street of the new Tower Insurance office building.

In 1948 Tower Insurance was purchased by current owners, the RSA Insurance Group, and shortly after, it acquired new offices in Athol Street, Douglas.

Tower Insurance has always maintained its focus on providing insurance for the needs of the people and businesses on the Isle of Man and has expanded over the years to become the market leader in general insurance products.

RATIONING BEGINS AND INTERNEES ARRIVE

1940
- Germany invades Holland, Belgium, France, Luxembourg and The Netherlands and The Battle of Britain commences
- Rationing introduced in Britain
- US magazine *Billboard* publishes the first record pop chart

Just two decades after the end of the Great War the Isle of Man is again feeling the full effect of the conflict in human terms. After a winter of "all quiet on the Western Front," the might of the German army has swept through the Low Countries and into France, encircling British and Allied forces around Dunkirk. We have seen the miracle of the evacuation in which the Steam Packet ships have played a valiant part, but at a cost of three fine vessels and the lives of many Manx seamen. We have followed the aerial battles over southern England as R.A.F. fighters withstood the onslaught of the Luftwaffe, and we have been moved by the inspiring oratory of Prime Minister Winston Churchill. Britain now stands alone, and many of our young men and women have left the Island to prepare for the long conflict ahead. Some of our young men have already been killed in action, while at home the war is aready beginning to touch our lives. We have this report.

Everyone recorded in the National Registration Census of last September has been issued with a National Identity Card and a Ration Book. January saw the War Committee, through the Food Division, introduce the first food rationing with sugar being limited to 12 oz. per person per week. Since then both tea and butter have been rationed. To help make the Island more independent for its food supplies, farmers are to be paid £2 per acre for bringing hitherto uncropped land into cultivation.

It has become clear that the Isle of Man is to become a place of internment for thousands of those with German or Italian connections. There will be no huge internment camps that swelled the Island population in the Great War; instead sections of boarding houses in various parts of the Island are being commandeered and fenced off.

The Island has experienced its first air raid alerts, while the threat of invasion by German forces massing across the English Channel has seen the formation of the Local Defence Volunteers, now the Home Guard. These are stirring times, but everyone seems to have adopted a grimly cheerful attitude to the situation and are determined to play their part, no matter what Adolf Hitler may have in store. In August the 'Isle of Man Times' launched an appeal to Manxmen everywhere to donate sufficient money to purchase a Spitfire. The response was overwhelming. Money poured in from many parts; Spitfire parties, dances and swimming galas were held. A total of £10,637 was raised, sufficient with a small Government subsidy, to purchase two of these fine aircrafr. Lord Beaverbrook, Minister of Aircraft Production, promised that the Spitfires will be named 'Manxland' and 'North Barrule' and will be in action with front line squadrons of the Royal Air Force.

HOLIDAY CAMPS TAKEN OVER
It appears that the well-laid plans of the War Office includes the take-over of many of the Island's facilities for use as training bases for the long conflict ahead. First to be taken over is Cunningham's Holiday Camp in Douglas for use by the Royal Navy. As early as last September, an advanced party of naval officers arrived to make preparations to receive hundreds of seaman boys transferred from training ships eleswhere, and brought together in what has been named H.M.S. St George. In fact, so many arrived that Howstrake Holiday Camp in Onchan was used as temporary accommodation. The boys are mostly aged 16 and are making the Royal Navy their career, having signed on for 12 years. At H.M.S. St George they will learn the basic rudiments of seamanship before specialising in such areas as communications. Already the young men in naval uniform have become a familar sight as they march from their 'ship' to the Ballakermeen High Schools. They are the first pupils of the new schools designed for the re-organistaion of secondary education on the Island which has now had to be delayed. The use of Ballakermeen classrooms for instruction purposes means that all the boys can be accomodated at Cunningham's Camp. The Howstrake Camp has become The Royal Marines School of Music, where the young musicians are trained for ceremonial occasions. The bright buildings have been camouflaged with drab paint.

OFFICER CADETS IN TRAINING.
The Villiers Hotel and neighbouring properties on the Loch Promenade are now occupied by officer cadets who have been selected for training as officers in infantry tactics, map-reading and administration. The car park in Lord Street is being used by military transport and Bren-gun carriers. The Island's varied terrain and weather is ideal, and the cadets undertake a rigorous 17-week course designed to develop physical fitness and leadership. The course ends with a Battle Week spent in remote parts of the Island in which the cadets are finally assessed for their suitability. Those who successfully complete the course are then commissioned and posted to regiments within the Army.

The realistic training results in serious accidents, especially when live ammunition and pyrotechnics are

A view of the Ballakermeen High Schools, taken last autumn. Upon completion, the classrooms are being used by H.M.S. St George to instruct young sailors who have chosen the Royal Navy as their career. (Frank Cowin Library)

being used. To cope with accidents and other medical cases from the O.C.T.U., the Hotel Majestic in Onchan has been converted into a fully-equipped Military Hospital staffed by the Royal Army Medical Corps and nurses from the Queen Alexandra's Imperial Military Nursing Service. The ballroom is now a surgical ward with 40 beds, while the dining room has been converetd into a medical ward with over 80 wards. Cases from other miltary units on the Island are also admitted.

A YEAR OF SHIPWRECKS
In severe weather which hit the Island in January, a Fleetwood trawler was wrecked at Bulgham Bay with the loss of her entire twelve-man crew. It was the first of a series of shipwrecks on the Island during the year. A Liverpool coaster went aground at Fort Island in a storm and two of her nine-man crew, father and son, were lost. A Northern Ireland coaster was wrecked at Maughold, fortunately without loss of life. One of the most dramatic rescues of modern times took place in February as a result of the passenger vessel 'Ulster Queen' running aground to the north of Maughold Head in thick fog. On board were 93 passengers and 53 crew. In the middle of a bitterly cold night three of the ship's lifeboats were lowered and transferred mainly the women and children to the Duke of Lancaster which was standing by two miles off shore. By 5.15 a.m. the Ramsey lifeboat Lady Harrison arrived and helped to transfer the remainder of the passengers. Nine of the crew were found in lifeboats and were picked up and brought into Ramsey. The rest of the crew were rescued by breeches-buoy by the Ramsey Rocket Brigade. Apart from an Alsatian dog, all lives were saved and the Ramsey lifeboat under Coxswain John Comish has been accredited with the saving of 60 lives. After nearly a month, the 'Ulster Queen' was refloated.

HEAVY SNOWFALL
In what has been one of the severest winters for many years, heavy snow fell at the end of January. In some places drifts of 10 feet blocked roads and railway lines.

Kirk Michael was marooned for eleven days and flying operations at Jurby were halted for a week because of the snow-covered airfield. In Douglas huge waves destroyed parts of the stone wall protecting the sunken gardens on Loch Promenade. And gales prevented the Steam Packet vessel 'Rushen Castle' from making port in Douglas. She was storm-tossed off the west coast of the Island for 71 hours. Her passengers included the Lieutenant-Governor, Earl Granville, and his daughter.

DISASTROUS FIRES
In February fire gutted a big private residence in Douglas. It was 'Knottfield' in Woodbourne Road, the home of Mr and Mrs Albert Rowell. Mr Rowell led three housemaids through the smoke to safety from their bedrooms on the upper floors. Albert and his brother Harold own a string of sweet shops in the town and are both keen competitors in the Manx Grand Prix. Riding Nortons, Albert came third in the 1937 Senior race while Harold came seventh. In May another fire badly damaged the premises of men's outfitters Lay and Company in Duke Street, Douglas. The fire occurred early in the morning and the upper floors of the building were gutted and the roof collapsed. The ground floor was flooded but most of the stock was saved.

FIRE BRIGADES REORGANISED
Amongst the many concerns of the War Comittee is the state of the Island's fire brigades. In February the Local Government (Fires) Act came into force, creating seven Fire Authority areas. Fire-fighting equipment has been pooled and spread equally throughout the Island. An Auxiliary Fire Service has also been formed and the call for volunteers resulted in 140 men coming forward for training by the Douglas Brigade in the Barrack Street Mission Hall. Equipment is very limited and it is likely to be some time before additional vehicles and trailer-pumps are received.

INCREASE IN AIR SERVICES
From April the skeleton service introduced last year has been substantially increased with seven daily flights from Liverpool, one of which continues to Belfast. The service is available to local residents but the majority of passengers are officers visiting the Island in connection with the many camps and stations set up on the Island by the War Office.

In March Ronaldsway became the home of the R.A.F.'s Ground Defence School. Men are billeted along Castletown Promenade and within the town itself. Officers taking the course are accommodated in the Fort Island (Golf Links) Hotel which is also used as a school for instruction in the use of Lewis, Browning and Bofors guns. Firing butts have been built on Langness and, near the Lighthouse, machine-gun positions have been built. Air-to-ground firing takes place here, firing at drogues towed by Wallace aircraft out to sea. The course is short and intensive, the airmen then being posted to defend R.A.F. airfields.

The 'Ulster Queen' high and dry on the rocks of Maughold Head. The Ramsey lifeboat 'Lady Harrison' assisted in the rescue of the 146 passengers and crew.
(R. and L. Kelly Collection)

BOOMING ECONOMY

In spite of the Island's wartime difficulties the Manx economy is booming. Presenting his 1940 Budget to Tynwald, the Governor said that the Manx exchequer had a record surplus of £100,000 for 1939-40 and the economy had performed beyond expectation. His Excellency admitted that the main reason was the boost given to Government revenues by the large number of German and Italian aliens interned on the Island.

In September steps were taken to follow the British Government which has introduced Purchase Tax to help off-set war costs. This will inevitably lead to higher costs of goods and merchandise in the shops. Cigarettes have gone up 2d a packet to 8_d. The new tax is estimated to bring in £70,000 to the Government exchequer.

DISMAL VISITING SEASON

The visiting season has already become a wartime casualty. In February the Publicity Board forecast optimistically the possibility of up to 50% of the usual visitor numbers arriving in the summer. In fact, there only 23,000. Nevertheless, the Steam Packet has had packed sailings bringing aliens for the internment camps. A local girl home on leave has reported that one of the crew of a German bomber, killed when it was shot down over the north-east of England, was called Georg Meier. Whether or not he is the winner of last year's Senior T.T. cannot be comfirmed, but it does beg the question: "Where is the valuable Senior T.T. Trophy?"

FIRST AIR RAID ALERT

For the purpose of giving air raid warnings the Isle of Man is part of the North-West area which includes Liverpool and Belfast. When an enemy or unidentified aircraft is reported in the area the sirens are sounded so that civilians can take cover and local defence members take up their positions. Practices have been organised by Chief Constable Major Young who is responsible for the Island's Air Raid Precautions. However, there was considerable confusion when the first real alert was given shortly after noon on Saturday, 31st August. Many regarded the sirens were being sounded for another practice and were not taken seriously. This led to a stern warning from the Chief Constable who complained about pedestrians walking the streets while cars and buses continued on their journeys. In future all alerts are to be taken seriously and there will be no more practices. Local people in the Dalby area have reported that on the night of 18th September a lone German aircraft dropped four high explosive bombs causing large craters, though without damage or injury. It is thought the crew were lost and jettisoned the bombs before returning to base.

FLEETWOOD TO BE WARTIME PORT

Heavy bombing has caused havoc in the Liverpool dock area which is often heavily congested with convoys of ships waiting to be unloaded. The Royal Navy has mined the Mersey to prevent U-boats approaching the port, and added to this are aerial mines dropped by the Luftwaffe. Since the outbreak of war a daily service has been maintained by the Rushen Castle supported by the Snaefell and Victoria. But on 27th December, when bound for Douglas with 200 passengers, the Victoria was struck by a magnetic mine and holed when nine miles north-west of the Bar Light. A nearby trawler took most of the passengers on to Douglas while the rest returned to Liverpool by a pilot boat. There were no casualties and the Victoria was towed back to Liverpool for repairs. This incident, together with the hazards and congestion of Liverpool, has resulted in the Steam Packet announcing that in future Fleetwood will be used for all services to and from the Island. All passengers are subject to strict security at the port.

FIRST WAR CASUALTIES

By the end of the year, notification has been received that 66 men and one woman have been killed by enemy action or are missing, presumed killed.

Totals from the Armed Forces are as follows:

BRITISH ARMY
12, including those lost in France and the evacuation

ROYAL AIR FORCE
3, in flying operations

ROYAL NAVY
11, lost when ships were sunk

MERCHANT NAVY
40, including 33 Steam Packet men at Dunkirk

W.R.N.S.
1, killed by enemy aircraft

In addition eight have died on active service, including two in accidents not connected with the war.

1940 NEWS IN BRIEF

FEBRUARY
20 - Water scheme for south of Island adopted by Tynwald.

APRIL
5 - Spanish Head has been purchased anonymously for the Manx nation and has been placed in the care of the Society for the Preservation of the Manx Countryside. The mystery benefactor bought the area from Mr J. T. Kelly of Port St Mary, who himself gave Harry Kelly's cottage to the Manx nation in 1937.
9 - Death of Miss Florrie Forde, one of the great ladies of music hall. She was 65, and collapsed and died after singing to an audience of Servicemen in Aberdeen. Appearing mostly at the Derby Castle during the past 36 years, she was a great favourite. She loved the Island and had a holiday cottage at Niarbyl.
9 - Germans invade Denmark and Norway.
18 - Poor Law Commission recommended Flat Rate for whole Island.

MAY
10 - Holland and Belgium invaded.
10 - Winston Churchill replaces Neville Chamberlain as Prime Minister.
22 - Local Defence Volunteers formed.

28 - DUNKIRK EVACUATION begins. Three Steam Packet vessels sunk.

JUNE
1 - Norman Lewis Daugherty of Bride, first conscientious objector, had his appeal refused by Tribunal.
11 - Mussolini declares war on France and Britain.
14 - Germans enter Paris.
16 - Two I.O.M. Air Services DH Rapides abandoned at Bordeaux. Captain Higgins and Captain Greenhalgh escaped to England by fishing boat.

JULY
5 - Honorary degree of M.A. conferred on Mr Wm Cubbon, Curator of the Manx Museum, at Liverpool University.
10 - Luftwaffe and R.A.F. meet in first air battles over Channel.

AUGUST
7 - Italians continue to advance into British Somaliland from Abyssinia.

SEPTEMBER
6 - 41st Battery of Manx Regiment credited with shooting down two German Dornier bombers.
7 - War Risks Insurance extended to Isle of Man.
30 - Blitz of London begins

NOVEMBER
30 - Blitz of industrial cities begins. Coventry devastated by a night of bombs.

MONA'S QUEEN

33 MANX CREW AND 3 SHIPS LOST AT DUNKIRK

Three Steam Packet vessels sunk, 33 crew lost, but over 26,000 British and allied troops rescued. These are the grim statistics of recent epic events. With the main part of the British Expeditionary Force trapped in northern France by the rapidly advancing German army, the order was given to commence the evacuation of surviving troops through the port and beaches of Dunkirk. Operation Dynamo began on 26th May and hundreds of ships of all shapes and sizes were involved - from large passenger ferries to paddle-steamers and even river boats. Many were lost in the great rescue bid by constant air attacks by the Luftwaffe. The first ship to arrive at Dunkirk was the elderly Mona's Isle under Royal Navy command. During an air raid she embarked 1,420 troops and set sail for Dover. She was fired on by shore batteries and machine-gunned from the air. There were casualties among those on her crowded decks but she reached Dover and was greeted as the first ship to complete the round trip. The Mona's Isle successfully survived a second trip and brought out a further 1,200 soldiers.

Another of the early arrivals was the King Orry which was also flying the White Ensign. She embarked 1,100 troops and left Dunkirk in the early hours of the 27th. She, too, was hit by shore batteries and suffered damage and casualties, but reached Dover by noon. She then returned to Dunkirk and, as she entered the port, came under heavy air attacks resulting in the steering and all bridge instruments being put out of action. It soon became clear the ship was in danger of sinking and, to prevent her being a hazard to other ships, the captain managed to take her out of the harbour. The engine room began to flood and the King Orry sank early the following morning. The crew, including four Manx engineers, were rescued.

Since the Blitzkreig of the Low Countries began on 10th May, the Mona's Queen, under Captain Radcliffe Duggan and manned by Steam Packet crew, had been on duty virtually non-stop. First, she was ordered to Rotterdam to take on Dutch soldiers but by the time she arrived the port was an inferno and covered in a pall of smoke. On the way back to Dover, Captain Duggan was diverted to Ostend and the Mona's Queen was loaded with soldiers and refugees of many nationalities who were brought safely to Folkestone. The Mona's Queen was sent next to Boulogne, this time loaded with 250 tons of explosives accompanied by Irish and Welsh Guards. Their mission was to blow up the port's installations before the arrival of the Germans. Arriving at Boulogne, a chain gang was formed by Chief Officer R. Clucas to man-handle the explosives onto the quayside. While this was happening, retreating troops, many in a sorry state, were scrambling on board. As they were leaving the quayside Stuka dive-bombers attacked the town, but Dover was reached in safety. The Mona's Queen was the last ship to leave Boulogne and, on 22nd May, Captain Duggan and his crew received a message from Admiral Ramsay of Dover Command congratulating them on their brave efforts.

On 26th May, the beginning of Operation Dynamo, Captain Duggan received orders to proceed to Dunkirk. When within two and a half miles of the port the Mona's Queen came under fire from the Calais batteries now in German control. Slight damage was done and after a change in course she was attacked by two dive-bombers, both of which were shot down by R.A.F. Hurricanes. At the pier the Mona's Queen took on board 1,200 soldiers and returned to Dover on the night of 27th May. Captain Duggan was then relieved for a well-earned rest. Under the command of the highly-experienced Captain Archibald Holkham, the Mona's Queen was ordered back to Dunkirk. At 5.30 a.m. on the 28th, she was hit by an aerial mine which struck her just aft of the funnel. The explosion split the vessel in two and she sank in 90 seconds. Of her 56 crew, the captain and 31 others reached the safety of one of the ship's lifeboats but 24, mostly from the engine room, were either killed or drowned; 20 were Manxmen.

The Fenella, under Captain Walter J. Cubbon and crewed by Steam Packet men, arrived in 'Hell's Alley' on 28th May and embarked 650 troops, She then came under a massive air attack during which she was hit by three bombs in quick succession. She was badly damaged and holed below the waterline by flying concrete, resulting in the engine room being flooded. The ship was hastily abandoned and sank soon afterwards. Of the 48 crew, 33 were saved and returned to Dover where one died from severe wounds. Of the 16 who perished, all but three were from the Island. Fenella's sister ship, Tynwald, evacuated more British and Allied soldiers than any other ship in-volved in Operation Dynamo. First under the command of Cap-tain Wilfred A. Qual-trough, and then Captain John H. Whiteway, the Tyn-wald made four perilous trips beginning on 28th May and ending on 4th June when the evacuation was brought to a halt. On that day she was the last to return to England, bringing with her 3,000 French troops. They brought her total which she saved from Dunkirk to 8,953.

The Manxman made two trips to Dunkirk and accounted for 2,394 men. Both the Lady of Mann and the Ben My Chree, the two largest Steam Packet ships played a major role in the Dunkirk evacuation, making good use of their speed and manoeuvrability. Each of these fine vessels

(Inset) Hit by an aerial mine as she returned to Dunkirk, the 'Mona's Queen' sank rapidly with the loss of 24 lives. (Main picture) Survivors from the 'Mona's Queen' escaped in one of the ship's lifeboats. (Photographs via Louis Bridson)

evacuated over 4,000 troops. On her first visit to Dunkirk on 31st May, the Lady, commanded by Captain Thomas C. Woods, was under fire for six hours while she loaded at the pier, suffering damage from both shore batteries and air attacks. Her gunners claimed one enemy aircraft shot down. The Lady was back at Dunkirk on 1st June, and was on her way again the following day when she was ordered to return to Dover because of a lack of waiting troops. Her final visit was made on 4th June when she returned with 1,500 casualties from the devastated port. The Ben was also kept busy and completed two round trips under Captain George Woods. It then became necessary to re-crew the ship and Captain Woods was replaced by Captain Thomas E. Cain, D.S.C. He had been Chief Officer on the Tynwald and was a veteran of the Great War. Captain Cain was mentioned in despatches on six occasions and was awarded the D.S.C. for the part he played in sinking a U-boat in 1917, when he was captain of the paddler Mona's Queen. On the night of 2nd June, and with his new crew on board, Captain Cain set out for a further visit to Dunkirk. However, when crossing the Channel, the Ben came into collision with a block ship and had to return to port as a result of the damage caused.

The success of the great evacuation in these dark days gives hope for the future. Already the evacuation is being called a miracle. Over 338,000 British and Allied troops have been saved and are ready to fight again some time in the future. Of these, 26,449, one in every 14, were saved by Steam Packet vessels and their gallant crews. Their normal peace-time duties are far removed from the horrors of being shelled, dive-bombed and machine-gunned. They have also had to endure endless hours at their stations with little chance of respite. Future generations will admire the men for their bravery and the part they played in another great chapter in the history of the Isle of Man Steam Packet Company. But the price has been high.

OPERATION ARIEL

Of the ten Steam Packet ships commandeered for war service, two were unable to play their part in the evacuation of Dunkirk. The Manx Maid, with a Royal Navy crew, and the Viking were both under repair at the time, the latter as a result of being bombed in the Thames Estuary. But both ships were to be involved in Operation Ariel, the evacuation of ports along the west coast of France. The Manx Maid embarked 3,000 French troops at Brest, nearly twice her normal passenger limit, and brought them to Southampton. Meanwhile, the Viking under Captain J. P. 'Ginger' Bridson, was present at the evacuation of both Le Havre and Cherbourg. She was sent later to Guernsey and evacuated over 3,000 islanders, including 1,800 children which was almost the entire child population. On her journey back to Weymouth the Viking was strafed by German fighters but the purser, Edgar Bishop, manned the anti-aircraft gun they had on board and helped keep the fighters at bay. The crew had been working non-stop for 18 hours and Captain Bridson dispensed what whisky was on board to fortify his men. Purser Edgar Bishop has been awarded the D.S.C. for the part he played in defending the ship.

Also taking part in the operation was the Manxman, with Captain Philip B. Cowley as master. Like other ships of the Steam Packet, the Manxman had operated as a 'personnel carrier' carrying troops to Le Havre and Cherbourg in the early months of the war. Now the process was in reverse. The Manxman was back again helping in the evacuation. On her final visit to Cherbourg she was fully laden at the pier when she came under fire from approaching tanks. A Royal Navy destroyer stood by to protect her as she made her escape, the last vessel to leave Cherbourg. On 16th June, the Lady of Mann joined in the operation and paid visits to Le Havre, Cherbourg and Brest. With 5,000 troops on board, and during an air attack, she was the last ship to leave Le Havre. Shortly afterwards, Operation Ariel was brought to a halt.

MEDALS FOR BRAVERY

In recognition of the tremendous courage and bravery shown by the Steam Packet crews, just a few have been chosen for awards. From the Mona's Queen, Captain R. Duggan and Radio Officer E. H. Ambler have both been awarded the Distinguished Service Cross, while the ship's bo'sun, Edgerton Watterson, receives the Distinguished Service Medal. Captain J. H. Whiteway of the Tynwald is awarded the D.S.C. together with his Chief Officer, A. Watterson and Radio Officer G. P. Mason, the latter of the Marconi Company. A/B Seaman T. Gribbin receives the D.S.M., and mentioned in despatches are purser W. E. Lister, carpenter J. Gawne and seaman A. J. Allen.

This dramatic photograph shows the 'Tynwald' flying the signal 'Full Speed' as she leaves Dunkirk with another load of troops. In the foreground can be seen the mast and funnel of the 'King Orry' which sank as the result of enemy air attacks. The 'Tynwald' had the distinction of rescuing nearly 3,000 soldiers, more than any other vessel taking part in the evacuation. Not so lucky was her sister ship 'Fenella' which was sunk by bombing during her first visit to Dunkirk. Sixteen of her crew perished.
(Photograph via Louis Bridson)

ISLAND ADJUSTS TO WARTIME SITUATION

The rationing of sugar in January (12oz) was followed in July by tea being limited to 2oz per person. This was followed in October by butter being rationed at 3oz per week, but this has since been reduced to 2oz. Apart from this there seem to be few shortages of other foods, though farmers are being subsidised to bring more land into cultivation, while a 'Dig for Victory' campaign is aimed at gardeners to make full use of allotments. Newspapers are now much slimmer and are only available to order. Imports of newsprint have had to be reduced because of Germany's U-boat blockade of Britain and the need to import more vitally important materials. Everyone is being encouraged to save waste paper to enable it to be recycled. Local authority workmen, scouts and guides are collecting bundles from home while children are playing their part in making school collections. One consequence is that very little paper is available in chip shops. People are collecting their meals in cooking basins wrapped in a cloth.

There is no petrol rationing as yet, but it is sure to come. One serious problem is that both petrol and fuel are being smuggled out of the Island, while private individuals or merchants have been caught trying to ship tea, sugar and other foodstuffs, presumably to sell on the black market. This is treated seriously and the authorities have warned offenders that they face imprisonment for breaking various emergency restrictions. The need for tighter controls has also been demonstrated by buyers from England buying up large quantities of fresh fish landed on the Island. People are being encouraged to stockpile at least one week's supply of food in their homes - in case there is an invasion. The authorities say they will try to keep deliveries of bread and milk going for 'as long as possible.' Provision has been made for the issuing of 'Iron Rations' for those unable to store a food reserve. They have been told to register their needs with the Food Executive Officer in their respective towns and villages. 'Iron Rations' will not be available in country districts, presumably because of problems of distribution.

THE BLACK-OUT

One of the effects of the black-out has been that many churches throughout the Island are holding Evensong in the afternoon this autumn. It means the churches will not have to finance black-out screens for their windows. The move also acknowledges that many people don't want to venture out in total darkness. There will be very little night time private motor traffic on Douglas promenade this winter, either. Speeds are being restricted to 10 m.p.h. and only side lights can be used. This is to to avoid light being seen out to sea from an area which has acquired considerable military significance. Public safety is also a logical reason for the restrictions, given the total absence of street lighting and the narrowness of the promenade now that barbed wire entanglements have been erected half way across the promenade to secure internment and military camps. The Government Order, applicable from half an hour after sunset or 7 p.m., whichever is the sooner, came into effect on 22nd October last. The masking of headlamps on all vehicles, whether private or on official duty, was made compulsory on 1st February.

FEAR OF PARACHUTISTS

Early in May, Mr Sargeaunt, the Government Secretary, received warning of the possibility of enemy parachutists landing on islands around the British coast and creating bases from which to attack the mainland. While nothing happened, local authorities and farmers responded to the Air Ministry request for obstructions to be placed on roadways and in large fields. This was to make it difficult for the landing of aircraft troop carriers. Port St Mary, for example, arranged to place lamp standards across roads. Motorists were warned to take extra care in the black-out. Fields were scattered with old farm machinery and oil drums.

To deny potential invaders knowledge of precisely where they are, the Highway Board removed all road signs including the historic ones dating back to the 1760s when the measuring of the Island's earthen roads began. Found throughout the Island, these ancient milestones, with details etched or cut into them, are made of limestone, sandstone or slate according to the locality in which they are found. About 50 were removed and it is doubtful if they will ever be returned. The more recent milestones with metal facings should be less of a problem.

AIR ALERTS

On moonlit nights the drone of German bombers can be heard overhead. There were alerts on the night of 26th October and on the nights of 20th and 21st December. On the latter nights the alerts lasted for five hours. Judging from the glare over the eastern horizon it was apparent that Liverpool was being heavily attacked. It has brought the horror of the Blitz a little nearer home and the chance of being bombed deliberately or accidentally cannot be ignored. Despite many demands there is still no properly organised A.R.P defence in place. There is plenty of advice to householders, such as covering windows with thin wire mesh or strips of sticky paper to prevent the hazard of splintered glass entering rooms. Meanwhile, many householders are building private air raid shelters in parts of their gardens.

Local authorities at last are providing public air raid shelters for those caught away from home which is still considered to be the safest place. Three large shelters have been built in the sunken gardens of Loch Promenade, roofed with concrete reinforced by railway lines. Other shelters in the town can now be found under the Villa Marina Colonnade, York Road bus depot, Shaw's Brow and next to Noble's Hall. Other designated shelters include hotel basements and the cellar of the Town Hall. Outside of Douglas, towns and villages are being provided with their own shelters. Peel now has five shelters capable of accommodating 900 people. Old tunnels under Castle Street, reputedly used by smugglers centuries ago, have been adapted for use. Probably the most exotic place of shelter of all is the old dungeons of Castle Rushen but they will not be available at night.

For the treatment of air raid casualties, 35 First Aid stations have been established throughout the Island by the St John Ambulance Association and the local branch of the British Red Cross Society. The stations are all equipped with beds for the injured and are manned by volunteer nurses whose uniforms now include trousers.

The Isle of Man has its own force of volunteers to fight any invader. In May the Secretary of State for War, Mr Anthony Eden, announced on the B.B.C. the Government's intention of raising an unpaid Local Defence Force as part of the defence of the United Kingdom. The raising of such a force in the Isle of Man was authorised immediately by the Lieutenant-Governor, its object being to prepare for any attempt by the enemy to land by parachute or any other means. The official notice from Government Office said that volunteers should be between the ages of 17 and 65, and of reasonable fitness. A total of 1,500 men responded and were asked to give details of their previous experience in weaponry and other military matters. The Island has been organised as a separate Zone under the control of Lieut.-Colonel G. S. Scott, O.B.E. of Western Com-mand. Organised in groups covering the whole Island, the men first attended parades in civilian clothing and wearing arm bands bearing the letters L.D.V. Uniforms of the denim overall type arrived by the end of June. For arms training, use was made of any firearms available including rifles of pre-Great War vintage found in Douglas Police Station, along with 90,000 rounds of ammunition.

With the German invasion fleet massing in French ports across the English Channel, Prime Minister Winston Churchill announced on 28th July that the Local Defence Force was to be re-named the 'Home Guard' and brought to a higher degree of preparedness. On the Island the Zone groups were divided into two Battalions. The 1st Manx Batallion, based in Douglas with about 1,200 men, was divided into A and B Companies, the latter also containing men from Onchan, Braddan and Santon. Officer Commanding 1st Battalion is Deemster S. J. Kneale with Mr A. D. McEvoy as Second in Command. Company Officers are Messrs T. C. Greenfield, J. W. Royston, J. M. Cain, R. T. Wetherill and R. J. Wilkinson. The rest of the Island sectors make up the 2nd Manx Battalion which consists of five separate detachments, each with a Commanding Officer. These are: Ramsey Company i/c Major A. W. Dobbin, D.S.O.; Castletown Company i/c Mr P. D. Kissack; Peel Company i/c Mr G. W. Howie; Laxey Platoon i/c Mr E. Corteen, and Ballaugh-Michael Platoon i/c Mr W. Cain.

The Isle of Man Rifle Association has made its nine rifle ranges available together with rifles and equipment to provide further experience. Other outdoor ranges have been constructed and the Government range at Balna-how, Santon, has also been made available. By the middle of July the more modern Lee Enfield rifle and ammunition became available. Village halls are being put to good use for training sessions and lectures which members attend in their spare time. In addition, most men are required to do guard duty on one night out of eight, from one hour before dusk to one hour after dawn. Fifty-two observation posts have been established to give warning of the landing of parachutists. Improvised road blocks are also manned and patrols are set up to watch over vulnerable areas such as reservoirs, harbour installations and the new telephone radio station at Creg ny Baa. The men now have full uniform and have been issued with protective clothing and blankets for night duties. An Order issued by Government Office forbids the ringing of church bells at any time. They are only to be rung as a method of calling out the Home Guard in an emergency.

Throughout the Island, men have come forward to join the Local Defence Volunteers, later renamed the Home Guard. Here, men of Onchan line up near the Commissioners' Office. Standing in front is Mr George Shaw, history master at the Douglas High School for Boys.
(Manx National Heritage)

ISLAND PROVIDES ACCOMMODATION FOR 14,000 ALIENS

Fourteen thousand enemy aliens have been interned on the Isle of Man. As the Germans swept into northern France at the beginning of May and occupied the Channel ports, a pressing need became apparent to ensure that anyone with German origins did not pose a threat to national security, especially should there be an invasion. The same applied to Italians when they became our enemies. There was little time to waste. Thousands of men and women, aged from 16 to 60, were summoned to appear before hastily convened tribunals. There they were classified roughly according to risk and then sent to make-shift transit camps. While many were shipped to Canada and Australia, the Isle of Man was selected as a secure place of internment within the British Isles. Under the Defence Regulations (Isle of Man) Act, Home Office officials, in co-operation with the Manx Government, created internment camps throughout the Island. Tynwald believed they would make an important contribution to the Manx economy while there was some consolation for boarding-house keepers who would be saved the deprivations of the last war. Nevertheless, there was considerable ill-feeling towards anyone seen to have German or Italian connections, even though they might be enemies of Nazism too. Another reason for hostility was the way Government officials commandeered properties without warning and required them to be vacated almost immediately.

An Internment Camp Division, headed by Government Secretary Mr Bertram Sargeaunt, was set up to administer the camps. Men, unlikely to be called up for military service, were employed as clerks and typists to deal with the mass of documents, forms and communications; others had the duty of arranging tenders with grocers, butchers and farmers for the supply of huge quantities of food. On 15th May, the Camp Division sent out the first batch of letters in buff envelopes marked 'On His Majesty's Service' to the occupiers of hotels and boarding houses along the Mooragh Promenade, Ramsey. The letters gave curt notification that occupiers were to vacate their premises by the end of the week. They had just five days in which to find alternative accommodation. They were permitted to take only the minimum amount of furniture, bedding and personal possessions. Everything else had to be left behind. Government valuers made lists of furniture, fixtures, bedding, cooking utensils and crockery etc. Those evicted were also informed that they would have the rents and rates of their properties paid, plus a small quarterly payment for the use of the household items according to the valuation.

That week the people of Ramsey became accustomed to the sound of pneumatic drills as hundreds of holes were made for the wooden posts which support the miles of barbed wire which now surrounds the MOORAGH CAMP. As the fever of activity came to an end, the *Rushen Castle* tied up at the Queen's Pier with 150 soldiers on board. They have been billeted in the town and guard the camp night and day. Everything was in position for the arrival of the first batch of 823 aliens on the evening of 27th May. They were brought by a Belgian steamer. Townsfolk turned out to watch them being marched from the pier, over the swing bridge and into the camp. The aliens appeared to be a strange mixture - young and old, rich and poor, each carrying from the transit camps what few possessions

they were allowed to keep, packed in suitcases, parcels or bundles. That day the evacuation of Dunkirk was already under way.

Two days later the Belgian steamer arrived at Douglas for the first of three visits, each time packed with the first women aliens. They were entrained for open internment in what is being called RUSHEN CAMP. It includes the whole of Port Erin and Port St Mary. By November, the number of women internees rose to 4,000, thus nearly doubling the local population. Landladies are responsible for organising the accommodation of their new 'guests' for whom they receive £1 1s. a week, well below the normal rate for full board. An additional allowance is paid for extra staff, such as cooks.

While the Mooragh Camp was being prepared, two further camps were being created. Occupiers of 60 boarding houses in the Royal Avenue West area of Onchan were put under short notice to quit while about 34 properties on and behind the Central Promenade, Douglas, were being vacated. The *Rushen Castle*, assisted by the *Victoria,* were kept busy and by the middle of June, ONCHAN CAMP had received 1,200 German aliens and the CENTRAL CAMP nearly 1,000, a number which would be doubled by the end of the month. A non-stop stream of arrivals saw the opening of the PALACE CAMP made up of 28 large boarding houses above the sea front. This camp became the most crowded of all with nearly 3,000 accommodated by the end of June.

The entry of Italy into the war resulted in a further influx of internees. The well-practised machinery saw the METROPOLE CAMP on Queen's Promenade and HUTCHINSON CAMP being made ready by the middle of July. Metropole was used mainly for Italian internees while the first to arrive in Hutchinson were Germans and Austrians. GRANVILLE CAMP and REGENT CAMP on Loch Promenade were also made ready. By October there were 750 men in Granville though Regent remained empty. The small SEFTON CAMP was also occupied though the group of properties known as the FALCON CAMP had not yet been used. The PEVERIL CAMP on Peel promenade was filled with Italian aliens. This brought the number of occupied men's camps to nine. An estimated 10,000 male internees are now being held, in addition to the 4,000 females in the Rushen Camp.

While the net has been cast far and wide to round up those thought to be of the slightest risk to national security there has, nevertheless, been much heart-searching about the inhuman treatment meted out to many of those now classified as aliens. The most dangerous have been put in Category A, including suspected Fifth Columnists, and will be detained for the duration of the war. The vast majority, however, are Categories B and C and are thought by many to be completely harmless. Many of these are refugees, including Jews, who were welcomed to Britain as they escaped the clutches of the Nazis. Others are old and sick. In July, despite the desperate war situation, questions were raised in the House of Commons. Was it right to keep these people behind barbed wire when many could be employed to help the war effort? This led to the Home Office taking the first steps to investigate each individual case through tribunals. The process began in October and already there has been a marked fall in the number of men now detained. Women have also been released from the Rushen Camp. Slow progress, however, is causing a high degree of restlessness in the camps.

MANX REGIMENT IN ACTION

Early in May, 55 gunners were detached from the Regiment and joined the expedition to support Norway against the German invasion. They landed in the Namsos fjord and immediately came under attack by Stuka dive-bombers. After five days the expedition was withdrawn and returned to England, surviving heavy air attacks on the way. The gunners have since been posted to another regiment and replaced by strangers, much to the disappointment of Lieut.-Colonel MacClellan. By then, the rest of the Regiment had been deployed in the south and west of England, 41st Battery providing Troops for the defence of the radar station at Ventnor on the Isle of Wight. All three Batteries undertook intensive firing practice at St Agnes in Cornwall.

August saw what is now being called the 'Battle of Britain' at its height. R.A.F. fighters were locked in battle with the Luftwaffe flying from France. Troops from the Manx Regiment took up defensive positions stretching from Kent to Devon, including Southampton and Portsmouth. While the Hurricanes and Spitfires were in action, the Bofors guns remained silent but there was plenty of opportunity for the gunners to open up. On 12th August, 'Z' Troop of 41st Battery was officially credited with shooting down two enemy aircraft during an attack on the R.A.F. station at Warmwell in Dorset.

During the autumn many changes took place within the Regiment. Major W. S. Valentine took over command of the 42nd and his place as Adjutant of the Regiment was taken over by Captain J. B. Mylchreest. In October, the Regiment was ordered to move to Glasgow, in preparation for embarkation to the Middle East. The men were given three weeks' leave and were given a warm reception back on the Island. They were entertained by the Mayor and Corporation at a civic dinner in the Villa Marina. A farewell dance held in the Palais de Danse was attended by 800 people.

The men returned to Glasgow and on the 15th November the 129th, separated once again from the main part of the Regiment, embarked at Gouroch on the troopship Strathaird filled to capacity with boisterous Australian infantry. The following day saw the 41st and 42nd Batteries and Regimental Headquarters board the Viceroy of India still in its peacetime guise. The ships departed in convoy on a six-week voyage to Egypt via the Cape of Good Hope, stopping at Durban for four days' shore leave. Christmas was celebrated on board the ships as they entered the Gulf of Aden and the Red Sea. The Regiment was re-united at Beni Yusef in the shadow of the Great Pyramid.

The Ben my Chree made two trips to 'Hell's Alley' and is seen here arriving at Folkstone loaded with troops evacuated from Dunkirk.

MANX MAID AT DOVER

BUSY SCENE AT R.A.F. JURBY

Jurby has settled down to a regular routine in the training of aircrew in techniques of bombing and air gunnery. The bombing ranges off Jurby Head are in use every day and the early Bristol Blenheims have been joined by Handley Page Herefords. The accuracy of practice smoke bombs dropped on the targets are recorded from observation huts positioned along the coast. Whitleys and Wellingtons are frequent visitors to the station. They arrive from Operational Training Units in England. Their crews are in the final stages of training before being posted to a Bomber Command squadron. They 'attack' the targets night and day from high, low and medium heights, both in formation and alone.

Air to air gunnery practice also takes place out to sea. Obsolete aircraft such as Westland Wallaces, Hawker Henleys and Fairey Battles are used as target-towers. The targets take the form of a drogue let out on wire from the rear of the aircraft. The gunners operate Vickers machine guns from a manually operated turret with which the short-nosed Blenheim aircraft are equipped. Each trainee gunner fires rounds which have been dipped in paint of different colours. Hits on the drogue can then be identified with individual gunners. The towing aircraft has to release its drogue over the beach or designated area. This operation is particularly dangerous because the pilot has to come in low and reduce speed before releasing the drogue. The danger lies in stalling the aircraft. Already there have been some accidents as a result.

The accommodation at Jurby is already over-crowded so when Manx airmen arrive from initial training stations, and are waiting a posting to a squadron, S.W.O. Radcliffe has no hestitation in allowing them to live at home. Most cycle home to Douglas or Onchan but have to be back at Jurby by 8.00 a.m. each weekday. Many of the staff pilots are Poles who escaped to England. They are accommodated mostly in farm houses in the district and have been befriended by local families despite the language difficulties. The Poles are noted for their fearless flying, and they love to join in a game of football organised on the station. They play with great gusto and are difficult to beat, even when playing in bare feet!

To add to the congestion, Jurby is now host to a night fighter squadron which arrived in November and brought more Poles to the station. Under an English squadron leader, and with British groundcrew, the pilots and gunners formerly belonged to the Polish Forces. They have been assigned to fly Defiant aircraft which have a four-gun turret and are being pressed into service as night fighters. They are sent into action to help in the defence of the North-West, now that Manchester, Liverpool, Belfast and Glasgow are threatened by mass formations of German bombers. They have the duty also of undertaking daylight convoy patrols which arrive north of Ireland as a result of the German occupation of France. One of the Defiants has been lost in a crash, fortunately without loss of life.

People in the north of the Island are becoming used to the amount of flying taking place. Aircraft are in the air every day and they are joined by others from other training stations around the Irish Sea, especially those of Silloth and Millom in Cumberland. It is noticeable also that the number of flying accidents is increasing. They are usually the result of engine failure, pilot error or because of bad visibility which hides the perils of Snaefell and other areas of high ground. It has been estimated that crashes occur on average once a month. Some of those involved are lucky to escape unscathed. Those badly injured or burned are attended to in the sick quarters at Jurby, which is in liaison with the Ramsey Cottage Hospital. During the year five Jurby aircrew have lost their lives including a sergeant pilot of the Polish Forces.

Heavy snowfalls affected the whole Island at the end of January, bringing flying operations at Jurby to a week-long halt. Here can be seen a Fairey Battle (below left) and a Bristol Blenheim Mk1 (below right) caught in snow drifts. (Flt. Lt. Norman Radcliffe)

1941
- Nazis advance through Balkans into Greece
- Death of James Joyce, Ireland's greatest literary figure

1941

PEEL SHAKEN BY RIOT AT 'FASCIST CAMP'

Hundreds of British Fascists detained in the Peveril Camp at Peel have run amok in a week-end of rioting and violence. The situation has become so serious that the Home Office has ordered 50 experienced London policemen to move to Peel and stiffen the military guard. We have this report.

In May the Italian internees in the Peveril Camp were replaced by some 600 so-called Regulation 18b detainees who are mostly members of Sir Oswald Mosley's British Union of Fascists - the 'Blackshirts' - while others are convicted I.R.A. terrorists. When they arrived in Douglas harbour they were greeted by the jeers and catcalls of local people who regard them as traitors. The camp is regarded by many as a hot-bed of intrigue and on Saturday, 20th September, the situation erupted in violence. On the previous Wednesday evening three of the internees, who had been attending a concert in a hall just outside the camp, slipped their guards and disappeared into the night. It was not until the following morning that their absence was discovered and a thorough search began both on and around the Island by the military and local police. It was discovered that a small fishing boat had disappeared from its mooring in Castletown harbour. Its engine was without sparking plugs, according to regulations, but two pairs of oars had been stolen from a warehouse in School Lane. On Saturday afternoon the escapees were picked up by a naval patrol boat seven miles off the Calf of Man and they were then returned to Peel.

Earlier on Saturday the camp had been inspected by an Under Secretary from the Home Office, accompanied by the Camp Commandant. They had been given a rough time and many of the detainees hurled abuse and obscenities at them. It was in this atmosphere that the three escapees, heroes to many, returned to the camp and were locked in cells. This sparked the riot. A demolished stone hedge was used for 'ammunition' along with dust bin lids and even lavatory seats. The guards were targets but they were not permitted to fire back into the camp. The Creg Malin Hotel, across Walpole Road, was an easy target and it took a battering. Many of its windows and slates were smashed and the whole area was littered with debris. As darkness fell the surrounding camp lights were switched on and the whole place was illuminated, making a dramatic and fearful sight for the hundreds of onlookers on the Promenade. It was not until midnight that things began to simmer down. The Home Office ordered an immediate inquiry, questions were asked in the House of Commons, national newspapers reported the 'scandalous affair' and the B.B.C. also reported the incident. The three 'heroes' were found guilty of the theft of the small fishing boat and sentenced to prison on the 'mainland.' A senior police officer from Scotland Yard visited Peel and it was announced that 50 London policemen, experienced in dealing with Mosley's Fascists, were to be drafted in to help the military guards keep control over what locals call the 'Fascists Camp.'

THE DETESTED WOMEN

Matters in Peel are made worse by the visits of women from Rushen Camp who, since May, have been permitted to visit their husbands on a regular basis. The women arrive by coach and are at liberty to shop in the town. Their display of arrogance is matched only by the amount of money they have to spend. Their buying up of large quantities of unrationed food is a sore point with the townsfolk. The women then congregate at the Creg Malin before being escorted into the camp. Hotelier Mr A. E. Ostick is so incensed by their behaviour that he has refused to serve them. Peel Town Commissioners are concerned about the large amounts of food being taken into the camp and it is noted that there seems to be no shortage of beer, judging by the number of deliveries being made to the camp. Another irksome feature is that locals are not permitted to be on the beach while the detainees are bathing. Following the riot, the women's visits have been suspended for a month and will be less frequent in future; also only one small parcel of food will be allowed each visit. The Creg Malin has now been commandeered and will be used for stores and interview rooms. A wooden hut behind the hotel will serve as a waiting room for the women.

MORE TROUBLE IN PEEL

Barely a week after the riot in the Peveril Camp, an Army officer noticed, by chance, a loose sod in a narrow footpath opposite the top end of the camp and passing the guard house. Beneath the sod was a short ladder leading from what appeared to be a tunnel. The hard-pressed Manx police were called to investigate and a team led by Inspector Kneen made an amazing discovery in the front room of No 13, Peveril Road. Floor boards had been cut and below there was a ten foot shaft. With great precision an 18" tunnel had been dug out leading for 25 yards under the road and wire fencing to the pathway directly opposite. The tunnel, through sand and clay, was timbered at intervals and illuminated by an electric light wired to the mains of the house. Obviously there were many collaborators and 18 men who are considered to be the ring leaders are to be transferred to Walton Gaol, Liverpool. They will be escorted by the newly-arrived Metropolitan police. Peel is also to be subject to tighter security and it has been declared a Protected Area. Only residents and those on legitimate business can enter the town; spot checks will be made and identity cards must be shown.

CHANGES AT RUSHEN CAMP

The work of the Tribunals has seen a considerable reduction in the number of internees being held on the Island, including the Rushen Camp. Much of Port St

Women interned in Port St. Mary have been transferred to Port Erin, apart from those who have husbands interned in other camps on the Island. They are now confined to Ballaqueeney and neighbouring boarding houses which have been wired off to form married quarters.
(Manx National Heritage)

the Douglas Head Hotel, Collinson's cafe and even the ticket office of the incline railway. A three-storeyed concrete building is also being built to provide 18 additional classrooms. The Principal Training Officer is J. L. T. Jackson who was a former chief instructor in wireless telegraphy. After recovering from a bout of dysentery which he contracted in Malta, he was commissioned to equip and operate the school. It is estimated the school has cost £3 million to establish and already the whole area is bristling with masts and scanners. Those who complete the course will be posted to Royal Navy ships from battle ships to submarines. Every vessel will require numerous radar operators to use this vital equipment which can locate enemy ships and aircraft beyond visual range.

Mary has been freed of the women held there, but the boarding houses along the promenade and the Ballaqueeney Hotel have been fenced off to form married quarters for the wives held in the Rushen Camp. They have been joined by their husbands from the men's camps. Up to now the wives have travelled on what locals call the 'love trains' to Douglas to meet their husbands in Derby Castle and its grounds. Commandant of the new camp, which opened in May, is Mr Cuthbert, a Divisional Inspector from Scotland Yard. The remaining women from Port St Mary have been transferred to Port Erin. The changes were not to the liking of the formidable Dame Joanna Cruickshank so she has resigned as Rushen Camp Commandant and returned to London. A nurse by training, she ran a strict, though caring, regime for the women in her charge. She had little time for the Chief Constable who has the ultimate responsibility for the camp, and no doubt Major Young will welcome Mr Cuthbert as the new Camp Commandant.

H.M.S. VALKYRIE

The Granville and Regent Internment Camps on Loch Promenade, Doug-las, have been taken over by the Admiralty and commissioned as H.M.S. Valkyrie. Here ratings are being accommodated as they train in the latest 'hush hush' technology of radio detection in what is called the Royal Navy's No 1 Radar Training School. Each morning ranks of the young sailors are marched up to Douglas Head where the school has classrooms in

AIR RAID VICTIMS

Many Manx homes have been bereaved by members of their families being killed by German air attacks on London and Merseyside. Some 14 are known to have lost their lives by the end of May. At the beginning of the month, babies from the bombed areas of Liverpool and Birkenhead were evacuated to the Island. About 90 under-fives are being looked after by members of the Manx Women's Guild either in private homes or hostels. It is estimated that nearly a thousand evacuated children from various parts of England and Scotland are now being cared for in Manx homes. Most of them have been found places in local schools. The Manx Women's Guild has been formed to provide knitted comforts and other articles for Manxmen serving in the fighting forces and also for the relief of civilians affected by the war.

TWO GIRLS DROWNED

Two 12-year-old Douglas girls were drowned while swimming in the sea near Victoria Pier. They got into difficulties after going into the water off the Peveril jetty. Hundreds of people watched as officer cadets and Navy men went to their rescue. But they were both dead from drowning by the time they were brought ashore.

Two Douglas boys had a remarkable escape from death after falling down cliffs below the Marine Drive. Eleven-year-old Dennis Ekin and 15-year-old Colin Savage landed on a ledge eight feet from the high-water mark. Both were injured and spent the night on the ledge. The next day the older boy, despite his injuries, climbed 200 feet to the top of the cliff and alerted Coastguards who rescued his friend.

FIRE DAMAGE

Fire caused serious damage to part of the White City amusement resort on Onchan Head, where thousands of visitors used to have summertime fun before the war. It destroyed the attraction known as the River Caves and threatened the timber-built Onchan Pavilion theatre. In September a fire caused £5,000 worth of damage in the projection room of the Strand Cinema, Douglas, after it had closed for the night.

The Douglas Bay Hotel is now bristling with aerials which are used in the highly secret art of radio detection. Here operators posted to H.M.S. Valkyrie are trained in the Royal Navy's No 1 Radar Training School.
(Manx National Heritage)

DARING ESCAPE FROM MOORAGH CAMP

On the night of Wednesday, 15th October, three Dutchmen, all pro-Nazi, made a bold escape from Mooragh Camp. Two officers in the Dutch mercantile marine and a civilian pilot had been planning the escape for some time with the help of a ladder to climb the barbed-wire fence, and a wooden plank to cross the two rows of fencing. The ladder had been discovered, however, so pliers were used to cut through the fencing. They had attended the six o'clock roll call and waited for dark before making a move. They headed for Ramsey Harbour where they had already noted the position of a small yacht when out on exercise walks. Its engine had been immobilised but they used a pole to get the yacht away and then raised its sails as they left the harbour. They met mountainous seas and had little hope of reaching Dublin where they planned to contact the German Consul. A strong south-westerly gale was blowing.

The absence of the three escapees was noted at roll call on Thursday morning and a massive search was carried out on the Island. Naval patrol vessels and aircraft from Jurby also joined in the search but were hampered by poor visibility. It was not until the next day, Friday, that the yacht was spotted from one of the aircraft. The Dutchmen were drifting helplessly towards St Bees Head where they scrambled ashore, ex-hausted and saturated. A military guard was waiting for them. They were given dry clothes and taken to Whitehaven police station. From there, Manx police escorted them back to Ramsey via Fleetwood. At their trial they were found guilty of stealing the yacht, valued at £300, and committed to Victoria Road Gaol for six months. After serving their sentence they are to be transferred to the Peveril Camp in Peel.

RATIONING BITES DEEPER

The U-boat blockade has started to hit everyone at their meal table. Towards the end of last year butter rationing was added to that of sugar, and the use of milk for the making of ice cream was banned. In January the making of synthetic cream was banned. Families now have to register with a grocer for their rations of preserves, syrup and treacle; sugar has been reduced to 4oz per person and cheese is also rationed at 2oz per person. The Island's food supplies are carefully regulated by the Food Control Office, bearing in mind that thousands of military personnel and internees have also to be fed. November saw the rationing of petrol begin with an allowance of six gallons per month per car. Motorcycles get two gallons. Many cars have been put away for 'the duration' and people are resorting to the steam railway for transport. The Government is also considering putting clothing on coupons. This follows the U.K. Board of Trade limiting the amount of clothing, cloth of all kinds and shoes. The announcement resulted in local shops being invaded, but Earl Granville put a stop to that by closing all relevant shops for three days. They had to report the

View of the Mooragh Internment Camp, Ramsey. In October, three pro-Nazi Dutchmen made a daring escape but were re-captured two days later off the Cumberland coast.
(Manx National Heritage)

exact amount of stock they held and must record all sales in future. Only those holding a Manx identity card can make purchases of reasonable quantities.

MANX GUNNER MEETS ROMMEL

Sergeant Ken Conibear of Douglas has met Field-Marshal Rommel. It happened in a hospital in Athens where Sgt. Conibear is recovering from serious wounds received during the evacuation of Crete. Rommel stopped at his bed and in perfect English enquired where he was from. The British doctor in attendance said he was a Manxman. Rommel seemed unsure what he meant. "Ah, Insel Man," he said when the doctor explained that Conibear was from the Isle of Man. Rommel then stood to attention and gave the Nazi salute.

AIR RAID ALERTS

On the nights of 7th, 15th and 16th April enemy bombers were again over the Island. On the first occasion the sky was illuminated by flares and an incendiary bomb landed near Port Soderick. On the 15th an h.e. bomb caused slight damage to the Cronk Ruagh Sanatorium near Ramsey and the following night a bomb fell near the radio detection station at Scarlett in the south of the Island. Considerable alarm was caused on the night of 8/9th May when two bombs fell on the outskirts of Douglas. One fell at Ballaoates. A bungalow on the corner had its roof damaged and windows blown in. The second bomb exploded in a field above Willaston Corner. A lady was blown out of bed and windows were smashed along Ballanard Road and as far away as Norwood Drive and Park Avenue. The only casualty was a frog whose seared body was found near the crater. The end of the year saw further alerts as Liverpool and Belfast came under heavy attacks.

LATEST WAR CASUALTY FIGURES

During the year news has been received of the loss of a further 60 lives of men from the Island as a result of enemy action.

BRITISH ARMY
21 casualties, including nine who were killed in Crete and one who died in hospital later.

MERCHANT NAVY
17, mostly lost at sea when ships have been torpedoed.

ROYAL AIR FORCE
13 killed on operations.

ROYAL NAVY
8 lost in ships sunk

In addition 4 have died whilst in service and 14 Manx persons are known to have been killed during air raids on London and Merseyside.

DISASTER FOR THE 129TH BATTERY IN CRETE

Towards the end of May, news filtered through to the Island, mainly via German propaganda radio broadcasts, concerning the fate of the 129th Battery. It was not good. In January the Battery had been sent to Crete to help defend the base at Suda on the north coast of Crete. The base had been set up following the Italian invasion of Greece last year and the 129th encamped among the olive groves on the surrounding hills. While Mussolini's soldiers were making slow progress, the situation changed rapidly with the German Blitzkrieg of Yugoslavia, and then Greece. Athens fell in April and it was imperative to support the limited British and Commonwealth force sent to aid the Greeks. Suda was the main supply port and protection was given by Royal Navy ships, including H.M.S. Warspite. The 11 Bofors guns were mounted in concrete and, together with a lone Vickers Mk11 gun, were positioned at various points in the hills around Suda Bay. Visits by Italian aircraft were made at a high level and caused little trouble, but matters changed for the worse with the arrival of the Luftwaffe. Swarms of Ju88 bombers and Ju87 dive-bombers attacked the port relentlessly. Following the collapse of Greece,

Heinkel and Dornier bombers together with ME 109 fighters joined in as German forces were massed to invade the island.

On the morning of 20th May the whole area was machine-gunned from the air. It was the prelude to the arrival of the German crack Airborne Division with hundreds of parachutists landing in the hills. They met stiff opposition from British and Commonwealth troops who were under orders to hold the island at all costs. But they were fighting against overwhelming odds and on the 26th the order was given to evacuate the island. The 129th had been in almost constant action for days and had succeeded in bringing down between 30 and 40 enemy aircraft. Orders were given to destroy the guns and to return to Suda Bay in darkness while hiding among rocks in the day. On the night of the 31st the men reached the beach. The wounded, 35 in all, were given priority and places for them were found on what turned out to be the last ship to leave Suda. The beaches were crowded with waiting troops, but they were strafed mercilessly by Me110s. Nine of the 129th were killed and more than 20 hospitalised with serious wounds. The remainder, some 110 including Major Cain and Captain Maley, were taken prisoner and sent to camps throughout Germany.

Meanwhile, the 41st Battery had been giving support to the 4th Indian Division. Together with the 5th Division, it had been sent to Abyssinia to halt the Italians adding to their East Africa Empire. The men had to endure desert conditions, snakes and scorpions and, the dreaded dysentery which claimed the life of one of the gunners. There was plenty of action against Italian aircraft and progress into Eritrea meant covering hundreds of miles of desert and mountain terrain. The Battery was present at the vital battle to take the town of Keren in March. Resistance began to crumble and the Italians surrendered at the beginning of June. Since then the 41st Battery has returned to Egypt and has joined the 42nd in the defence of the Suez Canal. Lieut.-Colonel MacClellan has been placed in charge of the defence of the Canal Zone.

Members of the Manx Regiment H.Q. staff photographed in the Suez Canal Zone. Seated in the centre is the Regiment's C.O., Lieutenant-Colonel G.P. MacClellan, now retired. On his right is Captain J. B. Mylchreest, and on his left, Captain Guy Pantin, the Regiment's medical officer. (Manx National Heritage)

One of the Bofors gun teams of 41st Battery which took part in the Eritrean Campaign in the early months of the year.

1941 NEWS IN BRIEF

FEBRUARY
21 - No 440 (1st Manx) Squadron of the Air Training Corps formed. Flights to be based at Douglas High School, King William's College and Ramsey Grammar School.

MARCH
18 - Tynwald grant £500,000 as war contribution to British Exchequer.

MAY
12 - Fascists arrive for detention at Peel.

JUNE
1 - H.M.S. Manxman commissioned.
13 - First news of Battery of Manx Regiment operating in Crete trapped when evacuation took place.
17 - British women Fascists arrive in Port Erin
17 - Higher income tax and surtax approved.
30 - GERMAN FORCES INVADE RUSSIA.

AUGUST
29 - All-Island A.R.P. scheme announced.
SEPTEMBER
20 - Night of riots at Peel following arrest of escaped Fascists.
30 - Keys approve shorter licensing hours.
OCTOBER
1 - London police arrive to take over Fascist Camp.
18 - National Savings Campaign : 'Warship Week' opens, £640,000 subscribed.
NOVEMBER
14 - Bigger National Insurance benefits announced, and higher weekly payments.
14 - 'Aid for Russia' Fund launched.
DECEMBER
7 - PEARL HARBOUR ATTACKED. U.S. ENTERS WAR - Japanese, Rumanian and Hungarian internees arrive.
12 - Order in Council extending Military Service Act (1941) to Island.

THE HOME GUARD AND THE CIVIL DEFENCE

1941
- Stalin becomes Prime Minister of the Soviet Communist Party
- The sinking of Germany's battleship *Bismarck*

During the year considerable improvement has been made in the training and preparedness of the Home Guard. Every opportunity has been taken to co-operate with the regular units and training establishments in contests and exercises. All Home Guard members have been equipped with army battle dress and boots as worn by the regular army, while there has also been a good supply of other items of equipment.

On 5th July the Manx Home Guard was honoured by a visit from the Director-General of the Home Guard, Major-General Viscount Bridgeman, D.S.O.,M.C., who arrived with his Staff Officers to attend the Tynwald Ceremony. A Home Guard detachment from Peel and St John's provided part of the Guard of Honour for the ceremony. The following day Lord Bridgeman inspected the 1st Battalion at Tromode and the Ballasalla Platoon, Southern Company, 2nd Battalion.

Tromode Drill Hall was designed originally for the Manx Territorial Regiment. Building had only just begun when war broke out. Work was stopped but, following approaches from the Manx Territorial Association, the War Office decided to complete the building. At the end of last year it was handed over to the 1st Battalion as a headquarters and training centre. The fine building has a large hall with social rooms, gymnasium, showers, Officers' and N.C.O.s' messes and canteen, with a parade ground and sports field alongside.

This summer a series of three week-end training camps under canvas were held at H.M.S. St George (Cunningham's Camp). Nearly 500 members took the opportunity of intensive training assisted by regular officers and sergeant instructors. One Sunday morning in August, the whole of 1st Battalion was involved in an exercise in which 150 'parachutists' attempted to capture Douglas, but without success. In October Castletown Company provided a cup and medals for a knock-out competition between fighting patrols. The final was held in December in the Baldrine area in atrocious conditions. The winners were Bride Patrol.

CIVIL DEFENCE (A.R.P.)

During last winter the schoolroom of Victoria Street Church in Douglas was a busy scene as unemployed men assembled thousands of gas masks, enough to supply every man, woman and child not already in possession of one. In March over 36,000 gas masks were distributed throughout the Island by members of the Manx Women's Guild. Younger children have been provided with gas masks with 'Mickey Mouse' faces.

After months of waiting, tentative arrangements already in place are to be put on a more efficient footing as a result of the Civil Defence Commission issuing plans for an all-Island scheme. An A.R.P. Executive, under the direction of the Chief Constable (Major J. W. Young, O.B.E.), will consist of a Staff Officer and Training Officer seconded from the Police Force. They will be responsible for directing Air Raid Precautions throughout the Island. Many of the Wardens are members of the Loyal Manx Association formed during the Great War for civil defence. They are the backbone of the scheme and will also train stirrup pump parties for every street. In the event of a bomb falling the Wardens will cordon off the area and summon the Ambulance or Fire service. A special Corps of Messengers, aged between 16 and 18, is being formed to maintain communications should telephones be put out of action.

Volunteers are required for the Ambulance Section to become proficient in first aid. The Masonic Temple in Douglas has been equipped as an emergency hospital. Instruction is also given in dealing with a gas attack and decontamination centres are being established where victims can be hosed down. Volunteers are also required in the Fire Section to undertake nightly fire-watching at the various posts being set up in the towns. The fire tenders ordered for the Auxiliary Fire Service are expected to arrive early next year. A new A.R.P. Headquarters and an all-Island Control Room has been set up in a four-storeyed building in Woodbourne Road, Douglas. It is linked to various points on the Island by 25 telephone circuits.

An architect's impression of the new Drill Hall at Tromode. It was due to be built for the Manx Territorial Regiment but was not completed until the end of last year. It is now the headquarters of 1st Battalion, Isle of Man Home Guard. (Frank Cowin Library)

1941
• Atlantic Charter drawn up between Great Britain and the United States
• US naval base, Pearl Harbor, attacked by Japanese air force

NEW AIRFIELD UNDER CONSTRUCTION AT ANDREAS

A new airfield is taking shape at Andreas. It is being built for Fighter Command as part of the R.A.F.'s defences of the North-West. Notices were served on landowners at the end of last year and 500 acres of fine fertile farmland have been commandeered. Ballaghaue, farmed by Mr Crellin, and Braust, farmed by Mr Callow, provide 200 acres with smaller amounts stretching into neighbouring Bride. These are needed to complete the extremities of the airfield and for the construction of a new road to replace the Ballacottier road to Bride. Other areas around the village will be used for the accommodation compounds, messes, station hospital and N.A.A.F.I.

The main contractor is the English firm of Moss and Co., though much of the construction work is being undertaken by local building and haulage firms, together with the Highways, Water and Electricity Boards. Many local men are employed and hundreds of Irish navvies have been brought in to assist. The airfield is being built to the full specification of Fighter Command. All buildings are of brick construction with asbestos roofing. The airfield has three intersecting runways. The main NE/SW runway is 1,100 yards in length. 'Deads' from the Laxey and Foxdale mines have been used for the 12" hard-core base of the runways which have been topped by 3" of tarmacadam. A total of 24 blast pens have been built at dispersal points around the perimeter track and the whole airfield has been surrounded by high roller concertina barbed-wire. The main entrance is from the Ballacottier Road before Braust Farm is reached. Concrete roads connect the buildings and lead to three maintenance hangars and flying control.

The Rectory is to be used as officers' quarters. As soon as they are completed, communals are being occupied to relieve the overcrowding at Jurby. which continues to host fighter squadrons. The Polish squadron was followed by three others during the year, each squadron flying Hurricanes. At present there is an Australian squadron of Spitfires and in October its groundcrew and administrative staff began the move to Andreas. The Spitfires, too, have arrived though operations are still undertaken from Jurby. Andreas should be fully operational early next year. December saw an unfortunate accident when a Spitfire coming in to land hit a truck which was crossing the runway. The driver was killed. The Spitfire nosed in and overturned, but the pilot escaped with minor injuries. Another Andreas Spitfire crashed whilst on a training flight at Aust Farm, Lezayre. The Canadian pilot, Flt. Lt. Edy jumped by parachute from a low height but was killed on hitting the ground.

In July R.A.F. Jurby was renamed No 5 Air Observers School and navigation was added to bomb aiming and gunnery instruction. Lysanders have joined the target towing flight and ex-squadron Hampdens have replaced the Herefords. They are being used for navigation and bombing exercises. A visiting Hampden from an O.T.U. caused quite a stir in December. It was on a training flight and flown by Pilot Officer Turner Chrystal of the well-known Ramsey auctioneering family. The aircraft was fully loaded and armed. On the approach one of the engines developed trouble and a tricky landing resulted in the aircraft slewing into the boundary hedge near Ballavarran Farm. The crew managed to escape before the fuel tanks erupted in fire and destroyed the aircraft. Fortunately the bombs were blown clear and did not explode. A few days later Turner Chrystal and the crew were collected by another Hampden and returned to their Saltby base accompanied by some turkeys prepared for Christmas!

The beginning of the year saw Wing-Commander Alford take over as Commanding Officer. One of his first tasks was to improve the defences of the airfield. There were no rifles available so a huge quantity of steel pikes were ordered from Gelling's Foundry in Douglas. Now every man is armed with one and has to carry it wherever he goes on the station. There are night exercises with the men taking up positions ready for a mock landing by parachutists in the light of flares. Apparently, the pikes are a source of much amusement but no one dare appear without one. The Officers' Mess now boasts silver and glass ware and is decorated with palms. The C.O. has also provided two blister hangars which have been converted into the Jurby Ritz Theatre. Through the efforts of S.W.O. Radcliffe a camp orchestra has been formed from musicians on the station. 'The Aeronautics' are trained by Jack Hart, the famous conductor from the Savoy, London. Local dance band leader Harold Moorhouse has been transferred to Jurby to take charge of the camp entertainments.

The grim side of life has been the number of fatal

Vicar and wardens of Kirk Andreas have been informed that the 120 feet tower and bell turret will have to be reduced by half. In line with the southern end of the main runway of the Andreas airfield, it is likely to be a hazard to aircraft taking off and landing. (Manx National Heritage)

flying accidents this year. The whole Island was saddened by the loss of four American flyers belonging to one of the Eagle Squadrons formed by volunteers. Five of them were on their way to Northern Ireland when they entered low cloud over the Maughold area. Completely lost, they circled and lost height to locate their position. The result was that four of them crashed with the loss of all four pilots. The aircraft were located at Ballaskeig Mooar, Corteen's Ballafayle, Cornaa above Corrany and in the Laxey valley below the Snaefell Mine Captain's house.

Above: Hawker Hurricanes of 312 (Czech) Squadron, which was based at Jurby during April and May for night fighter and convoy patrol duties. (Right) October 8th saw the tragic loss of four American volunteer pilots belonging to 133 (Eagle) Squadron who were caught in thick mist over the Maughold area. This particular Hurricane found its way into the upper Laxey valley before nosing into the hillside (below), a few yards from the former Snaefell Mine Captain's house. (Flt. Lt. Norman Radcliffe)

Ex-operational Handley Page Hampdens are replacing the unreliable Herefords at Jurby. The Hampdens will be used for navigational and bomb aiming exercises.

FATAL AIR ACCIDENT REPORTS, 1941

15th January. Lockheed Hudson aircraft from Silloth ditched in sea off Port Mooar. Only one crewman out of seven survived and only one body was recovered.

23rd February. Hawker Henley on target towing duty ditched in sea two miles south-east of Point of Ayre with engine on fire. Air Sea Rescue launch from Ramsey recovered the two drowned aircrew, including the Polish pilot.

27th March. Fully-laden Hampden on training flight from Cottesmore struck Mr J. R. Quilleash's farmhouse at Ballaragh, Lonan, with visibility down to 20 yards. Aircraft crashed in flames and Bomb Disposal Team from Jurby recovered six bombs and incendiaries. Three crewmen died as a result of the crash and one survived.

2nd May. Blackburn Botha from Squire's Gate, Blackpool, ditched in sea at north-east end of Carrick Point, Port St.Mary. The four crew died, two bodies being recovered by divers from sunken wreck.

10th June. Blenheim on gunnery practice from Jurby spun into field at Upper Geary Farm, Lezayre. Polish pilot and two trainee gunners killed.

9th September. Blenheim from Jurby on training flight was seen to spin into the ground with smoke coming from tail at Ballacregga, Bride. Pilot and three others killed.

9th September. Hudson from Silloth struck upper slopes of North Barrule in thick fog. Aircraft exploded on impact killing the four occupants.

8th October. Four Hurricanes out of a flight of five from American Eagle Squadron crashed in Maughold area with loss of the four pilots.

8th October. Wellington from Hawarden on flight to Aldergrove hit south-eastern flank of Snaefell. American ferry pilot killed.

18th November. Hampden on approach to Ronaldsway hit R.A.F. mail van on Balthane Road, killing one and injuring three. Aircraft recovered to land damaged.

1st December. Spitfire hit truck on runway when coming in to land at Andreas killing the driver. Pilot slightly injured after aircraft turned over.

5th December. Spitfire from Andreas during aerobatics nosed in from 2,500 feet at Vondy's Aust Farm, Lezayre. Canadian pilot killed when attempting parachute landing.

17th December. Avro Anson from Lichfield struck west flank of Snaefell and disintegrated. Three were killed with four survivors seriously injured.

1942
• World War Two continues throughout Europe
• The first electronic computer (ENIAC) is developed
• Frank Sinatra makes debut in New York

ROW OVER CONSCRIPTION: HOUSE OF KEYS IN REVOLT

As the Isle of Man enters the third year of the war, the question of extending conscription has led to a heated debate as to whether or not the Imperial Parliament's recent National Service Act (No.2) should be applied to the Island, as in 1939. The matter this time has been left to Tynwald and it has aroused an unseemly division between those in favour and those who believe the Island is already doing enough. We have this report.

Ever since conscription for National Service was applied to the Island in 1939, there have been consistent rumblings about those who have been exempted by the tribunals. Are they being too lenient? While some men in reserved occupations have been retained to carry out essential maintenance work, such as in connection with the many military establishments, others are being accused of escaping conscription for reasons which have nothing to do with the war effort. At a Home Guard dinner, the Lieutenant-Governor described such people as "the shirkers, the beastly rats" - a phrase that attracted instant, if not widespread, condemnation.

In January, His Excellency introduced in Tynwald the new Act which would make women between the ages of 20 and 30 liable for National Service, while the upper limit for men would be increased from 41 to 51. Immediate uproar ensued. To the Keys it seemed as if the Executive Government was determined to impose the new measures without regard to their opinions. They walked out and met separately to consider the matter. They decided on a number of amendments, one being that women should be excluded from the Act, and another that older men if called up should not be required to leave the Island. To many Manx people the arguments advanced by the Keys for their instransigence seemed insubstantial to say the least. Others, however, believe that the needs of the Island and its economy are unique; the removal of women will upset industry and deprive the Civil Defence organisations of essential numbers; in the U.K. women can undertake essential war work in the factories without leaving home; calling up the older men would deplete the Home Guard, and already young Irishmen are being called upon because of the shortage of labour. It can also be argued that the Island already contributes a higher percentage of its population to the Forces, Auxiliary Forces or war work than any other part of the Empire.

Nevertheless, the great majority take the view that it is imperative that the Island should be seen to be pulling its proper weight in the combined effort to defeat the scourge of Nazism. However, the Keys began to raise the standards of democracy and nationalism in the face of the dictatorial attitude of the Lieutenant-Governor and the Legislative Council. They remained adamant and would only accept the compulsory enrolment of unmarried women aged 20 to 30 provided that they could only be directed to war work in the Isle of Man. When the U.K. National Service Act was re-introduced at the March sitting of Tynwald, the Keys voted 18 to 3 against it being applied to the Island. They were supported by only one member of the Legislative Council. Many of the women in the age group are already involved in the Women's Services or in hospitals and factories. Those at home have the opportunity of joining the Woman's Land Army while others are now members of the 'Mannin Wrens' who undertake duties at *H.M.S. Valkyrie*. The whole affair may have been something of a storm in a tea cup, but perhaps the last word should be left to a local man serving with the Royal Army Service Corps. In a letter home he writes, somewhat cynically, that when the time for the victory celebrations at last arrives, the same 19 who voted against the Act will be in the forefront of the celebrations!

MORE SHORTAGES

Shortage of supplies is becoming increasingly difficult for traders and shopkeepers, especially with regard to paper, cigarettes and tobacco, chocolates and sweets. Beer is still plentiful but spirits are in limited supply and join other items 'under the counter' which are reserved for regular customers. Meat is also becoming less plentiful and 'beefless weeks' have been introduced when only mutton, lamb and pork can be bought. However, this is regarded as preferable to the strict rationing imposed in England where the habit of endless queues is now the custom. Nevertheless, it has been necessary for families to register with a butcher of their choice. He sees that his customers are treated fairly as regards meat and offal, including liver and sausages. The rabbit population of the Island is also the source of an alternative meat while the traditional 'spuds and herring' is coming back into fashion. In order to protect crops, those with shot guns are being issued with cartridges for the purpose of shooting rooks to lessen the number feeding on newly-sown seed. Food waste in the way of potato and vegetable peelings, and known as 'swill' is being scavenged by farmers for the feeding of pigs. One result of the shortages has been the considerable rise in prices for just about everything.

WOMEN'S LAND ARMY

As more and more men are being called up for the Armed Forces, women are being called upon to help on the farms. The Women's Land Army was formed in July last year to help hard-pressed farmers who are being pressured to bring more land into cultivation. Recruits receive six weeks' training at Knockaloe Experimental Farm. The training includes how to milk a cow, look after hens and chickens (including how to wring a chicken's neck) and generally attune themselves to undertake hard physical work on the land. This includes turnip-thinning, hay-making and mucking out. After training, the women are allocated to farms throughout the Island where some become 'livers-in' while others are 'mobiles' billeted at either Peel or Lezayre. From here they travel to work each day bringing packed lunches. Hours of work expected are 109 hours a fortnight, but often this is exceeded if a job is to be finished. Pay is 18 shillings a week plus meals for those staying on farms while mobiles receive 40 shillings. This year members of the Women's Land Army have been provided with two sets of clothes, one suitable for working in and a 'walking out' uniform which includes fawn riding breeches, shirt, green V-necked pullover, donkey brown great coat and brown shoes.

ARMY CADET FORCE FORMED

In January, sanction was given for the formation of the Isle of Man Cadet Force which is affiliated to the Isle of Man Territorial Association and units of the Home Guard. Commandant of the Cadet Force is Captain B. J. Pendlebury, M.A., Senior English Master at the Douglas High School for Boys. Recruitment began for boys between the ages of 14½ and 17 and the ceiling of 400 was quickly realised. The boys undertake a military-style training which will stand them in good stead when they are called up for Army service.

Boys with an interest in the Navy are well catered for by units of the Sea Cadets which are found throughout the Island. Flights of 404 Squadron of the Air Training Corps founded last year have become so numerous that a further squadron has been formed. This is 506 Squadron and is made up of the original flights belonging to King William's College, the Boys High School and Ramsey Grammar School.

DOUGLAS SCHOOL HIT BY BOMB.

Children attending Tynwald Street School had a frightening experience on the morning of 11th March. An aircraft from Jurby on a training mission accidentally dropped an 11 lb smoke bomb when flying over Douglas. The bomb pierced the roof of the upper hall where a class of seven-year-olds was in the middle of a P.E. lesson. The bomb then penetrated the floor and smashed through the infant assembly hall floor and imbedded itself in the earth. Incredibly, no one was hurt, not even by flying glass when the windows were shattered. Some girls were shocked but that was the worst of it. There were 240 children in the school at the time and fortunately the bomb missed the classrooms. The pilot of the aircraft came to school next day to apologise to the children. One of them said later that the Headmistress gave him a good ticking off!

CIVIL DEFENCE ENFORCED

While the air raid sirens continue to give warning of German aircraft in the vicinity of the Island, Tynwald has taken steps to ensure that the air raid precautions organised by the Civil Defence Commission are brought to a high state of efficiency. As a result of a shortage of volunteers, men between 18 and 60, and not already involved in Home Guard or A.R.P. duties, now have to register for Civil defence purposes and Fire Sections. Many have been enrolled as wardens. Whilst there is still an air of complacency, every step should be taken to protect not only the local population, but also the many thousands of military personnel at present in the Island being trained to play a vital rôle in the war effort.

SILK FOR THE LADIES

Drogues used as targets for those under instruction at the R.A.F. Gunnery School at Ronaldsway are being salvaged for unauthorised use. They are made of silk which is unobtainable in the shops. The drogues are towed by aircraft off Langness and are fired at from the gun emplacements near the lighthouse. The drogues are then released at Knock-y-Vriew where two aircraftmen are stationed in a wooden hut to collect them. Despite £5 rewards being offered for those which drift away, local women regard them as being much more valuable and are putting the silk to good personal use. The galvanised wire is also of great value.

DOING THEIR BIT

The staff and management of Clucas' Laundry at Tromode are doing their bit to help the war effort. They are cleaning bedding and blankets for the military stationed on the Island free of charge. A similar service is being provided for the hospitals and maternity home. Staff undertake the work after their normal working hours and sometimes turn in on Saturday mornings. They are not paid as management has told them the company is not charging for the service

RECORD COMPANY PROFITS

The Isle of Man continues to profit economically from the war. This year's Budget revealed continuing record surpluses arising from increased Customs and Excise duties as a result of the presence of thousands of service personnel and enemy aliens on the Island. A Budget for £1 million was introduced. The Steam Packet, Douglas Gas and Railway Companies and the electricity undertakings have all announced record profits. Meanwhile, as casualties mount among Manx servicemen, there was bitter anger in the Island when a London Sunday newspaper described it as a "Shangri-La of luxury in a world at war."

Tynwald's contribution to the war costs is another £500,000 and over £1 million has been raised from Island savers through War Savings and defence bonds. The Government has also issued a £500,000 War Loan at 3% for local investment.

JUVENILE DELINQUENCY

The Isle of Man Magistrates' Association has called for tougher measures to deal with the rising tide of juvenile crime on the Island. It has proposed compulsory membership of youth organisations, an evening curfew on young people and an extension of the birching powers of the courts. The Association blamed the increasing delinquency on lack of discipline in the home and lack of parental responsibility.

Recent cases have seen a 13-year-old page boy in a Douglas hotel being given six strokes of the birch for stealing £3 from a guest's bedroom. The court also ruled that his father had not met his responsibilities, and fined him £3. In another case a boy of 13 was given four strokes of the birch for stealing two pears from trees in the gardens of The Nunnery.

STEAM PACKET LOSES ANOTHER VESSEL

After playing a heroic part in the Dunkirk evacuation the *Tynwald* was commandeered by the Admiralty and fitted out as an auxiliary anti-aircraft ship and commissioned in

October 1941 as *H.M.S. Tynwald*. Manned by Navy personnel, she served in Home Waters on convoy escort duties before being assigned to Operation Torch, the recent Allied landing in North Africa. On 8th November she was involved in the attack on Algiers and three days later was part of a task force, including infantry landing craft, sent to capture the airfield at Bougie, 100 miles to the east of Algiers. While the harbour was successfully taken, further landings were prevented by adverse sea conditions and the attacking force came under heavy air attacks. On 12th November *H.M.S. Tynwald* was hit by a mine or torpedo and sank in about seven fathoms of water. It is believed ten of her crew were lost. This is the fourth Steam Packet ship to have been lost. They include the three newest ships in the fleet.

News of other Steam Packet ships is that the *Viking*, after a short period on the Fleetwood service, was requisitioned again and is at present serving as a Fleet Air Arm target vessel based in Scotland, where she has been joined by the *Victoria* carrying out similar duties. The *Manxman* has been fitted out as a Radio Direction Finding vessel and commissioned as *H.M.S. Caduseus*. Based in Douglas for a short while, she has been on patrol in the Irish Sea and has been used in exercises with the radar station on Douglas Head. The *Lady of Mann* is fully occupied as a troop transport operating around the Scottish coast and helping in the ferrying of American troops and Air Force personnel arriving at Belfast on the *Queen Mary*. Also in Scottish waters, the *Ben my Chree* has been a frequent visitor to Iceland with its vital North Atlantic base.

SAMUEL NORRIS DEMANDS MORE HOME RULE

The crusading M.H.K. for North Douglas, Mr Samuel Norris, has asked the House of Keys to adopt a series of demands to the U.K. Government for more Home Rule. He proposed a drastic reduction in the powers of the Lieutenant-Governor and the handing of executive power to a form of Manx Cabinet. But after three hours of debate at the December meeting of the Keys, the House decided to send his proposals to a committee for consideration. Angrily, Mr Norris said this was "the funkhole of the faint-hearted." In October, Mr Norris resigned from the War Committee.

MORE AIR ALERTS

The year saw by far the greatest number of air raid warnings. The sirens were sounded on no less than 32 occasions. The great majority of these were caused by lone high-flying Ju 88s sent to reconnoitre the Irish Sea in order to report the movements of convoys entering and leaving Liverpool. They follow a route which takes them northwards over the coast of Ireland, then turning southwards to their base in northern France. It is noticeable that cities in the North-West are receiving fewer attacks from the Luftwaffe.

Commissioned by the Royal Navy, 'H.M.S. Tynwald' took part in the North Africa landings but was sunk after being hit by a mine or a torpedo. She is the fourth Steam Packet vessel to be lost during the war. (Imperial War Museum)

1942 NEWS IN BRIEF

FEBRUARY
14 - Two meatless days weekly introduced.

MARCH
18 - Fat Cattle subsidy increased and £4 wheat subsidy offered.
23 - Wheatmeal bread introduced.
31 - Keys throw out Military Service Act in Tynwald.

MAY
27 - Miss W. S. Naylor appointed headmistress of Douglas High School for Girls in succession to Miss G. D. Hasler, M.A.

JUNE
25 - Tynwald pays tribute to Lieut.-Colonel MacClellan who has been retired from his position as C.O. of the Manx Regiment.

JULY
5 - Home Secretary Mr Herbert Morrison attends Tynwald Ceremony during visit to inspect Internment Camps. Lieut.-Colonel MacClellan acts as Sword Bearer for the Ceremony.
7 - Keys refuse to discuss Death Duties.

AUGUST
28 - Duke of Kent killed when Sunderland flying boat crashes in Scotland. He was the youngest brother of the king and, as Prince George, paid a memorable visit to the Island in 1932.

OCTOBER
15 - Agricultural Wages Board recommend £3 minimum wage for farm labourers.
23 - Canon John Ralph Strickland Taylor appointed Lord Bishop of Sodor and Man to succeed Rt Rev. W. Stanton Jones who has resigned.

MORE STRANGERS IN OUR MIDST

The beginning of the year saw the arrival of nearly 600 internees whose countries had joined the Axis powers. Over half of them were merchant seamen from Finland, while others were from Hungary, Romania and Japan. The Palace Camp was emptied of the few remaining Italians, and the new arrivals were placed in different sections of the camp. The 90 Japanese were mostly smartly-dressed bankers and press correspondents from London, but more recent arrivals included a dozen expert chicken sexers. They were soon released so that their skill in identifying pullets for egg laying should not be wasted to the poultry industry!

Despite these new additions, the number of male internees held has continued to decline as more are released, many to be employed in munition factories. During last year, 2,000 were freed bringing the total still held to about 3,500, including 500 detainees in the Peveril Camp. The stream of releases has meant extra work for the Manx Police who are responsible for visiting the camps and checking each individual's documents and escorting them to the boat for departure. Whereas the men's camps have military guards, mainly from the Pioneer Corps, the Police have also the responsibility for the security of women internees in the south of the Island. As constables are choosing to join the Armed Services, the Chief Constable is having to rely more and more on 'specials.'

The number of women confined to the Rushen Camp has also dwindled. It is now down to about a thousand, a quarter of the original total. In August Commander Cuthbert decided to move the married camp from Port St Mary to Port Erin. The move was made smoothly in a day with everyone, including the landladies, assisting. Couples who are pro-Nazi have been accommodated in the Towers and separated by a wire fence from the Italians who are in the Waverley. Uncommitted couples are housed nearby. The move means that Port St Mary ceases to be a restricted area. The former married quarters has been taken over by the Royal Army Pay Corps O.C.T.U., with the Ballaqueeney as its headquarters.

The occupation of Vichy French-controlled Madagascar by the British resulted in, perhaps, the strangest arrivals of all. They were the French women whose husbands were serving in the French colony. They were transported to Scotland and held pending a decision about their future. In September, about 60 women and children arrived in Laxey and were billeted in ten houses in the care of Miss Banks who had been transferred from Rushen Camp. She can be found now in the offices of the Village Commissioners where she deals with queries and complaints. A recent one was that four of the houses were without baths! An interpreter is available at the post office. While the women are free to move about the village, a permit is required to go beyond the three-mile limit. As they are all Roman Catholics, Mass is celebrated in the Pavilion of Laxey Glen Gardens, the priest being Father McGrath of St Anthony's, Onchan. Because they have come from a hot climate, Miss Banks has instructed the landladies to ensure that good fires are provided for the women. However, the sojourn in Laxey of these forlorn, though friendly, women is not to be for long. Their menfolk have decided to join the Free French Forces under General de Gaulle. Arrangements are in hand to transfer the women and children early in the new year to the warmer climes of northern Africa.

B Company, 1st Battalion Home Guard at Knockaloe after winning the Governor's Cup for general use of weaponry. Next to Earl Granville on the left is Lieut. J. B. Ritchie, holding the cup. On the right is Capt. B. J. Pendlebury, Commandant of the Island's Cadet Force. (Manx National Heritage)

MANX REGIMENT JOINS THE DESERT RATS

The beginning of the year saw the two Batteries continuing their deployment in the Suez Canal Zone, the survivors of the 129th having joined the 42nd Battery under Major Valentine. The vital sea link, its ports and R.A.F. bases were subject to frequent air attacks, especially when convoys arrived with troops and supplies in the great build up of British and Commonwealth Forces. The Bofors fired thousands of rounds and their tally of aircraft shot down continued to grow. Changes within the Regiment saw Captain Henry Kelly leave to take over command, as Major, of the 1st LAA Battery. The 1st had carried out most of the early trials with the Bofors gun and already had a distinguished war record, having served in France and the Western Desert. It had been with the Eighth Army which had routed the Italians. But the situation was reversed with the arrival of Rommel and the Afrika Corps. The 1st was retained to protect the withdrawal of the Eighth Army and was heavily engaged in the seige of Tobruk from where it was evacuated to Alexandria. During its time in the Desert it had accounted for 87 aircraft but had lost 100 men. After taking over command, Major Kelly was delighted to be signalled that the 1st was to be assigned to the 15th LAA, thus replacing the 129th and maintaining its regimental status.

In February, the three Batteries and Regimental HQ left the Canal Zone and entered the Desert to take up positions on the Gazala line in Libya which was being established by the Eighth Army in an attempt to halt the advancing German-Italian army. 41st and 42nd Batteries were soon in action against Messerschmitt fighters while the 1st was sent 200 miles to the south to help protect the left flank. In April more Manxmen arrived to reinforce the Batteries and were soon in the thick of the action. Lieut.-Colonel MacClellan was placed on the Retired List because of his age and returned to the Isle of Man where the veteran was given a hero's reception. Lieut.-Colonel T. Eustace Smith took over as Commander of the Regiment. The 1st Battery returned and the 15th LAA now became part of the 7th Division, which has been nick-named the 'Desert Rats'.

Field Marshal Rommel launched his expected offensive at the end of May. The 7th Division bore the brunt of the heavy fighting and when the R.A.F. was forced to withdraw from its forward airfield, the order was given to withdraw all guns to the El Alamein defensive position, just 50 miles west of Alexandria. The Regiment and the R.A.F. fighters joined in combating the constant air attacks to assist in the withdrawal which was successfully completed without heavy losses. At this point Major Clifford Kniveton left 41st Battery to become second-in-command of the Regiment and Major Brian Mylchreest succeeded him as Battery commander. Major Valentine (later to become Lieutenant-Colonel) was transferred to a Staff appointment and Major H. S. Balls took over command of the 42nd Battery. At the end of July, the Regiment came under regular attacks by Stuka dive bombers and suffered casualties including two killed and a number of wounded by shrapnel. The wounded were swiftly attended to by the medical staff, but it was necessary for Major Mylchreest to be invalided home to make a full recovery from his wounds. On promotion, Major T. W. Cain took over command of the 41st.

As the Eighth Army steadily built up its resources to face the inevitable attack on the El Alamein line, Prime Minister Churchill visited the area to assess the situation and make important changes in command. General Auckinleck was

CHANGES IN THE HOME GUARD

The legislation introducing compulsory enrolment for Civil Defence duties meant that Home Guard members were now committed to serve for the rest of the emergency period and would not be released without good cause. Attendance at parades and duties of up to 48 hours each month became obligatory. In February, the 2nd Battalion was organised on similar lines to 1st Battalion. Major G. W. Howie who, in civil life is the Island's Agricultural Organiser, and had commanded the Peel Company, was promoted to command the Battalion with the rank of Lieutenant-Colonel. At the same time, Major K. G. Groves of the Ramsey Company was made 2nd-in-command with the rank of Major. Following his retirement from the Manx Regiment, Lieut.-Colonel G. P. MacClellan, D.S.O., O.B.E., was appointed 2nd-in-command of the Isle of Man Home Guard in September.

The arrival of a number of Hotchkiss 6 pounder anti-tank weapons resulted in the formation of the Manx Troop Artillery under the command of Captain H. S. Cain of 1st Battalion. The unit made rapid progress and in April demonstrated their efficiency on Langness. Concerning medical matters, doctors were appointed to each Battalion under Lieut.-Colonel J. Wood and their first duties were to ensure that medical arrangements should be in force on all practical exercises. First Aid instruction and stretcher bearing are now included in the training manuals. Meanwhile, training on automatic weapons, field exercises, bayonet fighting, signalling and map reading is leading to higher degrees of proficiency.

On the Home Guard's second anniversary there were no ceremonial parades but, instead, the public were invited to attend training sessions and displays. The Colby Platoon put on an exhibition of weapons they first used two years ago. These included rusty old .22 rifles, billiard cues, hammers and sticks! July saw week-end training camps begin at Glen Wyllin which lasted throughout the summer with up to 100 men attending each camp. Also during the summer His Excellency the Lieutenant-Governor presented a cup for general efficiency in the use of weapons. Every Company entered and competitions were held on various ranges with the final taking place at Peel in August between 'B' Company, 1st Battalion and Ramsey Company, 2nd Battalion. The cup was presented by His Excellency in front of a large gathering to Captain J. B. Ritchie of 'B' Company which won by five events to three.

succeeded by General Alexander as Commander-in-Chief, and Lieut.-General Montgomery was placed in command of the Eighth Army. Their ordders were to repulse any assault on the El Alamein postions and prepare to go on the offensive. Rommel struck on the last day of August, his plan being to drive round the southern point of the line supported by hundreds of aircraft and then strike towards the coast. Montgomery pulled back units to prevent this and, despite a succession of all-out attacks, the German tanks were forced to a halt and turned tail. With the rest of the line holding, it was tempting to give pursuit but Montgomery called a halt in order to stabilise the situation. The three Batteries had played their part and scored many hits, though not without casualties. During the lull in the fighting, Lieut.-General Horrocks, commander of the X111th Corps, which included the 7th Armoured Division, ordered a First Aid Competition in which all units would be represented. The Regiment's M.O., Major Guy Pantin, hastily gathered a team together under the leadership of Bombardier Curwen Clague and prepared for the tests ahead. The competition went on for days and the 15th Regiment distinguished itself as not only being adjudged the best from 7th Armoured Division, but from all the 40 teams from the Corps!

The great barrage of the heavy guns, which was the prelude to the battle ahead, began on the night of 23/24th October as troops moved forward to clear passages through the minefields. The Regiment's job was to protect the 25 pounders from air attack and during the ensuing days fired 7,500 rounds, bagging more enemy aircraft. On the 31st the 7th Divison was taken out of the southern flank and moved northwards nearer to El Alamein ready for the planned breakthrough. The whole area was jammed with tanks, guns and supply vehicles and came under constant ground and air attack. Then on the morning of 4th November, came the great breakthrough with the Germans and Italians overwhelmed by the superior forces of the Eighth Army. By the 11th, advances of up to 300 miles had been made, 30,000 prisoners taken and hundreds of tanks, guns etc. captured. On the 13th November, 1st Battery reached Tobruk from where it had been evacuated over a year ago.

The beginning of December saw the 7th Armoured Division's progress come to a halt as they waited for reinforcements and supplies of ammunition and fuel. Time was also needed for the R.A.F. to move forward to bases within range of El Agheila where Rommel's forces had gathered. He was relying more and more on his aircraft to halt the advance and all Batteries were in constant action, meeting with considerable success but not without further casualties. Major-General Harding, the Divisional Commander, visited some of the gunsites and expressed his appreciation of the skill of the Batteries. By the middle of December the assault on the Agheila line had been successfully completed and the 15th's guns began the 300 mile trek to Tripoli. By the 23rd December the Batteries gathered in the Nofilia area where General Montgomery paid them a visit. He spent three hours touring the units and presenting medals. Christmas Day was a rest day and there was time to enjoy a full breakfast, beer and cigarettes supplied by the N.A.A.F.I., a celebration cocktail party, and an excellent Christmas dinner with roast pork, Christmas pudding and all the trimmings.

The three batteries of the 15th LAA (Isle of Man) Regiment have been playing a prominent part in the defence of the 7th Armoured Division ('The Desert Rats') as the Eighth Army pursues Rommel's forces following the decisive Battle of El Alamein in October. Here one of the Bofors gun teams digs in to meet further attacks by German and Italian aircraft. (Manx National Heritage)

R.A.F. ANDREAS BECOMES OPERATIONAL

The fighter station at Andreas became fully operational in March as a sector of 9 Group Fighter Command. Group Control was at Preston. When the first fighters arrived at Jurby towards the end of 1940, the newly-completed wing of Ramsey Grammar School was adapted as Sector Control. WAAF plotters use it to record the movement of aircraft. The Centre is linked to the radar stations at Dalby, Scarlett and Bride. Information is passed to Preston from where instructions are passed back to Ramsey and then to the operations room at Andreas.

The Spitfires of 457 Squadron were replaced by those of another Australian squadron, 452. Shipping patrols over the Irish Sea are maintained daily, while occasionally orders to scramble are received when hostile aircraft are detected. Much time is also spent over the air-to-ground firing range on the Ayres below Smeale. A large square is mounted on a rail and provides a moving target for practice. In May, two of the Spitfires, one with cine camera to take film of the other, collided head on, resulting in the attack plane diving into Farrant's Fort Farm, Close Lake, with its dead pilot. The other Spitfire was badly damaged and the pilot parachuted into a field at Andreas. June saw 452 leave Andreas. Villagers turned out to wave to the squadron as it made a final fly-past.

The Australians were replaced by 93 squadron which was converting to Spitfires and using the facilities at Andreas to work up to operational efficiency. The crisis which led to the formation of 9 Group has largely passed and the Andreas personnel of over a thousand have been posted out. While the future of this fine airfield is being determined, Air Sea Rescue aircraft are still present together with a detachment from the Fleet Air Arm which provide 'targets' for the trainee radar operators of H.M.S. Valkyrie on Douglas Head.

In August, another tragic accident happened when Andreas lost its Commanding Officer. On a quiet Sunday afternoon a Whitley bomber arrived to refuel. Wing-Commander E. F. Knowles, D.F.C. had served with Bomber Command and decided to take the Whitley up for a short flight. He was joined by his lady friend and six others, including four corporals who acted as ballast in the rear of the aircraft. The Whitley took off on the main runway but failed to gain sufficient height to clear the Bride Hills where it crashed in flames. The four corporals escaped from the rear but one died later from his burns. He and the four who perished in the nose of the aircraft were buried in Andreas churchyard.

The training at Jurby continues apace and is closely linked to the requirements of Bomber Command which, under Air Vice-Marshal Harris, is mounting a great offensive against German industrial targets. Developments on the airfield have seen the completion of two runways and the provision of additional hangars and improved accommodation for the airmen, and the hundreds of WAAFS now stationed at Jurby. Nearby Ballamoar Castle, which had been used as a rest haven for Battle of Britain pilots, is now the WAAF Officers' quarters. Most of the supplies for the station, including coal, are shipped in through Ramsey while local suppliers provide huge quantities of farm produce, fish, meat and bakery items. Shell and Esso tankers provide a constant supply of petrol from their depots at Douglas.

Spitfires of 457 (R.A.A.F.) Squadron line up at Andreas which became fully operational as a fighter station in March.

AIR ACCIDENT REPORTS, 1942

12th February. Avro Anson left Jurby at 7.00 p.m. and crashed near summit of North Barrule. Two were killed while there were two survivors found next morning in freezing conditions

2nd March. Hampden on training flight stalled and crashed at Ballagarraghyn after missed landing at Jurby in bad visibility. Canadian pilot and two airmen killed.

8th March. Australian pilot from 457 Squadron lost when Spitfire from Andreas broke up after exploding and then disintegrating over Ramsey Bay.

12th March. Blackburn Botha on training flight from Squire's Gate hit Cronk ny Irrey Laa in bad visibility. All five on board were lost.

24th March. Wallace aircraft from Ronaldsway crashed at Quayle's Orchard, Malew after colliding with another Wallace, killing the pilot and a cadet from King William's College Flight of 506 Squadron, A.T.C.

8th May. Two Spitfires from 452 Squadron, Andreas, collided in mid-air resulting in the loss of one of the Australian pilots.

25th June. Two Blenheims from Jurby on early morning gunnery practice crashed at Knockaloe Farm after colliding, with the loss of all six airmen. Parts of the wreckage hit Patrick School damaging the roof. No children were present at the time.

26th June. Anson from R.A.F. Bobbington on low flying exercise in vicinity of Douglas hit tree at Ballacreetch Farm and Ballanard Road junction and crashed at Scouts Glen, Castleward, Braddan. Aircraft went on fire and wreckage was widely spread. The five R.A.F. sergeants on board all perished in the accident.

29th June. Two Spitfires from Andreas on intercepting training at 25,000 feet became separated and one disappeared without trace. The body of the pilot was recovered eventually from the sea, two miles west of the Calf of Man.

10th July. Remains of German airman washed up on Peel side of Niarbyl Bay.

17th July. Anson from R.A.F. Cark struck North Barrule in thick cloud and driving rain. Pilot and two others were killed.

4th August. Bristol Beaufighter on fuel consumption test flight from R.A.F. Lynham, Wiltshire, to Jurby stalled on final approach and crashed at Ballacottier, Lezayre. Crew of two were killed.

23rd August. Whitley bomber flown by Wing Commander Knowles, C.O. Andreas, crashed at 400 feet into field of West Kimmeragh Farm, Bride. The Wing Commander and three others died in the impact. An R.A.F Corporal later died from burns.

21st September. Lockheed Hudson on morning training flight from Silloth crashed into Slieu Freoaghane, near Kirk Michael, killing all four occupants.

ADMIRALTY TAKES OVER RONALDSWAY

Throughout the year one of the biggest projects ever witnessed on the Island has seen Ronaldsway Farm and its two neighbours being transformed into a Royal Navy Air Station. This will train thousands of air crew to fly the Barracuda aircraft now in production for the Fleet Air Arm. The project has seen a massive 850 acres of farmland being commandeered; over 500 men are employed on the site, many of whom are Gaelic-speaking Irish navvies. We have this report.

Acting under the U.K. Defence of the Realm Acts, extended to the Isle of Man by Order in Council, the Lieutenant-Governor, Vice- Admiral Earl Granville, served notices of compulsory purchase on all the land and property-owners involved. Ronaldsway Estate is by far the largest area. Its 17th century farm house, once the home of Illiam Dhone, together with six farm cottages and three fine houses in The Crescent have been demolished, being in line with the runways. Subject to a separate purchase is the Turkeyland limestone quarry operated by C. Kniveton Ltd. The second farm is Ballagilley adjoining King William's College. It belongs to the historic Barrow Trust. Thirdly, the Creggans Farm, which stretches from neighbouring Ronaldsway to the Silverburn river, has also been taken over. Additional land acquired includes 70 acres of Balthane Farm north of the Balthane Road which has been now closed to traffic wishing to reach Derbyhaven from where the civilian air services continue to operate. Nissen huts for the accommodation of 2,000 personnel have been provided within Ballasalla for squadron staff and at Janet's Corner for administrative staff.

The main contractors for the airfield and hundreds of brick-built buildings are the Carlisle firm of John Laing and Sons, whose key workers are billeted in Castletown. Their heavy machinery has removed all hedges and levelled the area. Local hauliers are having another field day providing sand and gravel from as far away as the Point of Ayre, where concrete bricks are also produced. A major part of the scheme is the construction of four runways. The main 27/09 runway is 1,400 yards in length. This is intersected by three shorter ones. Over 16,000 tons of hardcore have been quarried from Turkeyland which is then crushed to size at Ballahot. The drainage problem has been solved by laying concrete channels on either side of the runways. The final coating of the runways is provided by the Paenmaenmayr Trinidad Asphalt Company and is laid by Laing's Berber-Greene tarmac pavers, the first seen on the Island.

Overlooking the airfield is the three-storeyed Control Tower built to standard Admiralty design. Nearby is the Creggans farm house which is to become headquarters for the Admiralty's Works Department. Here are found the generators which supply the entire area, while across the Ballasalla-Castletown road is the administrative site and communications centre. The whole of the Balthane corner of the airfield is devoted

to the maintenance section with stores, radio repair shop, and fuel dump. Still awaited are the prefabricated materials for 12 hangars of different types which are imported and will arrive early in the new year. Laing are extremely pleased with the progress made and are confident that the station will be ready for use at the beginning of next summer.

Another war victim. Ronaldsway House, once the home of the Manx patriot William Christian (Illiam Dhone) is to be demolished as part of the development of the airfield for the Admiralty.

BATTLE RELICS UNEARTHED
Local historians will be interested to hear that when the footings for the eastern end of the main runway were being prepared, complete human skeletons, together with swords and shields, were unearthed. It was on this site that the Battle of Ronaldsway took place in 1275 when emissaries of Alexander 111 of Scotland came to claim the Isle of Man for his kingdom. The Manx, leaderless since the death of Magnus ten years before, had refused to submit to Scottish rule. But here they were heavily defeated by the Scots. According to ancient records, some 537 Manxmen were killed. In order that the skeletons should not be further disturbed, it was agreed to raise the level of the runway at this end, thus protecting much of the battle area.

WELL-KNOWN FARMERS IN GAOL
The farmers of Ronaldsway, Ballagilley and The Creggans each had all of their farm equipment and livestock valued by the Government Property Trustees prior to public auction, where they would be guaranteed the valuation prices as fair compensation. During the auction of stock at The Creggans it was discovered that 31 cattle had already been removed and sold privately, and had been replaced by inferior Irish stock only recently imported. The scandal shook the farming community and the farmer, the highly-respected Mr Percy Kermode, together with two accomplices, were charged with conspiring to defraud the Manx Government. At a Court of General Gaol, George Percy Kermode, John Stanley Kermode and

Inside the Mooragh Camp, Ramsey. It was on the pavement in the foreground that the Finn internee was found stabbed to death. (Manx National Heritage)

James Martin were given a nine months' gaol sentence with hard labour.

R.A.F. REGIMENT FORMED

When the R.A.F. Ground Defence Gunnery School at Ronaldsway was disbanded in March, most of its personnel moved to Douglas where accommodation was provided in the vacant Central Internment Camp. It is next to the Empress Hotel which, since 1940, has been the Headquarters of the Gunnery School. In 1942 the many hundreds of those trained in airfield defence became members of the R.A.F. Regiment, and the Empress Hotel is now the Headquarters of this new branch of the Royal Air Force. New intakes continue to arrive for training and Douglas Corporation has made available part of the Villa Marina grounds for the construction of a large concrete dome. Inside, instruction in the use of the Bofors gun is given, using simulated 'targets' projected on the roof of the dome. Instruction is also given by infantry instructors of the O.C.T.U. based at the Villiers

MURDER AT MOORAGH CAMP?

An incident which took place in the Mooragh Camp has led to one of the Finnish internees being charged with murder. The remaining Finns held at the Palace Camp were transferred to Ramsey at the end of last year. There are about 140 of them, all merchant seamen and are noted for their boisterous and noisy behaviour. The majority are pro-Nazi because of their hatred for the Russians, while a few are supporters of the Allied cause. Shortly after noon on 20th April, one of the Finns, carrying a bucket of dirty water, approached another sitting on the steps and threw the water in his face. Taken by surprise, the man stood up and approached the man with the bucket and lunged at him with a blow to the stomach. But hidden in his hand was a shortened table knife and the Finn staggered backwards and died in a pool of blood. This caused uproar and the guards were soon on the scene. The body was removed on a handcart and the attacker was taken into custody and

ended up in Noble's Hospital with a broken nose after being badly beaten up in the camp.

The prisoner was charged with murder and the case came before Deemster Cowley in June. The Attorney-General, Mr Ramsey B. Moore, applied for the trial to be held in camera for security reasons. To outsiders, the case seemed clear-cut, but defence advocate, Mr R. Kinley Eason persisted with the argument that the killing was a result of provocation and that the man feared for his life. After the hearing which lasted for five days, the jurors returned a verdict of Not Guilty. The result led to rumours that the British Govern-ment had brought pressure to bear on the result for political reasons, but such rumours are without foundation.

HOME SECRETARY RETURNS

Britain's Home Secretary, Mr Herbert Morrison made a second visit to the Island in August to inspect the internee camps for which the Home Office is responsible. He stayed at Government House and, accompanied by His Excellency and members of the War Committee, made a speech to a gathering in the grounds of the Villa Marina. He said the Island's war effort was second to none. The number of Manxmen registered for military service was higher per head of population than anywhere else in Britain, something which was also achieved in the 1914-1918 War. In fact, over 5,000 of the Island's fit men up to 40 years of age are now serving with His Majesty's Forces in many parts of the world. While the women have not been conscripted, thousands have joined the women's sections of the Armed Forces, or, in the case of those up to the age of 30, are involved in essential work either here or outside the Island.

ISLAND POPULATION SOARS

Despite so many Manx people being off the Island on war service, the Island's population has soared to a record 93,205. It is an unofficial, but well-informed, figure which suggests that, with the internees down to about 2,000, over 40,000 service personnel are at present based on the Island. They are, of course, playing their part in maintaining the Island's buoyant economy. The Steam Packet's Rushen Castle and Snaefell are filled to capacity carrying personnel to and from the Island.

HOME RULE BATTLE CONTINUES

The battle over Manx Home Rule, begun by Mr Samuel Norris, goes on. The House of Keys has backed recommendations that a Cabinet of seven members should be formed to take over the executive powers of the Lieutenant-Governor. At the same time the Keys are angry that the British Government has seen fit to appoint a new Government Secretary without consulting them. Mr J. N. Panes is to succeed Mr B. E. Sargeaunt, M.V.O., O.B.E. who retires at the end of the year after 33 years in the post. The Keys wanted the position to go to a member of the Manx Civil Service and, as a result, have passed a vote of no confidence in the Lieutenant-Governor, Vice- Admiral Earl Granville.

RAMSEY CHILDREN IN DEATH FALL

Two small children have died tragically after falling from the top floor bedroom window of a house on West Quay, Ramsey. Five-year-old Ad-rienne Smith and her three-year-old cousin Cornelius Corlett, were playing in the room. They are believed to have fallen while leaning out of the window after climbing on a table. Both landed on the pavement below and died later in the Ramsey Cottage Hospital.

TRAGEDY AT KIONSLIEU

Six cadets from the 166 O.C.T.U. have been killed during a night exercise at Kionslieu Dam, some way above the Eairy Dam, Foxdale. On the night of 2nd November cadets were attempting to cross the dam by dinghy under cover of fire. Live ammunition was being used, machine guns opened up, mortar bombs exploded and the night sky was lit by flares. Then something went badly wrong as one of the dinghies was blown sky high as a result of a box of Mills bombs being detonated. Six cadets, in the final stages of being commissioned, died in the tragedy. At the enquiry, the exact cause of the explosion could not be explained but one theory is that a parachute flare landed on the dinghy. Onchan men of 'B' Company, 1st Battalion Home Guard witnessed the accident when observing the exercise.

BOMBER CRASHES ON RUSHEN FARM

While most air accidents occur in remoter parts of the Island, the horrors of such a crash have been brought home to people in the south of the Island. Eye-witnesses have described how, on the afternoon of Saturday, 6th November, a four-engined Halifax bomber passed over Port St Mary with one of its engines on fire and trailing black smoke. The Halifax was then seen passing over the bottom of Fishers Hill before it corkscrewed into the ground close to the buildings of Cronkmooar Farm. Wreckage was spread over a wide area and set light to several haystacks. Farmer Mr Bertie Qualtrough was leading a horse and cart but the noise of the impact caused the horse to bolt over a nearby hedge. Port St Mary fire-tender was soon on the scene and prevented the fires spreading.

LATEST WAR CASUALTIES

During the year notification of 53 war casualties has been received from the War Office. Details are as follows:

BRITISH ARMY	- 27, which includes 13 members of the Manx Regiment, one who died of malaria and one who died in a German P.O.W. Camp. Two others from the Army have died in Japanese P.O.W. Camps.
ROYAL AIR FORCE	- 10, mostly on operations over enemy territory.
ROYAL NAVY	- 6, including one in the Royal Marines and one in the Fleet Air Arm.
MERCHANT NAVY	- 10.

In addition, four have died while on active service.

It is believed the Halifax had requested to land at the new airfield at Ronaldsway, but as the latter had no facilities to deal with a fire it was diverted to Jurby. The aircraft was on a training mission from the O.T.U. at Topcliffe, Yorkshire and all but one of the seven crew were Canadians. On impact, the rear of the fuselage broke away and the rear gunner was found some distance away buried deeply in the ground with his parachute still unopened.

DECORATION AWARDS

During the year a large number of decorations for gallantry have been won by Manxmen serving in the Armed Services. Bombardier, now Acting Sergeant, Bill Watterson of Allan Street, Douglas, is the first member of the Manx Regiment to be decorated, winning the Military Medal for outstanding bravery when his anti-aircraft gun position was under heavy attack by German Stuka dive-bombers in North Africa. Also, Commander B. Bryant, D.S.C. of Ramsey, one of the Royal Navy's submarine aces, has been awarded the D.S.O.

VISIT OF LADY MONTGOMERY

Finally, a visitor to the Isle of Man has been Lady Montgomery, mother of General Sir Bernard Montgomery, commander of the Eighth Army. She stayed at Government House and visited the Manx Museum and King William's College. She also went to a dance at the Pool Ballroom, Ramsey, where she did the Lambeth Walk with a young R.A.F. officer from Jurby. When she left the Island she took a Manx kitten with her, and a Manx travelling rug for her famous son.

1943 NEWS IN BRIEF

FEBRUARY
2 - The new Lord Bishop, the Right Reverend J. R. Strickland Taylor, M.A., was enthroned in St George's Church, Douglas.

MARCH
3 - As a result of the first use of artificial insemination on the Island, a pedigree Friesian cow, owned by Mr R. G. Shimmin of Sulby Farm, Onchan, gave birth to a bull calf. The insemination was carried out by the Government Veterinary Officer, Mr Douglas Kerruish.

APRIL
4 - Jubilee of Main Road Wesleyan Church, Ballasalla.
16 - Keys challenge Governor on their right to consultation on Budget proposals.
18 - Lord Bridgman, Director of the Home Guard carries out inspection of all units. He expressed himself as being well pleased with what he had seen.

MAY
16 - Third Anniversary of formation of Home Guard. Celebrations took the form of Ceremonial Marches and Church Parades.

JUNE
6-13 'Wings for Victory' Savings Campaign raises £1,301,112 for war effort.
23 - Imperial Government decide to exercise right to purchase furniture in requisitioned boarding houses.
29 - Jubilee of Broadway Baptist Church.

AUGUST
6 - Mr J. R. Quayle appointed chairman of Isle of Man Bank Ltd. in succession to Mr T. Cubbon, J.P.
8 - St John's Battle Platoon, 2nd Battalion, beat Onchan Battle Platoon, 1st Battalion, in Final for Kissack Cup.

SEPTEMBER
19 - Governor's Cup for use of firearms won by Ramsey Company, 2nd Battalion after defeating 'E' Company, 1st Battalion by 5 wins to 3.

OCTOBER
26,27 Eight Manx prisoners of war, repatriated from Germany, given great reception on arriving on Island.

LIFE BEHIND THE WIRE

The number of internees continues to fall. Many have been released to undertake war work in Britain, while a few have been repatriated to Germany in exchange for our own people. Nevertheless, there are still over 3,000 males interned. These are in the Hutchinson, Metropole, Onchan, Mooragh and Peveril Camps. To satisfy outsiders who find the internees a source of curiosity, it is now possible to give some idea of what life is like behind the barbed wire fences, with special reference to Hutchin-son Camp which still has some 400 internees, about a third of the original total.

Hutchinson Camp in Douglas consists of the garden area of the Square on either side of which are two rows or terraces of boarding houses. Also included in the camp is the parallel row of houses facing Ballaquayle Road. The whole area is surrounded by a perimeter fence of barbed wire with the main gate into the camp found at the south-west corner by Ballaquayle Road. 42 houses are available for accommodation, all of which were built about 1890. The few properties overlooking the gardens at the top of the Square and facing seawards are wired off from the main camp, and form a separate compound which is used for administration and stores. A gap in the northernmost terrace has been used to provide showers and a laundry, and more recently a hall for recreation and indoor sports.

When the internees arrive they are allocated to one of the houses, but are free to rearrange themselves so they can be with relatives, friends or other interest groups. There are between 20 and 25 men in each house and each man is provided with a single bed, mattress, pillow and four blankets. Those in poor health can claim a fifth blanket. When the camp was first opened, only double beds were available. As married men were not used to sharing a bed even with their wives, sleeping with someone else, especially another man, caused considerable embarrassment and resentment. In the early days the top mattress was often dragged on to the floor for use by one of the room mates, while the other made do with the springs!

All the men are responsible for the cleanliness of their

rooms and have to undertake other duties. Every house has two cooks and three cleaners who are paid 3/6d a week pocket-money which is credited to their account with the camp bank. These are the regular workers but everyone still has to take a share. Each house elects a House Captain who is responsible for the good-running of his house and the general good order of everyone within. Then, each of the three rows of houses select a Row Captain who keeps in touch with the House Captains and passes on to the Camp Captain and the Works Organiser any requests or complaints originating from the men. The Camp Captain liaises with the Camp Commander who gives his approval to those elected as Row and Camp Captains. The Works Organiser is responsible for all work carried out by camp members, whether inside or outside the camp. Camp workshops produce items for sale either within or outside the camp, whilst outside work is in supervised groups on local farms. All work is paid for at nominal rates into the camp bank.

Each house cooks for itself with one of the daily tasks being to draw the house rations from the camp stores. The rations are issued according to a set scale and used at the discretion of the house cooks who are helped by the rota cooks. Soon after the camp opened, an internee chef and a doctor combined to publish a book of 100 recipes based on the camp rations. The book was soon circulated to other camps on the Island, and beyond!

The internees run their own canteen which is stocked with such necessities as soap, razor blades, writing paper, pencils, tobacco and some wine and beer. Additional foodstuffs are also available. The policy is to sell foodstuffs and essentials at little or no profit and to sell luxury items at an extra charge so that the overall enterprise makes a profit of just over 10%. A cafe is run separately and also makes a small profit which, with the profit from the canteen, provides pocket money and clothing for anyone who is destitute and unable to work.

Newspapers, both English and Manx, and periodicals are available by ordering through the camp post office. A camp newspaper has been produced on a regular basis since the camp first opened. Other camps also had their own publications, although many of these have now been lost since the closing of the camps. Some of the staff involved in producing these papers have joined The Camp as the Hutchinson Camp paper is called. Its No 1 issue is dated 21st September, 1940 and cost two pence. It carries an apology for the technical difficulties and admits the paper leaves a lot to be desired. While there is little mention of the daily life of the camp, a good deal of space is given to the hopes and dreams of the writers, and quite a lot about the cultural activities of the camp.

The day starts at 7.00 a.m. with roll call followed by ablutions, house cleaning and breakfast. Work, physical exercise, cultural activities, walks out of the camp accompanied by guards, and the occasional visit to a local cinema fill the days which end with another roll call. Within

One of the guards on duty in the Hutchinson Camp.
(Manx National Heritage)

the camp is a hospital for minor ailments in charge of a local doctor and an internee doctor. Serious cases are taken by ambulance to Noble's Hospital while those who require long-term treatment of a none too serious nature are taken to the special internee hospital at Falcon Cliff in Douglas. This serves all the camps, except Peel, and is staffed by the R.A.M.C., supplemented by both internees and civilians. Hutchinson has its own dental surgery run by an English dentist who visits daily and is assisted by an internee dentist.

The Cultural Committee has been an important influence in camp life since the start, and because of the constant arrivals and departures of internees, has changed frequently during its life. It arranges and encourages lectures on a variety of topics. In the early days lectures were given in the open in the central gardens, but the New Hall was available by Christmas, 1940. Lectures average attendances of 80 to 100, though one well-known historian attracted an audience of between 300 and 400. He left to go to America but was drowned when his ship was sunk in the Atlantic. The Debating Society meetings, musical performances and the Library are all organised by the Cultural Committee.

The New Hall is also used as a theatre. Already 40 performances have been staged. There is no admission charge. The actors have included professionals, while there are many helpers back stage. The plays have been mainly by English writers but there have also been Czechoslovakian and Russian works. The Library started with the gift of a few paperbacks, but has grown to 7,600 volumes on a wide range of topics. There is a well-appointed reading room and a loan service from Douglas Town Library and national organisations, including the Victoria and Albert Museum in London.

Music is also an important feature of camp life. With a large number of the internees being accomplished musicians, many being members of bands, concert parties, orchestras or soloists in their own right, it is not surprising that the standard is high and events frequent. The importance placed upon music can be seen, perhaps, from the incident when Captain Daniels, the Camp Commander, realised that the Austrian internee Marian Rawicz he had in his camp was one half of the pre-war piano partnership of Rawicz and Landauer. He traced the latter to another Island camp and arranged his transfer to Hutchinson. He then set about acquiring two grand pianos for them to play! Other well-known musicians include Charlie Kunz.

The camp roll also includes well-known names from the world of art and architecture. Within weeks of the camp opening, an art exhibition had been arranged and the first edition of The Camp reviews it. The report is dotted with names such as Kurt Schwitters, Markiowitz, Stern, Kahn and Uhlmann. Others with an equal or even greater claim to fame are recorded in later reviews here and in other camps. Some more simple work was even used to illustrate the various camp newspapers, perhaps most notably the now defunct Onchan Pioneer.

Meanwhile, life goes on in its regular routine behind the wire. Whatever interests are provided for the inmates, they all have the one abiding interest - freedom. While numbers continue to fall there is still no sign of the final release for all. They remain in a segregated community, and to schoolchildren passing by they are all prisoners of some kind about which fantastic tales are concocted. Perhaps now they will have a better idea of what really goes on!

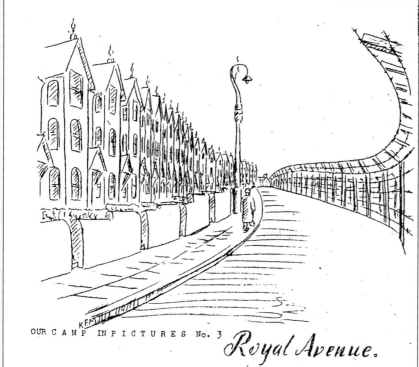

OUR CAMP IN PICTURES No. 3 *Royal Avenue.*

o. 21 THE ONCHAN PIONEER

Camp Picture No. 8.

HENRION

Illustrations from
The Onchan Pioneer
(Frank Cowin Library)

the "well-heated" cabin.

The CAMP CAFE is open from 10.30-12.45, 3.0-4.30 and 7.15-9.45.
Fridays closed from 3.0 to 4.30.

CRISIS OF FEEDING WARTIME POPULATION

The efforts to make the Island self-sufficient in the provision of basic food items for a population of over 90,000 are being intensified. Farmers are being forced to plough up meadowland and areas which have not been cultivated for many years. The scheme is being overseen by Agricultural Adviser, Mr George Howie who insists that every available acre is brought into cultivation for potato, corn and green crops. Douglas Corporation has been forced to give over seven acres of its prized golf course for cultivation. This urgency applies throughout the Island and farmers are desperate for tractors to supplement the hard-worked horses. Tractors and ploughs are supplied from the United States under the Lend-lease arrangements, but many have been lost in the Atlantic as convoys continue to suffer losses from U-boat attacks.

Farmers are being paid £2 an acre for bringing new land into cultivation, while the Board of Agriculture is paying an increasing amount of subsidies in order to expand production and to stabilise prices. For growing wheat, £4 an acre is paid to the farmer, and £10 an acre for potatoes which are in short supply, as evidenced by chip shops frequently displaying signs 'No frying tonight'. Consumption of milk and eggs is limited by the supplies available, but are not rationed. There are also subsidies for cattle, sheep and pigs; all imports of live-stock are prohibited, except under licence. Meat rationing at two shillings per person per week is now in force and is likely to be reduced even further, though not to the stringent levels in Britain.

Another side to the crisis is the shortage of manpower on the farms. While farmers and those employed full time in agriculture are exempt from military service, few casual workers are now available. An urgent appeal has been launched for more recruits to join the Women's Land Army. More and more internees, especially Italians, are being employed on farms. Groups of these with their guards are now a familiar sight in various parts of the Island. However, this valuable source of labour is diminishing as more of the internees are being released.

Posters asking us to 'Dig for Victory' have not gone unheeded. Spare land in the towns and villages has been given over to allotments which produce potatoes and vegetables to help with domestic supplies. Schools are closing for half-day holidays in September so that children can undertake blackberry picking. Thousands of pounds of berries are brought to school and then collected for taking to the jam factory at Rushen Abbey. Children are also being encouraged to collect cocksfoot grass seed for hay crops, now that supplies from Norway are no longer available.

WITH THE 15TH FROM TRIPOLI TO ITALY

The 15th LAA (Isle of Man) Regiment, as part of the 7th Armoured Division, continued to be in the vanguard of the victorious Eighth Army as it advanced across Libya. German and Italian aircraft were constantly doing their damnest to stave off the inevitable, providing plenty of action for the Bofors guns. On 23rd January the first troops entered a deserted Tripoli and early in February, the Prime Minister arrived to join in the celebrations and witness the Eighth Army's Victory Parade through the city. Lieut.- Colonel Eustace Smith, C.O. of the Manx Regiment, was presented to Mr Churchill.

The end of the month saw the Eighth Army take up positions for the advance into Tunisia. The fighting ahead was to be some of the hardest of the whole campaign, with the German and Italian armies desperately trying to survive as the American First Army advanced from the west. Rommel's counter-offensive inflicted heavy casualties, including gunners from the Regiment who were either killed or wounded. Then an attack on the German Mareth Line was repulsed and 1st Battery was forced to abandon its front positions. It was not until 20th March that a breakthrough was achieved and the Regiment passed through the Mareth Line. A link up with the First Army was made and time given for it to be reinforced. On the night of 30th April the final offensive was launched and Rommel's forces were overwhelmed after bitter fighting. On 7th May, Tunis was reached and the 1st Battery was the first to take up defensive positions to defend the port. Later they were joined by 41st and 42nd Batteries, but there was now little action following the surrender of the Germans and Italians.

In the ten months since August of last year, the Regiment had travelled 2,000 miles from Cairo to Tunis and its guns had been credited with 249 enemy aircraft destroyed, probably destroyed or damaged. The Regiment received many accolades for the part it had played, not least from G.O.C. Major-General Erskine of the 7th Armoured Division. In March, Sergeant W. H. Watterson was awarded the Military Medal for gallantry and later Sergeants R. Owen and L. C. Parry received similar awards.

Orders were then given to return to the Tripoli area for a rest period followed by intensive training, including landing craft exercises. By now, Major Clifford Kniveton had left the Regiment on being given command of the 34th LAA Regiment and was promoted Lieut.-Colonel. Major Henry Kelly took over command of 41st Battery and Major H. E. Hutton was given command of 1st Battery. Following the occupation of Sicily in August, the Regiment made ready to sail in support of 7th Division for the landing north of Salerno, near Naples. The first three days were critical as the Germans put up strong resistance, supported by ME 109s and FW 190s. Progress was made and the Batteries were operating together in the Vesuvius area when the vanguard of the Division entered Naples on 1st October. The Regiment continued to add to their score but not without further casualties. As the Allied advance continued, the Division was under orders to pull out and prepare for the sea journey back home. The Regiment left Naples on 20th December on its way to Gourock, Scotland. Earlier, in October, a group of 15 gunners and Captain J. J. Christian had left North Africa having been selected as 'battle experienced personnel' for home leave. They were given an emotional welcome as they landed on the pier at Douglas.

ANDREAS HOSTS NO. 11 AIR GUNNERY SCHOOL

After the winter lull, R.A.F. Andreas is once again bustling with over a thousand R.A.F. and W.A.A.F. personnel billeted in the compounds. Everyone has a bicycle issued so that they can get to and from their place of work. In May all was in place to open as an Air Gunnery School and the first intake of volunteer pupils, most of them in their 'teens, arrived to undergo an intensive ten-week course. The training huts are equipped with the latest power-operated turrets which are vital to the defence of the Lancasters and Halifaxes now coming into service in greater numbers. All the instructors are experienced gunners, having completed a tour of operations.

Air experience is gained first on Ansons with Martinets towing the familiar drogues. These are released by the side of Braust Farm, after the Martinets have come in low across the new road from Andreas to Bride which is being called the 'Burma' road. As the course advances, the pupils move on to the turrets of the Wellingtons which have been retired from operations. They are in the air daily with Spitfires providing targets for the cine-guns of the turrets. Practice takes place in allotted zones, care being taken to avoid the bombing ranges used by Jurby. Those who complete the course satisfactorily are then posted to an O.T.U. before joining one of Bomber Command's squadrons which are mounting the great offensive in the night skies over Germany.

For those off duty the N.A.A.F.I. along Smeale Road provides a place of relaxation, as does the Y.M.C.A. on the Bride Road which is run by local ladies. Here dances are held with visits from Jack Hart's Jurby Band, although Andreas has formed its own. Clegg's stores and Rainer's cafe in the centre of the village do good trade in providing cups of tea and 'sticky' buns while the Grosvenor is well patronised making Mrs Breadner a busy hostess. At week-ends, front rooms of many a home in the parish welcome the airmen for ham and eggs, in return for which help is given with the harvest. Crennell's coaches are available for a night out at the Plaza and Corner Cinemas, while the Pool Ballroom is a popular Saturday night venue.

Jurby has now become No 5 Navigation and Bombing School and is equipped with up to 80 Ansons which provide 'flying classrooms' for the students. Those on the navigation course set off from Jurby on long cross-country flights taking in many points around Britain and Northern Ireland. Exercises are undertaken both day and night. Flights last up to 3½ hours and each aircraft has a staff pilot, wireless operator and two trainees. For bomb aiming the Ansons are fitted with a perspex nose and the trainee bomb aimers take turns in a prone position over the ranges, using 22lb flash bombs. Results are recorded from observation huts positioned on the cliffs. The ranges in use are off Peel, Ballaugh, Jurby, Ballghennie and Cranstal. The Ansons have proved particularly reliable. Accidents are often the result of weather conditions or running out of fuel, especially when head winds are met on long navigation flights. There have been a number of accidents also involving aircraft from other stations.

Right: One of the elderly Jurby Blenheims used for gunnery practice seen here with groundcrew.

Far right: Newly-qualified aircrew pose in front of one of the Hampdens at Jurby. Proudly wearing the Observer 'O' and half-wing, they will be posted to Operational Training Units of Bomber Command.
(both Manx National Heritage)

AIR ACCIDENT REPORTS, 1943

18th April. Beaufighter on training flight from R.A.F. Ballyhalbert ditched in sea off south-west coast of Island. Crew of three were drowned.

28th April. Beaufighter from Crosby-on-Eden, Carlisle, crashed at Ellanbane Farm, Lezayre at 12.20 a.m. as a result of engine failure. Crew of two killed.

9th September. Wellington from R.A.F. Hixon on night flying exercise requested emergency landing at Jurby. Was seen from control tower but then disappeared. Caught wing tip on cliffs and crashed on Sartfield beach, north of Jurby Head. Exploded and burnt on impact with the loss of all five crew.

6th November. Halifax bomber crashed on Cronk Moar Farm, Rushen with engine on fire. Six Canadians and one R.A.F. crew lost.

14th December. Spitfire from R.A.F. Ballyhalbert hit the Rheast, near Kirk Michael, in bad weather. Polish pilot from 303 Squadron killed.

30th December. Anson from West Freugh, Wigtownshire, flew into cliff face above Horseleap Viaduct, Douglas Head Marine Drive at about 200 feet. Wreckage and remains fell back on to the railtrack below. All five Australians were lost.

D-DAY : DELIVERANCE OF EUROPE BEGINS

On the morning of 6th June, the Headquarters of General Eisenhower, the Supreme Allied Commander, issued a terse announcement informing the world that the long-awaited invasion of Europe had at last begun: "Allied naval forces, supported by strong air forces, began landing Allied armies on the northern coast of France this morning." Of the thousands of Manx personnel in the Armed Services, many are involved in the biggest operation of its kind ever staged. We have this report.

After almost exactly four years to the day, ships of the Steam Packet Company returned to northern France and were involved in the initial landings of troops early on the morning of D-Day. This time the *Lady of Mann*, crewed by the Royal Navy, acted as headquarters for one of the Assault Flotillas responsible for getting the first troops ashore. The Lady had been converted to carry six landing craft which were hoisted into the water. On the initial wave she carried 490 infantry of the assault force responsible for establishing the Juno beach-head. Similarly equipped, the *Ben my Chree* arrived off the Omaha beach acting as headquarters for another Assault Flotilla and carried some of the first U.S. Rangers to land. A third Steam Packet vessel to take part was the *Victoria* which had Steam Packet officers on board under the command of Captain Keig. The *Victoria* landed troops at Arromanches where stiff opposition was met. A footing was secured and here one of the Mulberry artificial harbours was established.

Not far behind were the three Manx Batteries. Major Henry Kelly, second in command of the Regiment, went ashore on D + 1 with five other officers to make arrangements for the arrival of the Batteries. The first Troops landed on the Juno beach-head on D + 3 to be followed later by the rest of the Regiment. It is part of the British Second Army and once again the Regiment finds itself with the 7th Armoured Division. The weather has been most unseasonal and moving along the narrow farm lanes has not been easy. Nevertheless, the troops have now been deployed to defend units of the Division whose immediate objectives are Bayeux and Caen.

HOME ON LEAVE

After leaving Italy at the end of last year, the Manx Regiment arrived at Gourock from where it had embarked over three years ago. Three weeks' home leave began on 10th January and members received a heroes' welcome from families and friends. An official welcome was given to them in the Villa Marina by Mayor of Douglas, Alderman S. A. Quirk. Special guest was Lieut.-Colonel MacClellan who received a great ovation. A special toast was given to 129 Battery which was represented by the wounded and repatriated Sgt. J. K. Conibear. In replying, he claimed that the 129th was the first Manx unit to enter Germany! Returning from leave, the Batteries began the work-up for the invasion -

'Operation Overlord'. On separate occasions the Regiment paraded with other units for inspection by General Sir Bernard Montgomery and H.M. King George V1. Captains K. C. Cowley and J. J. Christian, and Sergeant S. Cain have been Mentioned in Despatches.

FIVE PERISH OFF DOUGLAS HEAD

On the night of 11th January an Anson on a night navigation exercise from Wigtown, flew into bad visibility and ditched in the sea 100 yards south of the Coastguard hut on Douglas Head. The crash was heard from the Admiralty Civil Police hut between Douglas Head Hotel and Marine Drive tollgate, and Air Sea Rescue, Douglas was informed. The wind was south-east Force 5 and voices could be heard calling in the darkness for nearly an hour. It was later revealed that the R.A.F. rescue launch was aground at the top of Douglas Harbour because of the weather conditions. The Douglas lifeboat was informed but not requested to launch for another half hour. When it reached the scene of the ditching all cries for help had ceased. Steps are being taken to ensure that a rescue craft will at all times be available in the outer harbour.

HIGHLY SECRET

While the general public is unaware of what is going on at the 'radio' station on Douglas Head, it is also mystified by the aerials which were erected last year across the bay on the Douglas Bay Hotel. A large wooden structure on a circular mounting was bolted to one of the hotel's towers. The structure supports tubular aerials which can be rotated to ensure the best reception. The transmissions received are coded messages sent from German and Italian bases, and even from the Japanese 'Singapore Sam.' These interceptions are part of the work of the Special Operations Training Establishment set up by the Royal Corps of Signals. Its main base is in the former Palace Internment Camp including the Hydro. Because of the secretive nature of their work, the trainees are restricted in their movements and have the

1944
- The German V1 and V2 flying bombs launched over London during this year
- The Allied push for victory in Western Europe with a full-scale assault on Normandy beaches

(Above) A pre-war view of the Douglas Bay Hotel whose appearance has been altered by the construction of a huge aerial on its tower. It is used for wireless interception for training special operators for the Royal Corps of Signals. (R. and L. Kelly Collection)

1944
- The D-Day landings broke through the Atlantic Wall
- The liberation of Paris began on 19th August of this year

use of the Derby Castle Ballroom as a gymnasium and for recreational purposes.

Young men and women of high intelligence are selected to receive instruction in the Morse code. Headphones are linked to their instructors' Morse keys or tape machines. Proficiency is achieved when they are able to take down Morse at the maximum sending speed of 24 words per minute. They then move to the Douglas Bay Hotel to practise taking down the coded German messages until they can deal with 150 letters a minute. They are then posted as 'Y' signallers who continue the interception of enemy coded messages. The intercepts are then translated at the headquarters of British Secret Intelligence.

H.M.S. *SALAMANDER*

Stories are circulating that six weeks after the D-Day landings, R.A.F. Typhoons attacked a number of ships belonging to the 1st Minesweeping Flotilla. The Flotilla was engaged in sweeping the English Channel between Portsmouth and Arro-manches and, not having completed its task, was given permission to continue the operation. Shortly afterwards they were attacked by rockets and cannon fire from the Typhoons resulting in two ships being sunk and three damaged with loss of life said to be about 80, with another 150 wounded. One of the minesweepers, damaged beyond repair, is well known in the Island. It is H.M.S. *Salamander* which before the war acted as a Fishery Protection Vessel and was a frequent visitor to Manx ports. It is also known she was present at Dunkirk and saved some Manx servicemen who would otherwise have been trapped.

INTERNEE FINED

A fine of £10 has been imposed on an Italian alien who built a secret still in his detention camp in Douglas. The Court of General Gaol heard that he distilled a 44% proof spirit from fermented potatoes, beetroot, fruit and sugar. He was originally fined £200 because of the 1867 Act of Tynwald under which the charge was brought. However, the sum was reduced after a memorial was presented to the Lieutenant-Governor.

HALIFAX CRASHES ON LONAN.

The horrors of flying accidents were brought home to the people of Laxey and Lonan on the afternoon of Friday, 14th July. A Canadian Halifax bomber from R.A.F. Leeming was on a cross-country training flight and entered low cloud which covered the Island. As it passed over Agneash and Laxey, the bomber was seen to be on fire and shedding fragments of wreckage, some of which landed amongst schoolchildren enjoying their sports day in Glen Road. Five of the seven crew jumped from the aircraft but there was no time for the parachutes to open. At 4.20 the Halifax finally broke up and crashed near Lonan Church, spreading wreckage over two miles. Two of the engines landed near the vicarage and another in a field down Church Road where a farmer had just finished harrowing. Such was the violence of the impact, that the fourth engine, with part of the mainplane and undercarriage, crashed on Pinfold Hill, sending the wheel and undercarriage on to the rocks of Laxey beach. The engine hit 'Hokang' bungalow which went on fire, burning the three occupants who were taken to the Military Hospital in Onchan for treatment. A little boy, aged 3½, died from severe burns and shock. He had come from Newcastle with his mother for a holiday. The five aircrew who jumped from the stricken bomber have been buried at Andreas churchyard.

MORE DEMANDS FOR HOME RULE

The Manx Government has taken the unprecedented step of calling a Press conference in London to publicise its demands for Home Rule. It was given by Speaker of the House of Keys Mr J. D. Qualtrough and Middle M.H.K. Mr Eric Fargher, the well-known advocate. They received extensive coverage in the news-papers and on the B.B.C. The Government is to petition the Home Office for more control over the Island's domestic affairs.

FINANCIAL SUPPORT

The Manx Legislature this year voted another free grant of £250,000 to the British Government in support of the war effort. This makes a total grant of £1,250,000 in addition to the £750,000 already lent free of interest. These have been funded by increased taxes. The recent 'Salute to the Soldier' Week raised £1,204,405 in savings making a grand total of over £6,280,000 of Manx War Savings invested since the beginning of the war. The Island's buoyant economy is reflected in the high price for dwelling houses. Small houses with possession are fetching three times their pre-war cost.

NOT A 'DOODLE-BUG'!

The most sensational non-war event in the Island was the result of an 18-ton flywheel running out of control at the Douglas Power Station on the North Quay. Its rim, composed of six parts which were bolted together, disintegrated and parts were hurled through the roof up to a thousand feet before landing all over the centre of the town. One section of the wheel crashed through

(Below) Some of the 2,000 members of the A.T.S. special operators, photographed outside the Crescent Hotel. These well-educated and highly intelligent young women are trained to take down enemy morse messages which are then sent to British Intelligence for decoding. (Manx National Heritage)

the roof and floor of the stokers' mess room of the Douglas Gas Works and ended up near a boiler. A few feet more and there could have been an explosion and fire with serious consequences. Another piece hit the roof of the *Isle of Man Times* building in Athol Street, while a further piece hit a house and trapped two women in the debris. They were rescued by firemen and no-one was injured in the incident.

On duty at the power station was Roy Motion who had survived with an injured leg the sinking of the *Fenella* at Dunkirk. Subsequently, he served on a merchant ship which was torpedoed before he returned to the 'safety' of the Island! The resulting power failure spread to the entire Island and lasted for up to 14 hours in places. Cinemas and places of entertainment had to be evacuated and closed for the night. The noise of the airborne wheel was likened to that of the Flying Bombs, otherwise known as 'Doodlebugs' which the Germans are deploying against London. At first, some people thought Douglas had been hit by one. Hence the flying wheel being nicknamed 'The Kelly Bug'!

INVASION PLANS!
According to military maps discovered recently in a former German barracks in Belgium, the Isle of Man may have been in the direct path of the invasion of Britain, had it gone ahead. The maps suggest that the Nazis planned to seize the Isle of Man from Ireland and use it as a bridge-head to northern industrial England. R.A.S.C. driver George Hinds from Kirk Michael returned to the Island with the map of the Isle Man in October. He says the map indicates sea depths around the Island. It was revised with the other maps up to 1943.

MANXMAN WINS V.C.
It has been announced that Major Robert Cain, a Shanghai-born Manxman, has been awarded the Victoria Cross after taking part in the audacious attempt to capture the bridge over the lower River Rhine at Arnhem in September. In the desperate defence mounted by British paratroops against over-whelming German forces, Major Cain destroyed a tank single-handedly with an anti-tank gun at close range. His citation says he showed gallantry, endurance and leadership throughout the battle. Educated at King William's College, Major Cain worked for an oil company in the Far East before the war.

FIRST PRISONERS OF WAR ARRIVE
The first batch of 320 German prisoners of war arrived at the end of November. They were watched by crowds of curious local people as they arrived by sea at Douglas, looking sullen and very young.

LATEST WAR CASUALTIES

Up to the end of November next of kin have been informed of a further 71 casualties as being killed or missing on the war fronts.

BRITISH ARMY	- 40, including losses in Europe.
ROYAL AIR FORCE	- 18, mostly from Bomber Command.
ROYAL NAVY	- 1
MERCHANT NAVY	- 12
TOTAL	- 71

A total of 12 have also died on active service either by accident or illness, including two who are known to have died in Japanese P.O.W. camps.

Accommodation for the prisoners was provided at the Metropole and Onchan Internment Camps which were adapted by the War Office as prison 'cages.' It meant that every item of furniture in the two camps was removed for storage at Derby Castle. It is the policy of the War Office to provide its own items of basic furniture. As the Allies advance towards Germany it is estimated that 5,000 prisoners will be brought to the Island.

Meanwhile, further repatriation of internees has taken place during the year. On 1st September more than 600 men, women and children (including babes in arms) departed from Port Erin, leaving fewer than 400 in the resort. At the same time 100 from the men's camps left leaving less than 2,000 men and women still held on the Island at Port Erin, Mooragh and Peveril. Hutchinson was emptied in March when its last 300 inmates were transferred to Peel. Hutchinson Camp was checked over by the military ready for returning to the peacetime owners and tenants. The houses and contents were found to be in a reasonable state, and improvements had been made by the camp authorities such as the provision of shower-bath units and cubicles. Another sign of normality is the fair number of visitors arriving this year despite the limited space available on the Steam Packet vessels which have to give priority to service personnel.

A section of the Metropole Camp which is now rapidly filling with German prisoners captured by the Allied armies advancing into Europe. (Manx National Heritage)

WITH THE 15TH LAA REGIMENT INTO BELGIUM AND HOLLAND

By the middle of June the Manx Regiment was ready to play its part with the British Second Army in Normandy. The 1st Battery was in command of Major J. B. Mylchreest; the 41st was under Major T. W. Cain and the 42nd under Major H. S. Balls. The Second Army's task was to protect the left flank of the Normandy beaches at all costs against the XX1 Panzer Division counter attacks. Fighting was some of the fiercest of the invasion. The three Manx Batteries were constantly switched between units of the 7th Armoured Division. Initially there was not a great deal of enemy air activity, the Allied air forces having complete control. There was the constant threat, however, of low-flying ME 109s and FW 190s which kept everyone on their toes. There were the inevitable casualties as the score of aircraft shot down or damaged continued to rise. The month-long siege of Caen began on 18th June, the town being heavily shelled and bombed. The Division was in the centre of the final thrust, but on 10th August was pulled back and on the 17th joined the First Canadian Army to make the advance to the River Seine, some 65 miles away. On the last day of August the Regiment crossed the river south of Rouen in heavy rain. The task of 21st Army Group now was to clear the enemy from Northern France, destroy the Flying Bomb sites, capture the airfields in Belgium and take the port of Antwerp. Rapid progress was made until the Regiment was called to a halt as its supply vehicles were diverted to help other units. Six days later the Regiment was back with the Division as it approached Brussels. It received a rapturous welcome as each city was passed.

'Operation Market Garden' was to secure a footing in the Low Countries for a startline to attack the Ruhr. The Battle of Arnhem at the end of September was the focal point of the operation. The Airborne Division suffered disastrous losses and units of the Regiment were employed, not for the first time, in low-level shooting at enemy positions. Hundreds of rounds were being fired in a week. The Dutch people gave a warm welcome, but the onset of winter brought bitterly cold and damp conditions. Winter clothing was issued and this was supported by woollen garments arriving from the Island's Comforts Fund. By 28th November enemy gun positions overlooking Antwerp were neutralised and the port was opened to Allied convoys.

The Regiment moved across the River Maas into the Sittard area. A day later the Germans took the advantage of atrocious weather to launch its offensive in the Ardennes with bitter fighting lasting for a month and holding up 2nd Army's advance. The Regiment was soon called into action. It became the first Royal Artillery of the 7th Armoured Division to fire from German territory. The new ME 262 jet fighters put in their first appearance in large numbers. The Bofors continued the ground shoots. The 41st was particularly busy in the last week of December, some 3,500 rounds being pumped at the targets. There was little time for Christmas festivities but seasonal fare was available, and ENSA and cinema shows provided some welcome entertainment. More importantly, everyone is confident this will be the last Christmas of the war, at least in Europe.

1944 NEWS IN BRIEF

JANUARY
1 - New Year's Honours - Captain John Higgins, Supt. Isle of Man Air Services, M.B.E.; Sergt Walter L. Christian, Home Guard, B.E.M.; Wing Commander J. A. C. Karran, Air Force Cross.
21 - With an eye to the future, Steam Packet Company increases its holding in Isle of Man Air Services Ltd to 50%.

MAY
10 - Chief Constable Major Young is awarded £250 damages from the *Isle of Man Times* for libel. In an article the newspaper accused him of being a social climber and imposing a policing regime of 'unfairness and tyranny.'
12 - Douglas Corporation buys Willaston Estate (77 acres) for housing.
30 - Mr H. E. George, M.A., B.Sc., appointed headmaster of Ramsey Grammar School.
31 - Lieutenant-Governor's term of office is extended for one year.

JUNE
6 - D-DAY - ALLIED INVASION OF FRANCE.
20 - Decided to open Tynwald Court with prayer.

JULY
6 - Lady Louis Mountbatten visits Island
6 - Lady Baden-Powell opens new Scout and Guide headquarters (Cunningham House)
20 - Memorial to Miss Josephine Kermode ('Cushag') unveiled in Maughold churchyard.

SEPTEMBER
6 - Visit of Prince Olav, Crown Prince of Norway to meet Norwegians housed in the Onchan Camp who had escaped and were waiting to join their country's 'free' armed services.
17 - Blackout restrictions relaxed.

OCTOBER
2 - Ramsey Swing Bridge taken over by Harbour Commissioners.
26 - Four interned Manx soldiers who had escaped welcomed home.
30 - Government Commission's proposals for £250,000 Brine Spa at Ramsey outlined.
31 - Announced in Tynwald that agreement had been reached with Imperial Government for repurchase of requisitioned boarding-house furniture.

NOVEMBER
3 - L.G.B. approve Douglas Corporation's application to borrow £25,000 to acquire Glen Falcon House and garden for widening of Broadway.
17 & Manx women prosecuted and fined for failing to obey
24 Lieutenant-Governor's directive that they should join the Women's Land Army.
18 - Braddan Commissioners decide to purchase Snugborough estate for housing.

DECEMBER
3 - Home Guard Farewell 'Stand Down' Parade.

BLACKOUT RESTRICTIONS LIFTED : HOME GUARD STANDS DOWN

After five years of restrictions, street lighting has been restored on the Island and blackout curtains have become redundant. The big switch-on happened on the evening of Sunday, 17th September. Not having been used for such a long time and lacking maintenance because of shortage of manpower, it was not possible for all the lights to be made operational immediately. In Douglas, only 300 of its 671 lights were switched on and just a few of its 174 powered by gas. Even so, to a community accustomed to stygian darkness the event seemed like a light spectacular, particularly on Douglas promenade where hundreds turned out to experience the sight. Conservation of fuel and resources, however, meant that the amount of illumination, compared with pre-war days, was very poor. Light standards on the promenade, for example, were each fitted with one 150 watt bulb compared with the normal loading of two 300 watt bulbs. The lights were screened also from the sea as the risk from enemy attack from the sea still remains. The removal of the light restriction follows the lifting some time ago of the compulsory requirement for children to carry their gas masks with them on schooldays.

During the year the Home Guard Battalions continued to maintain a high standard of training. This was put into practice at the annual competitions and summer weekend camps at Glen Wyllin. A feature of the camps this year were battle simulation courses at which men were given the experience of advancing against a position whilst being under live fire. The summer over

and the Allied advance into Europe making steady progress, preparations were made for the possible Standing Down of the Home Guard. The compulsory drills and training introduced in 1942 were discontinued and all duties reverted to being voluntary. Attendance was little affected, but by the end of October arrangements for the Stand Down and withdrawal of arms and equipment were put into effect.

A grand Stand Down Parade was held in the Villa Marina on 3rd December. Over a thousand men from all parts of the Island belonging to the 1st and 2nd Battalions assembled in the Lord Street Car Park, wearing uniform for the last time. Led by the Band of the Royal Naval School of Music, based at the Howstrake Holiday Camp in Onchan, the men in Company formation marched along the Loch Promenade where His Excellency Earl Granville took the salute from the War Memorial. The Guard of Honour was made up of men representing all the Companies. Assembled in the Villa Marina, a short service was conducted by Archdeacon, the Ven. C. V. Stockwood. The singing of 'Guide me, O Thou great Jehovah' was most moving, especially the second verse which was sung unaccompanied. Earl Granville expressed the appreciation of all for the many hours the men had given to training and carrying out their duties, and paid tribute to the high standards that had been achieved since the L.D.V. was formed over four years ago. Then, armed with little more than 'patriotic spirit', the Home Guard had become a well-trained, well-armed and efficient military force.

The Maughold Platoon, 1944 winners of the Governor's Cup which is competed for by all sections of the Home Guard. Seated behind the cup is the Platoon Commander, Maughold farmer Lieutenant H. C. Kerruish. (Barry Quilliam)

Badge of the newly-
commissioned H.M.S. Urley. The
badge is surmounted by a 'crown'
of galleons and Viking ships and
incorporates the Eagle and Child,
ancient crest of the House of
Stanley whose family once
provided Kings and Lords of Man.
(The late Jack Callister)

The Royal Navy Air Station at Ronaldsway was commissioned on 21st June as *H.M.S. Urley*, taking its name from the Manx for 'eagle.' Its Commanding Officer is Captain W. P. Shirley-Rollinson, R.N. and over a thousand personnel are now resident in the accommodation huts at Ballasalla and Janet's Corner. The station is an Operational Training Unit for aircrew flying the Fairey Barracuda torpedo/bomber/reconnaissance aircraft now in service with the Fleet Air Arm. *H.M.S. Urley* is seen as an

important part of the preparations for the expected long campaign in the Far East, leading to the eventual capitulation of Japan. Many of those under training at Ronaldsway are from Australia and New Zealand.

The Barracuda is a complex aircraft which can be used either as a torpedo bomber or dive bomber. It is equipped also with air to surface radar and, with a weight of nearly eight tons, is powered by an up-rated Merlin engine which makes it particularly noisy, something the people of Castletown have learned to their chagrin. Three training squadrons, with a total of over a hundred Barracudas, are based at Ronaldsway. Each has a crew of three housed beneath a canopy over the wing, these being the pilot, observer/radar operator and the telegraphist/airgunner. The course lasts for 14 weeks during which each crew are in the air for about 90 hours. A third of this is at night, and either individually or in formation. Many hours are spent on navigation exercises around the Irish Sea. Torpedo dropping is

practised on targets towed by motor launches off the coast. The most demanding part of the course is the intensive dive bombing at targets found off Perwick and Port Soderick, where observation huts record results. At night a flare is released to light up the target which just gives sufficient time for the aircraft to dive down to 200 feet before dropping the practice bomb.

At Jurby the training navigation and bombing schedules continue, though the pace slackened before D-Day as pilots were posted out to take up positions in support of the Normandy invasion. Many of them flew Ansons which had been converted as air ambulances. More specialised training at Jurby involved navigators acting as bomb-aimers in the twin-engined Bostons, Beau-fighters and Mosquitoes. In the spring Wing-Commander Guy Gibson V.C, of Dambuster fame paid a visit to all R.A.F. establishments including Andreas and the radar stations. While Andreas continues to train air-gunners, its former Control Centre at Ramsey Grammar School has been given a new role. The Operations Room now plots all aircraft movements over the Irish Sea and wireless contact with the aircraft can be made to pass on information and instructions.

When an aircraft is 'lost' the Coast Guard is informed and Rescue Sections are summoned to undertake 'search and rescue' in a given area. The year has seen a number of crashes involving aircraft from the United States Army Air Force as they cross the Island on flights between their bases in England and Northern Ireland.

AIR CRASH FATALITIES, 1944

11th January. Anson from Wigtown ditched at night off Douglas Head. Air Sea Rescue unable to assist and Douglas lifeboat was later requested to launch, but was unable to find the five aircrew.

5th April. Anson from R.A.F. Cark ditched in sea between Mull of Galloway and Burrow Head. Air Sea Rescue Walrus from Andreas made search and recovered one body of the five aircrew.

8th June. U.S.A.A.F Liberator struck east shoulder of Snaefell, 50 feet from summit. Crew of four were fatally injured.

13th June. Anson from Wigtown struck North Barrule at night and disintegrated on impact. Four crew were killed.

6th July. U.S.A.A.F. Liberator flew into thick fog and struck North Barrule 100 feet from summit. Impact followed by explosion and fire. Four crew lost.

14th July. U.S.A.A.F. Marauder flew into thick cloud and struck Cronk ny Arrey Laa. Aircraft completely destroyed but two of the eight on board were found alive in the widespread wreckage.

14th July. Halifax on cross-country training flight seen on fire over Agneash and Laxey before crashing near Lonan Church. Wreckage spread over wide area, an engine setting fire to bungalow on Pinfold Hill. Small boy died from burns. The

crew of eight, including seven Canadians, was lost.

8th August. Anson from Squire's Gate struck Beinn-y-Phott at 1,100 feet and broke up. Pilot and navigator survived but two others were killed.

13th August. Anson from Wigtown flew into north-west face of Cronk ny Arrey Laa at full power killing all five on board.

27th October. R.N.A.S. Hurricane based at Andreas on exercise with Radar School on Douglas Head crashed near the incline railway, killing the pilot.

21st December. Barracuda from *H.M.S. Urley* dived on target in Port Soderick Bay when wing fell off. Pilot and observer were killed.

22nd December. Wellington from R.A.F. Shawbury, Salop, flew into South Barrule in thick fog, killing all four crew.

31st December. A mid-air collision involving two Ansons from mainland stations occurred during the morning over the south of the Island. One of the Ansons was able to land in a large field and the crew survived. The other Anson was seen to go into a dive and crashed at Ballabeg, Arbory, killing all four crew.

BONFIRES LIGHT UP VICTORY CELEBRATIONS

The news of the surrender of German forces came late on the morning of Tuesday, 8th May. That afternoon everyone, at home or at work, was glued to a wireless set to hear Prime Minister Winston Churchill make his triumphal address to the nation. The Manx Music Festival, which had just started the previous day at the Gaiety Theatre, was interrupted to enable the audience to listen to the broadcast from the stage. Everyone then sang the National Anthem and the rest of the day the whole Island joined in the celebrations. We have this report:

Church bells, which for long had been silent, pealed and were joined by ships' sirens and hooters. Air raid sirens sounded the 'all clear' for five minutes. Streets were gaily decorated with flags and bunting, and street parties hastily organised. Elsewhere, people went to church for special Thanksgiving services. Service personnel and locals joined in the merriment with much singing and music. At Ramsey black-faced Minstrels roamed the flag-decorated streets, one of them beating an enamel dish like a drum. The general noise everywhere was something one had to experience to believe. At night, the Island was lit by bonfires in the towns and villages, and on the beaches. Shopkeepers produced boxes of fireworks and rockets which had been hidden away since 1939. Little work was done on VE Day and the following day which was classed as a general holiday. Workers were either given the time off or, if their services were needed paid extra. There was no mail for two days because there were no postmen on duty!

At midnight on Tuesday, 14th August, Britain's new Prime Minister, Clement Attlee announced that Japan had finally surrendered. This brought huge crowds on to the promenades at Douglas as the Royal Navy ships fired their guns and lit up the night skies with flares. The following day was celebrated as VJ Day and a general holiday was proclaimed. There were more street parties in many parts of the Island and at night pubs had to close when supplies ran out. Many came in from 'the country' to join the festivities and the Villa Marina and Palais de Danse were packed with dancers. Billy Ternent and his band appeared on the roof of the Colonnade and, lit up by naval searchlights, played for thousands of dancers on the promenade opposite. It was a perfect summer evening which was also enjoyed by visitors already on the Island. It is estimated that 100,000 have arrived this summer - a welcome sign for the future.

VICTORY PARADES

The VE celebrations culminated on the following Sunday with a great parade in Douglas in which 2,000 took part, headed by a band of 70 musicians from the Royal Naval School of Music. The parade left the Victoria Pier Arcade and His Excellency Earl Granville took the salute at the War Memorial. The Guard of Honour was provided by officers and sailors from H.M.S. St George,

with the bugle band also in attendance. The parade consisted of detachments from H.M.S. Valkyrie, H.M.S. St George and H.M.S. Urley followed by the Wrens. Then came units from the O.C.T.U., Royal Corps of Signals, P.O.W. Camp guards, A.T.S., R.A.F. Jurby and R.A.F. Andreas, the R.A.F. Regiment with members of the Home Guard, Civil Defence, Army and Sea Cadets and A.T.C. Cadets taking up the rear. Weather conditions were dismal for the assembly in the Villa Marina Gardens and the parade was concluded by a short service during which the Lord Bishop gave a short address.

Glorious summer weather prevailed for the Victory Parade held to celebrate VJ Day. The proceedings were similar to those for VE Day, with all organisations again represented. The O.C.T.U. provided the Guard of Honour and the music was by the Douglas Brass Band conducted by Mr Sam Brough. In many ways it was also a Farewell Parade with the imminent closing of many of the training establishments and camps on the Island.

ROYAL VISIT

Adding to the excitement of the summer was the visit of Their Majesties King George VI and Queen Elizabeth - the first Royal Visit they had been able to undertake outside Great Britain since the war began. It was a three-day visit beginning on 4th July when they arrived at Victoria Pier, Douglas. The first stop was at the Villa Marina where 4,000 schoolchildren had assembled to greet them with massed singing. The rest of the day was spent touring towns and villages throughout the Island, before retiring to Government House. Thursday was Tynwald Day where record crowds assembled to witness the historic occasion

1945
• Massive bombing raid by US and British Air Force destroys Dresden in Germany
• The war in Europe officially came to an end at midnight on 8th May 1945

Following VE Day, a Victory Parade was held on Sunday, 13th May, with over 2,000 taking part. The Guard of Honour was provided by a contingent from H.M.S. St. George seen here being inspected by the Island's wartime Governor, His Excellency Vice-Admiral The Earl Granville, K.C.V.O., C.B., D.S.O. Much better weather was enjoyed for the Victory Parade following VJ Day in August.
(Manx National Heritage)

His Majesty King George VI presides at a meeting of members of Tynwald in St. John's Church prior to the Tynwald Ceremony. (R. and L. Kelly Collection)

1945
- US B-29 drops atomic bomb on Hiroshima in Japan in August
- Japan formally surrenders in September

Right: The historic occasion which saw, for the first time, a King and Queen take their places on Tynwald Hill. Their Majesties are seen accompanied by His Excellency Earl Granville and Lord Bishop Strickland Taylor, with Deemster R. D. Farrant, Clerk of the Rolls on the right. (Douglas Town Hall Archives)

Far right: Last engagement of Their Majesties before leaving the Island was an inspection of personnel at R.A.F. Jurby. Queen Elizabeth is seen here inspecting the parade of W.A.A.F.s in front of Flying Control. (via Laura Briggs)

when, for the first time, a King and Queen took their places on Tynwald Hill. In the afternoon a visit was made to H.M.S. St George, which was followed next morning by a visit to H.M.S. Valkyrie where the ship's company of 1,800 were paraded, watched by a huge crowd. Time was also spent at the machine shops of the Dowty engineering works at Castle Hill, Douglas, where 250 employees are engaged in making hydraulic undercarriages for aircraft. Then it was northwards to R.A.F. Jurby where over a thousand airmen and WAAFs were inspected. A Dakota aircraft left at 3 p.m. to return Their Majesties to London.

FISHING TRAGEDY AT PEEL
In January, two members of the crew of the Peel fishing boat Manx Lily died in drowning accidents within four days of each other. First, her acting skipper, Thomas Walter Quilliam, was dragged into the sea as the scallop dredge fell back into the water as it was being hauled inboard. Then the vessel's skipper, David Craine, died when he fell overboard while taking her to Scotland for overhaul.

ISLAND'S WORST AIR DISASTER
On the morning of 23rd April, a Boeing B17 Flying Fortress set off from its base in Essex to Nutt's Corner, Belfast. At 10.20 a.m. it was seen passing over Maughold at about 500 feet and entered low cloud which covered North Barrule. A moment later an explosion was heard as it crashed into the mountainside. Police and ambulance staff from R.A.F. Andreas were sent to the scene to recover the bodies. All 31 on board, including a dog, had perished, making it the most appalling aircraft accident on Manx soil. Every available space in the Fortress had been crammed with American airmen on their way for a rest period. The aircraft was found to be on automatic pilot while the mountainside was littered with playing cards and dollar bills.

Just nine days before, on 14th April, another Fortress on its way to Northern Ireland was seen flying very low in thick fog heading west over the Perwick Bay Hotel. The aircraft just cleared the trees beyond the swimming pool, banked left and crashed on Cronk ny Arrey, about half a mile from Glen Chass. All ten on board perished in the impact which was followed by an explosion.

NEW GOVERNOR SWORN IN

A great ceremonial occasion was staged at *H.M.S. Urley* when 2,000 of the ship's personnel paraded on 25th August. They were to witness the departure of the Island's wartime Lieutenant-Governor, Earl Granville and his wife, Lady Margaret Rose, sister to the Queen. Before they departed for Northern Ireland they greeted the incoming Lieutenant-Governor, Air Vice Marshal Sir Geoffrey Bromet, who had served with Coastal Command during the war. He arrived in a Lockheed Electra and the Marine Band played as the two Lieutenant-Governors inspected the Guard of Honour. The departing Lieutenant-Governor flew off in the Electra while Sir Geoffrey was driven to Castle Rushen to be sworn in as the Island's new Lieutenant-Governor.

FIRE CHIEF GAOLED

After a sensational trial at the Court of General Gaol, Douglas fire chief Stephen Albert Caugherty was sentenced to 15 months hard labour and fined £700. He pleaded guilty to stealing hundreds of ration books stored in Douglas Town Hall and selling them on the Black Market. Deemster Cowley said Caugherty had been a traitor to his country. The Manchester businessman who bought the ration books was also gaoled.

LEST WE FORGET

While most of those held in German Prisoner of War Camps had returned to the Island before VE Day, including men of the 129th Battery, Manx Regiment, it was not until the end of the year that over 40 survivors from Japanese camps returned to their families. Throughout the year further details were received about those who had been killed, were missing presumed killed, or had died as a result of accidents or illness. It has been difficult to get information from the Far East. The latest numbers include those who have had to be presumed killed after a considerable lapse of time. According to the latest local records, a total of 451 service personnel from the Island, including five women, have been killed in action or have died whilst on active service. Official figures show that 5,455 men from the Island served with H.M. Forces and Merchant Navy

FINAL WAR CASUALTIES		
BRITISH ARMY	-	22 (including 7 on Western Front, 2 in Italy and 4 in Burma and Malaysia)
ROYAL AIR FORCE	-	15 (on operations)
ROYAL NAVY	-	10
MERCHANT NAVY	-	5
TOTAL	-	52

In addition 13 have been killed in accidents or have died in hospitals. A further 16 have died in Prisoner of War Camps, 13 of whom were held by the Japanese.

Top right: View from the control tower of part of the parade of H.M.S. Urley personnel to mark the departure of the Lieutenant-Governor and the arrival of his replacement, Air Vice-Marshal Sir Geoffrey Bromet.

Middle right: Commanding Officer of H.M.S. Urley, Captain Shirley-Rollinson R.N., inspecting W.R.N.s based on the station.

Bottom right: His Excellency Earl Granville making a final tour of inspection before greeting Air Vice-Marshal Sir Geoffrey Bromet and departing for his new appointment as Governor of Northern Ireland on 25th August. (Photographs: The late Jack Callister)

The Royal Visit began with a welcome from 4,000 schoolchildren from Douglas who assembled in the Villa Marina Gardens. Their Majesties are seen here accompanied by the Mayor of Douglas, Councillor Stephen Quirk.

A stop in Royal Avenue Onchan, gave local children and villagers a chance to greet Their Majesties. Sergeant Fred Faragher of the Isle of Man Constabulary keeps a watchful eye over the proceedings.

An historic Tynwald Day. The Sword Bearer leads Their Majesties to Tynwald Hill upon which they became the first King and Queen to take part in the ancient ceremony.

Royal Visit
IN PICTURES

Right: Thousands of people from the north assembled in Parliament Square, Ramsey, to make the most of the Royal Visit.

Below: Members of the Women's Land Army based at Knockaloe are honoured by a visit by Their Majesties seen with Organiser Miss E. Teare. The W.L.A. played a vital part during the war in helping food production.

Below right: Their Majesties, in company with Captain Poland, Officer Com-manding H.M.S. St George, during an inspection of the entire ship's complement on the field adjoining Cunningham's Camp. Throughout the war, over 8,500 young sailors were taught at the Ballakermeen High Schools before being posted to ships of the Royal Navy.

(Photographs from Douglas Town Hall Archives)

PROUD RECORD OF THE MANX REGIMENT

The new year saw the 15th LAA Batteries in constant action on the German border, firing thousands of rounds as enemy fighters and bombers attacked R.A.F. landing grounds nearby. Then the guns were used to attack ground targets as units of the 7th Armoured Division pressed on with their relentless advance against stubborn German resistance. At the end of January, Earl Granville, accompanied by Lieut.-Colonel MacClellan, paid a two-day visit to the Regiment to see members in action and to discuss post-war matters.

The next major obstacle for Field-Marshal Montgomery's 21st Army was the crossing of the Rhine and on 22nd March 41st Battery was positioned in support of the vanguard and made the crossing on the 25th, to be followed by the other two Batteries. They were met by a mass of surrendering enemy, but carried on changing positions almost daily to defend bridges over the Dortmund-Ems Canal. The beginning of April saw the 1st and 42nd helping to marshal captured men and displaced persons from the concentration camps. Elsewhere, 41st was involved in resisting counter attacks. The 7th Division then turned south-east towards Nienburg and during the last weeks of April, the Regiment were involved in some of the most intensive anti-aircraft gunnery since the invasion. The Luftwaffe's ME 109s and FW 190s regularly appeared in force at low level to harrass the advance, and the Batteries were frequently called upon to wipe out pockets of resistance as towns and villages were entered. 1st Battery had the experience of moving through Fallingbostel where 10,000 British POWs (including some of the 129th Battery) had been freed.

Further progress brought the Divison within range of Hamburg. The Regiment was now more than 200 miles from the Rhine, after 27 days on the move during which they had fired 10,000 rounds with 27 'hits' scored. At this point Major Henry Kelly was made Lieut.-Colonel and took over command of the Regiment. Major H. S. Balls became Second in Command, handing over 42nd Battery to Major D. D. Lay. By the end of April, German resistance was waning and on 1st May, 42nd Battery made the last anti-aircraft firings of the war by the Regiment's guns. Hamburg surrendered on the 3rd and news of Adolf Hitler's suicide was followed quickly by the German surrender on 7th May. The regiment has the proud record of accounting for over 350 enemy aircraft destroyed or damaged - a total unrivalled by any other L.A.A. Regiment. Eighty of the Regiment lost their lives.

129TH BATTERY COMES HOME

Since that fateful day in Crete four years ago, the survivors of the 129th Battery endured the deprivations of German prison camps. Those who had been repatriated, and the three gunners who had escaped, told of the harsh treatment that had been meted out by their custodians who seemed to be unaware of the Geneva Convention. Red cross parcels brought welcome relief from the endless soup and black bread, while parcels from home helped to keep up morale.

The Americans were the first to reach the prison camps in Austria and by the end of April, groups were being welcomed home at the pier in Douglas. Among them was Major W. H. Cain, 129th Battery's Commander. A large number of the 129th were released in Bavaria on 17th April and were left to begin their trek southwards. They were picked up eventually by Americans and flown to an R.A.F. airfield adjoining Rheims. They were then allotted to one of the waiting Lancasters and made the flight back to England. The last of the 129th survivors landed in Douglas a week after VE Day.

1945 NEWS IN BRIEF

JANUARY
24 - Island in frost grip - 18 degrees of frost.
26 - Government announce financial assistance to local authorities and private enterprise for housing.

FEBRUARY
16 - Government to purchase Marine Drive, Douglas Head, for £14,000 from owners. It has been closed throughout the war and its electric railway fell into disuse.
23 - Agricultural Wages Board amended farm workers' wages to £3. 10s. per week.

MARCH
31 - Mr Ramsey Moore (Attorney-General) retired after 25 years' service. Succeeded by Mr Sydney Kneale, O.B.E.

APRIL
1 - Mr D. F. Barwell appointed manager of the Palace and Derby Castle Ltd.
27 - Cunningham's Camp, Britain's first holiday camp, sold by the Cunningham family for £400,000. A public company is to be floated to operate it.

MAY
4 - Castletown Brewery Company bought Clinch's Brewery, Douglas.
5 - VE-DAY - Germany capitulated.
10 - Proposed National Testimonial to Mr Noah Moore, Island's veteran conductor, on his retirement.

26 - Mr Herbert Morrison, Home Secretary, conferred with Tynwald deputation re Manx Constitution representations.

JUNE
1 - Basic petrol ration begins.
9 - Serious fire at Strand Cinema causing £7,000 of damage.
14 - His Honour Deemster Cowley awarded C.B.E. in King's Birthday honours.
19 - Earl Granville presented his last Budget showing surplus of £59,296 for the year. Reserves stand at a record £1,000,000, of which £700,000 is earmarked for post-war reconstruction.
22 - Okell's Brewery taken over by Heron and Brearley Ltd. at a cost of £250,000.
26 - Coal heavers' unofficial strike in Douglas regarding working practices. The strike was settled after a week when the Lieutenant-Governor ordered German PoWs to take over the men's work.

JULY
4 - KING AND QUEEN ARRIVE FOR THREE DAY VISIT.

AUGUST
14 - VJ-DAY - Japan capitulated. WORLD WAR ENDED.
24 - Palace and Derby Castle Company acquire Strand Cinema and Palais de Danse.

OCTOBER
27 - Thanksgiving Savings Week begins. £1,003,448 raised.

NOVEMBER
22 - *King Orry* launched at Birkenhead.

PROUD RECORD OF THE MANX REGIMENT

Although the hectic training programme for Barracuda aircrew continued unabated after the surrender of Japanese forces in August, it was only a matter of time before the training station would close down. In fact, the squad-rons on the base were disbanded by the middle of December. It has been announced now that H.M.S. Urley is to be de-commissioned early in the new year. After 18 months of day and night activity, peace has returned to Ronaldsway. Gone is the growl of the Merlin engines which were called upon to power the eight-ton aircraft, and gone are the many complaints to local newspapers about sleepless nights endured by the people of Castletown. Because of wartime censorship, such complaints were never published.

Schoolboys, however, found a holiday pastime in observing the antics of the Barracuda pilots who were required to undertake hazardous manoeuvres at low level when dropping practice torpedoes or diving on the targets located off Perwick and Port Soderick. Pilot error and mechanical failure of one sort or another caused many a crash landing on land and sea. Port Soderick Bay was nicknamed 'Barracuda Bay' because of the number of aircraft lost in its waters. There was always a rescue vessel in attendance and, although many aircrew were saved, many were lost.

On the afternoon of Wednesday, 17th July, a tragic accident happened involving a civilian. At 16.55 a general signal was sent to all aircraft to return to Ronaldsway at once. It had been a fine afternoon, but suddenly the weather began to close in. Dozens of Barracudas queued up to land on runway 13, the approach being across the road just south of the Creggans administrative site. Caught in a down-current, one of the Barracudas crashed through the hedge on either side of the roadway and slid to a stop just short of the runway. It was some time later that a body of a young man was found half buried in a hay rick. He had been hit by the wing of the Barracuda and carried on to the grass. The young man of 16 was David Kelly, son of Castletown's Police Sergeant. David worked at the Creggans which he left at five o'clock to walk home.

At the end of May, R.A.F. Jurby was re-designated No 5 Air Navigation School though it made no difference to

Two of the Fairey Barracuda torpedo/dive bombers from H.M.S. Urley. Seated behind the pilot are the observer and the telegraphist/air gunner. (R.A.F. Museum, Hendon)

its training programme. The Ansons still on charge were joined by numerous Wellingtons. It can be revealed now that Jurby was rocked to its foundations when a Sunderland flying boat crash landed on the airfield. Belonging to a Canadian Squadron based at Lough Neagh, Northern Ireland, it had taken off, fully armed, in search of surrendering U-boats when it clipped the top of a mountain, causing severe damage to its hull. Over the sea it let down through the cloud and spotted Jurby where it made an emergency landing. The crew scrambled to safety as the flying boat caught fire. Then four 1,000 lb depth charges exploded causing extensive damage to parked aircraft and buildings. Many windows were blown out, including the east window of Jurby Church. Much quieter was the visit of Their Majesties in July. The whole station was subjected to much 'spit and polish.' While King George inspected the parade of airmen, Queen Elizabeth inspected the WAAFS.

The routine of training air gunners at R.A.F. Andreas shows no let up. Numbers under training have been maintained by the arrival of gunners already wearing the AG flash but had been shot down over enemy occupied territory. Released from prisoner of war camps, they returned to England for rehabilitation and leave. Those arriving at Andreas have opted to re-train on the latest marks of gun turrets with a view to continuing serving in the R.A.F., either with a squadron or as instructors.

FATAL AIR CRASHES, 1945

6th February. Royal Navy Hurricane based at Andreas for training exercises with *H.M.S. Valkyrie*, crashed in East Baldwin valley. Wreckage spread over a wide area and body of pilot found under parachute, though he had not baled out.

14th April. Boeing B17 Flying Fortress on flight to Northern Ireland crashed in fog on slopes of Cronk ny Arree near Glen Chass, Rushen. None of the ten on board survived.

23rd April. Boeing B17 Flying Fortress on way to Northern Ireland with 31 on board crashed into cloud-covered North Barrule at 500 feet. Violent explosion killed all on board, making it the worst air disaster on Manx soil.

24th May. Firefly from R.N.A.S. Burscough, Lancashire crashed through deck barriers while landing on *H.M.S. Puncher*, ten miles south-west of Chicken Rock. Both aircrew were drowned.

12th July. Civilian killed on Ballasalla/Castletown road after being hit by Barracuda aircraft coming in to land at *H.M.S. Urley.*

7th August. Barracuda on night anti-submarine exercise at Port Soderick failed to pull out of dive through possible airframe failure and plunged into sea. Two of the bodies of the three crew were recovered.

Right: A Blenheim aircraft used for air-to-air gunnery practice at Jurby, 1943. Ballamoar Castle can be seen in the background.

Far right: Members of 54 Air Sea Rescue Unit seen at their base in North Shore Road, Ramsey. Launches are in constant readiness at the Queen's Pier and at Douglas and Peel.

Middle left: Trainee air gunners in front of the rear turret of a Wellington at R.A.F. Andreas.

Middle right: One of the Spitfires at Andreas used as 'targets' for cine-guns in the advanced stage of the gunnery course.

Bottom: Bomb aiming instructors pose in front of one of the many Ansons based at R.A.F. Jurby. (Flt. Lt. Ron Savage)

WARTIME MEMORIES

Left: One of the Lysanders used at Jurby for target towing seen in company with groundcrew, 1943.

Middle left: Officers and instructors of H.M.S. Valkyrie, the Royal Navy's No. 1 Radar Training School, which occupies the Granville Camp on Loch Promenade.

Middle right: Ratings from H.M.S. Valkyrie marching to Douglas Head to undertake training as radar operatives, vital to all ships in the Royal Navy.

Bottom: One of the many intakes of officer cadets of 166 O.C.T.U. based at Clarendon House, Loch Promenade. The cadets undertook a gruelling 17-week course in infantry tactics before being commissioned in one of the Army regiments.

TYNWALD MATTERS : THE AFTERMATH OF WAR

Looking to the future, Lieutenant-Governor Air Vice-Marshal Sir Geoffrey Bromet, K.B.E., C.B., D.S.O., who will work with Tynwald to solve the Island's post-war problems.
(Manx National Heritage)

Early in the war, indeed in 1940, the Douglas Dilettante Debating Society, in an act of supreme confidence, chose as a subject for discussion the possible post-war needs and problems that might confront the Island. Well, now the time has come and actions, not words, are needed. One thing is imperative - the hardships endured by many people after the Great War must not be repeated. The major issues are readily identified - the de-requisitioning and restoration of hundreds of boarding houses; the rapid release of Steam Packet vessels; and the provision of work and financial assistance for the 5,500 returning ex-servicemen and women.

A hopeful start was made in June when Earl Granville, in presenting the last wartime Budget, claimed that the Island was in its strongest financial position ever, with over £1,000,000 in the Reserve Fund. Up to £700,000 was earmarked for reconstruction and housing, while £250,000 was noted as an interest-free loan to the Imperial Government. Wealth indeed, and while the contribution to the war expenses was far more speedy than the shameful procrastination of the 1920s, many would argue it was still insufficient. Another development, perhaps not totally unexpected, has been the apparently insatiable desire of war-weary people to celebrate the first summer of peace by taking a holiday. Despite travelling difficulties, accommodation problems and shortages of all kinds, something like 100,000 arrived in June and July alone. The visiting industry has clearly a very bright future indeed.

One of the most pressing problems concerns the boarding houses which have been freed of servicemen and women, while the internees, detainees and prisoners of war have departed. But many of the houses have been found to be in an absolutely deplorable condition and their restoration has become a major burden for the occupiers. Furniture and fittings have vanished in many cases, and inadequate records of their disposal and storage were kept. Wartime austerity means that replacements are hard to come by. The Imperial Government still, of course, remain in possession of great blocks of such houses. *H.M.S. Valkyrie* continues to hold sway on Douglas promenade, and elsewhere on the Island service establishments still maintain an active presence. Many voices are heard urging Tynwald to be more active in securing the release of accommodation and in pursuing the many claims for compensation.

A similar view is being taken over the release of Steam Packet vessels which provide the Island's life blood. Everyone has been delighted to see the early return of the *Viking* and *Mona's Isle*, still in their war paint, with the *Manx Maid* soon joining them. Better news came in November with the launch of the *King Orry*, one of two new passenger ships being built in Birkenhead for the Steam Packet Company as replacements for wartime losses. Some, however, are looking to an alternative system of travel, perhaps more important for the future. Civil aviation has great potential and, now that *H.M.S. Urley* is to be de-commissioned early in the new year, Ronaldsway could well play an increasingly important part in bringing visitors to our shores.

In human terms by far the major concern is still the absorbing of the returning ex-servicemen and women into the economy of the Island. The visiting industry, which is the major employer, is unlikely to be back to pre-war levels for some time. Already, Tynwald is being heavily criticised for what is seen as its lethargy, although it is difficult to see what can be done swiftly, apart from the much-maligned winter works schemes which seem to have become a permanent part of Manx life! Still, despite this year's Budget with its vast sum marked for reconstruction, few construction work plans have been announced as yet. Over three months after the war ended, a Resettlement Advisory Officer was appointed, but it was late and he was to be guided by Voluntary Advisory Committees that were to be formed later! By this time many of the unemployed had decided to take matters into their own hands. A Government Vigilance Committee was set up to press for immediate action, and they were not disappointed. Tynwald almost immediately provided funds for the completion of the promenade widening scheme at Derby Castle which had begun in 1938. It will find work for 100 men during the winter months - a short term measure it is true, but it is a start. Other important matters of state have already surfaced, as well. Constitutional reform is still uppermost in the minds of our leading politicians, while the innovative plans, introduced in 1938, to provide a new and exciting secondary system of education for all demands immediate attention. Many of the answers to our post-war problems will be addressed by the new House of Keys, which will be formed after the General Election to be held sometime in the new year.

ACCOMMODATION CRISIS: FOOD SHORTAGES CONTINUE

The first full year of peace has seen an encouraging revival of the Island's visiting industry, with more than 400,000 arrivals during the summer, nearly up to pre-war numbers. But there were accommodation problems as hotel and boarding house owners re-occupied their premises after they were used as PoW and alien detention camps and found that extensive damage had been caused. And with food shortages and rationing there were often long queues at cafes and shops. We have this report:

The aftermath of war left the visiting industry infrastructure in disarray. Hoteliers struggled hard to get ready for the summer in the face of a shortage of building materials and new furnishings. There were also food shortages in spite of efforts by the Manx Government to get increased quotas in order to feed its visitors. This led to complaints about quantity and quality of meals. But nearly all the main places of entertainment in Douglas were open again and June saw an all-time record arrival of nearly 90,000 visitors as war-weary Britons rushed to take holidays. The shortages included beer and spirits, and in the absence of imported beer the visitors eagerly drank the local brews of Okell's and Castletown Breweries which faced record demand. There was also a clear sign of thankfulness among visitors that the war was over. There were congregations of up to 16,000 people at the Sunday open-air services at Kirk Braddan.

EDUCATION REFORMS

The Education Authority has carried through the biggest ever reform of the Island's school system, to provide secondary education for all. A spokesman said this would eliminate "snobbery and class distinction." Up to now elementary school children had to pass a scholarship exam to get to secondary school - or pay fees which parents could not always afford. Under the new multi-lateral system all 11-year-olds will go into the new single system operated by Ballakermeen and the Douglas High Schools for Boys and Girls. Children in the north of the Island will attend Ramsey Grammar School when the new 'wing' is made ready.

LADY OF MANN RETURNS

On 9th March the *Lady of Mann*, pride of the Steam Packet fleet, returned to her home port after completing her war service. Bedecked in flags which contrasted with her drab camouflage the '*Lady*' was greeted by a large crowd and emotional singing of 'Ellan Vannin' and the Manx National Anthem. The fine vessel had gone to war in 1939 under the command of the Steam Packet's Commodore, Captain T. C. Woods who vowed to bring her back. Mayor of Douglas, Councillor Tom Cowin, greeted him and his officers at the pier and took them by bus to the Town Hall for a Civic Reception. Captain Woods was awarded the O.B.E. in the New Year's

Honours List in recognition of his achievements throughout the war, including Dunkirk and the D-Day landings. Aged 66, Captain Woods is to retire and will be replaced by Captain J. W. Cubbon as fleet Commodore. After her brief visit, the *Lady* departed to be made ready for the coming season.

DANGER OF SEA MINES

Sea mines were swept ashore around the Manx coastline early this year. Several exploded but upwards of a dozen others were made safe by Royal Navy experts. The mines are believed to have been swept by a storm from their moorings in a minefield to the south of the Calf of Man. Some reached as far as Kirk Michael. This has led to agitation that the minefield should be cleared as quickly as possible.

CONSTITUTIONAL REFORM

In April, Tynwald gave unanimous approval to a resolution seen as a big step forward to Manx Home Rule. Instead of absolute control of the Island's domestic affairs being vested in the Lieut-Governor, a Manx 'Cabinet' is to be introduced consisting of seven members of Tynwald. The Lieut-Governor, however, will still be in a strong position as chairman of the new Executive Council.

INCOME TAX REDUCED

The Island has finished the war in its strongest financial position for many years. As a result income tax is to be reduced to 2 shillings in the pound. The first post-war Manx Budget showed revenues of more than £1 million. The presence in the Island of thousands of aliens, PoWs and British Service personnel doubled the amount of indirect taxation coming in from the Common Purse.

DOUBLE-DECKER BUSES

Isle of Man Road Services Ltd took delivery in August of its first double-decker bus - a Leyland Titan 56-seater. It is one of ten on order and the remainder are expected to arrive by passenger boat next year. However, the use

1946
• Birth of the United Nations with delegates from 51 countries meeting
• Nationalisation in Britain with the newly elected Labour Party leader, Clement Attlee

Lieutenant-Governor, Sir Geoffrey Bromet, attended his first Tynwald Ceremony this year. His Excellency is preceded by Sword Bearer, Lieutenant-Colonel A. H. Kissack, and is followed by his A.D.C., Major J. M. Cain. (Frank Cowin Library)

The "King Orry IV" which, along with "Mona's Queen IV", entered service with the Isle of Man Steam Packet Co this year, the first vessels to replace wartime losses. They are both of similar design and, with a tonnage of 2,485, are certified for 68 crew and 2,163 passengers. Speed capability is 21 knots. (R. and L. Kelly Collection)

of the first is being confined to the Douglas-Onchan route until the relative road traffic law is amended so that double-deckers can be used throughout the Island. At the same time, current law only permits the carrying of 34 passengers and the double-decker now in service operates with only eight seats on the upper deck, the rest being sealed off. The required amendments of the Island's Highways Acts is being opposed by some M.H.K.s on the grounds that the new buses would be too big for Manx road conditions. Nevertheless, it is confidently predicted that Royal Assent will be given to the amendments next year, so that Road Services Ltd. will be able to fully utilise the double-deckers. Douglas Corporation Transport introduced the first of six AEC double-deckers in 1933 and last year acquired a further three, these being diesel-engined Daimlers with wartime utility finish including wooden slatted seats.

NEW STEAM PACKET VESSELS

Two new passenger ships, built by Cammell Laird, Birkenhead, and named *King Orry* and *Mona's Queen* have joined the Steam Packet fleet as the first replacements for the four vessels lost during the war, and the *Snaefell* which has been scrapped. Each of the new ships, with a tonnage of 2,485, have twin-screw

turbines and are certificated to carry 2,163 passengers. They join the *Lady of Mann*, *Ben my Chree*, *Viking*, *Mona's Isle*, *Manx Maid* and *Rushen Castle*, the latter due to be scrapped at the end of the year. The *Victoria* returns next year while the *Manxman* will remain on war commission as a personnel carrier and is not likely to return.

T.T. TROPHIES SAFE

While the A.C.U. found it impossible to stage the T.T. Races this year, the trophies which went to Italy and Germany in 1939 have been found. The Lightweight Trophy, won by Benelli, was discovered at the end of last year. It had been taken to Italy by Giovanni Benelli and hidden in a garden away from potential looters. Appropriately, it was found by a former T.T. rider, E. A. Simcocks who discovered it under a hen coop. The Senior Trophy was discovered earlier this year by an officer stationed at Hochst, near Frankfurt. He was informed by a former senior B.M.W. executive that he had last seen the trophy in Vienna at a B.M.W. agency. At first the manager claimed it had been plundered by the Allies but after "a little gentle persuasion", however, he produced it. Meanwhile, there is news about Georg Meier and the B.M.W.s which did so well in 1939 T.T. All have survived, the racing machines hidden to prevent them being lost in Germany's war effort. Meier hopes to return to the Island one day. The report that Meier had been killed in an air accident early in the war was mistaken.

MANX GRAND PRIX

The news that the Manx Motor Cycle Club was to stage the September races was greeted with immense enthusiasm. It had been made possible by the Manx Government overcoming petrol rationing by making sufficient low-octane 'pool' petrol available. Winner of the Junior race was Ken Bills who showed he had lost none of his pre-war touch. He was followed by Peter Aitchison and Denis Parkinson, all on Nortons. L.W. Parsons (Rudge) won the Lightweight class with Ben Drinkwater and R.S. Simpson, on Excelsiors coming second and third.

H.M.S. Manxman was completed in 1940 and 'adopted' by the Isle of Man. Designed as a high speed minelayer of 2,650 tons, she is said to be the fastest ship in the Royal Navy, being capable of cruising at 44 knots. She paid an official visit to Douglas in December. (Frank Cowin Library)

The Senior M.G.P. was run in atrocious conditions - thick mist and heavy rain. The bravery and fantastic riding of Dubliner Ernie Lyons rode a Triumph-twin to victory, but at the end of the race it was discovered that the down tube of the frame had been completely severed! Ken Bills had to be content with second place, while local rider Harold Rowell (brother of fellow-rider, Albert) was third. Over 7,000 race fans flocked to the Palace for the prize presentations, each rider receiving tumultuous applause. A sad note was the news that popular rider Peter Aitchison had died after crashing at the 33rd Milestone.

GENERAL ELECTION

The results of the General Election on 27th and 28th September brought to an end the Island's 'Long Parliament' elected in 1934. The elections were held in May but the results were delayed in order to account for the many absentee voters still on national service. There were 54 candidates, 18 representing the Manx Labour Party. The poll, however, has shown a massive defeat for Labour which won only two seats. The new member for Garff, Mr. Charles Kerruish, is by far the youngest M.H.K. Mr. J. D. Qualtrough (Castletown) was re-elected Speaker. Elections of Keys' members to the Legislative Council resulted in Mr. Samuel Norris, for long the champion of Constitutional Reform, being unseated.

DESPERATE HOUSING SHORTAGE

The severe post-war shortage of housing in the Island, especially for newly-married ex-servicemen, has been relieved by the Government's purchase of former Nissen hut encampments at Janet's Corner, Castletown, and in Ballasalla. The huts at Ballasalla, arranged in avenues, have been converted into two-, three- and four-bedroomed habitations and will accommodate 92 families. Huts at Janet's Corner have been made ready for 120 families. The conversion was completed in the autumn and each has an allotment as a garden. However, the accommodation is very basic and is reported to be rat-infested. Separate cooking and washing facilities have been provided after a petition against the communal system. A typical hut consists of a living room with a curtained-off kitchen and two small bedrooms at one end. Heating is provided by a round combustion stove with a pipe acting as a 'chimney' through the thin corrugated roof. On cold days everyone has to wear heavy clothing. Dampness is another problem about which there have already been many complaints. Every hut has an outside toilet a short distance from their entrances, and blocks of lockable bathrooms, one per hut, are dotted about the estates. Hot water is only available on certain days.

LAXEY WHEEL PURCHASED

Finally, the man credited with saving the Laxey Wheel from dereliction, Laxey builder Mr. E. C. Kneale, has now become its owner. He first leased it in 1938 from a local family which had owned it since 1918 and allowed it to fall into decay and disrepair. Mr. Kneale restored it to showpiece condition - and now he has bought it outright. This summer the Wheel was visited by about 40,000 people.

1946 NEWS IN BRIEF

JANUARY
24 - Island in grip of 18 degrees of frost.
26 - Government announce financial assistance to local authorities and private enterprise for housing.
21 - Dr. C. Guy Pantin appointed first honorary pathologist at Noble's Hospital.

FEBRUARY
4 - Manx People's Political Association formed.
5 - Launch of *Mona's Queen* at Birkenhead.
13 - Mr. S. A. Perry appointed Entertainments Manager for Douglas Corporation.

MARCH
2 - Golden Jubilee of incorporation of Douglas as a borough celebrated at a civic luncheon in the Villa Marina.

APRIL
10 - Diocesan Conference approves Tithes Bill providing redemption of tithes in the Isle of Man.

MAY
16 - Lieutenant-Governor re-opened Douglas horse tram service.
17-23 House of Keys General Election.
28 - House of Keys Election Bill, introduced by Mr. Samuel Norris to effect re-distribution of seats, "shelved" for six months by Legislative Council
31 - Victory Ball held in Villa Marina.

JUNE
16 - Payment of Members Bill passed, giving members of the Legislature increase from £100 to £150 a year.
24 - Lieutenant-Governor laid inauguration stone of widening scheme at Victoria Pier.

JULY
2 - Anson from Jurby, involved in evening search for a missing R.A.F. aircraft off the south of the Island, struck and carried away the mizzen mast of *Boy Alex* which was in company with other herring boats out from Peel. The Anson ditched five miles off Chicken Rock; only two bodies of the five airmen on board were recovered.
5 - Air Vice Marshal Sir Geoffrey Bromet presided at Tynwald Ceremony for the first time as Lieutenant-Governor.
18 - Arrival of *Millie Walton*, new Douglas lifeboat, most up-to-date of its kind in British Isles.
28 - Bread rationing scheme introduced on the Island.

AUGUST
6 - Family Allowance scheme began.
21 - Douglas Corporation accept tender for £166,511 for erection of 110 houses at Spring Valley.
26-27 Manx General Election results announced.

OCTOBER
16 - Provisional Order constituting new Island Water Board approved by Tynwald. Mr. A. J. Teare, J.P., M.H.K., M.B.E., appointed chairman.
23 - First reunion celebration of 15th Light Anti-Aircraft (Isle of Man) Regiment, R.A., held with Earl Granville as special guest.
28 - Manx Hotels Ltd fined £50 for obtaining unauthorised supply of rationed preserves for Majestic Lido Hotel.

NOVEMBER
9 - Following Douglas municipal elections, first since 1938, Councillor T. C. Cowin, J.P., M.H.K. elected Mayor for second term.

DECEMBER
6 - *H.M.S. Manxman*, 'adopted' by the Isle of Man at the beginning of the war, anchored in Douglas Bay for official visit. Receptions and cocktail parties were held on board and at the Town Hall. Members of the crew were treated to coach trips, ending with a dance in the Villa Marina.

HOTELIERS BATTLE WITH SHORTAGES

Anger and frustration marked the re-birth of the Island's tourist industry this summer. It was a remarkable transformation: from a place of barbed wire fences, military, internment and prisoner of war camps, to a traditional seaside holiday resort. The rushed hand-over of commandeered hotels and boarding houses and the quest, not only to repair damaged furnishings and equipment, but to locate much of what had gone missing led to raised tempers. Hoteliers and boarding house keepers were furious with the military over the slow decommissioning of their properties - and when the latter were handed over they were found in many cases to be in a terrible condition: some altered beyond recognition. One hotelier found that his entire lift system had vanished! Assessors brought in by both the military and property owners disputed what compensation should be paid. The military offered only 50% of what was claimed.

Whilst that issue rumbled on, the rush to get what properties were available in a fit state for the season was not easy. Many windows were boarded up and glass was not readily available. Interiors needed repainting but before that could be done damaged walls needed repairing, and there was a shortage of basic materials like plaster. Plumbing and electrics had been changed to suit all-male establishments and the old equipment had been apparently discarded. In some cases furnishings used by internees or prisoners of war had been defaced with deep carvings of "Heil Hitler" or "Il Duce". Cupboard doors and drawers had been removed as raw material in the making of toys. Stores of linen and equipment, believed to have been securely locked away, had been plundered. One hotelier found a missing gas range eventually but all its jets had been removed. Iron bedsteads were badly damaged, caused, reputedly, by being thrown out of buildings during decommissioning.

Thousands of mattresses removed from requisitioned properties were found to be either verminous, moth-eaten or damaged by poor storage. Some were capable of re-use after disinfecting but many had to be replaced. Large quantities were made last winter and early summer this year at Derby Castle. The ballroom and theatre complex was established by Tynwald's Furniture Restoration Division as a clearing and main repair centre for furnishings and equipment. It was manned by a staff of 100, 30 of them joiners. Hoteliers were invited there to claim what they believed to be theirs. Some identified items but there were rival claims. Consequently, many items had to be auctioned. Indicative of the chaos was a mound of rusting, fat-caked frying pans which the Derby Castle team had to clean and disinfect for re-use.

Bureaucracy in England delayed the production of all the required mattresses and pillows. Earlier this year Tynwald sent a buyer to England to acquire the necessary ticking for a further 930 mattresses. Delays in official paper work prevented the seller sending the material on time. Other supplies did get through, however. These included 25,000 yards of curtaining material bought by Tynwald for re-sale, and large quantities of linoleum and some blankets made at the Tynwald Mill, St. John's. Even so, there were insufficient floor coverings. Some hotels had to settle for the simple staining of bedroom floorboards. Combined with the absence of clothing coupons to provide hotel staff with proper clothing, hoteliers were worried about the impression this would make on tourists. The Hotel Alexandra reported using cut-down pieces of old curtaining as aprons and its waitresses wore trousers. Tynwald managed to ease the situation further by buying war surplus stores and equipment from the services as they vacated their bases on the Island and then re-selling them to hoteliers. When the latter did not want the items, they were offered to householders who had accommodated servicemen in their private homes during the war.

Planning for the summer season was preceded by a highly speculative property market. This was led by the floating of a new public company to operate the Douglas Holiday Camp. The scramble for shares in January led to a temporary suspension in dealing in the shares by the London Stock Exchange. The fact that Admiralty use of the camp had devastated its facilities and chalet accommodation for 1,000 campers had been destroyed, did not deter the speculators. A spirit of regeneration was in the air, typified by the arrival at the camp of 120 builders shortly before and during its de-commissioning by the Admiralty in January.

Buyers of hotels and boarding houses, who anticipated a sudden post-war tourist boon in which quick fortunes could be made from tourists not too fussy about standards were reported to have paid "fantastic prices" for holiday property, despite their poor condition and the chronic shortages of plaster, bricks, wood, glass and paint to repair them.

Among the hotels which changed hands were the Majestic in Onchan, which had been used as a military hospital between 1940 and January this year, and the Fort Anne on Douglas Head which had remained an hotel during the war. Both were bought by the London theatrical, Archie Shenborn, who also leased the wooden Pavilion Theatre in Onchan's amusement park. Shenborn got the Majestic restored in time for opening on 1st July.

Food for holidaymakers was another problem. There was no crisis, claimed the Government, anxious to avoid a scare which would deter visitors from coming to the Island, but, equally, the Island was no "food paradise". In fact, the summer was dogged by every conceivable shortage, despite the importation of Irish cattle, 148 tons of potatoes from Belfast and other goods. Hence, perhaps, a surprise decision by Lieutenant-Governor Bromet to spend a night with the Peel fishing fleet to see how it was managing to land much-needed herring. He spent the night with Peel's M.H.K., George Moore, aboard the 50 foot fishing boat, *Manx Fuchsia*, skippered by Stanley Gorry. Next morning, after attending the auction of the herring, he returned to Government House with some herring on a string.

At the height of the season, on 28th July, one week behind the U.K., even bread rationing had to be introduced. Bakers and hoteliers hoped that it could be delayed until the autumn but problems with national flour supplies meant it had to be imposed. The ration of nine ounces a day for the average consumer, 15 ounces for a male manual worker and between four and 12 ounces for children, depending on their age, was reckoned to be not much less that what an average person ate in a day - and there was provision for people to gain more bread in exchange for other ration coupons, such as cakes or sweets. It did not seem to offer the prospect of much hardship but it was another major headache for the tourist industry.

At least there were enough eggs for breakfast. Anticipating problems in respect of eggs, hoteliers started "putting down" all the unrationed Manx eggs they could get direct from Manx farmers last spring. "Putting down" involved preserving fresh eggs by placing them in metal barrels filled with a mixture of water and a substance known as 'Water Glass'. This forms a white sealant around egg shells.

Problems with food supplies meant that most hoteliers and boarding house keepers had to confine their services to tea, bed and breakfast. Visitors had to queue for their principal meals in cafes and restaurants which seemed to be able to get better supplies. Reports of food shortages were believed to have reduced August Bank Holiday arrivals. Despite the chaos, some normality crept back into Manx life this summer. The Palace Ballroom, which had been used as a naval dining room during the war and a training centre for D-Day visible signalling, throbbed to the sound of dance music again.

Now planning has begun to get the tourist industry launched properly in 1947. It will not be easy. Some hoteliers and boarding house keepers are still waiting to gain possession of their properties from the military. This is notably so in respect of the £3 million radar instruction camp H.M.S. Valkyrie I. The camp is not due to be decommissioned until the end of December. A Royal Navy landing craft is expected in Douglas some time after that to collect the station's secret equipment. Even then it is estimated that some of the H.M.S. Valkyrie I properties on the promenade

will not be available for civilian use until May, 1947. Douglas Head, meanwhile, which is still sealed off from public use and is littered with mysterious aerial systems, is not likely to be restored to tourist use until 1948.

To help equip hotels and boarding houses, three factories have been established for the local manufacture of basic short-life furniture like wardrobes and beds which is desperately needed. One is on Douglas Head, another at Kirk Michael and a third in the former Victorian paper mill in Glen Road, Laxey.

One of the holiday places which should be ready next year to take visitors is the former Howstrake Holiday Camp. It was de-commissioned in August-September. Since July 1941 it had been used as the Royal Naval School of Music. Four hundred of Britain's most musically-talented youngsters aged between 14 and 18 were trained by 24 instructors for membership of the navy's top bands. From its very beginning the school provided a band for many functions, the Tynwald ceremony and for morale-boosting summer afternoon concerts in the Villa Marina gardens. Now it is reported that many of those taught here, and who learned to swim in the nearby Groudle Bay, are likely to become the top players in Britain's dance hall bands.

During its occupation of the holiday camp, the school adapted the tennis courts for drill. A parade ground was added on and the chalets were adapted to serve as dormitories for groups of between 20 to 30 young men. This included the installation of central heating.

Howstrake Holiday Camp served as the Royal Naval School of Music and hundreds of young bandsmen were trained here for service in the Navy. Now decommissioned, preparations have begun to make the Camp ready for next season. (Frank Cowin Library)

TYNWALD MATTERS: THE 1946 GENERAL ELECTION

A year ago the voters of the United Kingdom gave unequivocal backing to the British Labour Party and its programme for post-war reconstruction in one of the biggest election victories ever recorded. No doubt encouraged by this, our own Manx Labour Party has made its most determined effort yet. It would seem from its public statements that it was not content with aiming for, say, half a dozen seats to form a significant pressure group. Rather, its intention was to produce a House of Keys in which Labour members were so numerous and dominant that it would be able to form a party government. Its programme was the Socialist one: nationalisation of essential services, a comprehensive social and health system and so on. This message was trumpeted out at the many public meetings held all over the Island in April and May as the Island was gripped by election fever. In all, 18 Labour Party candidates took the field.

Needless to say, this bold and determined assault produced its counterblast. As early as February many citizens, especially those of the business class, were perturbed enough to embark on forming their own political party. A public meeting was held at the Villa Marina attended by over 200 people and presided over by the ex-Attorney-General, Mr. R. B. Moore. Out of it came a new political party representing, it may be fairly said, the more conservative sections of the community. Perhaps clumsily, it named itself the Manx People's Political Association but there was little doubt about its character. Candidates sponsored by this new party were identified in the Isle of Man Weekly Times as "Anti-Socialist"! The election days in May, lasting from the 17th in Rushen to the 23rd in Garff, saw scenes of great excitement although this was tempered by the knowledge that because of the difficulties in gathering in the servicemen's votes the results would not be announced until September.

The issues were certainly no major considerations of principle.

On the contrary, the Manx electorate seemed far more concerned with practical affairs: employment and the need for industries to complement the visiting industry; farming subsidies; rural housing. There are still 239 farms with no piped water. As far as public housing is concerned, no new house should be built without a bath; the boarding houses must be modernised and so on. Big political ideas seemed unwelcome and now, at the end of September with the results, exactly how unwelcome is clear. Of the 24 members returned it can reasonably be said that 22 are anti-socialist. Only 2 Labour candidates were returned out of 18 and those two were of such stature and worth that any label would have sufficed.

The new House is assembled. Half of its members are new-

Mr J. D. Qualtrough, who has been re-elected Speaker of the House of Keys following this year's General Election. (Frank Cowin Library)

comers, and their overwhelming character is conservative. The problems facing the House are great, not least the constitutional developments which were announced secretly. However, the Island has just experienced a prosperous season and in this, at least for the foreseeable future, the prospects are excellent. Our new House must see that they are fulfilled.

THE MANX CABINET

For a considerable time voices have been raised in the Island demanding more participation in our Executive. The position of the Lieutenant-Governor and the Legislative Council and, indeed, the complete authority vested in them, have been under attack from many quarters. Indeed, in the recent election campaign one of the planks of the anti-Socialist campaign, even if not pressed too hard, was an extension of Home Rule.

Perhaps the return of a Labour Government in the United Kingdom provided a heaven-sent opportunity for those who advocated a reform of the old ways. The new Home Secretary, Mr Chuter Ede, no doubt acting upon comments from his predecessor, Mr. Herbert Morrison, has proved sympathetic to the demands for an extension of democratic control.

In April the Home Secretary expressed his interest in the establishment of an Executive Council to assist the Lieutenant-Governor in the performance of his duties vis a vis the government of the Island. Having considered his proposals, the Speaker of the House of Keys moved that they should be adopted and this was agreed unanimously. The essence of these proposals was that the Lieutenant-Governor should be guided and assisted by seven

members of Tynwald, five of whom should be the Chairmen of the main Boards of Agriculture and Fisheries, Highways and Transport, Social Services, Local Government and Education. Two other members would be recommended and appointed by resolution of Tynwald. An important condition was that the Lieutenant-Governor, Legislative Council and the Keys should be consulted prior to the appointments.

Now, following the first meeting of the new House of Keys after the General Election, history has been made. The Executive Council has been nominated and accepted, the one exception being that it was felt that the Speaker, although Chairman of the Board of Education, should not take a place. Another member of the Board has become a member instead. Some have carped that only three members of the Keys are on the Council. It is less than the democratic revolution anticipated, but the fact remains, the Island does have a "Cabinet", it is an important part of the Executive and nothing in Manx Government can ever be the same again.

Home Rule it may not be, but a sizeable stride towards it, it certainly is.

A REVOLUTION IN EDUCATION

1946
- National health service founded in Britain
- War crimes tribunal (The Nuremberg Trials) begin in Berlin

On the 25th October the Home Secretary, Mr. Chute Ede, officially opened the new multi-lateral School at Ballakermeen in Douglas. This represents a radical transformation in the educational system of the Island and happily a transformation that has been welcomed and applauded across the entire spectrum of the Manx nation. It may be as well to remind ourselves of the system it replaced. At the age of 11 all pupils, boys and girls, sat for the "Scholarship" examination. Those fortunate and clever enough to pass, a generous 25% or more, then went to the two High Schools in Douglas and the Grammar School in Ramsey. The remaining 75% or so, not being selected, were in fact rejected and remained at their Elementary Schools. Thus was established an 'education snobbery and class distinction', and the futures of whole generations of pupils were decided irrevocably at the age of 11.

The Island was very fortunate indeed in that just before the outbreak of war two brand new buildings, one in Douglas, one in Ramsey, were constructed to form part of the old system, both doing valiant war service. Both could be fitted into the new system. In this every pupil boy or girl would transfer to the new multi-lateral or comprehensive High School. There in classes that could be streamed according to ability they would all complete their education, in the same school in the same uniform, playing in the same school teams.

The administrative problems in effecting this revolution have been great. Not only have the pupils and their parents had to be informed of events, but the teachers in the old elementary schools have had to be redeployed now that their upper classes have gone to Ballakermeen or Ramsey Grammar. Furthermore some old schools, notably Hanover Street in Douglas, part and parcel of the fabric of their communities for more than half a century, are now seen to be superfluous to requirements and one supposes at some point must close. Still, these new schools are magnificent. They are superbly equipped, light and airy, ideally situated in their playing fields, a credit to the Island. And on September 16th all roads led to them. Long crocodiles of youngsters, marshalled by their teachers marched no doubt with some apprehension to their futures. Indeed one lady living near Ballakermeen said that she had stood at her window all morning watching, and no doubt hearing, hundreds of children flood the hitherto quiet streets and avenue. The Dining Room staff at Ballakermeen didn't have time to stand and stare. They started at 8 a.m. peeling hundreds of pounds of potatoes and carrots.

Like first days everywhere there was no doubt a little confusion but the staffs in Douglas and Ramsey by dint of exceptional care and devotion ensured that not only was it kept to a minimum but that the vital element in any school, namely the teaching of the pupils, got under way with remarkable speed and efficiency.

Today has seen the official ceremony. In the Boys Hall at Ballakermeen 100 boys, 100 girls, 100 parents and 100 politicians, officials and guests heard Mr. Chute Ede speak glowingly of the new school and the system it represented. "Few schools can more fittingly represent the spirit of modern education". The facilities he remarked were for everyone and in conclusion he made a formal request for a school holiday, a plea heard with delight by the 500 or so pupils in the Girls Hall. They may not have been able to see him, but hear him they certainly could, and favourable comments were heard on all sides about the behaviour and appearance of the children.

There can be little doubt that the term "educational revolution" so often misapplied now totally accurate. It is a revolution and dramatically different from the tripartite and divisive arrangement in operation in the United Kingdom. Is it the pattern for the future? Too early to tell. Of one thing the Island can be sure, the progress and achievements of these Manx Bi-laterals, or Comprehensives as they are increasingly being called, will be scrutinised with eagle eyes. If they are successful it may be that the Island really has formed the pattern for the future.

Completed in 1939 and used throughout the war as part of the H.M.S. St George training ship, the Ballakermeen High School was officially opened in October and is now part of the Education Authority's policy of providing secondary education for all children of 11 and over.
(R. and L. Kelly Collection)

AIR SERVICES NATIONALISED

One of the most immediate effects on the Isle of Man as a result of the Labour Government's policy of nationalisation concerned the Island's air services. All airlines and airports came under the control of the Ministry of Civil Aviation. Isle of Man Air Services Ltd is a Manx registered company operating from an airport outside the United Kingdom, albeit controlled by the Ministry of Civil Aviation now that Ronaldsway has been vacated by the Admiralty. A Commission set up by Tynwald last year to make representations to the U.K. Government regarding the future ownership of Ronaldsway has made little progress, though it was made clear that the Ministry of Civil Aviation would continue to operate the airport for the foreseeable future. This involved the provision of safety factors including the installation of Standard Beam Approach (VHF D/F) on the main runway which makes Ronaldsway one of the best equipped in the British Isles. As regards the air services to and from the Isle of Man, it has been made clear these are to be taken over by British European Airways Corporation next year. For the present, Isle of Man Air Services Ltd will operate the routes established before the war as an associate of B.E.A. The local airline has three de Havilland Rapides available and on 15th July this year Captain John Higgins, M.B.E. flew the first post-war inaugural flight of Isle of Man Air Services on the Manchester route.

R.A.F. ANDREAS TO CLOSE

The one and only opportunity the general public had of visiting R.A.F. Andreas was on Battle of Britain Day this September. Already it had been announced that the station was to close and that the Gunnery School would transfer to Jurby after being vacated by the Air Navigation School. The Commanding Officer of Andreas, Group Captain Crawford, and his personnel made every effort to present the activities of the station and many had the opportunity of operating the gun turrets on display in the training huts. Low cloud and rain, however, put a dampener on the proceedings. The Y.M.C.A., run by local volunteers since the station was opened, dispensed welcome hot drinks, though the public was warned beforehand to bring their own food because of rationing difficulties. Much of the flying programme had to be abandoned but one of the station's Wellingtons and a Spitfire gave a brave demonstration in what was some of the last flying from the airfield. Until the lifting of wartime censorship, many Manx people in other parts of the Island were unaware of its existence!

By the end of September, the transfer to Jurby was completed and the gates of R.A.F. Andreas finally closed. Immediate steps were taken by the Local Government Board to acquire three of the communal sites near the village for conversion into badly needed family accommodation. Built of single brick, the huts are in some ways better than Nissen huts, but are still cold and damp in wintry conditions. Every effort is being made to convert the huts into attractive two- and three-bedroomed homes, with electrically heated living rooms and kitchens. Each will have a toilet but bathrooms have to be shared. In the new year it is expected that 81 families will be accommodated as a temporary measure until proper housing can be provided sometime in the future. The old gymnasium cum church on the Smeale Road is to become a useful Parish Hall.

DOG RESCUES INJURED AIRMAN

A Manx dog has won an award for saving a life. An Anson aircraft on a navigation exercise was returning to Jurby on the afternoon of Thursday, 3rd January. On board were the normal crew of four, plus two Avro technicians who had been picked up at Hooton Park, Wirral. The Anson was due to arrive at 4.50 p.m. but it failed to appear and, as darkness fell, search and rescue operations began without any indication of the whereabouts of the aircraft. Coastal fog covered the Bulgham area and low cloud hid Slieu Ruy, which rises steeply to 1,500 feet and is known locally as Red Mountain. The Anson struck the hillside 150 feet below the summit. The

search was abandoned that night but continued the following day without success, hampered by fog and low cloud.

On the Saturday morning, Mr and Mrs Shooter, living at Fern Cottage, Agneash, were alerted by the whining and growling of their Alsatian, Peg-leg, so called because it had lost one of its feet when a puppy. When let out, it went straight to a little glen nearby, but Mrs Shooter could hear nothing above the noise of the stream and the wind in the trees. Back indoors, Peg-leg kept growling and eventually Mrs Shooter, keeping hold of her dog, was led a hundred yards up the hillside. It was then that she saw a hand reach out above a bush. The frightened Mrs Shooter discovered a cold, wet and terribly injured airman. He was the wireless operator, Warrant Officer Charles Jones, the sole survivor of the six on board. His right leg was shattered with bare bone exposed, but he had managed to cover a mile and half using a piece of wood to climb over a stone wall and barbed wire. The Shooters summoned help from neighbours who supplied brandy, tea and blankets. There being no telephone in this remote area, another ran down to Laxey to inform the police and Jurby. Transport arrived and the injured airman was stretchered down the hillside and taken to the Navy Hospital on Glencrutchery Road, Douglas. Wireless operator Jones was immediately operated on and, mercifully, his leg was saved.

Now that the war is over, it is possible to give further details about air accidents on and around the Isle of Man. Records indicate that over 200 military aircraft were involved in accidents up to the end of this year. Some of the airmen involved were fortunate to escape uninjured, while many survived their injuries. Nevertheless, a total of over 250 died, including British, Canadian, Australian, Polish, Dutch and American airmen. Overlooking Jurby airfield is the parish church of St. Patrick. The east window, replaced by R.A.F. Jurby, looks down upon three neat rows of white headstones marking the graves of 42 airmen. A further 24 are found at Kirk Andreas. All are in memory of the airmen who died on Manx soil.

Mrs Shooter of Ag-neash, with Peg-leg.
(Manx National Heritage)

MANX GOVERNMENT PURCHASES RONALDSWAY AIRPORT

The Isle of Man is ready for the expected post-war boom in civil aviation after the Government's purchase of the wartime Fleet Air Arm training station at Ronaldsway. The pre-war aerodrome, where aircraft used to land on the grass, has been turned into a fine modern airport with tarmacadamed runways and all necessary safety facilities. We have this report:

When His Excellency Air Vice-Marshal Sir Geoffrey Bromet was informed that the Ministry of Civil Aviation had changed its mind about ownership and administration of Ronaldsway, it left the way clear to reaching agreement over a purchase price. It was conditional that the Ministry of Civil Aviation would continue to provide and operate the technical services subject to a percentage of landing fees and a financial arrangement whereby the British taxpayer would be alleviated of any charges. Second Deemster Percy Cowley, was given the task of thrashing out a deal with the Admiralty. It was pointed out that the cost of construction had been £1 million, and that £105,000 had been spent on the purchase of the 825 acres of land. The Deemster's offer was £100,000. He said that the airfield was not to the design of the Manx Government and that maintenance costs would be heavy. Deemster Cowley returned with an agreed purchase price of £200,000 for the airport, land and buildings. That was put before Tynwald in July and accepted unanimously, the Deemster being showered with congratulations. This paves the way for the Island having its own national airport - and at a bargain price!

COLDEST WINTER

The Island endured its coldest winter for 70 years with heavy snowfalls which halted road and rail traffic. Passengers were trapped by drifts in a train near Ballasalla for three hours before being rescued. Temperatures remained below freezing for days on end, and February was the coldest since records began, recording a mean for the month of 31.6 degrees Fahrenheit. This was followed by March recording a record 7.84 inches of rain.

B.E.A. TAKE OVER

Isle of Man Air Services Ltd was taken over by British European Airways in January. The three partners, Olley Air Services, Railway Air Services and the Isle of Man Steam Packet Company, were re-imbursed to the full share value of £75,000. The local airline had carried 137,000 passengers during its 13 year history, without loss of life and setting high standards of regularity and safety. In February, B.E.A. took over all scheduled passenger routes from Ronaldsway. These were to Blackpool, Liverpool, Carlisle, Newcastle, Glasgow and Belfast. Passengers for Manchester and London change at Liverpool. Mr R. L. Carter, who was originally with Olley Air Services, was appointed Isle of Man area manager. Aircraft being used are De Havilland Rapides. One was involved in an accident shortly after the summer schedules got under way. Fortunately, the five passengers and two crew were not seriously injured. Bad weather resulted in a diversion to Jurby and the aircraft crashed into the mist-covered slopes between Greeba and Slieau Ruy. One of the passengers was able to make his way down to Crosby where he summoned help from the post office. The police alerted the Jurby Rescue Party

A view of the wartime buildings, taken from the Control Tower and looking towards the Creggans farm, which now serve as part of the airport terminal. The tall white building was formerly the parachute house which has been converted by British European Airways as offices and waiting hall. (Terry Faragher Collection)

The bespectacled Harold Daniell who won this year's Senior T.T. He is sitting astride the Norton which has been little altered since he set up the record lap of 91 m.p.h. during his win in 1938.
(Keig Collection)

T.T. RACES RETURN

The first post-war Tourist Trophy Races were held in June. They attracted a total of 169 entries, of which 64 were for the newly inaugurated Clubman's T.T. The entries included many pre-war stars who were joined by a new generation of young men anxious to make their name on the world famous T.T. Course. Victory in the Junior Race went to Bob Foster (Velocette) and the Lightweight was won by Manliff Barrington (Moto Guzzi). The Senior was dominated by Nortons though there was a strong challenge from the A.J.S. 'Porcupines', ridden by Les Graham and Jock West. The A.J.S. twins are so named because of their distinctive cooling fins. The race was won by Norton teamster Harold Daniell, holder of the 91 m.p.h record lap from 1938. Speeds were predictably slower than pre-war days because of the use of low-octane 'Pool' petrol. The fastest lap time of 84 m.p.h. was set up jointly by Artie Bell (Norton) and Peter Goodman (Velocette), who came second and third respectively.

which made its way to the scene of the accident. Though badly cut and bruised, the passengers were able to complete their study visit to the Marine Biological Station at Port Erin.

FAREWELL TO *H.M.S. VALKYRIE*

Nearly two years after the end of the war, H.M.S. Valkyrie was decommissioned at the end of March. The Royal Navy's largest radar training school had provided thousands of operators for all ships of the Navy. Millions of pounds worth of equipment has been removed from Douglas Head and the boarding houses along Loch Promenade have been vacated. The closure of the station has opened Douglas Head for the first time since 1941. Many of the visitor attractions are being brought back into use although some, like the old incline railway, are in serious need of repair and renovation. The Marine Drive has also been re-opened but although the property of the Marine Drive Company has been purchased by the Manx Government, no attempt is to be made to resurrect the electric railway.

RESTORATION OF CATHEDRAL

The Archbishop of York, Dr. Cyril Garbett, called for the restoration of the ruined St. German's Cathedral on St. Patrick's Isle at Peel. He was on the Island for the 1,500th anniversary celebrations of the Manx Church. He told a big public meeting in Douglas that restoring the cathedral would be a wonderful expression of the noble heritage of the Manx diocese.

VICAR DEFROCKED

A Manx clergyman made national headlines when he was sentenced to 18 months hard labour at Wiltshire Assizes after admitting a charge of bigamy. The Revd. Harry Lamb, 36-year-old chaplain of St. John's, who was born at Santon, was alleged to have married a member of the W.A.A.F. at Salisbury when he was serving in the R.A.F. as a wartime chaplain in 1944. At the time, his wife, Dorothy, was living at home in the Island with their son. Lamb has been excluded from the Church by the Lord Bishop of Sodor and Man.

STATIONMASTER KILLED

The Isle of Man Railway's stationmaster at Union Mills, Mr. George Henry Hogg, was killed in July when he stumbled and fell under the wheels of a Douglas bound train passing through the station. The train was travelling at only 10 miles an hour as he went under the leading coach. Mr. Hogg had more than 60 years service with the railway company - and was the oldest stationmaster in Britain. In another tragedy two elderly sisters were burned to death in a fire at their home in Malew Street, Castletown.

SUCCESSFUL SUNNY SUMMER

As if to compensate for the bad winter, the Island enjoyed one of its best summers. August enjoyed a record 305 hours of

British European Airways' de Havilland Rapide which crashed in bad weather on the slopes between Greeba and Slieau Ruy. Miraculously, the crew of two and the five passengers escaped without serious injury.
(Terry Faragher Collection)

sunshine, with just a trace of rain. This was a great help to the tourist industry as it got back to near normal, despite many difficulties. A total of 602,230 visitors arrived during the season, including 10,000 delegates to the conferences staged by Rotary International and the British Legion. The Douglas entertainments were in full swing with 'Two Ton' Tessie O'Shea starring in the Summer Show at the Palace Coliseum, while Joe Loss and his Orchestra proved a big attraction for dancers at the Villa Marina.

CAR RACING RETURNS

Car racing returned to the Isle of Man in August and an estimated 50,000 people turned out to see it. There were not many cars (33 starters in all spread between two races) and the available fuel was poor - just 72 octane - but excitement was intense nevertheless.

The two events were run over the 3.8 mile Willaston Circuit. One was the British Empire Trophy Race for cars up to 4.5 litres unsupercharged; the other, the Manx Cup Race for lighter weight cars with a maximum of two litres. The British Racing Drivers Club had organised the British Empire Trophy Race at Donington prior to the war. It switched its ninth race to the Isle of Man because of a lack of suitable circuits in post-war Britain.

Winner of the Empire Trophy race over 40 laps was Bob Gerard at the wheel of a supercharged 1,488 c.c. E.R.A. His average speed was 68.02 m.p.h. Earlier it had been speculated that the international favourite, Prince Bira of Siam, might achieve the double. In fact, he came fifth in the major race in a supercharged 1.5 litre Maserati then won the 12 lap Manx Cup race in a 1,100 c.c. Simca-Gordini, averaging 66.05 m.p.h.

VISIT OF DE VALERA

The President of the Irish Republic, Eamon de Valera, paid an informal visit to the Island while on a holiday cruise round the North British Isles in an Irish Navy corvette. It was a low key visit which attracted little public attention, at Mr. de Valera's wish. He went to Peel Castle, Tynwald Hill and Cregneash - where he met Ned Maddrell, one of the Island's last surviving native speakers of Manx. The two men conversed in their respective Gaelics. As a result, Mr. de Valera arranged for the Irish Folklore Commission to come to the Island to record the voice of Mr. Maddrell and other Manx speakers.

Famous dance band leader Joe Loss, whose orchestra proved a big attraction to visitors and locals at the Villa Marina this year. (Douglas Town Hall Archives)

T. E. BROWN ANNIVERSARY

The 50th anniversary of the death of our national poet, on 29th October, has not engendered celebrations of the sort seen in 1930 on the centenary of his birth. Indeed, the only noteworthy event has been the appearance of the book 'Two Men of Manxland', written by Samuel Norris and published by his printing firm, Norris Modern Press Limited. It will be remembered that Mr Norris, who is a reporter and politician, recorded the political turmoil of the early years of this century in his book 'Manx Memories and Movements'. His latest book deals separately with the lives of Hall Caine and T. E. Brown. Inevitable comparisons are drawn and Mr Norris is seen to clearly favour Brown. Great interest has been shown in the book and a second print is planned for next year.

R.A.F. JURBY TO CLOSE

The post-war contraction of the Royal Air Force has led

Below left: T. C. Harrison in his pre-war Riley cornering at the Manx Arms, Onchan, during the Manx Cup Race for smaller cars.

Below: Popular pre-war E.R.A. racing driver Prince Bira of Siam returned this year with a Maserati. He is seen here at Cronk ny Mona during the British Empire Trophy Race in which he finished 5th.

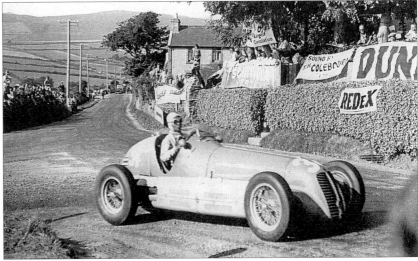

to the closure of R.A.F. Jurby. The Gunnery School, which transferred from Andreas last year, is to be disbanded. The station will retain a care and maintenance staff while its future is being decided. Since 1939, R.A.F. Jurby has trained thousands of navigators, bomb aimers and gunners for Bomber Command. It has a proud record, and the station has played a prominent part in the life of the north of the Island. It is hoped that another role for the station will be found in the not too distant future.

It is sad to record that in March a Spitfire being flown to Jurby crashed into Maughold Head which was covered in low cloud. It struck the headland just below the lighthouse and was thrown against the gable end of the keepers' quarters, scattering debris over a wide area. A car inside the garage was set on fire and destroyed. With the telephone not working, help was summoned from the vicarage. Ramsey Fire Brigade soon had the fires under control, but Dr. Paton was unable to help the badly injured pilot. He was a highly respected pilot who lived in Ramsey with his wife.

Fortunately, the keepers' children were at school at the time and their wives were attending a sale of work in the church hall.

PURCHASE OF ANDREAS AIRFIELD

Negotiations with the Air Ministry have resulted in Tynwald agreeing to purchase Andreas airfield for £23,750, the original price paid to the landowners. The Air Ministry agreed to this as a gesture of appreciation for the co-operation shown during the early years of the war. Conditions are that the runways are to remain intact and no building should take place within the perimeter track. The majority of Tynwald agreed that they had got a bargain, though Mr. H. C. Kerruish lamented the loss of two prime farms whose fields would never be the same again.

When put up for auction by the Government, the airfield was purchased by Mr. Morrey for £33,000 who plans to revert to the original farms of Ballaghaue, to be farmed by the owner's son, and Braust to be farmed by a tenant. It is understood that some of the buildings are to be used as a Landrace pig farm.

It was always the intention of the Air Ministry to restore the upper part of the tower of Kirk Andreas church, which was removed as a hazard to flying. The keystones were carefully numbered to help in the restoration. However, the church wardens have agreed now to accept a sum of money instead, so that the fine old organ can be equipped with an electric blower.

1947 NEWS IN BRIEF

JANUARY
14 - Rotary Club of Ramsey inaugurated.

FEBRUARY
10 - Mr. T. C. Greenfield, Water Engineer to Douglas Corporation, appointed Engineer Manager to new Isle of Man Water Board.

MARCH
20 - Territorial Army presence in the Isle of Man to continue with the formation of the 515th (I.O.M.) Light Anti-Aircraft Regiment, R.A. Lieut.-Colonel J. B. Mylchreest appointed Commanding Officer.
25 - *Tynwald V* launched at Birkenhead.

MAY
7 - Mr. Robert Nicholl (tenor) won Cleveland Medal at Manx Music Festival for second time.
22 - Mr. W. A. Kirkpatrick won Manx Golf Championship for third successive time.
24-26 Revival of Manx Air Races at Ronaldsway. Veteran Major Tommy Rose won the Manx Air Derby in his Miles Hawk.

JUNE
19 - Record entry of 213 for International Bicycle T.T.

JULY
10 - New list of magistrates included for the first time the appointment of women justices on the Island.
19 - Retirement of His Honour Deemster R. D. Farrant, Clerk of the Rolls. Deemster W. P. Cowley is elevated to succeed him. High Bailiff Mr. R. G. Johnson, O.B.E., appointed Second Deemster and Mr. Howard D. Lay appointed new High Bailiff.

AUGUST
26 - Tynwald approve resolution to implement five-year plan for all-Island water supplies costing £200,000.

SEPTEMBER
9-11 Manx Grand Prix drew record entry of 284 for the three events. Lightweight race marred by death of B. B. Russell in crash at Ramsey when in the lead. The race was won by Austin Monks (Moto Guzzi) while Eric Briggs achieved the 'double' by winning the Junior and Senior races on Nortons.
11 - Title of 'Mona's Queen of Beauty' won by Miss Joyce Lewis of Douglas in final contest of successful season of competition

organised by the June Effort and Season Extension Committee.
22 - Island milk exported to Liverpool to relieve mainland emergency. In all, 26,000 gallons were sent in 41 days.
27 - Manx farm workers receive new weekly wage of £5.0s.4d. for 56-hour week.

OCTOBER
9 - New multilateral school at Ramsey opened by His Excellency the Lieutenant-Governor.

NOVEMBER
1 - Potato price fixed at £12. 10s a ton, an increase of £4.3s.4d over 1946.
3 - By 21 votes to one, Douglas Corporation reject motion to abolish the horse tram service as a result of huge public support.
5 - Education Authority approve recommendation from Reorganisation Committee that Andreas School be transferred to former R.A.F. communal site, and that Bride and St. Jude's Schools should be closed.
11 - Potato rationing scheme, inaugurated in England, extended to the Island.
14 - Tynwald adopted main provisions of Imperial Government's interim budget increasing Purchase Tax on wines and spirits, estimated to produce £100,500 a year for the Island.
16 - For the first time in 26 years Island has snowfall in November.
18 - Lieutenant-Governor announces that basic petrol rationing is to be ended.
20 - Wedding of H.R.H. Princess Elizabeth and H.R.H. Prince Philip, Duke of Edinburgh. Island's wedding gifts are a carved oak chest, designed by Mr. W. T. Quayle, made at the Kirk Michael workshops of Messrs. Kelly Bros., and a supply of woollen rugs and blankets from Tynwald and Sulby Mills.

DECEMBER
10 - Plans to carry out £300,000 extensions to electricity power station and change distribution to alternating current, adopted by Douglas Corporation.
16 - Tynwald appointed committee to inquire into position regarding National Service after Keys rejected adoption of Imperial Government's National Service Act, 1947.

GETTING BACK TO NORMAL

Newly-weds, and others who are setting up home for the first time, are to be given the chance to buy Manx-made furniture tax free. As Purchase Tax accounts for 50 per cent of the price, it is a significant gesture by Tynwald. The concession includes a restriction on retail pricing to prevent the imposition of higher profit margins by shops. It is to be targeted at people who are furnishing a home or some rooms for the first time, have married since the outbreak of war in 1939, or are having to cater for the needs of a growing family.

The Manx plan is an up-graded version of a U.K. one which is encouraging the manufacture there of cheap, inferior 'utility' furniture but there will be no emphasis on low quality here. Tynwald members want something better. That is why there are going to be delays in implementing the Manx scheme. Initially, the plan was to introduce it this year but problems arose over getting advice from the U.K.'s Board of Trade on furniture specifications. Now supplies will not be available until about mid-1948. Those who want to take advantage of the concession will have to apply then to the Clothing Control Division of Government Office for a Buying Permit.

Foreign imports have started to arrive, of course, principally from Scandinavia, but prices are high. Hence the need to provide assistance for people setting up home. Hence, too, the protests by hoteliers in their negotiations for compensation for furnishings damaged or lost by the military during the commandeering of hotels during the war. One Douglas hotelier says he was offered £2 recently for a chair which had been valued at £1 at the outbreak of war. The offer sounded good until he realised that it would cost £4 now to replace it.

The local manufacture of furniture - mainly tables, chairs, wardrobes and beds - has been underway for some time. As yet, however, it has concentrated on satisfying the urgent needs of hoteliers and boarding house keepers. There are now 56 craftsmen and 34 women and apprentices involved in the work, using timber imported on their behalf by Tynwald to overcome chronic national shortages. The builders, Kelly Bros., at Kirk Michael are one of the main manufacturers. During World War I and the recent war they made strap-on wooden clogs because of the shortage of leather for shoes. The French polishing of its furniture is undertaken by specialists in Douglas.

SUPPORT FOR HOTELIERS

During the year outright grants totalling £10,000 were voted by Tynwald for hoteliers and boarding house keepers who missed all or part of last season and, perhaps, some of this season also, because of military occupation of their premises. Assessment of losses proved to be difficult because many hoteliers were unable to provide proper accounts to show the sort of business they had experienced prior to the war. Some said their books had been lost or destroyed. In investigating what grants

should be given, a Tynwald team established that profits at hotels which were not requisitioned by the military are now 100 per cent up on their immediate pre-war level. Those hotels which managed to open last summer after overcoming repair and equipment difficulties, are experiencing a growth of 90 per cent in profits.

Complaints about the condition of properties continued this year with the decommissioning of hotels occupied by H.M.S. Valkyrie in Regent Street and Granville Street on Loch Promenade. There were protests about broken walls, panelless doors, sagging ceilings, cracked washbasins, and brown and grey paint daubing over wall coverings. This was particularly so in respect of the Mayfair Hotel. Other faults listed by its proprietor included the asphalting of some bedroom floors, so they could be used for showers and urinals, and the absence of door knobs. They had been replaced by bolts and padlocks.

The repair of hotels in the H.M.S. Valkyrie camp marked a significant advance in the Island's struggle to normality. Advances elsewhere included the re-opening of the Metropole Hotel, the recommissioning of Peel's swimming pool and the building of additional accommodation at Douglas Holiday Camp on the Falcon Cliff side. Niarbyl with its radar station, may remain sealed off by the military. Douglas Head Minstrel shows may still be impossible until a new stage and dressing room is built.

LOW STANDARDS

Weather-wise, the past summer was good, hence the crowded scenes on Douglas beach. Not everyone was pleased, though. It was too fine for indoor entertainments to thrive, it was reckoned. Still, such problems seemed small in comparison with the crises which marked the early days of the year. In February national fuel stocks were so low consumers were warned that unless they consumed less voluntarily there would be official cuts in gas, coal and electricity supplies. That meant the Island shivered. Public transport was so poor, meanwhile, that there was barely standing room at times on many buses. Residents at Foxdale even had to walk to and from the Eairy Dam to use a bus at all - a practice which looks like continuing for some time!

In this austere age, of course, people are having to tolerate lower standards. During the season's peak, some boarding house keepers split families so as to maximise bedroom use: so many men to one room and so many women to another. Queueing at cafes remained an accepted part of life. One had to queue for most things. The queues at local cinemas were sometimes hundreds of yards long.

During the August Bank Holiday rush when only about half as many people came here as in 1939, some people slept in charabancs on Douglas Promenade or under the Villa Marina colonnade. At 5 a.m., when early morning arrivals had nowhere to go, the Villa Marina

1947
• Marriage of Princess Elizabeth to Philip Mountbatten in Britain
• New land speed record of 634 km/h (394 mph) set by John Cobb in California
• Independence for India (separating India and Pakistan)

café opened and cups of tea were served to visitors seated on deck chairs on the ballroom floor.

FRUSTRATIONS

Shortages continue to frustrate. Some people may have made a good profit in the re-born tourist industry but there is little for them to spend it on. The shortage of new clothing is such that the re-making and re-styling of old clothes is flourishing. Material taken from second-hand men's suits is being used in women's fashions. New cars cannot be bought. Almost all are being exported to save Britain from bankruptcy. A new model was announced recently by a British manufacturer but its Manx agent received just one token model for the year. Inevitably, second hand pre-war cars are commanding ridiculous prices and even they are a rarity.

Hoteliers face 1948 worried about feeding visitors. Demand for eggs was such this summer that they sold at six shillings a dozen compared with a subsidised two shillings in England. Whilst the situation in respect of meat may not have reached the stage that whale meat is evident in Manx shops as it is in England, hard pressed butchers are appealing for freshly-caught rabbits. Even the basic potato is in short supply. Amid bitter attacks on farmers for failing to grow enough and their protests that they are not being paid sufficiently to do so, shortages this autumn resulted in potatoes being rationed. Everyone is asking now: Will there be no end to the misery?

HOPEFUL SIGNS

In fact, perhaps one is in sight. The first post-war lemons from Sicily, grapefruits from Texas, oranges from South Africa and bananas arrived in shops this year. Because none were rationed and quantities were small, the Government appealed to shopkeepers to ensure a fair distribution. It meant only a small amount for everyone but at least their arrival provided a foretaste of better times. Manx people who managed to holiday in Dublin this autumn, meanwhile, found that shops there were well-stocked with 'luxury' goods - from fully fashioned nylon stockings to mouth-watering tinned salmon. Some of the latter were smuggled back to the Island, which suggests that extensive smuggling could develop once regular steamer services are re-established with Dublin.

In anticipation of better times, Tynwald has adopted a plan to spend £100,000, about a tenth of its reserves, on a brine spa at Ramsey. Critics reckon that the costings are over-optimistic and the spa will never materialise. They are probably correct but at least Tynwald's apparent willingness to invest in the future suggests that there is one there in which one can have some confidence. Too many are beginning to fear that we could all disappear overnight in World War III. Ten years ago poison gas was the bogeyman. Now vaporisation by the atom bomb is the nightmare as the world polarises between the democratic west and the communist east.

Those who can imagine the after-effects of an atomic war in which the Island is not hit but is isolated in a devastated world and suffers from radioactive fall-out are persuading the authorities of the continued need for a Manx Home Guard and Civil Defence. Others are wondering: Would such a world be worth living in?

Seen at Douglas Railway Station are a few of the 1,312,780 passengers carried by the Isle of Man Steam Railway last year. With petrol rationing in force, the railway has enjoyed a post-war boom and passenger returns are the best since 1925! The Manx Electric Railway has seen figures return to normal and is now carrying over 750,000 passengers a year. But the steam railway is facing a crisis with the track, engines and rolling stock badly in need of repair. Materials are in short supply and costs are rising. The railway carried over a million passengers a year throughout the war and provided 14,000 'specials' to meet service requirements. (I.M.R.)

NEW RAMSEY MULTILATERAL SCHOOL OPENED

The multilateral School in Ramsey was officially opened on 9th October by the Lieutenant-Governor Sir Geoffrey Bromet. The north of the Island was thus formally incorporated into the new comprehensive system of education that has been meeting with widespread approval, not only here but in the United Kingdom. A problem at Ramsey, as in Douglas of course, is that this new school will occupy two separate buildings, Fortunately they are only 100 yards or so apart. It will be remembered the new building was designed in 1937 and completed shortly before the outbreak of the war. It was commandeered immediately by the R.A.F. and remained under their control until recently. The conversion, it is believed, has cost some £44,000. Together with the existing Grammar School on Lezayre Road, it has been in existence for the past year catering for some 300 boys and girls with Mr. H. E. George M.A. as the Headmaster. The Lieutenant-Governor has praised this new concept in education as giving 'more opportunity' - as he put it - to the ordinary boy and girl. It was remarked also by some that as the school had had such an important

association with the R.A.F. during the war, it might be seen as appropriate, especially as the school had been given no official name as yet, to commemorate this important part of its history in whatever name was finally chosen.

The new west wing of Ramsey Grammar School.
(R. and L. Kelly Collection)

1,500TH ANNIVERSARY OF THE MANX CHURCH

May 11th to 18th was chosen as the period to celebrate the 1,500th Anniversary of the Manx Church. On the opening Sunday, all churches were encouraged to celebrate with an early Communion and then to join in special services during the day. The Archbishop of York preached at St. George's in the morning and at St. Mary's, Castletown in the evening, which was broadcast by the B.B.C. Home Service. At this service the Archbishop was joined by the Bishop of Sodor and Man who had earlier conducted a service at St. Thomas's in Douglas, this being broadcast for overseas listeners. The Bishop of Nidaros (Trondheim) preached at Peel in the morning and at St. Thomas's in the evening.

Monday saw a Diocesan Conference and a public meeting at which the visiting Archbishop and Bishops took part. On the Thursday, a service was held at Peel, which was addressed by the Archbishop of Dublin. On the closing Sunday a series of services were addressed by the Archbishop of Dublin and the Bishop of Argyll and the

Coat of Arms of the Diocese of Sodor and Man.

Isles. The celebrations were based on the traditional date for the introduction of Christianity to the Isle of Man by Patrick of Ireland. However, the date calculated uses somewhat dubious evidence produced by James Ussher, Archbishop of Dublin, in the 17th century.

The programme published for the celebrations contained a short summary of the history of Christianity in the Isle of Man written specially by Canon E. H. Stenning, Vice-Principal of King William's College. In it he divided the 1,500 years into six periods beginning with the coming of Christianity from the Patrick Church of Ireland in the fifth century. This was followed by the suppression of the Celtic Church by the Norse Vikings beginning about the end of the seventh century and lasting until the tenth century. It was towards the end of that century that Christianity was reintroduced by the Norse Church. This was followed by the establishment of the Diocese of Sodor and Man and its progress from the eleventh century until the Reformation. This was followed by a difficult period until the revival in the nineteenth century, partly attributed to the preaching of John Wesley. This revival led to the re-building of many of today's parish churches.

Canon Stenning ended by stating: "One may look back over fifteen centuries of Christianity in Man and see therein a very interesting miniature survey of Christianity in the civilized world. There have been the ebbs and flows of the spirit, the same mistakes and misguided zeal of men, and the same over-ruling certainty of the power of God that one may see in the world at large."

Top: The Conferment of the Honorary Freedom of the Borough of Douglas to Field Marshal the Viscount Montgomery of Alamein was a splendid occasion. The presentation took place in the Villa Marina Royal Hall, in May, before an invited audience from all parts of the Island. The Mayor, Councillor F. M. Corkill, J.P., was joined on stage by the Aldermen and Councillors of the Borough.

Above: Field Marshal Montgomery received a warm welcome on his arrival at Victoria Pier.

Right: In company with His Excellency The Lieutenant-Governor, Air Vice-Marshal Sir Geoffrey Bromet, Lord Montgomery inspects members of the Manx branch of the Royal British Legion outside the Villa Marina.
(Photographs from Douglas Town Hall Archives)

WORST YEAR FOR CIVILIAN AIR CRASHES

The Island has had its worst year ever for civilian air crashes. Seventeen people died in three plane crashes. The worst was in the River Mersey when a Mannin Airways' charter aircraft from Ronaldsway had to ditch in the sea. We have this report:

One of the seven who died in the Mersey crash was the pilot, 48-year-old Captain John Higgins, the best known of all Manx civil aviation pioneers. The others killed were the radio officer, Manxman Noel Clucas, Douglas jeweller Mr. Louis Jacobs; British Army Lieutenant Juan Kelly, son of the late High Bailiff Kelly; Mrs. Doris May Bridson and her daughter Alice Winifred Bridson, of Douglas; and Mrs. Joan Cannan whose 26-year-old husband Matt, of Belmont Hill, Douglas, was the only survivor. The aircraft, a de Havilland Rapide, was on a flight from Dublin to Ronaldsway on 11th November but bad visibility forced air traffic control to divert Captain Higgins to Speke Airport at Liverpool. Three miles short of Speke he ran out of fuel and came down in the Mersey near Garston Docks, quarter of a mile off the beach. The plane stayed afloat and its occupants got out and clung to it in the dark, cold November evening - until, after 25 minutes, it sank, leaving everyone in the sea. Mr Cannan tried to save his wife, unsuccessfully, and was the only person who managed to swim to shore, shocked and exhausted. The Ministry of Civil Aviation report on the accident said Captain Higgins had miscalculated the amount of fuel he had to get him safely to Speke. Another pint of petrol would have enabled him to reach Speke which was in view.

The other accidents happened on the Island. One involved a Rapide on charter for the Senior T.T. race. Early in the morning it overflew Ronaldsway and shortly afterwards crashed high on the slopes of Cronk ny Arrey Lhaa and burst into flames. Also on Senior Race Day, an Avro XIX ditched in Port Erin Bay when out of fuel. The seven passengers, pilot and radio operator climbed out on to the wings and were saved by local lobster fisherman Mr. F. Watterson before the aircraft sank.

At the end of September, Cronk ny Arrey Lhaa claimed another victim when a converted Halifax bomber on the 'milk run' from Nutt's Corner to Liverpool crashed in thick fog. All four of the crew were killed. The Halifax was loaded with 1,100 gallons of milk and wreckage of the aircraft and milk churns were scattered over a wide area.

NINE LOST AT SEA

Early in January, nine men were lost when the 300 ton motor vessel Teasel of Cardiff, carrying cargo from Belfast to Manchester foundered in heavy seas off the Point of Ayre. She got into difficulties when her cargo shifted. The Ramsey lifeboat Thomas Corbett went to the scene and Coxswain E. Starkey had a lucky escape after being washed overboard. In July, the ketch Sarah Latham foundered in rough seas off Langness Point. The

five on board were rescued by Port St. Mary lifeboat Civil Service No. 5.

FIRST WITH RADAR

Douglas harbour has become the first in the world to be equipped with radar. A 60 foot high steel mast was erected on Victoria Pier with a scanning range of three miles. It will enable vessels to leave and enter port safely in bad visibility. One of the guests at its inauguration was Sir Robert Watson Watt, one of the pioneers of the development of radar as a secret weapon in the Second World War.

HONOUR FOR MONTGOMERY

Field Marshal Lord Montgomery of Alamein was made a Freeman of the Borough of Douglas at a special meeting of the Town Council held in the Villa Marina. Britain's most successful wartime general was mobbed by admirers when he got off the boat in Douglas. The Manx Regiment served under him in the Eighth Army and in his speech he said Manxmen were descended from Vikings and had inherited the qualities that go into the making of good soldiers.

ROBBED OF VICTORY

Racing star Reg Parnell was robbed of victory in the British Empire Trophy Race held in May. He was comfortably in the lead when his Maserati ran out of fuel at Parkfield Corner on the last lap. Geoffrey Ansell in an E.R.A. swept past to win the race. Winner of the Manx Cup Race was George Nixon in a Riley Special. The Castletown Cup, a new race for pre-war cars, went to Kenneth Bear in a Bugatti.

NATIONAL HEALTH SERVICE

Britain's Welfare State, introduced by the U.K.'s Labour Government this year, is to be followed in the Island. Though the service started unofficially in July, delays in passing the necessary legislation meant that the service was not legally operational until 16th November. The Health Service offers free medical treatment by doctors, dentists and opticians, while there will be no charge for prescriptions. This means that the many Friendly

Most fortunate were the five passengers and crew of this Anson XIX which ditched off Port Erin after running out of petrol. They were rescued by local fisherman, Mr F. Watterson, a Dunkirk veteran. The passengers went off to watch the Senior T.T. race and one of them had this dramatic photograph published later on the front page of the Daily Express.

Members and Executive Officers of the newly-formed Isle of Man Airports Board. Seated, centre, is its chairman, Mr T.C. Cowin, M.H.K.

On the left is aviation pioneer Captain John Higgins who, earlier in the year, formed Mannin Airways Limited. Standing next to him is comedian Norman Evans who plays to packed audiences at the Palace Coliseum. On the right is Airport Manager Gwynn Griffiths. Later in the year, Captain Higgins was drowned following a tragic accident in the River Mersey.

Societies that abound on the Island, such as the Rechabites and Oddfellows, are likely to fade away. Also, Manx hospitals will not have to rely any longer on charity as their Management Committees will be financed by grants from the National Health Service. It will be possible also to eliminate deficiencies at Noble's Hospital which has only two specialist surgeons and one specialist medical man to satisfy hospital requirements. The hospital only has one ambulance which is not manned all the time.

DISASTROUS FIRES

Four people died in a fire at a lodging house at 2, Mona Terrace, Douglas, in August. The dead were an Irish labourer and three women. There were 11 people in the house when the fire started on the ground floor at 5 a.m. The dead were trapped on the upper floors. Eight days later fire devastated the Douglas Head Hotel in the early hours of the morning. No one was hurt but the only part of the premises to escape destruction was the concert hall.

NEW AIRPORTS BOARD

The new Isle of Man Airports Board, nominated by the Lieutenant-Governor, held its first meeting in August. Under the chairmanship of Mr. T. C. Cowin, M.H.K., it is entrusted with the development of Ronaldsway Airport and air services from the Island. Mr. Gwynn Griffiths is confirmed as Airport Manager and Commandant. He arrived at Ronalds-way with I.O.M. Air Services in pre-war days and his services were retained by the Admiralty during the war.

The monopoly of B.E.A. has done little to dampen the enthusiasm of the independents to operate charter services for passengers and freight on routes which the national airline regards as unprofitable. Last year Manx Air Charter Experts Ltd was formed by Mr. George Drummond and his agent, Mr. Leslie Vondy. It was soon found that there were many deficiencies in the B.E.A. service and the company was expanded and renamed Manx Air Charters Ltd. Mr. G. S. Hankinson was appointed managing director and plenty of work has been provided for the four Rapides which were named after Manx glens.

Earlier this year a second charter company was formed. Mannin Airways Ltd was formed by the redoubtable Captain John Higgins, the pre-war pioneer. Three Rapides were acquired and the company was granted a licence to fly a scheduled service to Newcastle via Carlisle this summer. However, the future of Mannin Airways is uncertain following the loss of Captain Higgins at the end of the year.

BUS CREWS ON STRIKE

Douglas bus crews staged a four day strike in protest at the sacking of eight men by the Corporation Transport Department. They went back to work after a court of inquiry set up by the Lieutenant-Governor upheld their grievance and ordered the sackings to be withdrawn. However, it added that in going on strike the men had shown a lack of concern for the travelling public.

DIVORCED VICAR

Mrs. Dorothy Lamb, wife of the disgraced former chaplain of St. John's, the Reverend Harry Lamb, who was gaoled for 18 months at Wiltshire Assizes last year for bigamy, has divorced him. The Douglas Divorce Court was told that she is living now at Barrow-in-Furness with their son. She left the Island after her husband lost his living at St. John's. He admitted bigamously marrying a WAAF while he was an R.A.F. padre during the war.

MANX SPEAKERS RECORDED

Last year's proposal by Eamon de Valera, Taoiseach of Ireland, during his brief holiday visit to the Isle of Man, that the Irish Folklore Commission should undertake to record the voices of the last native Manx Gaelic speakers had unexpected results. It was discovered that the Irish Folklore Commission did not possess the

necessary mobile equipment and this had to be rectified by the special provision of a van and battery-operated recording equipment. The van was craned aboard a cattle ship and stowed in the hold. Unfortunately, the cattle were housed at a higher level and by the time the van arrived on the Island it was well camouflaged! When Mr. Basil Megaw, director of the Manx Museum, saw it arrive he ordered the crew to stay in the van while it was hosed down. The visit has resulted in the first good sound recordings of Manx speakers, including the voices of John Kneen (95), Ned Maddrell, Harry Boyde and John Tom Kaighin. Assisting in the recordings were the present few 'custodians' of the language who are keen to preserve Manx Gaelic for posterity.

NEAR-RECORD SEASON

The huge post-war rush of holidaymakers to the Island continued during the past season. The 1948 summer arrival figure was 624,737 which included 36,000 arriving by air. The overall total was more than last year, but was 10,000 short of the all-time record of the 634,512 figure established in 1913. One of the highlights of the season was 18-year-old Joyce Lewis winning the Miss Isle of Man Bathing Beauty Competition for the second year in succession.

SUCCESS AT BLACKPOOL

Over 400 Manx competitors took part in the Blackpool Music Festival in November. They returned with a long list of successes, including: Miss Barbara Taggart, open pianoforte solo winner; Messrs. J. Miles and N. Kaighin, duet winners; Messrs. A. W. Quirk and R. R. Nicholl, winners of bass and tenor lieder classes respectively; Miss Mavis Kelly, winner sight reading, singing; Mr. Bert Gray, second in tenor class; Miss S. Corlett, third in girls' solo; Miss Eileen Peters, winner, soprano class, and third in Rose Bowl contest; Lhon Dhoo choir, conductor Douglas Buxton, third in male voice choir class, and Mr. C. Jones, second in baritone lieder.

Recording the voices of Manx language speakers John Kneen (95) and Harry Boyde (78). Making the recordings are enthusiasts Bill Radcliffe and Mark Braide with the help of the Irish Folklore Commission's van. (Manx National Heritage)

1948 NEWS IN BRIEF

JANUARY
20 - Tynwald rejected resolution to introduce universal suffrage for all local elections.
20 - Constitution for Whitley Council for civil servants approved by Tynwald.

FEBRUARY
3 - Keys pass third reading of the Rent Restrictions Bill after record session of eight hours.
11 - Mr. Maurice Holmes, M.A., (41) appointed Headmaster of Douglas High School for Boys to succeed Mr. A. H. Sykes, B.Sc., upon his retirement in March after being head for 27 years.
23 - Rev. R. H. Reid, M.A., elected chairman of the Manx Motor Cycle Club in succession to Alderman Robt. Cowell, chairman of the club for 25 years.

MARCH
30 - W. H. Kelly, of Onchan, won the North of England 26½-mile marathon championship.

MAY
4 - House of Keys adopt amendment to Education Bill depriving school teachers of representation on the Education Authority, and carry amendment that universal suffrage apply to Authority elections in place of restricted voting by ratepayers.
5 - Mr. A. W. Quirk wins Cleveland Medal at the Manx Music Festival.
17 - Football history made when Sheffield United and Sheffield Wednesday played a match at King George V Park.

JUNE
8 - Memorial seat, erected on Quarterbridge Road at junction with Alexander Drive, in honour of the late W. L. Handley, famous racing motorcyclist, unveiled by Mr. Graham Walker.
12 - Death of 'Noel' Christmas from injuries received the previous day at Michael in the Senior T.T. The race was won by Artie Bell (Norton) and the fastest lap at 88 m.p.h. was set by O. Tenni (Moto Guzzi).
15 - During Cycling Week Reg Harris, amateur sprint cycling champion of the world, took part in grass track meeting at King George V Park.
23 - Important decision by Deemster Johnson at General Gaol in ruling that Manx law did not give legal power to the police to hold a man for being found drunk and incapable.

JULY
5 - Earl of Derby among the distinguished visitors to the Tynwald Ceremony, and later a guest at the World Manx Association gathering.
19 - Snaefell V, latest addition to the Steam Packet's fleet, arrived in Douglas for the first time. Mona's Isle is to be sold after 28 years' service.

SEPTEMBER
8 - Miss Doris Oakley (17), of Douglas, swam Douglas Bay from Port Jack to Port Skillion in 63 mins 48 secs.
12-16 Centenary celebrations of the Douglas Town and Seamen's Mission (The Bethel).

OCTOBER
1 - Standard 44-hour week for general workers came into force.
7 - Commission recommends that a new Electricity Authority be set up for the Island to take over the assets of the Douglas Corporation and the Electricity Board.
18 - Mr. Jack Nivison (Labour) elected to the House of Keys in Middle Sheading bye-election caused by the resignation of Col. Clifford Kniveton, M.C..

NOVEMBER
16 - Tynwald adopted recommendations to amend income tax law, including introduction of a standard rate of 4 shillings in the pound.

1948
• David Ben-Gurion, first Prime Minister of Israel, reads the Jewish Declaration of Independence
• North Korea proclaims independence

TYNWALD MATTERS: THE MANX NATIONAL HEALTH SERVICE

In little more than six months this year one of the most momentous and far reaching pieces of social legislation made its way through the various stages of Tynwald. Although the Royal Assent to the legislation is not expected until November, the medical community has started to implement its terms already. The establishment of the Manx National Health Service will surely be seen in years to come as one of the great achievements of a civilised society.

Initial stages occurred in April when a Bill detailing the establishment of a comprehensive Health Service in the Isle of Man was circulated. While it was true to argue, as some did, that it merely represented an extension of the Health Insurance Scheme of the 1920s, it was also true that its real genesis lay in the National Health Service introduced in the U.K. Here on the Island, however, our Bill differed in some respects from the English scheme. Voluntary hospitals, for example, were permitted to continue as independent charity-funded organisations, if they wished, though none has done so. The various professional societies, such as the Medical Society, will have representatives on the administering committees.

The Health Services Board of Tynwald is to be assisted by an Advisory Council which, it is proposed, will consist of the Medical Officer for Health, the Medical Superintendent of Ballamona and nine other members -three doctors, one consultant, one dentist, one chemist, and a midwife, an experienced manager and an official of a government department.

It is probably true to say that it was the composition of this Advisory Council that occasioned the greatest unease and, in some cases, fairly vitriolic criticism. Claims that this would give the doctors more or less complete executive control of the scheme were widely expressed and there were fears, unlikely though they may be, that the doctors would operate a closed shop. Indeed, some argued that the Manx Bill had been acceptable to the medical profession only because all the points to which the doctors in Britain objected were deleted from it! Any objective view of the situation would suggest that many of the worries were unfounded. Apart from a general consensus that professionals are the best people to oversee the working of the new scheme, it seems inconceivable that highly respected and regarded doctors would act in an irresponsible manner.

There were other concerns, too, not least the fate of the various charitable endowments that exist throughout the Island for the relief of distress. These are being transferred to the Health Services Board 'free of any trust' but that has not allayed the doubts of the several groups of trustees. The Corrin Endowment in Peel was directed towards the establishment of a Peel and District Cottage Hospital. Agreement has been reached now that a clinic or home for the elderly will be provided.

Another problem was the reluctance by Manx doctors to have their private practices nationalised. Initially, the Manx legislation omitted this U.K. plan, but in mid-May, when the Bill was in the middle of its parliamentary stages the doctors said they now wanted the same provisions. The reason for this change of mind was that in the United Kingdom certain alterations had been made to the British Scheme largely to do with the acquisition, sale or not of medical practices and other conditions of service which were more acceptable to the medical profession here than had hitherto been the case, particularly with regard to the compensation to be paid when practices were acquired. Despite the upset that this caused, the Legislative Council accepted the doctors' amendments and in early June gave the third reading to the Bill.

Matters progressed swiftly from that point. On Tuesday, 29th June the Bill was given its second reading in the Keys and passed by 15 votes to 8. There was a hard core of opposition in the House but it is probably fair to say that such opponents directed their fire not at the principles of the Bill, but at the financial consequences of its introduction. There were predictions that income tax could soar to 10 shillings or 17s 6d in the pound. It did not stop the opponents being described as eight 'Canutes' standing in the way of progress, however. During this debate doctors, dentists, opticians and chemists were well represented in the public area and they had already made it known that if the second reading was passed they were prepared to start the scheme the following Monday without waiting for the third reading.

This generous spirit on the part of the medical professionals was very well received by the population at large and from all over the Island reports were received that many doctors were already treating patients under the new system. There was some confusion as people were urged to register now with a chosen doctor but when, on 13th July, the Bill received its third reading and passed without a division, the message that came across was to get on with it. A new government form, HS1, for people to register with a doctor, appeared on the Island. By 30th July the Legislative Council had accepted the Bill.

There will be growing pains. Such a gigantic scheme will certainly produce immense organisational and administrative problems and the professional officers of the Health Services Board will be working long hours and at full stretch to find solutions. But already, in September, it is clear that the basic structure has not only been put in place but is working with remarkable smoothness and efficiency. Already over 35,000 people, some 65% of our population, have chosen their doctors, and each doctor has approximately 2,000 patients on his list. Concurrent with the launch of the new Health Service, a new Social Security system for the payment of benefits during times of hardship has also been introduced, partly financed from the Island's Income Tax fund. Employers and employees will have to pay higher contributions, but this is not begrudged because now the Social Security and Health Service will care for everyone 'from cradle to the grave'. These represent the most beneficent measures ever introduced by the Manx Legislature.

TYNWALD MATTERS: NATIONAL SERVICE TO CONTINUE

Young, fit Manxmen will be legally obliged to give 18 months National Service in one of Britain's armed services - but only after considerable hesitation by the House of Keys. It will be recalled that last November, when the proposed extension of the U.K's 1947 National Service Act to the Isle of Man came up for discussion, a resolution extending it to the Island was passed in the Legislative Council but fell in the House of Keys. The reasons for this apparent disarray were varied. For a few, a very few, the fact that the United Kingdom was not at war seems to have had some weight. But for the majority the complications arose when the Imperial Government amalgamated all its previous legislation dealing with National Service but left the Island under the jurisdiction of the existing National Service Act. This suggested that Manxmen could be called up and asked to serve under conditions more onerous in some respects than those called up in the United Kingdom.

As the reality of the situation dawned upon Tynwald members, this, coupled with increasingly forthright demands that the Island should follow the 'path of duty', led to the setting up of a Commission to enquire into the position regarding the extension of National Service to the Isle of Man. The views of the Committee became available recently and in October, Tynwald Court was asked once again to give 'most careful and favourable consideration' to a resolution asking His Majesty to extend to the Isle of Man by Order in Council the National Service Act 1947. When the matter was debated in Tynwald, the majority of the members were fully aware of all the implications of their decision. An impassioned speech by a new Labour member may well have swung the doubters - 'I appeal to you as a conscript, and as a young man likely to go again, to adopt the resolution'. The resolution was adopted and young Manx men, like their peers in the United Kingdom, will now find that their careers and aspirations will be put on hold, as it were, while they serve King and Country all over the world.

BLINDED OFFICER ADMITTED TO MANX BAR

One man's triumph over adversity should be an inspiration to other war-wounded. Despite being blinded, 28-year-old Howard Simcocks of Rushen Abbey, Ballasalla has qualified as an advocate. He did it through his indomitable courage and with the support of his family and friends. Before the war he was studying to be an accountant, then joined the Manx Regiment and served with it in Egypt until being commissioned and being transferred to another Light A.A. regiment. It was during the battle for Monte Casino, after the Salerno landings, that the jeep in which he was travelling was blown up by a mine. Lieutenant Simcocks was badly wounded in the head, rushed to hospital in Naples and, from there, to St. Dunstan's. He was told that he would never see again.

Whilst at St. Dunstan's, Mr. Simcocks learned to type and read Braille. This was particularly difficult for he was left handed, and his left hand had been damaged so badly he could not use his fingers for such delicate work. It was now that he began to develop what is now regarded as an amazing memory. Accountancy was out of the question, so he decided to embark on a career as an advocate. He sought the help of former Attorney- General, Mr. Ramsey Moore, who was more than willing to accept the challenge. He undertook to provide daily lectures in Manx law and Lieut-Colonel Henry Kelly, the Commanding Officer of the Manx Regiment, agreed to accept Mr. Simcocks as an articled student in his law firm of Kelly, Moore and Kelly. Mr Simcocks was able to make some notes from Mr. Moore's lectures and each night these were read to him at Rushen Abbey. He was then able to transcribe them into Braille on thick brown paper using a machine supplied to him by St. Dunstan's.

Despite many frustrations, Mr. Simcocks passed his intermediate examination after eight months. He then attended courts and sat in on interviews with clients. Law was read to him by advocates Arthur Luft and Stanley Allen. Mr. Simcocks noted some points, others he simply memorised. His prodigious memory enabled him to walk about home and office so long as no furniture was moved. Now it enabled him to memorise the whole of the prospectus for his final six hour examination. In the Rolls Office the questions were read to him and his answers were taken down in shorthand and transcribed. Mr. Simcocks passed, and was sworn in as a member of the Manx Bar in August by Deemster Cowley.

It is understood that Mr. Simcocks now aspires to be a member of Malew Parish Commissioners and the House of Keys, too. Given his determination, no one doubts he will succeed. Before the war Mr. Simcocks was a keen motorcyclist. Now he rides pillion when his secretary, 18-year-old Helen Kinvig, takes him to his office in Castletown. Occasionally they visit clients and sometimes travel as far as Douglas. Truly, he is a remarkable man and an example to us all.

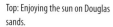

Top: Enjoying the sun on Douglas sands.

Middle left: The popular bathing beauty competitions.

Middle right: Mooragh Park, Ramsey.

Bottom left: Relaxing in the Villa Marina Gardens.

Bottom right: The Swimming Pool, Ramsey

Top: Peel Sands and Castle.

Middle left: Chapel Bay, Port St. Mary.

Middle right: Information Bureau, Victoria Pier, Douglas.

Bottom: Port Erin Sands
(Illustrations from Publicity Board Guide, Frank Cowin Library)

ISLAND TO RECEIVE TELEVISION?

People in the Isle of Man could soon be watching television for the first time. A new high-powered transmitter is under construction in the Midlands and will start beaming the television transmissions from Alexandra Palace in London next year. Its range will come close to reaching the Island. We have this report:

Britain's first television service was started by the BBC in 1936. It could be seen only in the London area, and only a few thousand people could afford a television receiving set. During the 1939 to 1945 war years the service was suspended, but now it is expanding rapidly. The new transmitter at Sutton Coldfield will have a range conservatively estimated to be a hundred miles - and the Isle of Man is only 150 miles away. Local radio dealers, notably Harold Colebourn, Ernie Dickinson and Russell Fox, plan to test local levels of reception and provide public demonstrations. Mr. Fox, who came to the Island during the war to work in the radar installations on Douglas Head, worked in television in London before the war. He says he believes the new developments in television technology are bringing the Island close to being able to receive reasonably good television pictures. That means something that is rather sparkly, shadowy and inclined to fade. Screens will be no bigger than nine inches. Even so, he believes television will be highly popular in the Island, especially when major sports events are screened. In the meantime, the BBC's Controller of Television, Mr. Norman Collins, has said his long-term intention, backed by a £12 million development programme, is that television will reach out across the whole of the British Isles. The problem is that the emphasis at first will be on providing good reception in areas of high population. Because of post-war shortages it could be years before transmitters are provided to give better reception in the peripheral areas.

STRIKE AVERTED
Last minute intervention by the Government saved the Island from a potentially disastrous general strike at the start of the visiting season. After six months of negotiation between employers and unions had failed to reach a settlement on improved pay and conditions, a deputation of M.H.K.s brought the two sides together at the eleventh hour. The strike was called off when the employers conceded the main demand of an increase in basic pay for the Island's 5,000 general workers.

INDEPENDENT AIRLINES TO THE RESCUE
In February, the Lieutenant-Governor, reported the results of a meeting with the Minister of Civil Aviation following the announcement that B.E.A. was to make drastic cuts in the summer services to the Island because of heavy losses. Only Liverpool and Belfast would be served, with a week-end service to London. His Excellency said these cuts had to be accepted, but to compensate for what could have been a calamitous situation, independent airlines would be permitted to provide services to the Island on other routes. Many willing and eager private companies responded. One of the first was North West Airlines (Isle of Man) Ltd. It was formed out of Mannin Airways, now without Captain Higgins, combining with Ulster Aviation. Immediate

An aerial view of Ronaldsway Airport showing a multitude of aircraft parked near the terminal buildings. Many of the aircraft are operated by independent airlines which have been permitted to fly on routes which are not the preserve of British European Airways. Connections with many parts of the British Isles have boosted the number of passengers handled at Ronaldsway over the 100,000 mark for the first time. (Aerofilms Limited)

steps were taken to add two Dakotas to their fleet of smaller aircraft and licences were granted to provide services from Manchester, Blackpool, Carlisle and Prestwick. Other independents appeared and services were provided from Leeds, Birmingham and Newcastle. It was these independents that boosted the number of passengers handled at Ronaldsway over the 100,000 mark for the first time.

ACQUITTED OF MANSLAUGHTER
Applause and cheering broke out in Douglas Court House when the jury returned a verdict of 'Not Guilty' at the trial of William Henry Wattleworth, a 22-year-old painter from Liverpool who also boxes professionally under the name of Bill Watts. He was involved in a violent brawl in Strand Street, Douglas, involving nine men. One of them, 29-year-old Henry Yates, of Wellington Square, Douglas, died of head injuries after being punched to the ground by Wattleworth. The latter entered a plea of self defence, saying he had been provoked by Yates.

PRISONER ESCAPES, TWICE!
A London criminal, 20-year-old Raymond Henry Spicer, escaped from the Island's prison in Victoria Road, Douglas - not once, but twice in two months. He was on remand on a burglary charge when he made his first escape. He was recaptured by the police after 54 hours on the run as he tried to get away from the Island in a stolen motor boat. His second break for freedom lasted 42 hours until he was recaptured in a hay loft near Castletown. He is serving two years imprisonment with hard labour.

WARDEN QUITS CALF OF MAN
The man who has been the English National Trust warden on the Calf of Man for the last 10 years is giving up. Forty-nine-year-old Robert Mitchell and his wife Norah said it had been the loneliest job in Britain, suitable only for a Robinson Crusoe. They farmed on the Calf but found it a hard life with bad weather cutting them off for up to five weeks at a time. A Manx National Trust is now being formed and this is to take over a long lease on the Calf.

DROWNED IN CALF SOUND
A Scots holidaymaker drowned while trying to swim across the tidal race in the Calf Sound. Twenty-seven-year-old Andrew Young had swum across to Kitterland but got into difficulties when he tried to make the return trip. His body was washed up later at Port Erin. A plucky but unsuccessful attempt at rescue was made by Port St. Mary art student Edward Cannell who was among scores of people who witnessed the tragedy.

In another sea tragedy a young man, Michael Walker from Blackpool, lost his life following the capsizing of a small yacht in which he and his uncle James Norris were fishing in Ramsey Bay. Mr. Norris, practically a non-swimmer, was picked up after clinging to the upturned boat for over two hours. Michael, a powerful swimmer, lost his life when trying to swim ashore for assistance.

NEW RACING STARS
Two bright new British sports stars emerged in the Island during this year. Geoff Duke, a 26-year-old motorcyclist from St. Helens, won the Senior Manx Grand Prix at record speed and set up a new lap record of 87.5 m.p.h. Second was Cromie McCandless who beat Duke in the Junior Race after a terrific battle. Duke first appeared in June this year when he won the Senior Clubman's T.T.

In the Manx Cup Race on the Willaston Circuit, 18-year-old Stirling Moss attracted much attention for his spectacular driving in a Cooper J.A.P. He was well in the lead until forced out with magneto problems. He recorded the fastest lap in the race which was won by John Heath driving an H.W. Alta. In the main race, Bob Gerard won the British Empire Trophy in an E.R.A. for the second time.

In June, Senior Race Day was honoured by a visit from H.R.H. The Duke of Edinburgh, Patron of the A-C.U. He witnessed the massed start of the Lightweight Race which was won again by Manliff Barrington riding for Moto Guzzi. The Duke flagged off Artie Bell to start the Senior Race which had a dramatic finish. Les Graham, on one of the A.J.S. 'Porcupines', started the last lap with a comfortable lead but had to stop at Hillberry with magneto failure. Les managed to push the heavy machine to the finish where the ex-fighter pilot received a standing ovation from the crowded grandstand. He

With local farmers unable to meet the huge demand for milk this summer, supplies have had to be ferried in from Northern Ireland. Here, one of the Miles Aerovans being employed in the operation is being loaded with the car of a local resident intent on holidaying in Ireland.

During the year Isle of Man Road Services Limited added a further 18 56-seater Leyland double-decker buses to their fleet, bringing the total to 28 of this type. The new buses arrived together as 'cargo' for a large tank-landing craft employed in the D-Day landings. Here, four of them can be seen after being craned on to the King Edward Pier. (Frank Cowin Library)

finished tenth. His misfortune allowed Harold Daniell to notch up another win for Norton.

This year the Isle of Man T.T. was the first round of the new World Motor-Cycling Championships being held in various European countries. Enthusiasts followed the fortunes of British riders and it is good to report that two T.T. favourites have become World Champions. Freddie Frith, this year's Junior T.T. winner, is the first World Champion in the 350 c.c. class while Les Graham is the first 500 c.c. World Champion.

DOUGLAS ILLUMINATIONS RETURN

The attractive feature of the illuminations along Douglas promenade made a welcome return this year. They had not been seen since 1939. The steam ferries across Douglas harbour which take thousands of visitors to the attractions of Douglas Head, also made a welcome return as did the incline railway towards the end of the

season. The steam ferry owners are objecting strongly to the proposed bus service to Douglas Head which the Corporation plan to introduce next year. The number of visitors to the Island this year once again topped the 600,000 mark but was slightly down on last year's figure. The season was marked by a shortage of milk. Extra supplies had to be ferried in from Northern Ireland.

ISLAND'S CONTRIBUTION TO WESTMINSTER SETTLED

After a political row lasting six months, Tynwald has settled at last the basis on which a contribution to the cost of Imperial Defence, diplomatic and other common services should be paid. In May it was decided unanimously that five members of the Finance and Consultative committee should accompany His Excellency the Lieutenant-Governor to London to discuss the matter with His Majesty's Government, and to agree on the amount of the annual payment with a further reduction in the National Debt arising from the cost of the war. In June the deputation's report on the Defence Contribution recommended that the Island should pay the British Exchequer a sum based on a percentage of our Common Purse receipts. The suggested rate was 61/2%. At present, that would have amounted to £100,000. The proposal was that as these receipts rose or fell the contribution would vary with a minimum limit of £50,000. It was recommended also that the sum of £500,000, the balance of money loaned to the U.K. Government during the war, should be converted into a gift. The report was considered by Tynwald twice during June, but a decision was deferred until October.

The October meeting of Tynwald resulted in stalemate when Keys and Council failed to agree on the final details of the contribution. This led to a series of private meetings, and in November a compromise solution to the controversy was agreed without a division in Tynwald. The decision means that the Isle of Man will make an annual payment to the Imperial Government of a sum equal to 5% of the Common Purse receipts, currently approximately £80,000. This may be decreased or increased in any year by resolution of Tynwald. It was agreed also that the £500,000 on loan to the U.K. Government free of interest should not be converted to a gift at this stage. In response, the U.K. Government said it would accept the offer but only reluctantly because the offer did not truly reflect the services the Island received at the expense of U.K. taxpayers.

Above left: Newcomer Geoff Duke relaxes after winning the Senior Clubman's T.T. in June. A few weeks later he returned and took the Manx Grand Prix by storm, coming second in the Junior and winning the Senior. It could be that a T.T. star of the future has been born. (Keig Collection)

Left: H.R.H. The Duke of Edinburgh, Patron of the A-C.U., chats with Harold Daniell before the start of the Senior T.T. The Norton rider went on to win his third Senior race. (Manx National Heritage)

BLESSED ARE THE PEACEMAKERS

Last minute intervention by the House of Keys saved the Island from being paralysed by a major strike in late June. It was in the Spring that what had been vague flickers of discontent amongst the Island's workers, particularly those in the T.G.W.U. and the Electrical Trades Union, seemed ready to burst into a serious conflagration. Union demands for both wage increases, some 3 shillings a week for general workers, and zonal upgradings in conjunction with other requirements, had produced a head-on clash with the Employers' Federation. General workers, municipal passenger and transport workers, Gas Company and Steam Packet Company employees, laundry and quay workers - all the wide spectrum of T.G.W.U. members - meant that should the issue fail to be resolved then the subsequent strike would to all intents and purposes shut down the entire Island.

From March, despite the Lieutenant-Governor's proposal for arbitration, which was accepted by the unions but not by the employers, continuous talks had got nowhere. The main sticking point seemed to be that the employers wanted the case of the General Workers dealt with first, before moving on to the rest, while the unions wanted the whole package to be considered. Negotiations ended in acrimony in May with the employers finally accepting arbitration but the unions rejecting the notion. On 10th June the unions issued a formal notice of strike action. This would expire at midnight on Sunday, 19th June and a general stoppage would be implemented.

The effect of such a stoppage would have been catastrophic. This undoubtedly played a great part in the decision of the House of Keys to depute three of their members - Messrs. A. J. Teare, H. K. Corlett and J. C. Nivison - to make one final attempt to bring the parties together. On Wednesday morning, 15th June, they met representatives of the unions involved, and by early evening they had discussed matters with those of the Employers' Federation. At 8 p.m. a joint meeting was held in a Tynwald Committee room. This continued until midnight. On the following morning the meeting was resumed and at 2 p.m. the unions withdrew their notice of strike action.

The outcome was that the general workers would receive their rise, from 97 to 100 shillings a week, but not their upgrading. Other workers received modest increases, all retrospective to 1st March. Most people believe that this result could, and should have been achieved without the months of tension, and perhaps some good will come out of it. Certainly, some form of machinery should exist before they threaten the economy. There is a reasonable case for setting up a cost of living index for everyone's guidance. It might end the uninformed comparisons that always seem to add fuel to whatever fire is burning - although human nature being what it is, even that seems 'pie in the sky'!

In October, His Excellency the Lieutenant-Governor announced to Tynwald his intention to make an Order giving the necessary powers to safeguard public interests in connections with trades disputes. The Order came into effect on 14th November.

1949 NEWS IN BRIEF

JANUARY
1 - Manxman Sir Ralph Stevenson, British Ambassador to China, awarded the Grand Cross of St. Michael and St. George.

FEBRUARY
16 - After having been on Government service for over nine years, the steamer *Manxman* docked in Barrow. She is to be sold for breaking-up purposes.

MARCH
1 - Tynwald agrees to appropriate money to support industries which promise to provide employment. The Court also authorised the Electricity Board to set up its own generating station at an estimated cost of £212,000.
8 - Legislative Council rejected by five votes to four, a Bill designed to give women the right to serve on juries.
22 - Fiftieth anniversary of the founding of Yn Cheshaght Ghailckagh, the Manx Language Society.
22 - Manx Operatic Society founded.

APRIL
22 - Mr. Bryan Kneale, a student at the Royal Academy Schools, awarded the 1949 Rome Scholarship in Mural Painting.

MAY
4 - Mr. Lewis Gale (baritone) scored a notable 'double' by winning the Cleveland Medal and the new 'F. M. Cubbon' silver rose bowl in the final of the Lieder classes.
22 - Centenary of St. John's Church commemorated by special services.
28 - Visit of Lord Rowallan, Chief Scout of the British Empire, and the Hon. Lady Cochrane, Chief Guide Commissioner for England.

JUNE
9 - Speaker of the House of Keys, Mr. J. D. Qualtrough, awarded the C.B.E. in the King's Birthday Honours List. Superintendent Alfred Kelly, Deputy Chief Constable, awarded the King's Police Medal.

JULY
13 - Douglas Town Council adopt plan for the lay-out of King George V Park to provide a stadium and football pitch, and running and cycle tracks.
14 - Ramsey's new lifeboat, the *Thomas Corbett*, named by Lady Bromet.

AUGUST
16 - John James Foster (46), living at Ballaghaue Housing Estate, Andreas, lost his life by a fall of sand when working at the Kimmeragh sand-pit.

SEPTEMBER
14 - Mr. William Teare (66), of Ballaghennie Farm, Bride, accidentally killed when duck-shooting near the farm.
16-19 Douglas bus services stopped by unofficial strike of drivers and conductors following the suspension of driver Thomas Gale for failing to observe the compulsory stop on Prospect Hill. He was reported by Councillor T. C. Cowin, chairman of the Tramways Committee. The strike ended when the Tramways Committee, acting on a legal opinion in respect of Councillor Cowin's occupancy of the chair when Driver Gale appeared before them, rescinded the suspension of the driver.

OCTOBER
31 - Francis Thomas Cubbon (aged 2) died in a fire which destroyed Glen View Cottage, West Baldwin.

NOVEMBER
7-12 Many successes by Manx competitors at Blackpool Music Festival.
12 - Mr. William Hughes of Peel killed when thrown into crankpit of Ramsey Steamship Co's vessel *Ben Jee*, during severe gale in Preston Bay.
16 - By 13 votes to 5 in the Keys, a resolution asking for approval to a proposal that the Airports Board provide licensed catering facilities at Ronaldsway Airport rejected in Tynwald.

NEW SECONDARY SCHOOL FOR THE SOUTH

The new secondary school for children in the south of the Island was formally opened on Friday, 6th May by British Home Secretary, Mr. Chuter Ede. He referred to the Island's bilateral (or comprehensive) educational system as 'one of the great educational ventures of our time'. The Manx system is the brainchild of our Director of Education, Mr. H. L. Fletcher, O.B.E., M.A., who envisaged in pre-war days all children of secondary school age being educated together, rather than being separated by passing, or failing, a scholarship examination. As a symbol of stability and security, the new school has been named Castle Rushen High School. It is unique in that it makes use of wartime single-brick buildings of Admiralty design, built to accommodate personnel of the highly secret Air Radar School. Here thousands of personnel were trained in the intricacies of radar. The school operated in conjunction with the radar stations at Scarlett and Dalby.

The task of converting the site into a school was given to the firm of Davidson, Marsh and Co., architects and surveyors. All the main classrooms were linked by a long corridor. Three other corridors which linked the offices, dining room, staff room, music room, art room and handicraft workshop and additional classrooms, formed a garden quadrangle for use as a rural science centre. Other rooms were fitted out for general science and domestic science. Another unique feature of the school was that all rooms were linked by a tannoy system, enabling the headmaster to communicate with the whole school. A new assembly hall/gymnasium was completed this spring. It was here that the formal opening took place. Mr. Chuter Ede was joined by His Excellency the Lieutenant-Governor, the Ven. Archdeacon C. V. Stockwood (chairman of the Education Authority) and Mr. J. D. Qualtrough, S.H.K. (Member for Castletown and chairman of the Board of Education).

The school actually received its first pupils last September when those already attending the lower two forms at the Douglas High Schools were joined by those of eleven years and over attending the elementary schools in the south of the Island. Children living outside Castletown are 'bussed' from Port Erin, Port St. Mary, Colby, Ballabeg, Foxdale and Santon. The school, opened with 147 boys and 116 girls who met in the dining hall for the first assembly under the school's headmaster, Mr. Godfrey Cretney, B.A. He held up a blank piece of paper and emphasised that everyone was making a fresh start. 'This school has great potentialities,' said Mr. Cretney, 'but it needs prestige, and that is what I want to give it.' The pupils have been streamed in mixed forms according to suggested ability, but flexibility will allow transfers to be made as pupils progress through the school.

The establishment of this school in the south fulfils the aspirations of those who had argued long ago that such a school was essential not only to counterbalance the preponderance of Douglas interests, but also to put the south on a parity with the north of the Island. It is seen as the last stone in implementing the revolutionary concept of secondary education pioneered on the Island. But perhaps it is not quite the last stone. People living in the west of the Island will dispute that! How long will they have to wait? Ten years? Fifty years? Surely not half a century!

Below: Pupils line up in the main corridor which links the former buildings now used as class rooms and specialist rooms.

Below right: The first members of staff of Castle Rushen High School. Standing centre is Headmaster Mr Godfrey Cretney, B.A.

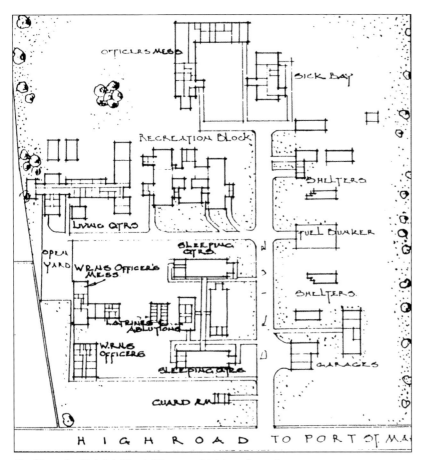

Plan of the wartime Admiralty buildings built to accommodate trainee radar operators.

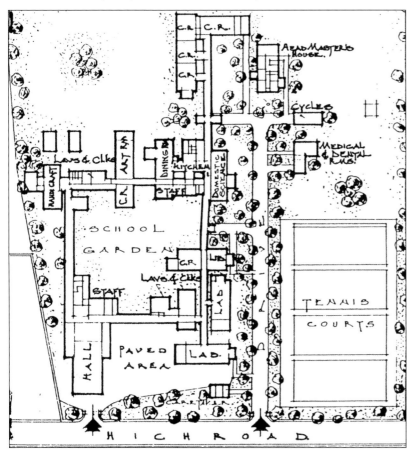

Plan of the school showing the ingenious use of corridors to link the buildings now converted into classrooms and specialised rooms. (Photographs by kind permission of Mr W. C. Callister)

School entrance.

Nissen huts used for metalwork, and the groundsman's hut.

The quadrangle forming the school garden.

Building being used as the chemistry lab.

The domestic science room.

CRISIS IN HEALTH SERVICE: CHEMISTS GO ON STRIKE

The Isle of Man's fledgling National Health Service, launched in July, 1948, was brought close to collapse this year because of the cost to the taxpayer of dental treatment and prescriptions. When the Government introduced tough new regulations under which patients would have to pay a charge of sixpence for prescriptions, the Island's chemists rebelled and withdrew from the N.H.S. Only crisis talks with the Health Services Board saved the situation. We have this report:

At a secret session of Tynwald in April, members were shocked to discover that the cost of the all-free N.H.S. had soared to an estimated £800,000 a year, well beyond expectations. It was decided that there would have to be cutbacks, and the public would have to contribute to the cost. The charges, announced by Mr. T. C. Cowin, chairman of the Health Services Board, came into effect on 1st October. They provide for a charge of sixpence for each form of prescription; a charge for medicine or drug containers; the payment of 10% of the excess over £1 of the cost of dental treatment, and that all children under school leaving age should receive free treatment only by the School Dental Officers. The moves were opposed strongly by the Island's doctors, dentists and chemists, but only the Manx Chemists Association stood out against the Government. With over 40 members, all but seven decided to pull out of the N.H.S., as they felt the collection of the charges would be unworkable. It amounted to a strike and led to the Isle of Man Medical Society issuing a statement that the N.H.S. was in chaos and on the brink of collapse. The situation forced the Health Services Board to bring in the police. It was arranged that patients' prescriptions would be collected at police stations and brought to Douglas to be dispensed, Atkinson's Pharmacy in Granville Street and Boots the Chemists in Victoria Street not having joined the boycott. The dispensed articles were then returned to the various police stations for collection by or on behalf of the patients. The situation persisted for 18 days during which 150 prescriptions a day were processed. The deadlock was broken after talks between the Chemists Association and the Government although no official details of the agreement have been made public.

TRAWLER LOST ON ROCKS

A Lowestoft trawler, the Mary Heeley, was lost when she went aground in fog on the rocks north of Onchan Harbour in April. Her crew of 10 were rescued by the Douglas lifeboat, the Millie Walton. She was making her first service call in charge of coxswain Mr. Robert Lee. It happened at midnight and the trawler's S.O.S. was picked up by a radio ham in Douglas who raised the alarm. The Island was hit by the worst storms for years in September with 80 mile an hour winds and torrential rain. Steam Packet sailings were delayed, but not halted.

DAMAGES AWARD REVERSED

A schoolboy has been awarded £760 damages in the High Court at Douglas for the loss of the sight in one eye during a game of conkers on a school train. Fourteen-year-old John Donald Bridson, of Glen Maye, was hit by a conker wielded by another boy while the train was travelling from Peel to Douglas. The Education Authority was held responsible for failing to exercise proper supervision on the train. However, the Court's decision was reversed on appeal.

STREET PARKING PROHIBITED

A major clamp-down on all-day car parking in Douglas has been launched by the Town Council. Restrictions have been imposed on all the town's main roads and streets under which cars will not be allowed to park longer than it takes to drop off or pick up passengers and goods. Works Committee chairman Alderman J. C. Fargher told the Council: "Streets were never made for the parking of motor cars".

LICENCE FOR SPIRITS REFUSED

The Douglas Licensing Bench has refused to allow boarding houses to serve their guests spirits in addition to wine and beer. The Bench refused to accept the argument of 91 applicants that drinking habits had changed and spirits were more in demand. The Manx Temperance Federation opposed the applications. It is questionable that the decision will have much impact on the majority of guesthouses. They are unlicensed but are selling drinks to their guests even so, under a dubious scheme that argues that the drinks have been bought in on behalf of the guests and are, therefore, the property of the guests. Meanwhile, the Island's Appeal Court has upheld a decision by the High-Bailiff that publicans who instal juke boxes in their pubs must have a music licence.

T.T. RECORDS SMASHED

All pre-war records were smashed in this year's T.T. Races. Irishman Artie Bell set up new race and lap records in the Junior T.T., raising Stanley Wood's 1938 lap of 85.3 m.p.h. to 87.3 m.p.h. in a time of 25 mins 56 secs. The new Lightweight records were set up by Dario Ambrosini on a Benelli. Kluge's 1938 lap record of 80.35 m.p.h. was lifted to 80.9 m.p.h. by the Italian rider. But it was the brilliant riding of newcomer Geoff Duke which caught everyone's attention on Senior Race Day. He won last year's Senior Clubman's T.T. and Senior M.G.P., and had been enlisted into the Norton works team along with Artie Bell, Harold Daniell and Johnny Lockett. They were riding the new 'Featherbed' Nortons, so called because of the suspension of the revolutionary frame designed by Cromie and Rex McCandless. Duke astonished the crowd by being the first to lap at under 25 minutes and, in the process, breaking team-mate

1950
• First Formula One motor racing championships held
• Death of novelist George Orwell and writer/playwright George Bernard Shaw

Harold Daniell's lap record of 91 m.p.h. which had stood since 1938. On the fifth of the seven laps, Duke sped round at 93.33 m.p.h., altering the record books with a time of 24 mins. 16 secs. Geoff Duke was the main topic at teatime in the boarding houses that day. It is confidently predicted that he is a World Champion in the making.

CONTRABAND FROM IRELAND

Customs officers who boarded an Irish cargo ship when she called into Douglas while on passage from Dublin to Silloth in Scotland found thousands of pounds worth of contraband on board. A hundred thousand cigarettes and a thousand pairs of nylons were seized. The ship was detained in Douglas for six days. Her owners denied all knowledge of the contraband and the ship was released after they paid £2,500 demanded by H.M.Customs.

COUPLE FOUND SHOT

A Douglas inquest has decided that a retired Army officer murdered his wife by shooting her and then turned his Service revolver on himself. The bodies of 54-year-old Captain Ernest Thompson and his 48-year-old wife Margaret were found at their flat in Finch Road. Captain Thompson was posted to the Island during the Second World War and stayed on afterwards. He was said to have had business worries and concerns about his wife's health. In another tragic case of suicide, Mr.

and Mrs. William Kelly, formerly of Ballachrink, Bride, were found gassed in their home 'Millway', Lezayre Road, Ramsey. Verdicts of suicide through financial worries were recorded.

OBJECTIONS TO HOTEL INSPECTIONS

The Island's hoteliers and boarding house keepers have rejected proposals that their premises should be subject to Government inspection and registration in future. They say they know the requirements of visitors best and they do not need any kind of Government interference. It was in the House of Keys that Mr. Spencer Kelly (Ramsey) sought to bring about the registration of visitor accommodation by an amendment to the Publicity Bill. He withdrew the amendment later, but intends to introduce a separate Bill to deal with the matter.

GRAMMAR SCHOOL SAVED

The Island's oldest building has been saved from demolition. Castletown Grammar School has been given to the Manx Museum by the Town Commissioners. It had been intended to demolish the school in a clearance scheme to create car parking. Preservers of the Island's past will be relieved to hear of the change of mind as this ancient building dates back to the middle of the 13th century when it was built as St. Mary's Chapel by the monks of Rushen Abbey. In 1698 it became the Academic School for the training of

1950

• Regular colour TV broadcasts begin in the US

• First 'universal' credit cards issued by Diner's Club

Below left: After escaping a dramatic three-car pile up involving Prince Bira's Maserati at Parkfield Corner, Bob Gerard went on to complete a hat-trick of wins in the British Empire Trophy series. Here he is seen cornering at Parkfield in his 1,488 c.c. supercharged E.R.A. (Doug Baird)

Left: Harold Daniell's 1938 Senior T.T. lap record was finally eclipsed this year by rising star Geoff Duke of the Norton team. Here he is flat out on the new 'featherbed' Norton at the bottom of Bray Hill during the Senior race when he set up a new lap record of 93.33 m.p.h., in a time of 25 mins 56 secs. (Island Photographics)

Bottom left: The trawler 'Mary Heeley' which was wrecked after going aground in fog on the rocks to the north of Onchan Harbour. The Douglas lifeboat rescued all ten of the crew.
(Frank Cowin Library)

Bottom right: It has come as a relief to many that the ancient Castletown Grammar School (left foreground) is to be placed in the charge of the Manx Museum. Some of the nearby buildings have already disappeared, while the rest await demolition to provide a car park for the town.
(Frank Cowin Library)

clergy and is the forerunner of King William's College. The Grammar School continued in use until 1930.

DRASTIC ATTEMPT TO ERADICATE TUBERCULOSIS

The most determined bid yet to eradicate tuberculosis - one of the most feared diseases this century - is underway. It involves the wholesale slaughter of Manx dairy cattle. Better housing and improvements in hygiene have helped to reduce the incidence of T.B. but contaminated milk supplies continue to perpetuate the disease.

It has been known for most of this century that milk is one of the main causes of spreading the disease, hence repeated attempts to eliminate bovine T.B. These have failed, however, as evidenced by the fact that at least a third of the Island's cattle population and between 60 and 100 per cent of dairy herds have been tested as carriers. Now it has been decided that the only way to eradicate the disease is to slaughter systematically, parish by parish,

all cattle which test positive. It is expected to take between seven and eight years.

This will be a costly exercise for Tynwald, which is to provide compensation for farmers, and for the farmers too, for they say the compensation is not enough to cover the purchase of replacement stock which must be T.B. free and is, therefore, quite rare and expensive.

One benefit for the Island, of course, is that there should be more beef than usual available for summer tourists at a time when food shortages are still a problem. There is concern about milk supplies, however. In the last two years milk has had to be imported from Northern Ireland during the height of the summer. This led to suggestions that local ice cream production should be curbed to release Manx milk for drinking purposes. Such a proposal, however, would have encouraged the importation of ice cream for tourists and that would have helped destroy the local industry.

1950 NEWS IN BRIEF

JANUARY
1 - Retirement, after 37 years incumbency of Kirk Braddan Parish, of Rev. Canon W. A. Rushworth, M.A. He is to be succeeded by Rev. Bertram Kelly, formerly Chief Electrical Engineer to the Borough of Douglas.
12 - Completion of a year's work by the British Mission Micro-Film Unit in micro-filming of Manx archives totalling 350,000 facsimiles of separate scripts.
24 - Rev. F. M. Cubbon inaugurates start of work on the Thomas Cubbon Wing at Noble's Hospital made possible by the £20,000 bequest of the late Thomas Cubbon, J.P., and a similar amount by himself.
25 - Appointment of Mr. Emrys Griffiths as headmaster of Murray's Road School in succession to Mr. T. C. Corris who retired.
31 - House of Keys pass Fire Services Bill providing for the appointment of a Chief Fire Officer for the Island.

FEBRUARY
3 - Mr. Nigel Kneale, of Douglas, and brother of Bryan, awarded the Somerset Maugham Award for his book of short stories, "Tomato Cain", which has a strong Manx connection.
12 - Report of Local Government Commission recommends abolition of village and parish commissioners by amalgamation of local districts on a sheading basis for administration by rural district authorities.

MARCH
1 - Tynwald approves £29,585 scheme for undergrounding by Electricity Board of electric cables in the out-district districts.
29 - Dr. A. K. Soutar, School Medical Officer for 27 years, resigned. He is to be succeeded by Dr. S. V. Cullen, M.B., Ch.B.

APRIL
6 - Resignation from Legislative Council of Mr. J. H. L. Cowin, chairman of the Board of Agriculture since July, 1944.
28 - Mr. J. R. Bregazzi, chief reporter of the *Isle of Man Times*, completed 60 years in Manx journalism.

MAY
2 - Opening of new Castletown Sports Stadium by the Lieutenant-Governor with a match between South Liverpool F.C. and an Island XI selected by ballot of *Green Final* readers.
3 - Cleveland Medal at the Manx Music Festival won by Eileen Peters of Douglas, first lady to win the award for 16 years.
6 - John Edward Moore (64) of Braddan electrocuted and died when an overhead cable carrying 33,000 volts was touched by tipping gear on a lorry he was working at Pulrose.
18 - W. A. Kirkpatrick won the Manx Golf Championship for the fourth time.
20 - Bob Gerard achieved his hat-trick of wins in the Manx series of the British Empire Trophy Races.

JUNE
1 - The Mayor of Douglas (Councillor T. Radcliffe, J.P.) speaking at the Junior T.T. presentation of awards, vigorously attacked the Lord Bishop (Dr. J. R. Strickland Taylor) for his remarks on the organisation for T.T. practising as expressed in an interview with

the representative of a national newspaper. Two riders were killed during the practices.
14 - For the second time, Douglas Town Council rejected a recommendation from the Estates Committee that refrigerators be made available for tenants in Council houses.
20 - For the first time in 30 years Budget proposals submitted by the Lieutenant-Governor came under criticism. Tynwald retired until the next day and the proposed increase of a shilling in the pound income tax was reduced to sixpence. The Court agreed to raise the duty on Manx brewed beer by 2d a pint.
25 - Well Road Methodist Church, Douglas, closed after being used for 113 years, the last sermon being preached by Mr. J. J. Kerruish of Laxey.

JULY
14 - Local Government report reveals that 1,449 families have been housed since the war. Permanent houses completed totalled 1,148, erected by private enterprise and local authorities.
19 - First excursion sailing to Dublin since 1939.
20-21 - Visit to R.A.F. Station, Jurby, of the Rt. Hon. Arthur Henderson, Secretary of State for Air. The station was partially re-activated in November last year for ground combat training and this year became the base for No. 1 Initial Training School for pre-flying training of pilots and navigators.

AUGUST
17 - First two houses on the Willaston Estate occupied by selected tenants.

SEPTEMBER
19 - With seven members of the House of Keys opposing, Tynwald carried a resolution extending the period of National Service by six months to two years.
27 - Peel Commissioners protested against rejection by Public Works Commission of a project to construct a new pier at a cost of £200,000.

OCTOBER
12 - Launch of the *Mona's Isle V* at Cammell Laird's shipyard, Birkenhead. Due to be launched later this year is the new cargo vessel to be named *Fenella III*. She is the company's first motor ship and is being built by the Ailsa Shipbuilding Company at Troon. The *Manx Maid* is to be sold for breaking up.
20 - Announcement made that a Nurses' Home, costing £160,000, is to be built on land opposite Noble's Hospital.
24 - Onchan Village Commissioners abandoned a proposal to seek town status for the area under their control.

NOVEMBER
6-11 - Among further successes by Manx competitors at the Blackpool Music Festival, Mr. Arthur Quirk (bass) won the Rose Bowl, the premier award.

DECEMBER
5 - House of Keys pass final stages of National Assistance Bill which abolishes Poor Law Guardians and the poor rate, and passes administration to the Board of Social Services.

1950

• Briton Roger Bannister runs the first sub-4 minute mile

• North Korean troops invade South Korea: start of the Korean War

CHORAL UNION SURVIVES . . . AND CELEBRATES!

Douglas Choral Union, the Island's longest established amateur operatic society, has been saved from closure after a dispute over auditions led to the formation of a rival Manx Operatic Society. The central issue which tore the D.C.U. apart was a tendency by the "old guard" to operate a "closed shop" in respect of principal parts. They expected to be given the parts, almost as a right, because of their proven record with the Society. This meant that new blood was unwelcome unless needed for a specific part.

Recently the music teacher and choir conductor, Douglas Buxton, son of Fred Buxton, the former operator of pierrot shows in Douglas, was appointed as Musical Director. He accepted the post, however, only on the condition that he could institute auditions for the principal parts and thereby open the way for new blood. This was accepted begrudgingly - until the D.C.U. started to plan for this year's golden jubilee celebrations. Inevitably, all the veteran members wanted to play significant roles.

Trouble erupted early last year at the annual general meeting of the Choral Union in the Savoy Restaurant in Victoria Street, Douglas. One faction, representing veterans who had refused to submit to auditions and, therefore, had ceased to be given principal parts, proposed that the society should get rid of the recently introduced "audition nonsense". Douglas Buxton said this would not happen as long as he was Musical Director. When the proposition carried, therefore, he left the meeting vowing that he would have no more to do with the Choral Union. Others followed.

Supporters of Mr. Buxton resigned their membership and, almost overnight, formed a rival Manx Operatic Society, with a target of February this year for their first show. The disaffected included the D.C.U.'s chairman, Stephen Quirk, former London dance school operator, Eira Elma, Rene Gibson (a talented producer) and Dan Minay, brother of the dynamic veteran star of so many D.C.U. productions and, more recently, its producer, Margaret Minay. There was such a movement of younger talent to the Manx Operatic Society that there were fears that the D.C.U. might collapse. Indeed, it is estimated now that the Operatic Society is 75 per cent ex-D.C.U.

The D.C.U. owes its survival principally to the efforts of Margaret Minay - one of the veterans who had refused to submit to auditions. An emergency meeting of the society filled all the committee posts such as chairman, treasurer, librarian, which had been vacated, then, undeterred by the loss of membership, the members committed themselves to the production for the society's jubilee of Gilbert and Sullivan's The Mikado.

Frank Bull was given the title role. Three of the society's founder members, who played principal roles in The Mikado when it was staged by the D.C.U. in 1901, were invited to the show as special guests. They were Winifred Adams, Fred Minay and Willy Craine.

Young singers who had never appeared on stage before were recruited at the Manx Music Festival and from elsewhere, then coached at Margaret Minay's home before appearing for an obligatory voice test which precedes confirmation of D.C.U. membership. Recruits included a number of potential stars for the future. Among them were Onchan butcher Jack Hampson, Marie Dawson, Fran Quirk, Thea Craine, Marion Hampton, Harry Butterworth, Cranston Laidlaw, Marsie White and Shirley Currie.

The 79-year-old former bandmaster and Musical Director, "J. T." Wood, came out of retirement to act as Musical Director. Despite his age, he stood "as straight as a die" at the Gaiety Theatre every night of the show - and afterwards he walked unaided up the steep Crellin's

Hill to his home in central Douglas! He must have felt well satisfied. On the opening night, the show received a standing ovation.

The Choral Union has thus been re-born and the Island has gained two thriving amateur choral societies, each striving to better the other. Typical of this rivalry was a pre-show promotional stunt undertaken by D.C.U. secretary, Jack Cretney, and Tom Humphrey. They used a rickshaw which had been brought to the Island as a stage prop to give each other rides through Douglas. The stunt worked well as an attention-grabber until three days before the show when the rickshaw lost one of its wheels after hitting a kerb.

This sort of new spirit will raise standards, says Mr. Buxton. Although the division has been painful, he believes the result to have been beneficial. The noted singer and music teacher, Gladys Skillicorn, says that the Choral Union had become too big anyway. Sometimes there had been so many on stage that anyone with lines to say had to squeeze past others.

MANX OPERATIC SOCIETY

(Amateur Operatic & Dramatic Society)

Under the distinguished patronage of His Excellency the Lieut.-Governor, Sir Geoffrey Bromet, K.B.E., C.B., D.S.O., and Lady Bromet, His Worship the Mayor of Douglas (Councillor T. Radcliffe, Esq., J.P.) and Mrs Radcliffe, and members and officials of the Insular Legislature, Town Council and other public bodies.

Present their First Production—for 6 Performances Only

"The Vagabond King"

(By arrangement with Samuel French Ltd.)

A Musical Play founded upon Justin Huntly McCarthy's Romance: "IF I WERE KING."
Book and Lyrics by Brian Hooker and W. H. Post. Music by Rudolph Friml.

GAIETY THEATRE :: DOUGLAS

FEBRUARY 6th, 7th, 8th, 9th, 10th and 11th, 1950

Overture 7-10 p.m. : Curtain 7-15 p.m. prompt : Final Curtain approx. 10-30 p.m.

COACH AND PRODUCER
Rene Gibson

CHORUS MASTER AND MUSICAL DIRECTOR
F. D. Buxton

HON. LIBRARIAN
Margaret Killip

DANCING MISTRESS
Eira Elma

STAGE MANAGER AND CHAIRMAN
Dan Minay

HON. SECRETARY
S. G. Quirk

HON. TREASURER
J. H. Cowin

ACCOMPANIST
Ethel Barrow

KEYS DEMAND HOME RULE CHARTER

The House of Keys has made its most forthright demand ever for more Home Rule for the Isle of Man. It is enshrined in an eight-point Home Rule Charter drawn up by the Keys after a major constitutional clash with the Lieutenant-Governor, Air Vice Marshal Sir Geoffrey Bromet. The situation led to an invitation from Home Secretary Sir David Maxwell Fyffe for a Keys deputation to have talks with him in London.

The situation blew up out of a dispute between the Keys and the Lieutenant-Governor over the relatively minor issue of salary increases for senior police officers in the Island. His Excellency recommended increases to the Home Secretary in spite of protests by the Keys that they were too high. When the increases were accepted by the Home Secretary, overruling and ignoring the Keys, matters led to the consultative committee of the House drawing up its Home Rule Charter which said it was wrong that the elected representatives of the Manx people should have no control over financial matters. The committee said the situation was undemocratic. It also added that the Executive Council, or Manx Cabinet, set up in 1946 in the last major constitutional development in the Manx Government, had turned out not to have the executive powers hoped for it. It had become apparent that the Lieutenant-Governor's control over Manx affairs had remained paramount. The committee's report was placed before the Lieutenant-Governor and he reported to the Home Secretary, who issued the invitation to talks, saying that he was concerned that difficulties of such magnitude had arisen in the Island. The meeting took place at the end of 1951, but no public statement was issued afterwards.

DRINKING HABITS CHANGING

Three Douglas private hotels won the right to serve their guests spirits as well as beer and wines. They were The Hydro, Milne's Waverley and Ducker's Trevelyan. Sixteen other applications were refused by the licensing bench. Last year there were 91 applications and all were refused. It is argued that drinking tastes are changing and there is now more demand for spirits.

WOOLWORTH'S DESTROYED BY FIRE

The Woolworth's store in Strand Street, Douglas, was almost completely destroyed in a fire which caused £300,000 worth of damage. Staff and customers doing their morning shopping on 11th April were evacuated and no one was hurt. But, fanned by a stiff breeze, the entire building was engulfed in ten minutes.

Later in the year, in October, a fire occurred at 73 Strand Street, but this time with more tragic results. The fire was in the living quarters above the shop of R. Hotchkiss and Sons Ltd., nurserymen and florists. Two sisters died in the blaze, one of whom had been among the last to escape from the Woolworth's fire. Twenty-one-year-old Miss Peggy Ledwidge could have escaped

this one too, but she sacrificed her life by trying to rescue her two younger sisters. Trapped upstairs by a blazing and collapsing staircase, she left her bedroom to collect her sisters from an adjoining room and managed to get them back to hers. She pushed her 14-year-old sister through the window to safety but before she and her other sister, aged 11, could leave, they were overcome by smoke and flames. Mrs Ledwidge and a lodger were treated at Noble's Hospital.

FESTIVAL OF MANN

Though excluded from this year's Festival of Britain, because the Isle of Man is not part of Britain, the Island staged its own Festival of Mann as a tourist promotion. Tynwald gave a grant towards the cost of producing an elaborate pageant depicting the Island's history with scenes from earliest times to the present. Mr L. Du Garde Peach was commissioned to write the text, with music for songs and dances by Haydn Wood. The producer was Heath Joyce. There was no shortage of participants from all over the Island for the many acting and solo parts, with local choirs providing the chorus. In addition, many were employed in making the costumes and creating the scenery and properties. In June the pageant, with a cast of 600, was performed in Ramsey, Peel and Castletown, with a final performance in the Nunnery Grounds, Douglas. The latter was spoilt by wet weather but everyone agreed that the mammoth production had been worthwhile and brought together many facets of the Island's long and varied history.

POPULATION CENSUS

The first population census in the Island for 20 years has revealed that there are 54,499 permanent residents. This is more than 5,000 up on the figure recorded in 1931, a rise of over 10%. The population of Douglas has risen nearly a thousand to more than 20,000. But the main feature is the growth of Onchan village where the population has risen from 1,700 to 3,300. The census also revealed that there are nearly 5,000 more women than men in the Island.

ONCHAN'S NEW STADIUM

The Civic Opening of Onchan Park and Stadium took place on Tuesday, 19th June. It was the culmination of an ambitious scheme, begun by Onchan Village Commissioners four years ago, to develop the rough ground on the seaward side of Summer Hill Road, part of which was used by Onchan A.F.C. The

1951 CENSUS

At the Census taken in 1939 for the purpose of National Registration the total of persons in the Island was 50,829. At the last Census proper, in 1931, the total was 49,308. Details of the recent Census are given below together with the percentage increase or decrease since 1931.

DOUGLAS	- 20,288	(+5.0%)
RAMSEY	- 4,607	(+9.7%)
PEEL	- 2,582	(+4.3%)
CASTLET'N	- 1,749	(+2.1%)
Port Erin	- 1,435	(+27.8%)
Port St. Mary	- 1,399	(+20.0%)
Laxey	- 1,341	(+10.4%)
Onchan Village	- 3,359	(+95.7%)
Michael Village	- 370	(+11.1%)
Andreas Parish	- 1,095	(+11.6%)
Arbory	- 781	(+2.0%)
Ballaugh	- 544	(-3.2%)
Braddan	- 2,120	(-33.1%)
Bride	- 404	(-10.4%)
German	- 1,081	(+8.8%)
Jurby	- 330	(-14.5%)
Lezayre	- 1,349	(+18.2%)
Lonan	- 1,067	(+25.8%)
Malew	- 2,321	(+51.6%)
Marown	- 919	(+12.6%)
Maughold	- 787	(+0.4%)
Michael	- 423	(+31.3%)
Onchan	- 1,671	(+97.3%)
Patrick	- 1,129	(+4.9%)
Rushen	- 967	(-1.1%)
Santon	- 381	(-3.8%)
TOTAL	- 54.499	(+10.5%)

Left: During the building of a major extension to Woolworth's in April, a disastrous fire gutted the building. The Palais de Danse is being used as temporary accommodation.

Centre: In October, a fire in living accommodation above the shop of R. Hotchkiss and Sons at 73 Strand Street, adjacent to the Waterloo Hotel, resulted in the tragic death of two sisters.

Right: This summer has seen the opening of the Nautical Museum in Castletown. On display is the schooner-rigged yacht Peggy, built for Mr George Quayle of Bridge House in 1791.
(All pictures: R. and L. Kelly Collection).

1951
- Death of British popular composer and theatre producer Ivor Novello
- Festival of Britain opens

ground was levelled and, in a unique scheme, serviced building plots were provided for use by either the Commissioners or private builders. These houses are now highly regarded properties and front open spaces for games and a children's play area. At the opening of the park, Commissioners' chairman, Mr J. C. Nivison, M.H.K., J.P., welcomed guests in the afternoon and they were given a guided tour of the facilities of the Pavilion and the new bowling green, tennis courts and boating pool. The guests then watched cycle heats on the banked track surrounding the football pitch in the centre of the Stadium. Afternoon tea was then taken in the Pavilion café. In the evening the stands were packed to witness World Champion Sprint Cyclist Reg Harris complete a lap to open the track officially. Afterwards he declared, "It compares favourably with Continental tracks and is quite as good as Hearn Hill." The Stadium and its environs have cost £60,000.

NEWSPAPER 'PLANE LOST
One of the two de Havilland Rapides on charter to fly the UK morning newspapers to the Island was lost in

July. Because of bad visibility at Ronaldsway the pilots opted to fly to Jurby which was clear. One of the Rapides landed safely at 6.45am but there was no sign of the other one. Coastguards and Rescue Units were activated but no trace of the missing plane could be found. The following day, a farm worker at Skinscoe Farm on the coast just to the north of Laxey, found a wing tip at the top of the cliffs. With no further wreckage found, it is assumed that the aircraft and pilot crashed into the sea below. In another incident, in June, two officers from No. 1 Initial Training School set off from Ronaldsway at noon to fly to Blackpool in a light Aeronca aircraft. By mid-afternoon the aircraft was posted overdue and an intensive search over the sea during the next two days failed to locate any sign of wreckage.

DEATH OF MR COLBY CUBBIN
One of the Island's richest men has died, leaving nearly half-a-million pounds in his will. Mr Colby Cubbin, a 53-year-old bachelor, was the son of a Liverpool property magnate. He lived a reclusive life, with his mother, in a mansion on Strathallan Road, Onchan. He owned a private yacht, a converted steam trawler called Glen

With Douglas Corporation Transport permitted to operate outside the town boundary, summer bus services have been extended to the White City Amusement Park. Here, one of the Corporation's pre-war AEC Regent double-deckers is seen returning to Victoria Pier. (Frank Cowin Library)

Strathallan, which he kept moored in Douglas harbour, but never put to sea in the last years of his life.

WIN FOR STIRLING MOSS

Stirling Moss, Britain's up-and-coming racing star, took his 1,971cc Le Mans Replica Frazer Nash to victory in a new-look 35-lap British Empire Trophy Race in May. He was able to benefit from a multiple crash at the 'S' bend near the Nursery Hotel, Onchan. Five of the leading cars were involved and one of the drivers was taken to Noble's Hospital with a fractured skull. This put Moss in second place and when the leader, Pat Griffith, lost the oil of the fast Lester-MG, he was able to finish over three minutes ahead of second man Bob Gerard, also in a Frazer Nash.

The new-style race has been introduced because of a shortage of Grand Prix cars, and the growing popularity of sports car racing. The British Racing Drivers Association argued that the general public was more interested in seeing how the latest sports cars, which could be readily purchased, performed in racing conditions. It also gave manufacturers the opportunity to test new cars in competitive conditions. Sports cars entered must satisfy the same requirements as for the classic 24 hour Le Mans Race. Cars are handicapped according to engine capacity with cars up to 1500cc being given a start of four laps over those of more than 3,000cc.

NAUTICAL MUSEUM OPENED

The opening of a Nautical Museum in Castletown follows an amazing discovery in a cellar in 1935. The cellar, backing on to Castletown harbour and adjacent to the Quayle's family home of Bridge House, concealed an 18th century schooner-rigged and armed yacht. Named Peggy, it was built for George Quayle in 1791, and is a survival from the period of the French Revolution. It had remained hidden and untouched for nearly a century and has attracted great attention from scholars of nautical history. In 1942 it was offered to the Manx Museum by a descendant of the Quayle family, and gratefully accepted. Since the war, remedial work has been carried out to what is now the Nautical Museum. It is open to the public and the Peggy, the oldest surviving Manx-built boat, is already attracting considerable attention.

T.T. FATALITIES

The high death toll of riders this year - five in June and one in September - has led to U.K. Press criticism of the risks on the T.T. Course. In the Daily Mail the Archbishop of York said the fatalities had been a waste of young lives, and he called for the races to be stopped. This year there was a record entry of 290 for the T.T. and the Harbour Board have announced that a record 4,762 motor-cycles were brought to the Island during the race period.

Changes in the format of the races this year saw the Lightweight race revert to the interval start and the introduction of a race for 125cc machines. It was no longer necessary to use low-octane 'pool' petrol. The

Junior and Senior races were dominated by Norton rider Geoff Duke who broke all existing records in achieving a notable 'double'. In the Senior he broke the 24 minute barrier and lifted the lap record to 95.22 mph. He went on to become a unique double World Champion by winning both the 350cc and 500cc classes. Geoff returned to the Island in September to marry Pat Reid, daughter of Rev R. H. (Bertie) Reid, chairman of the Manx Motor Cycle Club. Geoff rounded off the year by being voted the B.B.C's 'Sportsman of the Year'.

TELEVISION ARRIVES

The first clear television pictures were seen in the Island when the new B.B.C. transmitter at Holme Moss in Yorkshire opened in September. As the transmitter is over a hundred miles away, the Island is officially outside its range. But pictures did get through, although with some interference - to be watched by hundreds of people standing outside the shop windows of radio and TV dealers in Douglas.

LON DHOO CHOIR TRIUMPH

Success for the Manx participants in the Blackpool Music Festival continued this year and there were wild scenes of excitement when the Lon Dhoo Choir, conducted by

Onchan's new Park with its Stadium, was officially opened in June. Behind the bowling green is the café and grandstand overlooking the Stadium.

After completing a record-breaking Junior and Senior T.T. 'double', Geoff Duke is congratulated by Norton's managing director Mr Gilbert Smith. Behind Geoff is a smiling Joe Craig, Norton's engineer and team manager. Also smiling is local girl Pat Reid who later married Geoff in September at St George's Church, Douglas.

The successful Lon Dhoo Choir which won the premier award for male voice choirs at the Blackpool Music Festival. Sitting behind the Grundy Trophy is conductor, F. D. Buxton, A.R.M.C.,L.R.A.M. On his right is Geo. Higgins M.L.C., president, Barbara Taggart, accompanist and J. N. Halsall, secretary. On Mr Buxton's left is chairman H. Corkill and treasurer P. Gatfield. (via George Kinrade)

Douglas Buxton L.R.A.M., won the prestigious Grundy Challenge Trophy for 'A' class male voice choirs. They competed against over 30 of the finest men's choirs in Britain. The Lon Dhoo Choir, with 50 voices, set their sights on winning this award when they first appeared in Blackpool after the war. It is a brilliant personal triumph for Mr Buxton who founded the choir in 1937 and named it after the Manx Gaelic for 'blackbird'. Mr Buxton is also the founder and conductor of the ladies' Lon Vane Choir which is named after the Manx for 'whitebird'.

1951

- Death of American newspaper tycoon William Randolph Hearst
- Conservative Party wins British General Election: Winston Churchill PM again

1951 NEWS IN BRIEF

JANUARY
26 - Civil Defence Scheme for Island was announced.

FEBRUARY
20 - Tynwald authorises expenditure of £10,000 to carry out preliminary investigations on a £2,000,000 scheme to extend the Douglas breakwater to make Douglas an all-weather port.
20 - Lieutenant-Governor sets up a committee to enquire into the position of the Island with regard to television and sound broadcasting.
23 - South-east storm causing erosion resulted in the sea reaching the front gardens of houses at Port Cranstal, near Point of Ayre.
28 - Education Authority adopts Burnham Scale of salaries for school teachers.

MARCH
7 - Noble's Hospital Management Committee and the Health Services Board announce plans for extensions to the Hospital incorporating a children's wing with accommodation for 50 patients and an operating theatre.
13 - Steam Packet Co's new ship, *Mona's Isle,* arrived in Douglas from Cammell Laird's shipyard, Birkenhead. She is similar to the four ships built since the end of the war.
15 - Lieutenant-Governor laid foundation stone of £157,000 Nurses Home for Noble's Hospital.
19 - Announcement in Tynwald of end of Douglas harbour swing bridge toll.

APRIL
11 - Douglas Town Council decide to allow parking of private cars on Loch Promenade during evenings.
17 - Tynwald approve Health Service costs of £1,200,000 for current year, including £600,000 capital expenditure.

MAY
2 - Cleveland Medal won by Ena Gelling of Ramsey at Manx Music Festival.
10 - Manx Golf Championship won by W. A. Kirkpatrick for the fifth time.

JUNE
19 - Budget presented by Lieutenant-Governor to Tynwald resulted in petrol being increased by 3d to 3/3 a gallon and the standard rate of income tax by 6d to 5/-. For the first time in 30 years there was a budget deficit during the past year and members warned the Court that a curb on spending was needed.
28 - New Thomas Cubbon wing at Noble's Hospital for the accommodation of incurable and chronic cases opened by Lieutenant-Governor.

JULY
5 - Country dancing was a feature of Tynwald Fair for the first time in over 300 years.
9 - Local Government report shows that 1,658 new houses have been built since the war.

AUGUST
6 - First diesel-engined ship to be built for the Steam Packet Company, the new cargo ship *Fenella III,* launched at Troon.

SEPTEMBER
1 - Visit of *HMS Manxman,* mine layer adopted by the Island during the war.
28 - Large scale unemployment threatened for the winter owing to cut in winter work schemes. Single men and women advised to seek work available in England as a result of the national defence programme.

OCTOBER
23 - Season arrivals figures published show that 542,065 visitors came to the Island this year, compared with 535,560 last year.
29 - Mrs Catherine Teare, of Peel, the Island's only centenarian, dies aged 100 years and two months.

NOVEMBER
20 - New House of Keys assembles after this month's General Election.

THE SEARCH FOR URANIUM

Large scale claims to mining rights on the Island were lodged recently with Tynwald's Forestry, Mines and Lands Board, when it emerged that uranium - the radioactive ore which provided the power for the atomic bombs dropped on Japan in 1945 - had been found on the Island. These developments were partly the result of the chance activation of a geiger counter which someone was carrying through a geological museum in South Kensington, London. The source of the radiation was a sample of ore which had been supplied by the Laxey Mining Company in 1860. This led to an amateur geologist going public over his secret prospecting on the Island during the previous two years. He is electrical and mechanical engineer Douglas Bannock, who came to the Island to manage the Manx Engineers Ltd factory in Mines Road, Laxey. He has already lodged claims in respect of the old mining sites at Snaefell, North Laxey, Great Laxey, Maughold Head and Slieu Chiarn.

Financed in part by local catering entrepreneur John Marsland, Mr Bannock has been prompted by a U.K. Government appeal to locate British deposits of uranium and other ores which could save having to import expensive ores from foreign sources. As uranium is found with lead, copper and zinc, and all of these have been mined on the Island until earlier this century, Mr Bannock reckons there is a good chance of finding uranium here. He also believes that by sifting through the old 'deads' from the mines that quantities of lead and zinc can be retrieved - lead being in demand for screening devices against gamma radiation, and zinc for Britain's armaments industry.

Mr Bannock's research has led him to believe the old

Snaefell mine is the most likely site for uranium. While others have failed to record any significant radioactivity here, Mr Bannock is convinced that underground deposits are being shielded by the overburden of the 'deads.' Recently, he submitted ore samples to the British Atomic Energy Department. It confirmed that they contained between 10 and 15 per cent of uranium oxide. In April a senior geologist from the Geological Survey Museum in South Kensington came to the Island to investigate the matter further. He found that while most existing mine sites are devoid of uranium, there is some at the Snaefell mine but only in too insignificant quantities to be of any economic value.

Mr Bannock remains undeterred, however. He is now working on plans to get rid of the overburden by the re-processing of left-over ore. This will thus remove the shield of any uranium deposits beneath. His plan is to site a processing unit at Snaefell Mine and transfer sifted and concentrated ores to it from the other mining sites on the Island. Even if this does not reveal radioactivity below ground, Mr Bannock believes the venture to be a financially viable one. As far as the Isle of Man is concerned, meanwhile, even if this is not financially successful, the removal of the mountains of rubble which disfigure the countryside would be a welcome transformation.

A view of the Snaefell Mine before it closed in 1912. The mine is to be the scene for reprocessing the 'deads' to retrieve any remaining lead and zinc ore. It is hoped that the removal of the 'deads' will enable possible deposits of uranium to be detected.
(R. and L. Kelly Collection)

CASTLETOWN THERMOSTATS

Castletown looks like becoming the base for a new industry which intends to supply the world's electrical manufacturers with heating control devices known as thermostats. Castletown Thermostats owes its existence to the invention during the last war of a thermostat to control heated uniforms worn by bomber crews at high altitudes. In 1946, Eric Taylor, an old-boy of King William's College who had invented the thermostat, established a business with others at Higher Buxton to manufacture the thermostat. The company was known as Otter Controls Ltd and the two old coach houses used by the company was dubbed 'Otter's Ole.'

Thermostats look like being important components in the electronics industry when post-war shortages have been overcome and people are given access to the same gadgetry as the Americans already know, but the directors see little future in the high-taxed U.K. Recently they almost bought an uninhabited island in the Channel Islands so they could re-locate there. Instead, they chose the Isle of Man and settled on the top floors of Bridge House in Castletown as their factory location, a primitive location with just one toilet which empties directly into the harbour.

If the business expands, sewers will have to be provided but this could be tricky for the excavators, for the site around Bridge House is reputed to be an old graveyard.

Shortages of post-war materials were evident from the outset. Timber-rationing meant that work tables had to be adapted from second-hand kitchen tables bought in a Douglas sale room. A cast iron clothes mangle, meanwhile, had to be found in a Douglas junk shop to use as a winch to raise and lower materials from the premises. Since its acquisition, winching has become a popular spectacle for the people of Castletown.

The top floor of the fine old Bridge House in Castletown is providing space for the manufacture of thermostats. The 18th century building was the home of the Quayle family. On the right in the picture is the walled boatyard and house of the re-discovered 'Peggy' which is now the main attraction of the newly-opened Nautical Museum.
(R. and L. Kelly Collection)

1952
- Death of King George VI of Britain; daughter succeeds as Elizabeth II
- Death of Italian educational reformer Maria Montessori
- Britain's first singles chart published

N.A.L.G.O. WINS BATTLE WITH DOUGLAS CORPORATION

Douglas Corporation has lost an eight-month-long power struggle with one of Britain's biggest trade unions, the National Association of Local Government Officers, which represents town hall officials nationwide. The Corporation decided to refuse to recognise N.A.L.G.O. at Douglas Town Hall on the grounds that the town could not afford the pay and working conditions demanded for N.A.L.G.O. members. Eventually, however, the Corporation had to give in and restore union recognition.

It was a battle the Corporation had little chance of winning because of the power of N.A.L.G.O. with its more than 200,000 members, over the appointment of local authority staff. It started when the Town Council withdrew recognition of the union and broke off all relations with it. Councillors complained that the pay expected by N.A.L.G.O. members sent the Corporation's wage bill soaring from £31,000 to £36,000 last year with negotiations on pay and conditions taking place off the Island instead of locally. The Council decided to appoint a committee of its own to handle future negotiations. The Council felt N.A.L.G.O.'s wrath almost immediately. Advertisements of job vacancies in Douglas were blacklisted and N.A.L.G.O. officials said the Council's action was a major challenge to the trade union movement which had to be fought out to the end. At the same time, Council officials in Douglas were ordered by N.A.L.G.O. not to sign the new employment agreements drawn up for them. The union also abandoned its plan to hold its highly lucrative national conference in Douglas in 1953. The stand-off lasted from March to November when the Council decided in private to restore recognition of N.A.L.G.O.. It also invited the union to hold its 1954 conference in Douglas.

An aerial view of Douglas Holiday Camp (formerly Cunningham's) which is now open to men and women and has been granted a public house licence for the summer. In pre-war days the camp catered only for men and was strictly teetotal.

DEATH OF KING GEORGE VI
The death of King George the Sixth in February caused deep sorrow in the Isle of Man. Six days later it was followed by a joyous response to the proclamation of his daughter's succession to the throne as Queen Elizabeth the Second. Large crowds gathered for the proclamation from Douglas Town Hall and Tynwald Hill.

In the Queen's first Birthday Honours List she conferred a knighthood on First Deemster and Deputy Lieutenant-Governor Percy Cowley, now Deemster Sir Percy Cowley, Kt, C.B.E. As Second Deemster, he was chairman of the Island's War Committee and has since served the Island with distinction.

CONSTITUTIONAL REFORMS ADOPTED
The Island's strong demands last year for more Home Rule appear to have met with some success. After a Manx Government deputation went to the Home Office for talks a report setting out new constitutional reforms was adopted by Tynwald. It is understood the Government has won more control over the Island's financial affairs.

INCREASE IN CRIME
In his annual report Chief Constable Major J. W. Young said the Island had its worst ever year for crime in 1951. There were big increases in both adult and juvenile offences. It was also a bad year for road deaths - a total of seven - and there was a 40 per cent increase in drunk driving. The prison in Victoria Road had a total of 68 prisoners during the year - but it was completely empty for one night.

TELEVISION AERIALS BANNED
Douglas Town Council has banned its house tenants from erecting television aerials on their homes. Television is banned under a condition of their leases. A test case was fought by Mr Norman Clark, a labourer, of 16 Springfield Avenue, who put up a television aerial and refused to take it down. The Corporation won a house possession order against him in the High Court.

The Steam Packet's *Snaefell* acting as a tender for the *Ascania* which arrived at Douglas on 5th June from New York. On board was another party of Homecomers from America and Canada.

LICENCE FOR HOLIDAY CAMP

Douglas Holiday Camp - the former Cunningham's Camp - is no longer teetotal. It has been granted a public house licence by Douglas licensing bench - for summer season guests only. When Cunningham's started in 1904 the camp was confined to men. Drink and women were banned. Meanwhile, in spite of strong opposition, Douglas Town Council has decided that its tennis courts and bowling greens should be open on Sundays from next summer. This is in spite of one councillor's warning that there would be calls for the Island's pubs to open on a Sunday next.

SHOOTING RANGE TRAGEDY

A teenage boy has been accidentally shot dead in a tragic accident at a shooting range of Douglas Head. Fourteen-year-old Tony Bevis, of James Street, Douglas, who worked there as a change attendant, was shot by another boy, 14-year-old Patrick Joseph Moffatt. He pointed a .22 Winchester rifle at Bevis in fun, not knowing it was loaded, and pulled the trigger. The inquest decided there was no criminal negligence.

SIR GEOFFREY RETIRES

His Excellency Air Vice-Marshal Sir Geoffrey Bromet left

Members of the Manx Civil Service assemble for a photograph prior to the departure of His Excellency Sir Geoffrey Bromet. He is seen seated centre with principal officers, who are from left to right: W. B. Kennaugh ('A' Division), W. A. Latham ('C' Division), J. N. Panes (Government Secretary and Treasurer), Sir Geoffrey Bromet, T. Nesbitt (Assistant Government Secretary), W. T. Harvey (Assessor of Income Tax) and W. F. Cringle (Finance Division).

IN TRUST FOR THE NATION

As a result of an Act of Tynwald passed last year, the formation of the Manx National Trust has now been completed. It is largely due to the efforts of Deemster Sir Percy Cowley that this has come about and the object of the Trust, a voluntary body, is to preserve wildlife and areas of outstanding natural beauty. Almost immediately some 212 acres around Spanish Head have passed into the possession of the Manx National Trust. The area, with majestic cliffs rising to 400 feet, provides secure nesting sites for such rare birds as choughs, ravens, peregrine falcons and fulmars. The land had been acquired by, among others, Sir Mark Collet of Ballamanagh, Sulby, in the hope that one day it would be placed in the care of a national trust. Sir Mark was Governor of the Bank of England and has connections with prominent Manx families. The area also includes the famous chasms which are deep fissures in the Manx slates. They are 300 feet deep overlooking Bay Stacka and vary from a few

inches in width to a few feet. The large detached rock, known as the Sugar Loaf, is 100 feet high. The Trust hopes to acquire the coastline of Maughold Head and Eary Cushlin in the near future, and it has already taken over the 14th century Franciscan Chapel at Friary Farm, Ballabeg.

The Calf of Man has been leased from the National Trust of England and Wales to whom it was donated in 1937 with the object of preserving its 600 acres as a bird sanctuary. The Manx Trust has appointed well-known farmer Mr Frederick James Faragher as warden for the Calf. He will occupy the original 18th century farm buildings and he intends to graze sheep on the walled fields which cover some 150 acres. It has been described as the loneliest job in Britain but Mr Faragher and his wife have the option of a 21 year lease. As well as farming, Mr Faragher will also act as resident bird observer and one day it is hoped that the Calf of Man will be recognised as an official Observatory by the British Trust for Ornithology.

1952
- First Holiday Inn built in the USA
- Rhone Valley dam officially opened in France
- Leo Fender develops the Fender Stratocaster electric guitar

The Island's new Lieutenant-Governor, Sir Ambrose Dundas Flux Dundas, K.C.I.E., C.S.I. He was sworn in at Castle Rushen at the beginning of September. (Manx National Heritage)

(Below) Lieut.General Sir George Erskine with Lieut. Colonel G. P. MacClellan, first C.O. of the Manx Regiment, and Colonel Henry Kelly at the unveiling of the Regiment's War Memorial in the Drill Hall, Tromode.

fostering of good relations with Home Secretary Chuter Ede, and the latter's successor, Sir David Maxwell Fyffe, who was guest of honour at this year's Tynwald Day. He has seen ambitious new housing schemes begun and the opening of new secondary schools. The years have seen rationing and austerity continue and in his last Budget he was not afraid to add an extra shilling to the petrol tax. One of his last acts was to set up an enquiry into the poor television and radio reception the Island has to endure. Sir Geoffrey and his wife Margaret have grown fond of Government House and he hopes that improvements to the house and grounds will continue. He and his wife are to settle in Kent for their retirement.

NEW GOVERNOR INSTALLED

The new Lieutenant-Governor, Sir Ambrose Dundas Flux Dundas, K.C.I.E., C.S.I, was sworn in at Castle Rushen at the beginning of September. He comes to the Island after a distinguished career in the Indian Civil Service ending as Governor of the North West Frontier Province. It was there that he witnessed the end of British rule and he returned to England in 1949. With his wealth of administrative experience he is well suited to becoming the Island's next Lieutenant-Governor. Aged 52, he is joined at Government House by his wife, Mary, and his teenage daughter. Sir Ambrose will benefit from Tynwald's recent decision to increase the salary of the Lieutenant-Governor from £3,000 to £5,000 a year, tax free.

the Island at the end of August after completing seven years as Lieutenant-Governor. He has presided over the Island as it successfully re-established itself as a leading holiday resort. He has also been involved in constitutional changes which have been aided by his

TOURIST BOARD FORMED

The promotion of the Island as a holiday resort has been streamlined. Publicising the Island began in 1894 with the setting up of a Board of Advertising supported by a small Government grant. A change of name came in 1931 when the Publicity Board was formed and continued to be served by members of Tynwald and representatives from local authorities. They coped with the ever-increasing demand for holiday literature and purchased a van for their travelling agent. Now the Isle of Man Tourist Board has been formed. It will consist solely of seven Tynwald members. They have been given a grant of £40,000 for their first year. Mr Leonard Bond is the Board's first secretary.

RISING WINTER UNEMPLOYMENT

Now that the summer season is over, winter unemployment has reached a record level with over 1,500 men out of work. As a result, the Government has decided that in future employers must give job preference to men who have lived in the Island for at least five years. Tynwald has also instructed Government Boards to submit schemes to provide work for the unemployed.

WINTER STORM

The seven-man crew of the Ramsey Steam Ship Company coaster *Ben Jee* had to be rescued by breeches buoy by the Ramsey Rocket Brigade when she was driven ashore near the Point of Ayre in fierce gales. It happened shortly before midnight during severe November weather. Wind speeds were more than 100 miles an hour and there was heavy snowfall. Sea and air services were halted, roads and railway lines blocked, and there was extensive structural damage to property.

1952 NEWS IN BRIEF

JANUARY

15 - Tynwald adopt report of committee investigating financial relations with the United Kingdom with a view to constitutional reform.

16 - Pulrose Tenants Association challenge Douglas Corporation decision to ban television aerials on Corporation houses.

FEBRUARY

6 - Death of His Majesty King George VI.

12 - Queen Elizabeth II proclaimed on Tynwald Hill.

18 - Tynwald approves scheme to compensate doctors for loss of practices stated to be likely to cost Government £100,000.

26 - House of Keys approve in principle, aims of the Douglas Boundaries Extension Bill to extend Douglas boundaries by taking in Willaston and Port-e-Chee Garden City.

MARCH

19 - Mrs Annie Catherine Green, 3, Roslyn Terrace, Douglas, a pioneer of the covered-wagon days in the American West, celebrated her 100th birthday.

25 - Mrs Mary Graves, 16, Patrick Street, Peel, celebrated her 100th birthday.

APRIL

22 - House of Keys refused to remove right of creditors to arrest debtors attempting to leave Island.

MAY

7 - Arthur Quirk won the Cleveland Medal at the Manx Music Festival.

20 - Lieutenant-Governor in Tynwald repealed bread delivery charge, but increased price of bread.

JUNE

2 - 20 m.p.h. speed limit imposed in Onchan Main Road.

5 - Homecomers from Canada and America arrived in Douglas Bay on Cunard liner *SS Ascania*. They were given a great reception and feted for a fortnight in every part of the Island.

9 - World Champion Geoff Duke wins Junior T.T., his fourth successive T.T. win.

11 - Fergus Anderson wins Lightweight race for Moto Guzzi, and M.V. Agusta gain their first T.T. victory when Cecil Sandford wins the 125cc race.

13 - Friday proved to be a lucky day for Irishman Reg Armstrong when he won the Senior race for Norton, despite the primary chain snapping as he crossed the finishing line. Les Graham was second on the M.V. Agusta. Earlier Geoff Duke retired with clutch trouble whilst in the lead.

JULY

26 - Accommodation crisis in Douglas when 55,000 visitors were expected for Bank Holiday week-end and Tourist Board issued an appeal to private householders to give temporary accommodation.

AUGUST

7 - Royal Manx Agricultural Society Show marred by ban on cattle and sheep classes, owing to danger of foot and mouth disease, and by heavy rain.

19 - Dispute over 13 tons of cheese, made on instruction from Milk Marketing Association from surplus milk, was discussed in Tynwald following refusal of Lieutenant-Governor to permit sale off the ration.

SEPTEMBER

20 - Jet aircraft showed their paces at Jurby during Battle of Britain 'At Home' day.

OCTOBER

1 - Statistics published show Ronaldsway was busiest provincial airport in the United Kingdom in August when 32,383 passengers were handled.

8 - Capt. Peter Aldcroft Downward, of Douglas, awarded D.S.C. for distinguished service and gallantry in Korea.

10 - Local Government Board reports that 2,778 permanent houses have been built since the war, 1,057 by Government departments and local authorities.

10 - Protest by Victoria Methodist Circuit against Douglas Town Council's decision to open Corporation tennis courts, bowling and putting greens on Sundays next season.

15 - Federation of Women's Institutes press for establishment of a crematorium for the Island.

17 - Three Government Bills circulated to implement plan to give more Home Rule in the Island.

31 - Local tradesmen express dissatisfaction at decision to place new Nurses Home furnishing contract off the Island.

NOVEMBER

18 - Grant of £1,000 made by Tynwald to farmers towards loss of £1,581 on disputed 13 tons of cheese.

DECEMBER

23 - Memorial to fallen of Manx Regiment unveiled at Drill Hall by Lieut-General Sir George Erskine.

1953
- First successful open-heart surgery carried out
- Death of Soviet dictator Joseph Stalin
- Egypt's monarchy abolished, now declared as a republic

NATIONAL NEWSPAPER SLAMS 'BLOODBATH ISLAND'

The Island has been struck again by a wave of bitter criticism in the British national press over deaths on the T.T. Course. Race officials were particularly outraged by a headline carried in the Sunday Pictorial - BLOODBATH ISLAND.

Four riders, including top British competitor Les Graham, were killed in this year's T.T. He died in the Senior race when his works MV Agusta went out of control as it came out of the bottom of Bray Hill. The front wheel came off the ground, the machine went into a high-speed wobble and Graham was thrown into a garden wall and died instantly. Immediately after the races the Sunday Pictorial and the Daily Sketch led a barrage of criticism that the T.T. Course was too dangerous. They recorded that over 20 riders had been killed in accidents on the course since the war, and the Manx people were accused of caring nothing for the riders but only for the profit that the T.T. brought in. It is not, of course, the first time that the British press has criticised the races. There were six T.T. Course deaths in 1951 and this led to a condemnation by the Arch-bishop of York, in an interview in the Daily Mail of what he called the waste of young lives. It is known that our own Bishop Strickland-Taylor has similar views.

There is no doubt that questions are being asked all over Britain about the safety factor of the T.T. races, and whether or not they should be banned. It appears that as speeds continue to rise, so does the number of deaths. Mr Sam Hugget, secretary of the Auto-Cycle Union, denied that the stewards are considering ways of controlling speeds. "You can't have a race in which speed is restricted," he said. Norton works rider Jack Brett remarked, "Of course racing is a risky business, but there has been too much scare-mongering about T.T. fatalities. If one considers the number of miles covered at high speed the ratio of accidents is very low." Geoff Duke had these comments to make: "To suggest that T.T. racing is not worthwhile is sheer stupidity. Improvements to machines developed through racing have helped to save hundreds of lives. Les Graham's death came as a big shock to me but racing motor-cyclists know the risks and are prepared to accept them. There are also risks in other sports, such as mountaineering, but do we ever hear it suggested that people should be stopped climbing mountains just because several climbers are killed every year?"

Perhaps the most threatening aspect of the situation is the growing criticism of the Course within the sport's international ruling body, the F.I.M. It is understood that the Italian delegates are leading the opposition. While Moto Guzzi give enthusiastic support to the races, there have been no works entries from the Mondial and Morini concerns, as anticipated this year.

'SPORTSMAN OF THE YEAR'

The Isle of Man's first 'Sportsman of the Year' - is a woman. Racing cyclist Millie Robinson, who competes successfully both on and off the Island, won the title in a competition launched by the *Isle of Man Examiner* and its sister sports paper, the *Green Final*. Nearly 5,800 votes were cast by readers and well over half were for Millie. Runner-up was motorcyclist Derek Ennett of Castletown who came 4th in last year's Junior Manx Grand Prix and 5th in the Senior. Young Donald Jones of Onchan came third after making his mark in both badminton and golfing circles.

DISASTER AT SEA

Six bodies were washed up at Castletown following the disaster in the Irish Sea in which the British Railway steamer Princess Victoria sank with the loss of 128 lives at the end of February. It happened in rough weather when she was on passage from Stranraer in Scotland to Larne in Northern Ireland.

Below: Sword-bearer Lieutenant-Colonel A. H. Kissack leads His Excellency Sir Ambrose Dundas for his first Tynwald Ceremony as the Island's Lieutenant-Governor. (Frank Cowin Library)

Bottom right: T.T. favourite Les Graham on the four-cylinder MV Agusta in the Senior race. It was on this machine that he lost his life after the machine went out of control while leaving the bottom of Bray Hill.

There was also a near disaster when a bulkhead door on board the Steam Packet ship *Mona's Queen* burst open on the way from Liverpool to Douglas in August. Thirty passengers were injured. And the 23-strong crew of a French trawler were rescued by Douglas lifeboat when she went aground on rocks below Douglas Head after being in collision with another French vessel.

CORONATION CELEBRATIONS

The Coronation of Her Majesty Queen Elizabeth the Second was celebrated with a massive demonstration of loyalty to the Crown. All winter plans were being made and in January a highly successful Coronation Trade Exhibition was staged in the Palace Ballroom and opened by His Excellency Sir Ambrose Dundas. In May the *Isle of Man Examiner* Coronation Year Beauty Queen contest final was held in the Villa Marina. Thirty-six competitors, chosen from photographs submitted by 176 girls and young ladies, took part. Winner was Miss Norma Hudson of Douglas with Mrs Shirley Druggan of Ramsey second, Miss Pauline Lace (Douglas) third and Miss Joyce Lewis (Douglas) fourth. Adjudicators were film stars Zena Marshall and Guy Middleton, assisted by Mr Philip Ridgeway.

Coronation Day, 2nd June, dawned sunny and blustery but nothing could spoil the many carnival processions and street parties held throughout the Island. Children received the customary Coronation mugs and medals. In Douglas all public buildings were decorated and floodlit and a novel re-enactment of the Coronation was staged. The elderly were entertained in the Villa Marina and the children enjoyed a tea party at Douglas Holiday Camp. Highlight of the celebrations was the Carnival parade followed by a fancy dress ball at the Palace Ballroom. At night Scouts from King William's College lit a bonfire on South Barrule which, fanned by a strong breeze, lit up the night sky as one of a chain of beacons throughout Britain.

Those lucky enough to have a television set were able to follow the proceedings in Westminster Abbey. Better reception was achieved thanks to the efforts of Douglas television dealer Mr Harold Colebourn. Frustrated at the Island being a 'fringe' area for television coverage he erected an unlicensed booster station at Carnane! The excitement of Coronation Day was heightened by the news that New Zealander Edmund Hillary and sherpa Tensing Norgay had reached the summit of Mount Everest, making it a Coronation Day triumph. It is believed that Edmund Hillary is a great-great-grand nephew of Sir William Hillary of Fort Anne and founder of the R.N.L.I.

MANX AIRLINES LTD

Manx Air Charters Ltd, formed by Captain Drummond in 1947, has changed its name to Manx Airlines Ltd. This is thought to be more appropriate now that the airline has been granted licences to operate regular scheduled services to Glasgow and Newcastle. The company has invested in two ex-R.A.F. Dakota aircraft which have been fitted out for 34 passengers. The Dakotas join the four Rapide aircraft which have been kept busy on charter work. Manx Airlines now has a staff of 27 under managing director Mr Hankinson and operations manager Tom Kavanagh. By the end of this year the number of passengers carried soared to nearly 15,000, more than double the combined total for the last two years. B.E.A. have taken back the Manchester schedules and have changed their Rapides for 'Pionair' class Dakotas.

Cyclist of international renown Millie Robinson, who has been acclaimed the Island's first 'Sportsman of the Year.' (Manx National Heritage)

Centre right: Residents of Hillside Avenue, Douglas, got together to organise a bumper street party as part of their Coronation celebrations. (R and L Kelly Collection)

Right: Douglas Coronation Carnival in full swing as it passes along the promenade. Paul Aldridge is dressed up as a box of Manx kippers and is with his aunt, Linda Morrison who is dressed as a kipper girl. (R. and L. Kelly Collection)

The two immaculate Dakotas which have been purchased by Manx Airlines to operate the newly-granted scheduled services to Glasgow and Newcastle.

T.T. RECORDS

At the end of the T.T. fortnight the Steam Packet announced that a record number of motorcycles had been shipped over and the Company's entire fleet of nine vessels had been kept busy ferrying in visitors, with Senior Race day being the busiest ever. Despite the controversy over racing on the T.T. Course, this year's races attracted more riders from outside Britain that ever before, including seven from Australia and six from New Zealand. But it was the daring riding of Southern Rhodesian Ray Amm which caught everyone's attention. As a member of the Norton works team he won both the Junior and Senior, setting up new race and lap records in both events. Geoff Duke, now riding for Gilera, led in the early stages but was hotly pursued by Amm. When Duke slid off at Quarterbridge, it left the

The wreckage of the Anson found near the summit of Clagh Ouyr, in which Jurby's Commanding Officer, Group Captain Worthington was killed along with three other senior officers, including the incoming Jurby C.O.

way clear for Amm to complete the 'double.' In doing so he recorded the fastest lap ever at 97.41 m.p.h. Jack Brett was second for Norton and Reg Armstrong was third for Gilera. In the 250cc Lightweight Fergus Anderson gained his second victory for Moto Guzzi, though he was strongly challenged by Germany's Werner Hass (N.S.U.) and S. Wunsche (D.K.W.). The Ultra Lightweight race gave Les Graham (M.V. Agusta) his one and only T.T. victory. Afterwards the highly popular rider said, "It seems I've broken the jinx at last." Local riders Eddie Crooks of Douglas and Alan Holmes of Castletown finished second and third in the Senior Clubman's T.T.

AIRPORT GRANTED LICENCE

The controversy over whether Ronaldsway Airport should have a liquor licence is over. Castletown licensing court has agreed that the restaurant can serve drinks with meals and drinks can be served in a smoke room. But a public bar was refused. The court was told that Ronaldsway was the third busiest airport in Britain during the summer months and passengers often asked for a drink.

SPECTACULAR THUNDERSTORM

A spectacular summer thunderstorm at the end of June caused serious flooding in low-lying parts of the Island in the central valley. There were several feet of water in houses at Greeba, St. John's and Glen Helen. Parts of the T.T. Course were under six feet of water and roadside stone walls at Laurel Bank collapsed. At the same time the flagpole on top of Tynwald Hill was split down its length when it was hit by lightning.

OBSCENE PUBLICATIONS

Five Douglas shopkeepers have been fined £2 each by the High-Bailiff, Mr Howard Lay, for selling allegedly obscene novels. The books were bought during visits to the shops by plain clothes police officers. They included "No Orchids for Miss Blandish" and "Death Wore a Petticoat" written by Hank Janson. The High-Bailiff reserved judgement until he had read all the 34 books involved. In two other cases fines of £1 were imposed on Boots Cash Chemists, Douglas, for issuing books from its lending library which were obscene literature.

TRAGIC DEATH OF JURBY C.O.

In May the Air Ministry announced that it was to make further use of the facilities at Jurby when it was to be taken over in September by Technical Command in order to transfer No 1 Officer Cadet Training Unit from R.A.F. Millom in Cumberland. While this was good news which secured the future of Jurby, the transfer was saddened by the loss of Jurby's Commanding Officer, Group Captain F. R. Worthington. On the morning of 6th September he had flown in the station's Anson to Millom in order to pick up Group Captain G. A. Robinson, C.B.E., who was to take over as Jurby's C.O. He was accompanied by two other senior officers. They left Millom at noon in clear conditions but they never reached Jurby. Thick mist covered the Snaefell area and it was not until the following day that the wreckage of the Anson was spotted near the summit of Clagh Ouyr by Mr G. Quayle of Fairy Cottage, Laxey. He informed Sgt Kneen at Laxey Police Station who immediately contacted Mr Rhodes Tate of Keppel Gate, a shepherd who knows the area well. They began their search from the Black Hut and discovered the remains of the Anson about 100 feet below the summit of Clagh Ouyr. The wreckage was strewn over a wide area, together with the bodies of the four occupants. Group Captain Worthington, aged 46, lived at Ballamoar Farm, Jurby and was a popular figure in social circles. He had chosen St. Patrick's, Jurby as his last resting place. Amongst the mourners were His Excellency Sir Ambrose Dundas and Lady Dundas.

INCREASE IN WINTER JOBLESS

The Island's perennial winter unemployment problem is worsening. For the second winter in succession the number of men out of work has gone over the 1,000 mark. Many Manxmen are now being forced to emigrate or join the Armed Forces. Job offers available in the UK are listed at Douglas employment exchange and there is Government assistance for those willing to leave the Island.

TV RECEPTION IMPROVED

The Island has won its battle with the British Government for good quality television reception. The Postmaster General has given in to insistent Manx Government demands that priority should be given to building a TV booster station on the Island. A temporary one has been erected on the Howe, on Douglas Head, and was operational in time for Christmas. Meanwhile Douglas Corporation repealed its year-old ban on the erection of TV aerials on council houses.

1953
- Edmund Hillary and Tenzing Norgay reach the summit of Mount Everest
- Coronation of Queen Elizabeth II in London
- Death of Welsh poet Dylan Thomas

1953 NEWS IN BRIEF

FEBRUARY
17 - Tynwald approve an increase of one shilling in the charge for prescriptions under the National Health Service.
24 - House of Keys accept amendment by Legislative Council to Shop Hours Bill extending summer proposals for Sunday opening of tobacco and sweet shops to the winter period.

APRIL
1 - Maughold Head and Glebe presented to the Manx nation.
2 - £170,000 Nurses Home at Noble's Hospital opened by the Lieutenant-Governor.
21 - Return to Island of the Manx Girls' Choir and conductor Mr Harry Pickard after successful concert tour of Norway.

MAY
6 - Mrs Gladys Skillicorn of Douglas wins Cleveland Medal at Manx Music Festival.
7 - Industrial Tribunal rejected claim by Employers' Federation seeking revision of agreements so that wages would not be tied to variations negotiated in England.
16 - Everton XI defeated I.O.M.F.A. XI 7-0 at Onchan Stadium.
28 - New Clothworkers School at Peel opened by the Lieutenant-Governor.

JUNE
2 - CORONATION DAY. Mr J. N. Panes, M.A., Government Secretary and Treasurer, awarded C.B.E. in Coronation Honours list.
16 - In his first Budget, Sir Ambrose Dundas warns that this will be the last year that the Island could live on its accumulated balances.
18 - James Neilson of Largs received fatal injuries in a crash at Cronk-y-Berry during the British Empire Trophy Car race which was won by Reg Parnell (Aston Martin).
24 - New airport terminal building at Ronaldsway opened.
30 - House of Keys agree to increase payment to members by £50 to £200 a year, with additional increases for Board chairmen.

JULY
7 - Resolution passed by Tynwald calling on Boards to effect economies in view of the Island's financial position.
13 - Miss Maureen Brown of Peel crowned 'Herring Queen' at Peel.

16 - Board of Education disapprove of Education Authority's proposal to close temporarily schools at Kewaigue, St Mark's and St Jude's.
26 - Rev Canon E. H. Stenning, M.A., retired after 44 years service for King William's College.

AUGUST
7 - Seven fish merchants summoned at Peel for purchasing herring privately from fishermen instead of through official auction. Six were fined 10s with costs.

SEPTEMBER
2 - Miss Marion Joyce Lewis, of Douglas, won 'English Rose' contest at Southport.
8 - Dennis Christian of Douglas came second to Frank Fox in Junior Manx Grand Prix.
10 - Dennis Parkinson of Wakefield realised his ambition of winning the Senior M.G.P. On a Norton he became the first 'amateur' rider to lap the course at 90 mph. He has already won the Lightweight race on three occasions and the Junior once, in 1948.
27 - Centenary of Marown Parish Church celebrated.

OCTOBER
2 - B.B.C. engineers begin survey and tests for the provision of a television 'booster' station in the Isle of Man.
5 - High Court approved petition to use £63,000 held by the Corrin Trustees for the building and endowment of a convalescent home for Peel and district.
14 - Douglas Town Council decided to put contracts for season bands at Villa Marina out to tender.
18 - W. H. Kelly of Onchan, the noted marathon champion, ran one lap of the T.T. Course in 4hrs 10 mins and 58 secs, unpaced.
26-29 Among many high results by Manx competitors at the Blackpool Music Festival, Miss Eileen Peters won the open soprano lieder class and was third in the soprano class.

DECEMBER
31 - Retirement of Mr T. Nesbitt, MBE, Asst. Government Secretary and Treasurer. Mr W. F. Cringle appointed his successor.

RONALDSWAY'S NEW AIRPORT TERMINAL

The war-time buildings pressed into service to provide a terminal for passengers arriving at and departing from Ronaldsway have gone. They have been replaced by a fine (some say 'palatial') modern Air Terminal designed to meet the growing numbers using the airport, especially during the summer season. The Terminal building was officially declared open on 24th June by the Rt Hon Lennox-Boyd, M.P., Minister of Transport and Civil Aviation. He was introduced by His Excellency Sir Ambrose Dundas, and other guests included Lord Teddington, chairman of the Air Transport Advisory Board, Lord Douglas of Kirtleside, chairman of British European Airways, and Sir Geoffrey Bromet who

had done so much to guide Manx aviation in the post-war years. It was a proud moment for the members of the Airports Board and its chairman Mr T. C. Cowin, M.H.K.

Great thought has gone into the design of the Terminal; many such buildings have been visited by members of the Board and its architect, Mr T. H. Kennaugh. By 1951 the first part of the new building, comprising lounge, restaurant and medical wing had been completed. Work then began on the main part of the building which is the two-storeyed traffic hall with a frontage of 180 feet. On the opposite end to the restaurant, is the customs and immigration wing with luggage handling facilities. Side entrances to the main hall give access to the Board's office and offices for B.E.A. and charter company staff. Overlooking the airfield is an observation gallery for the general public. During the summer 30,000 passengers are handled each month, and Ronaldsway is ranked as the third busiest airport in Britain, behind Northolt and London. Work has begun on extending the main runway at either end in anticipation of the arrival of the new Viscount aircraft now coming into service with B.E.A.

A Manx Airlines' Dakota receives a pre-flight check as passengers assemble at the departure gate of the new Terminal Building.

1954

FEAR OF STEAM PACKET COMPANY TAKE-OVER

A take-over bid for the Steam Packet Company sent shock waves through the Isle of Man early this year. It was launched by a London syndicate led by Lloyds underwriter Mr Michael Jay, and there was widespread alarm at the prospect of the Island's long-standing lifeline passing out of Manx control. This led to a vigorous defence of the company by the Steam Packet's board of directors.

Mr Jay's announcement that he was offering £1.8 million for the Steam Packet's share capital came out of the blue. He followed it up with a promise to invest £10 million in developing the Island's visiting industry, with new hotels, a helicopter service - and a gambling casino. But the directors, under their chairman, Captain J. F. Crellin, M.L.C., responded with a strong appeal to shareholders not to sell out. To encourage them the directors approved a large bonus share issue and an increased dividend of 171/2 per cent. Meanwhile, the Douglas Hotel and Boarding House Association responded by calling for the Government to step in and nationalise the Steam Packet, to safeguard it. But the Island's large number of winter unemployed came out in support of Mr Jay, welcoming his promises of more jobs. The situation was one of high drama in the weeks leading up to the annual meeting of the Steam Packet in February. However, the threat of take-over evaporated as suddenly as it appeared. Mr Jay suddenly announced that he would not be making a cash offer to shareholders after all because of the antagonistic attitude of the directors. He said the idea of fighting a battle for control was repugnant to him. In response Captain Crellin said Mr Jay's withdrawal had not come as a complete surprise - but it had come earlier than he thought. This was followed in April by a lively debate in Tynwald when the Executive Council was instructed to consider the question of Government control over the Steam Packet fares and freightage. Subsequently, following consultations with Steam Packet directors, the Government announces that it proposes no further action at present.

PRISONER HANGS HIMSELF

A prisoner in the Island's prison in Victoria Road, Douglas hanged himself in his cell while on remand charged with the attempted murder of his 11-year-old daughter. Harold Ernest Killen, a 32-year-old labourer, of Laburnum Road, Pulrose, used string and twine tied to a ventilation shutter in the cell ceiling. Meanwhile the Chief Constable reported the lowest crime figures for eight years in 1953. He said one of the reasons was increased use of the birch by Manx courts.

THREE DROWN AT SEA

A Port Erin man, Mr John Ernest Clague, and his 14-year-old son Colin were drowned when their 50-foot ketch

"*Hold on, Yessir.*" by Dusty

was sunk in the Mersey in a collision with a tanker. They had just left Liverpool for Douglas. In another tragic incident a newspaper photographer, John Stubbs, who worked for the Isle of Man Examiner, drowned when his 14-foot dinghy was hit by a sudden squall near the Point of Ayre. Mr Stubbs, who joined the paper from Liverpool two years ago, was trying to make an overnight passage from Douglas to Peel.

HEALTH SERVICE COSTS

Tynwald has decided that the National Health Service, launched in July 1948, is costing the Manx Exchequer too much. This year's Health Services Board expenditure estimates of more than £550,000 have been cut back by £100,000. A commission of inquiry has been set up to decide on future economies. This may result in charges being imposed on services which have been free up to now.

END OF RATIONING

War-time rationing came to an end in May, nine years after the end of the Second World War. There has been no problem with butter for some time because of the popularity of new and tasty brands of margarine. Competi-tion between 30 different brands has reduced the price to 1s 9d per pound compared with 4s 3d for butter. The de-rationing of meat has provided the greatest headaches. Whilst the Island's sheep and pig population has increased, cattle have declined because of the long-term slaughtering scheme to eradicate TB carriers. Arrangements were made for a 'floating reserve' of Irish cattle which could be imported if necessary.

The most contentious issue has long been the amount of fat in locally-produced meat, and a proposal

The introduction of the Clypse Course also saw the return of sidecar racing. It caused great interest and here crowds have gathered at Parkfield Corner to witness Eric Oliver and 'Pip' Harris lead the charge on the first lap.

After nearly 50 years' service, including two World Wars, the Viking left Manx waters for the last time in August. She is the last coal-burning passenger ship of the Steam Packet fleet and was used on the Fleetwood route. When built, she was fastest of all Manx vessels and made a crossing to Douglas in a record 2 hours 22 minutes, averaging over 23 knots.

that butchers should pay a minimum price at auction, notwithstanding the possible fat content, has not helped. The butchers are threatening to import prime cuts from England unless something is done about local supplies. Part of the problem lies in the inadequate cold storage facilities on the Island, which means that local butchers cannot buy meat by 'dead weight' after examining carcasses. Manx meat is sold 'on the hoof'. The solution to the problem could well be in the de-controlling of meat prices which has followed the end of rationing. Butchers can now charge more for better quality, less fatty, cuts.

COLLEGE DAMAGED BY FIRE

A fire caused £7,000 worth of damage at King William's College in May. It started at night in the attic of Dickson House and all the boys had to be evacuated in their night clothes. Two dormitories were damaged. The college fire brigade fought the blaze until fire-engines arrived from Castletown and Douglas. It is thought that the fire might have been started by somebody smoking in the attic.

T.T. CONTROVERSY

There was considerable controversy following the announcement in the middle of the Senior T.T. that the race was to be stopped at the end of the fourth lap of the seven-lap race. The start had been postponed until noon because of the dismal conditions which showed little sign of improving. This was reflected in the slow times of all riders who were contending with rain and mist. Geoff Duke (Gilera) had a slender lead over Ray Amm (Norton) at the end of the second lap and at the end of the third

lap came in to refuel. Ray Amm sped through without refuelling, and then came the announcement that the race was to be stopped at the end of the fourth lap because of the conditions. Four laps was sufficient to count for the World Championship. The sun came out as Ray Amm was adjudged the winner at 88 m.p.h., but Duke had to be content with second place. Despite bitter protestations, the result was final - and once again the British single-cylinder Norton had held off the challenge of the faster Italian 4-cylinder machines.

The year saw the introduction of the 10.79 mile Clypse Course, the first race being the Lightweight 125cc event, which was won by German Rupert Hollaus for N.S.U. This was followed by the return of sidecar racing in the T.T. after nearly 30 years. Huge crowds turned out to watch Eric Oliver and Les Nutt (Norton) win after the retirement of 'Pip' Harris. German riders on B.M.W outfits finished second and third.

GOVERNMENT WINS MORE FINANCIAL CONTROL

The Manx Government has won more control over its financial affairs following talks at the Home Office in London. The Manx deputation was led by the newly knighted Sir Joseph Qualtrough, C.B.E., Speaker of the House of Keys. He was first elected to the Keys for Castletown in 1919. But the Island's new fiscal freedoms led to criticism of its low income tax - five shillings in the pound - in the House of Commons. Socialist M.P.s said the Island was becoming a "funkhole for refugees from high taxation in the U.K." and it should be brought under increased control from Whitehall. The House of Commons passed the annual Isle of Man Customs Bill by 146 votes to 40.

WARNING ABOUT TV

As television reception in the Island continues to improve there's been a warning that watching TV is affecting the health of children. In his annual report the Principal School Medical Officer, Dr S. V. Cullen, said children were staying up too late watching TV. He said parents should restrict their viewing time and encourage them to get out in the fresh air more.

BID FOR SUNDAY OPENING FAILS

When a Bill was introduced in the House of Keys to permit limited opening of licensed premises on Sundays, it was heavily defeated by 18 votes to 3. Thus were dashed the hopes of many who have pressed for Sunday opening during the season as vital in keeping the Island in the forefront as a holiday resort. Douglas Town Council had supported, without division, such a proposal. However, strong opposition came from those who attended a protest meeting in Douglas which was addressed by the Lord Bishop and Speaker Mr Joseph Qual-trough, a strong Methodist and Temperance campaigner. In a plebiscite organised by the Isle of Man Examiner as to whether or not Sunday opening was desirable, voting showed 4,852 were in favour, with 2,339 against.

MYXAMATOSIS HITS ISLAND

Myxamatosis has spread to the Island from the UK. It appears to have been introduced deliberately by farmers trying to keep down the rabbit population, despite Government banning the import of rabbits to prevent the spread of a particularly nasty disease. The north of the Island seems to be the worst affected. During the war rabbits became a useful food resource and butchers couldn't get enough of them. Farmers added to their income by renting out trapping and shooting rights on their land. Now, with the ending of rationing for meat, bacon, cheese and other foods, rabbits are regarded as a pest again. Perhaps, given time, what remains of the rabbit population will develop a resistance to the disease. In the meantime, consumer demand for rabbit flesh has collapsed.

PROFESSIONAL BATHING BEAUTIES?

The future of the bathing beauty competitions held in the Villa Marina grounds is being reviewed as a result of claims that many of the entrants are professional models. They are said to be 'freezing out' ordinary girls and some would like to see the models banned. The problem is that their very professionalism makes the competitions so entertaining for the thousands of holidaymakers who watch the competitions whilst seated in hired deckchairs.

MGP 'DOUBLE' FOR MANX RIDERS

This year's Manx Grand Prix was the best ever for local riders. Derek Ennett, of Castletown, began the week by winning the Junior Grand Prix. In practice he had become the first Manx Rider to lap the T.T. Course at over 90 mph. This was followed by George Costain, also of Castletown, causing a sensation by winning the Senior race in atrocious weather conditions. The early leaders, including Ennett, were sidelined and by the sixth lap John Hartle was in the lead by five minutes. Then he ran out of fuel and a surprised and delighted Costain found himself winner of the Senior trophy. He thoroughly deserved his victory after riding six laps in such appalling conditions. Dennis Christian came fourth and Bob Dowty was sixth. The two victors were given a civic reception in Castletown along with members of the Southern Motor Cycle Club who won the team prize.

A grimly determined Ray Amm gingerly guides the partly streamlined Norton round Quarterbridge in the wet conditions for the Senior T.T. The Southern Rhodesian star went on to win the race which was controversially stopped after four laps.

1954 NEWS IN BRIEF

JANUARY
1 - Isle of Man Airports reported a record total of 149,381 passengers using the airport last year, with arrivals of 65,602, also a record.
9 - Donald Jones of Onchan won the All-England Junior Badminton Championships for men's singles, men's doubles and mixed doubles, at Wimbledon, being partnered in the latter event by Joan Quilliam of Onchan.
19 - Tynwald discontinues the private enterprise building scheme.
28 - Mr J. Arthur Cain, M.A., appointed Second Deemster following retirement of His Honour R. G. Johnson.

FEBRUARY
2 - Legislative Council pass Entertainments Duty Bill under which there was an estimated annual yield of £44,000 from cinemas, theatres and ballrooms.
6 - W. H. ('Bill') Kelly, champion marathon runner, elected 'Sportsman of the Year' by *Examiner* and *Green Final* readers. Donald Jones was second and Mildred Robinson, cyclist, third.

APRIL
19 - Opening of the new Football Stadium at King George VI Park when Peel defeated St. George's in the Association Cup Final.

MAY
5 - Arthur Connan, tenor, wins Cleveland Medal at Manx Music Festival.
20 - Donald Jones (17) won the Manx Golf Championship at Castletown when he defeated the holder Will Kirkpatrick by 5 and 4. This puts Jones in the unique position of being both Junior and Senior champion.

JUNE
7 - The Jane Crookall Maternity Home closed down when there was an outbreak of paratyphoid infection. While fumigation took place, patients were housed in Noble's Hospital and the Home was opened again two weeks later.
10 - In the Queen's Birthday Honours, Mr Joseph D. Qualtrough, C.B.E., Speaker of the House of Keys, was knighted.
15 - In Budget speech Lieutenant-Governor reports a "considerably happier position than faced the Court a year ago."

AUGUST
16 - Departure from Douglas for the last time of the *Viking*, veteran ship of the Steam Packet Company fleet. A new vessel is now under construction by Cammell Laird, Birkenhead.
19-26 Spectacular Carnival parades staged in Douglas by a voluntary Carnival Committee, with over 100 vehicles and 1,000 performers taking part on each occasion.

25 - Castletown featured in the B.B.C. programme 'Going Your Way'. Among those taking part was Sir Ralph Stevenson of Balladoole, H. M. Ambassador in Cairo.
25 - Tynwald Race Committee rejected proposals for staging a production car race over the T.T. Course on account of cost. Top British drivers like Stirling Moss and Reg Parnell were to take part.
29 - Opening by Dr Godfrey, Archbishop of Liverpool, of new Roman Catholic hall and presbytery at Willaston estate.
31 - Death of Major J. W. Young, O.B.E., Chief Constable of the Isle of Man for 18 years.

SEPTEMBER
25 - Bill Kelly won the London to Brighton 52½ miles marathon in 5 hrs 39 mins 46 secs, and was given Civic receptions in Douglas and Onchan on return.
27 - Centenary of Laxey Wheel - 'Lady Isabella' - celebrated in Laxey with ceremony and pageantry, and the unveiling of a plaque by Lady Dundas. Over 4,000 attended, many in Victorian costume.

OCTOBER
5 - Legislative Council pass Bill proposing the fixing of standard measure for the sale of spirits in the Isle of Man.
7 - 150,000th passenger passed through Ronaldsway Airport - the first time this figure has been achieved in a year.
23 - Marathon runner Bill Kelly laps T.T. Course in 4 hrs 8 mins 8 secs - better than his performance last year.
25-30 Miss Eileen Peters wins Rose Bowl at Blackpool Music Festival. Lon Dhoo Choir came second in Male Voice 'A' class.
27 - Official farewell at St George's Church to the retiring Lord Bishop, the Rt Rev J. R. Strickland Taylor and Mrs Taylor.
31 - Avenue Cinema, Onchan, closed for winter months because of insufficient public support.

NOVEMBER
10 - Miss Jean Burns of Ramsey won British National Championship for tractor-mounted ploughing.
12 - New primary school at Ballasalla opened by Sir Joseph Qualtrough, C.B.E., S.H.K.

DECEMBER
22 - Mr J. R. Smith, M.A., appointed headmaster of Castle Rushen High School as successor to Mr Godfrey Cretney, who is leaving to become head of a new comprehensive school near Wolverhampton.

TYNWALD MATTERS : THE CIVIL DEFENCE COMMISSION

Two years ago Tynwald set up a Civil Defence Commission which empowered local authorities to take steps to ensure that some sort of organisation was in place to help survivors in the event of a nuclear bomb being dropped in the Irish Sea area. When the matter was raised again in Tynwald this year it was seen that there was considerable apathy and that very little had been done, with only Ramsey taking the matter seriously. General opinion seemed to be that there was little that could be done and it was useless to provide protection; others thought that 'it would never happen,' while others were of the opinion that the Island was so unimportant that an enemy would not waste expensive bombs on it.

When Sir Percy Cowley presented a new Civil Defence Bill in the Legislative Council he pressed strongly for an adequate civil defence organisation which should be under a central administration with direct responsibility to the Lieutenant-Governor. He argued that the Island was in a strategic position with regard to food supplies to Britain. As the Cold War continued we had to be prepared for such an attack which Sir Percy thought highly likely and "if no preparations are made it will be a damning indictment of our modern civilisation." He was supported by Mr J. F. Crellin, chairman of the Local Government Board under whose direction the Commission at present operates. The Bill was then passed through all stages by the Council.

In the House of Keys the Bill was introduced by the Chairman of the existing Civil Defence Commission, Mr T. A. Coole. He referred to the advent of the hydrogen bomb and said "it was dangerous to assume that the Isle of Man will escape the implications of what that means." He paid

tribute to the few officers who had volunteered to undertake the work despite lack of public interest and support in the way of training and equipment. While there was general support among members for centralising control of civil defence, there were many who had misgivings about the expense. There would have to be a headquarters manned by permanent staff; uniforms and equipment would have to be provided. Once under way, who could tell how the expenses of such a scheme would escalate. One of the main objectors was Mr C. C. McFee who visualised an expensive and unnecessary organisation. He was supported by Mr H. C. Kerruish who said, "This is going to be another white elephant." He thought it better to continue civil defence on its present "reasonable lines." But it was Mr L. Gerrard who summed up the feelings of the majority "It is time we tried to make a go of civil defence. We have been dallying with it for two years. It has been said that if an atom bomb was dropped near the Island it would be wiped out, but if one were dropped near Liverpool the Island would be affected by radiation fall-out, and it was in a case like that that civil defence would be needed." The second reading of the bill was passed by 19 votes to two.

When it came to the third reading the last word in opposition to the Bill was from Mr McFee who said it should be noted that it placed the whole control of civil defence in the hands of the Lieutenant-Governor. The aim of the House was to restrict the latter's power and take on responsible government, not shed it. Despite a choppy passage, the third reading of the Bill was passed without a division. It remains to be seen how much money will be granted to set up a proper Civil Defence organisation, and how long it will take.

THE ANSWER TO RISING UNEMPLOYMENT

The Isle of Man could well be facing a crippling recession. The completion of the new 'town' of Willaston has left many out of work as the number of unemployed men soars above 1,500. Tynwald is giving allowances to married men to seek work in England and about 250 have found work with the sugar beet farms in East Anglia. Entire families have started to emigrate to Canada, Australia and New Zealand. There is an atmosphere of gloom and impending disaster. Many houses now lie empty. Property prices have dropped by 25% since the post-war boom. A modern semi-detached house with garage can now be bought for around the £2,000 mark. The problem of a diminishing population, especially in young people, was emphasised in April with the closure of St Mark's school which was reduced to just three pupils. Other country schools are threatened with closure despite strong protests.

Hopes of averting an economic disaster have led Tynwald to supporting the establishment of light industries on the Island. One of the first to benefit is Metalliferous Holdings Ltd under the supervision of Douglas Bannock who raised hopes of a uranium bonanza three years ago. Machinery imported from Africa's Gold Coast will be operated 24 hours a day to sift through the estimated 80,000 tons of spoils that lie on the surface, searching for lead and zinc which may have been overlooked.

Other speculative new industries, established with Government assistance, have been launched during the year with remarkable frequency. Jobs for between 70 and 80 girls have been created at the Continental confectionery sweet factory of Tres Bon, in premises at the top of St George's Street, Douglas. It is targeting the American market and capacity has risen from 20 tons to 50 tons a week.

A coal briquette factory at Hills Meadow, Douglas, is the brainchild of industrialist and aspiring Manx politician, Harcourt Matthews of Parville, Ballabeg. The raw material for the briquettes will be the large quantities of coal dust which arrive on the Island with every coal shipment. Mr Matthews has also launched a company at Balthane which is making aluminium ladders in the war-time buildings.

Other ventures have seen two carpet factories being commissioned. One is at Hills Meadow. It occupies the first purpose-built factory provided by Tynwald for an industrialist. The other is at Laxey, one of whose products is 'The Mannin Homecomer' - a hearth rug depicting the Three Legs. In December the first half mile of export carpet left Laxey for Wellington, New Zealand. At Union Mills a new business plans to manufacture cotton yarn on the former Cowen's Laundry site with hopes of employing up to 70 girls.

At Peel the development of a fish meal factory in the kipper yard brings hope of revitalising the fishing and kippering industry. One of its aims is to attract the landing of herring there by non-Manx fishermen, principally the Scottish ringer fleet. This will not only create some local work but will help to maintain supplies for the kipperers. Currently there are only three fishing boats operating out of Peel. Despite the poor employment situation, local crews cannot be found.

Giving a lead to attracting new industries, is the Lieutenant-Governor. For example, Sir Ambrose has visited Yorkshire to meet businessmen to point out the benefits of setting up work places on the Island. He has also introduced an official trade mark - 'Manxmark' - for Manx-made goods and a committee has been set up to consider applications from manufacturers to use it.

HELICOPTER IN DRAMATIC MISSION OF MERCY

When Mrs Williams, the expectant wife of the Calf of Man warden Mr Frank Williams, began to go into labour ahead of schedule, a mercy mission was put into action. She had planned to go into the Jane Crookall Maternity Home for the delivery. But she was marooned in the storm-bound farmhouse and the near-hurricane force winds had raged all night. At first light the lighthouse keeper on Chicken Rock had sighted a pre-arranged signal from the Calf calling for immediate help. Distress flares were then fired as orders were sent out for the Port Erin and Port St Mary lifeboats to stand by. But the waters around the Calf were a seething cauldron, ruling out the remotest possibility of launching the boats.

When it was realised that a helicopter was the only means of helping the distressed mother-to-be, Group Captain Burnett, Commanding Officer of R.A.F. Jurby was contacted. From thereon the R.A.F. directed the mercy operation. At the Fleet Air Arm station at Eglington, Northern Ireland, a Dragonfly helicopter was airborne within minutes of the emergency call and proceeded to Ronaldsway. The helicopter was accompanied by an Avenger whose task was to keep them in contact with the land.

The helicopter reached Ronaldsway at mid-day and picked up a doctor from the station hospital at Jurby. Also waiting at Ronaldsway by now was an ambulance with midwife, Nurse E. B. M. Heath in attendance. The helicopter then battled its way to the Calf and touched down only yards from the farmhouse. Leaving the doctor it then returned to fetch Nurse Heath. At 1.50 p.m. - less than two and a half hours after leaving Ireland - the helicopter approached the control tower at Ronaldsway and dropped down in front of the main buildings. Mrs Williams, accompanied by Nurse Heath, stepped down from the helicopter and soon she and the midwife were on their way to the maternity home where, later, a healthy seven-pound baby girl was born.

The weather at Ronaldsway began to deteriorate and it was not until late afternoon that the stranded R.A.F. doctor and helicopter crewman were picked up and taken to Jurby. The mission of the helicopter had been completed, and history had been made.

Former Royal Navy Officer Commander Frank Williams took over the wardenship of the Calf of Man in October after being appointed by the Manx National Trust. He succeeded Mr Frederick Faragher who was forced to retire earlier in the year because of ill-health. He and his wife had spent two years in the post.

DROP IN ARRIVALS CAUSES ALARM

The number of visitor arrivals this season is causing great concern within Government circles and within the tourist industry itself, the mainstay of the Island's economy. The season's arrivals figure of 518,983 is a drop of nearly 100,000 compared with five years ago. There are also indications that holidays in sunny Spain and other parts of re-built Europe have started to become popular among the Island's traditional visitors. Foreign holidays are cheaper and have guaranteed sun.

The blocks of hotels mushrooming in the Mediterranean resorts offer guests their own toilets and bathrooms, while Manx hotels and guest houses provide pre-war standards which, even then, were far from ideal. Some have started to advertise 'H and C Running Water.' That means rooms are equipped with mains-supplied hot and cold water. The majority are not, however. Water jugs for washing and hot water for shaving have to be delivered to rooms every morning. Slopping out with buckets remains a common practice for staff afterwards - and that includes emptying chamber pots which are kept under the beds. Continental hotels have much higher standards and guests are free to come and go as they please. There are no landladies standing at the door waiting to lock up at midnight.

Local businessmen, led by Clifford and Frank Irving, formed an Action Group this autumn. At a meeting in Douglas the Action Group endorsed a programme calling for redistribution of seats in the House of Keys in favour of the towns; a commission of inquiry into the visiting industry; support for progressive candidates in elections and the setting up of a scheme to support worthwhile ideas with vigour. This includes the opening of public houses and the selling of cigarettes on Sundays which will be welcomed by holidaymakers.

The situation does not bode well for the relationship between the tourist industry and the Church. The issue as to whether Sunday should be preserved as a traditionally sacred day, as the Lord's Day Observance Society would have it, or be allowed to be commercialised has split the Island. Throughout the last 50 years the Church has been forced to give ground in such matters as the use of motorcars and motorcycles on Sundays, the sale of newspapers, the staging of concerts and the opening of cinemas - albeit only after church services. During the immediate post-war years most churches were packed. Sunday Schools were well attended and Anniversaries were great social occasions. This gave the Church tremendous influence over people's habits. While the older generation accepted attending church services, some by compulsion, and respect the Sabbath, this is being questioned by the younger generation. They have been influenced by two horrifying wars and now the constant atomic threat of instant destruction has made them rebel against being told what they must do. It would appear then that the power of the Church is beginning to wane and that many restrictions now in force will be removed as society changes.

1955
- Walt Disney opens his first theme park in California
- Death of Nobel prize-winning physicist Albert Einstein
- Convicted murderer Ruth Ellis hanged, first woman to be hanged in Britain

VISIT OF QUEEN ELIZABETH AND PRINCE PHILIP

The big event in the Isle of Man this year was a one-day visit by the young Queen Elizabeth II and her husband the Duke of Edinburgh. It was just over two years after her Coronation that she sailed into Douglas Bay aboard the Royal Yacht Britannia accompanied by her children, Prince Charles and Princess Anne. As with all royal visits to the Island throughout this century, Manannan's Mist played its part.

The Island had had five weeks of unbroken sunshine until the August morning that Britannia appeared off Douglas. A thick mantle of mist, Manannan's Cloak, suddenly shrouded the Island. Then the following day as *Britannia* left, the sun came back. The only disappointment of the visit was that the royal children did not come ashore. But people in small boats who went out to Britannia were rewarded by the sight of them playing on deck. Meanwhile, the Queen and the Duke were taking part in a packed programme which took them by car to every town and village in the Island, stopping at Castletown, Peel and Ramsey. They were met everywhere by thousands of people in a tremendous demonstration of Manx loyalty to the Crown and the cheers of summer visitors. One of the main occasions was at Noble's Park where the royal couple made a Land Rover tour among 2,000 excited schoolchildren. Her Majesty also attended a special session of Tynwald. She told members that her father, King George the Sixth, who visited the Island in 1945 with the Queen Mother, had told her of its beauties. She went on to end her speech in excellent Manx saying: "And now good morning and good luck." The Queen also indicated that she hoped one day to preside over the Tynwald ceremony at St. John's. A reception for Island V.I.P.s was held on board Britannia in the evening, with a huge firework display on Douglas beach, to bring the visit to a close.

One of the highlights of the Royal Visit was a tour of 2,000 schoolchildren assembled in Noble's Park. Afterwards the children were given a tea party at the Douglas Holiday Camp. (Town Hall Archives)

DRINKS IN THE PALACE

People who went dancing in the Palace Ballroom this summer were able to also buy a drink - for the first time ever. Douglas Licensing Court granted the Palace Company a liquor licence for a bar - after being told that all other similar ballrooms in the British Isles were licensed. However, the campaign to get the pubs open on Sundays in the summer suffered setbacks with the House of Keys rejecting a private member's Bill for the purpose by a large majority.

WOMAN IN GAOL FOR MURDER

A Douglas seaside landlady was sentenced to three months imprisonment at the Court of General Gaol for killing the man with whom she lived. Fifty-four-year-old Mrs Amy Margaret Walker, of Christian Road, admitted a charge of manslaughter but pleaded extreme provocation and mental stress. The court heard that she stabbed Frederick Arthur Shirt with a bread knife when he attacked her in the kitchen.

NO BEER GARDEN FOR ONCHAN

Plans to provide a Continental-style beer garden at the Nursery Hotel in Onchan have been scotched following the refusal of Douglas Licensing Court to grant a licence. Hotelier Mr Chafer planned to turn the hotel's bowling green into a beer garden despite opposition from the village commissioners and a petition drawn up by villagers. Members of Onchan Bowling Club also objected to the loss of the green, the only one in Onchan. The hotel grounds were the former Nursery Gardens until 1909 when the gardener's house was extended and turned into a hotel. Walks in the grounds were popular with villagers and children used part of it as a play area. But this is no longer possible following Mr Chafer's decision to deny the public a right of way.

MANXMAN JOINS THE FLEET

Manxman II, the latest addition to the Steam Packet fleet, arrived in Douglas for the first time in May, ready for the summer season. She is the sixth to be built since the war for the Steam Packet Company by Cammell Laird, Birkenhead. All six are of similar design with the same dimensions and are driven by twin-screwed turbines. Tonnage of the *Manxman* is 2,495, speed is 21 knots, and she is certified to carry 2,393 passengers with a crew of 68. The nine passenger ships in the current fleet are: *Lady of Mann, Ben-my-Chree, Victoria, King Orry, Mona's Queen, Tynwald, Snaefell, Mona's Isle* and *Manxman*. Cargo vessels are the *Peveril, Conister* and the new diesel-engined *Fenella*.

Soon after the Fleetwood service was resumed in June, a trawler skipper was drowned when his fishing boat was run down by the *Mona's Isle* as she left the Lancashire port with holidaymakers in the early hours of the morning. The trawler was cut in two and sank, but

1955

Top left: Manxman II is the latest addition to the Steam Packet's fleet. She is the sixth vessel of similar design which has been built since the war.

Left: Geoff Duke at speed on the 4-cylinder Gilera during the Senior T.T. The cheers that greeted the news that he had completed the first 100 m.p.h. lap turned to groans when it was announced that the lap speed had been corrected to 99.97 m.p.h. (Island Photographics)

the remaining crew of three were rescued. The *Mona's Isle* stopped to search for the men and went aground when caught by the ebb tide. She was left high and dry for several hours.

T.T. MARATHON

British Olympic runner Tom Richards won the first ever marathon round the T.T. Course at the end of May. In sweltering conditions, he recorded a time of four hours 13 seconds. Later, he said it had been the toughest race of his career, especially in making the climb up the Mountain. Second was the Island's top runner and Sportsman of the Year, Bill Kelly. At 42 he was slowed by cramp in the closing stages of the race. In September the two runners met again in the London to Brighton 52 1/2 miles marathon. Bill repeated his second place to the Olympic Champion.

RICHEST WOMAN DIES

The richest woman in the Island, Mrs Ellen Cubbin, died in June. She left personal estate of £850,000 in the Isle of Man and a large amount of real estate. In her will she made bequests to charities of £193,000 and divided the residue between 16 other charities. She was the widow of a Liverpool property magnate and lived in a mansion on Strathallan Road, Onchan. Her 53-year-old bachelor son, Colby Cubbin, died in 1951. His main interest was in his fishing boats and he would be up all night in radio contact with them. He built a luxury yacht, the Glen Strathallan, in which he would sail to the Western Isles to escape the noise of the T.T. period. The yacht was moored alongside Douglas Quay for many years but it has now left for Chatham, having been bequeathed by Mrs Cubbin to the Shaftesbury Home and the Arethusa Sea Training School. One of the main beneficiaries of Mrs Cubbin's will is the R.N.L.I., money being left to provide four of the latest Watson-type lifeboats.

DUKE NEARS THE 'TON'

Run in perfect weather conditions, it was expected that the Senior T.T. would see the magic 'ton' achieved for the first time. Favourite was Geoff Duke on the Gilera and when, at the end of the third lap, it was announced that he had lapped in 22 mins 39 secs - exactly 100 m.p.h. - there was great jubilation at the grandstand and around the course. But 40 minutes later the jubilation turned to groans following a dramatic announcement by the Clerk of the Course that Duke's time of 22 mins 39 secs

equalled a speed of 99.97 m.p.h. Three fifths of a second would have made the difference, but many people felt that morally the credit for the first 100 m.p.h. lap should have gone to Duke. His team-mate Reg Armstrong came second, with the Australian Ken Kavanagh on a Moto Guzzi in third place. Thus the decades of dominance by the Norton factory in the Senior T.T. was broken, works rider Jack Brett finishing in fourth place.

CUT IN INCOME TAX

A major improvement in the Island's finances led to the Lieutenant-Governor cutting income tax in this year's Budget. It went down by sixpence to four shillings and sixpence in the pound. There was an increase also in the Government rebate which keeps down the price of petrol in the Island. His Excellency said there had been an unexpected increase in Government revenues during the financial year with indirect taxation receipts up to more than three quarters of a million pounds.

FREEDOM FOR R.A.F. JURBY

There was an impressive ceremonial occasion in Ramsey at the end of April when the Freedom of the Town was granted to R.A.F. Jurby. Group Captain Burnett, D.S.O., D.F.C. accepted the Scroll of Freedom on behalf of the station, witnessed by officers and cadets of the O.C.T.U. Market Square was the scene of the Ceremony. There was a march-past through Parliament Street and a service in St. Paul's Church. This was followed in July with the granting of the Freedom of Douglas. The ceremony took place in sweltering heat on Harris Promenade followed by a parade of 400 cadets past the Town Hall. The unique gesture by both towns is in appreciation of the long and happy association of R.A.F. Jurby with the Island. About 500 cadets at any one time are based at the R.A.F's only Officer Cadet Training Unit, and many of

The bowling fraternity of Onchan are delighted that the licensee of the Nursery Hotel has been refused a licence to turn the bowling green into a beer garden.

The opening of the Ronaldsway
Right: Aircraft Company's factory
is a major boost to the
Government's efforts to attract
light industries to the Island. The
factory will produce components
for Martin Baker ejector seats now
being used in jet aircraft.

Far right: High maintenance costs
are adding to the problems of the
Manx Electric Railway, placing its
future in doubt. Only minimum
maintenance is possible, such as
the re-timbering of the track on
Ballure Bridge, Ramsey.

them are commissioned during their National Service. Wearing their white cap flashes, the cadets are a familiar sight at week-ends and attend the Pool Ballroom in Ramsey in great numbers, while others travel by coach to Douglas for dancing at the Palais de Danse and the Majestic La Tonelle Ballroom. Later in the year a stained glass window was presented to Douglas Town Hall by R.A.F. Jurby to commemorate the granting of the Freedom of the Borough.

SOUTHERN "100" RACES
The inaugural motorcycle races of the Southern "100" were run in July over the Billown Circuit with the start and finish on the Castletown by-pass. The races were suggested by the Southern Motorcycle Club and it was only after Tynwald reversed an earlier decision not to support the races financially, that the club was able to go ahead. Tynwald members thought the races would "not be in the same category as the T.T. and M.G.P.," and that the season did not require any "build up at that time." However, once approval was given club members worked with enthusiasm to organise the races and prepare the course. They were rewarded by attracting many star riders and it was fitting that one of their members, Derek Ennett, won the Junior race on an A.J.S. Lightweight winner was Dave Chadwick on a Norton and Terry Shepherd won the Senior race, also on a Norton. There is no doubt the races have proved a popular attraction and are likely to run and run.

MAJOR FACTORY OPENS
Government measures to deal with the Island's worsening winter unemployment problems are taking effect. At an emergency session of Tynwald extra funds were committed to winter work schemes. There will also

In recognition of the part played
by R.A.F. Jurby in the economic
and social life of the Island, the
station was granted first the
Freedom of the Town of Ramsey
and then the Freedom of the
Borough of Douglas. In Douglas,
the impressive ceremony took
place on Harris Promenade in the
presence of 400 officer cadets
from No 1 O.C.T.U.
(Town Hall Archives)

be extra work in the Government's £227,000 plans for reconstructing the Marine Drive which was left derelict after the Second World War. Meanwhile, Government subsidised factories are opening to encourage light industry to move to the Island and provide all-year-round employment.

A major boost to the employment situation has been the opening of a large factory on a site opposite the entrance to Ronaldsway airport, once occupied by the war-time administrative buildings of the Admiralty. The factory has been built by Ronaldsway Aircraft Company Ltd to produce components for Martin Baker ejector seats which have become standard equipment for jet aircraft in use by the Royal Air Force and other air forces. The site has plenty of room for expansion and the factory will employ hundreds of local men in the future.

VISITING INDUSTRY COMMISSION
For the first time Tynwald has appointed a special commission to plan the future development of the Island's visiting industry. This follows concerns that the Island is falling behind other resorts. The commission is at present taking views from all interested parties and individuals and is to make its report next year. There has been an upturn in arrivals this season but there is no guarantee that this will continue.

M.E.R. GIVES NOTICE
The Manx Electric Railway Company has given notice that it will be unable to continue services beyond the end of next season. High maintenance costs have resulted in another working loss for the year. A further loss is the result of trying to maintain the unprofitable winter service. People in the Maughold area have long been dependent on the electric railway. Last year the railway company applied to suspend its winter services and to raise fares. The House of Keys deleted the winter closing clause from the Manx Electric Railway Bill, but allowed an increase in fares. It was revealed that the company might be forced into voluntary liquidation, but no solution was provided as to how the company's financial crisis could be averted.

END OF 'SHAMATEURISM'
A practice which has angered many in amateur music for over half a century has been ended, thanks to a Government tax. The practice, condemned as 'shamateurism,' has seen the Island's top singers and

show organisers, though classed as amateurs, receive payments either in the form of 'expenses' or 'honorariums.' Douglas Choral Union, the Manx Operatic Society and others like them are all classed as amateur but, whilst the chorus members have received little for their services other than a free or subsidised annual dinner, the leading members have received payments of one kind or another. Former Choral Union Secretary, travel agent Mr Jack Cretney, recalls the practice as a long-standing tradition - a way of helping performers perhaps to pay for such things as singing tuition or lost work time when required to attend rehearsals. The demise of the practice has been brought about by Tynwald following the U.K's Entertainment Tax on admission tickets to theatres, cinemas and dance halls. Tynwald had to impose it because of its Customs Union with the U.K. Societies tried to absorb the tax at first but fear of lowering standards and charging higher admission prices has led them to abandoning payments to show 'stars.' Instead they are now truly amateur and are exempt from the tax as non-profit-making concerns.

SAD CHRISTMAS FOR MANX AIRLINES

One of Manx Airlines' two Dakotas, which had been chartered to bring R.A.F. personnel and families from Germany to England for Christmas, has been lost. It was crewed by the highly-experienced Captain John Fisher and First Officer Reg Cowin. By the toss of a coin Shirley Cole of Douglas was assigned as the air hostess. The Dakota arrived over Dusseldorf on time but in poor visibility, and on the final approach crashed into a beech forest, killing all three on board. As soon as the news was received at Ronaldsway, airline directors Hankinson and Vondy flew to Dusseldorf to assist in the investigation. No cause of the crash could be found, apart from the bad visibility. It makes for a sad Christmas for all concerned at Manx Airlines and it will be difficult to find a replacement aircraft now that Dakotas are in scarce supply.

1955
- Commercial TV broadcasting begins in Britain
- Death of US film actor James Dean
- Military coup ousts Juan Domingo Peron from power in Argentina

---

1955 NEWS IN BRIEF

JANUARY
4 - New Willaston Infant's School opened to pupils for the first time.
11 - The Housing Bill, enabling local authorities to sell municipal housing, passed by the House of Keys.
25 - Tynwald agreed to support the Deemster Johnson Fat Stock Marketing Scheme by means of deficiency payments at rates near as practicable to those in force in the United Kingdom.
26 - Manx Fair and Trades Exhibition at the Palace Ballroom attracted more than 26,000 visitors in seven days.
26 - Dr Benjamin Pollard, D.D., M.Sc., T.D., installed and en-throned as the 75th Bishop of Sodor and Mann before 1,000 people in St. George's Church, Douglas.

FEBRUARY
2 - Famous marathon runner Bill Kelly awarded the 'Sportsman of the Year' trophy for the second year running. Runners-up were motorcyclists Derek Ennett and Eddie Crooks.
23 - House of Keys refuse to ban 'gin traps' designed to catch rabbits.
23 - Blizzard hits Island. Thousands of sheep missing.

MARCH
3 - 400 people at a meeting in the Villa Marina demanded relaxation of laws governing the opening of shops and public houses on Sundays.
18 - The Island's 'Grand Old Man' Mr Richard Cain, 93-year-old founder of the World Manx Association, received the O.B.E. at an investiture in Douglas.

APRIL
21 - Mr Clifford Irving, a founder member of the Action Group, elected to the House of Keys for North Douglas in a bye-election caused by the death of Mr T. C. Cowin. He had a majority of 2,440 votes over his Labour opponent, Mr R. C. Stephen, and was the third man ever to receive over 4,000 votes in a Keys election.
22 - Announcement that the Manx Regiment of wartime 'Desert Rats' fame is to be reformed as a Counter-Bombardment Staff Troop (T.A.)

MAY
5 - Norman Kaighin, baritone, wins Cleveland Medal at 'The Guild.'
8 - B.B.C. radio broadcast 'Down Your Way' from the Island, with interviews by Franklin Engelmann.
14 - A ten-year-old boy, Robin Hughes of East Foxdale, died in Noble's Hospital after falling 40 feet down cliffs at Glen Maye.
28 - 'Invasion' by 250 hockey players from England to take part in a Whitsun Hockey Festival.

JUNE
9 - Memorial unveiled on Snaefell Mountain Road to Les Graham, former world champion motorcyclist who was killed in the 1953 T.T.
11-16 First National Football Tournament promoted by the I.O.M.F.A. and the June Effort Committee won by Bishop Auckland F.C. which defeated Cliftonville F.C. 2-1. Second half of final was broadcast by the B.B.C.

JULY
5 - Speaking at the World Manx Association Gathering the Lord Bishop, Dr. Benjamin Pollard, hinted that the Isle of Man - "the oldest see in the Anglican Church" - should have a cathedral.
8 - Television reception at Ramsey and the north of the Island improved by newly-opened station at Divis, Northern Ireland.
19 - Highland Games revived at Onchan Stadium. 5,000 people attended.
23 - Marathon runner Bill Kelly came 4th in A.A.A. Championships at Reading.
31 - Two 16 year old Douglas girls, Rene Huntley and Janet Alexander, swam Douglas Bay in 56 minutes.

AUGUST
1 - Miss Mildred Robinson (Manx Viking Wheelers) won the first three-days international road cycling race for women in France.
1 - Island had the busiest Bank Holiday week-end for years. Over 30,000 visitors landed at Douglas, and an all-time record 5,500 at Ronaldsway.
9 - One-day visit of Her Majesty Queen Elizabeth II and H.R.H. the Duke of Edinburgh.
26 - A practically complete 1,500 years old Celtic fort revealed by remains uncovered during excavations at Scarlett, near Castletown. Mr Peter Gelling, M.A., of Crosby, directed the work.

SEPTEMBER
22 - Announcement of the formation of the £100,000 Isle of Man Exploration Company Ltd to survey the Island in search of minerals.
24 - I.O.M. Cycling Association team of R. Killey, S. Slack and R. Quayle finished second in an international cycling meeting held on Aintree circuit.
24 - Manx Girls' Choir conducted by Mr Harry Pickard gave a recital in St. Paul's Cathedral, London.
28 - Miss M. G. Dickson appointed headmistress of Douglas High School for Girls in succession to Miss W. S. Nayler.

OCTOBER
1 - Beginning of the dismantling of the Douglas Head incline railway. It has not been used since last season, and with a total length of 450 feet was the shortest railway in the British Isles.
2 - Miss Mildred Robinson won the five-day international women's cycling road race in France.
6 - Commission on electricity recommended one authority for the control of generation, transmission and distribution of electricity on the Island.
13 - Lieutenant-Governor switched on new turbo generator at the Pulrose Power Station.
14 - West Baldwin Reservoir water level at its lowest since the reservoir was opened in 1905.
24 - At Blackpool Music Festival Miss Margaret Curphey won girls solo class, and with Mr T. Gelling won the open duet class. Lon Dhoo Choir placed fourth in the principal male choral contest.
25 - House of Keys passed Bill to extend franchise to local authority elections to all over 21 years of age. The property vote was retained in the new measure.

NOVEMBER
2 - Great storm at Douglas smashed sea wall on Promenade and caused £2,000 damage to the wall of the sunken gardens.
23 - Keys to the last two houses to be completed at Douglas Corporation's 600 house estate at Willaston handed over to their first tenants.

MR WILLIAM CUBBON - MANX SCHOLAR AND PATRIOT

Flags on the Manx Museum and Govern-ment buildings were flown at half-mast on the occasion of the death of Mr William Cubbon, who died early in January. His life was devoted to preserving all that is best in the heritage of the Island and his work will be invaluable to students of Manx history in the future. He was born in 1865 at Croit-e-Caley, the son of a master mariner who was involved in the local fishing. As a boy he grew up surrounded by farmers and fishermen from whom he absorbed the Manx language, customs and folk lore. Leaving school, he was apprenticed to a printer in Douglas, but he soon changed his interest in printing to that of writing. As a journalist with the Isle of Man Examiner he rose to be its manager and acting editor. In 1900 he became joint owner of the Manx Sun. This placed him in a better position to promote Manx interests and ideals among its readers.

His love of Manx books led him to accepting the post of Borough Librarian of Douglas. In 1916 he left to become manager of the Manx Labour Exchange. He was a great friend of Mr P. M. C. Kermode and they realised their mutual ambition with the establishment of the Manx Museum in 1922. William Cubbon was appointed its first Secretary and Librarian under the Curatorship of Mr Kermode.

Mr Cubbon was a founder member of Yn Cheshaght Ghailechagh - The Manx Language Society - and became its President in 1916. As a member of the Antiquarian Society since 1898 he became its President in 1925. Apart from his own writings he encouraged others and was instrumental in the publication of J. J. Kneen's 'Place Names of the Isle of Man,' the 'Grammar of the Manx Language' and 'Manx Personal Names.' Cubbon's work as Librarian led him to compiling two volumes of the invaluable 'Bibliography of the Literature of the Isle of Man.' He was editor also of the 'Journal of the Manx Museum.' When Mr Kermode died in 1932, William Cubbon was the automatic choice to become the next Curator.

It was during this time that he instigated the use of Harry Kelly's Cottage at Cregneash as the basis of a Manx National Folk Museum, the first 'open-air' folk museum in Britain. In 1940 Mr Cubbon retired as Curator at the age of 75 and was succeeded by Basil Megaw, the present Director. The University of Liverpool conferred on him the degree of M.A. in 1940 and the Norwegian Government made him a Knight of their Order of St Olaf in 1947. Mr Cubbon continued to give of his time in the interests of the Museum as Honorary Consultant. He helped in the interior design of the Manx Farmhouse Kitchen, now one of the most popular exhibits in the Museum.

In his book 'Island Heritage,' published in 1952, he presents a series of essays which has proved extremely popular with the lay person who wishes to know more about the Island's past. This sums up the lifetime's work of William Cubbon, who will be remembered as one of the Island's greatest scholars and patriots.

One of the most popular exhibits in the Manx Museum is the Manx Farmhouse Kitchen, designed with the help of Mr Cubbon. It typifies the type of house occupied by a quarterland farmer, and the chiollagh, or open hearth, came from the 200-years-old Collane Farm, Jurby. All the articles of furniture and household possessions were formerly used on Island farms and crofts.

MR WILLIAM CUBBON - MANX SCHOLAR AND PATRIOT

A disgraced former member of Tynwald and disbarred advocate is to go down in history as the man who revived the ancient right of Manxmen to present petitions for redress of grievance to the open-air sitting of Tynwald. He caused a sensation on the St John's Fair Field when he tried to present a petition calling for a Government inquiry into the circumstances of his enforced resignation from Tynwald six years earlier. Ironically, his case was not accepted for examination. But his dramatic action opened the way for grievance petitions to become a regular feature of Tynwald Day.

Fifty-six-year-old Mr Harry Cowin resigned from Tynwald in 1950 and was disbarred from practising as an advocate the following year. This was after he gave evidence in a fraud trial at Manchester Assizes involving a development company based in the Isle of Man. The trial judge said Mr Cowin's evidence was not to be trusted. After his resignation from the Government - he was a member of the Legislative Council - Mr Cowin went to live in London. But he returned to the Island to make his dramatic appearance at St John's. As members of the Court were leaving Tynwald Hill at the end of the ceremony he shouted out from the crowd: "Your Excellency, I have a petition to present." It was a great sensation, but the procession continued back to St John's Church - and that seemed to be the end of the matter. Then Mr Cowin appeared in the public gallery at the next monthly sitting of Tynwald in Douglas and again tried to get his petition accepted for investigation. In the event, he failed in spite of the fact that his petition contained allegations that collusion by senior members of Government forced him to resign in 1950. His allegations, however, were dismissed out of hand. But Tynwald had not missed the significance of what he had done. The ancient practice of presenting grievance petitions, going back to the Norse Kings of Man, had fallen into disuse. In fact, it had been rescinded many years back. Tynwald decided now that it should be restored as a cherished right of all Manxmen and women.

LIGHTHOUSE KEEPERS MAROONED

Three lighthouse keepers were marooned in the Chicken Rock lighthouse, missing Christmas at home with their families in Port St Mary. Persistent gales prevented the relief boat reaching them and they were eventually taken off on 3rd January - 25 days late. It was the longest ever delay to be experienced by the keepers on the Chicken Rock. One keeper, Neil Squire, actually had to spend a total of 67 days there.

COMMISSION'S REPORT

Sixty recommendations for boosting the Island's visiting industry were made in the report of the Commission of Inquiry set up by Tynwald last year. They included improved accommodation standards, Sunday opening of pubs and shops and a new indoor swimming pool for Douglas. All were accepted by Tynwald - apart from the report's most sensational recommendation: that the Island should have a Continental-style gambling casino. Only one member of Tynwald voted in favour of it - Garff M.H.K. Mr Charles Kerruish. The report was passed to the Tourist Board to consider and make recommendations.

TUBERCULOSIS ELIMINATED

The risk of tuberculosis being spread in milk has been overcome. In 1950 the Board of Agriculture embarked on a scheme to eradicate bovine tuberculosis from Manx cattle herds. Following the slaughtering of 1,010 infected cattle in 1949, the Board's first and only veterinary surgeon, Mr Douglas W. Kerruish, suggested that the only way to eliminate the disease was to

Will such scenes on Douglas beach be a thing of the past? Concern about the future of the Island's vital tourist industry has resulted in far-reaching proposals being suggested in the Report of the Commission of Inquiry into the Visiting Industry.
(R. and L. Kelly Collection)

Manx Airlines' two Bristol Wayfarers which have been leased from parent company Silver City in order to maintain the scheduled routes from the Island.

must sell all carcasses at Liverpool prices which, say Manx agriculturists, is the cheapest meat market in England. Slaughtering takes place in two abattoirs - one owned by Douglas Corporation in Lake Road, and the other in the heart of Ramsey's shopping thoroughfare, this being viewable by passers-by. Both abattoirs are regarded as antiquated and unsuitable in the light of modern-day hygiene standards. A new abattoir will have to be built eventually by Tynwald for lease to the Association. Without it, all dreams of exporting Manx carcass meat, rather than cattle on the hoof, will evaporate.

introduce regular testing of all herds by vets. Any animal reacting to the test, even if only a carrier, should be slaughtered. Often whole herds had to be killed. Compensation equalled the market value of the animal but took no account of the farmer's loss of earnings before he could re-stock - often months or even a year later - because the premises had to be disinfected and replacement cows were scarce and costly. However, the Island has now been cleared of bovine tuberculosis, parish by parish. The sea around us is an effective barrier and provides full control over the importation of livestock and raw carcass meat. Regular tests will continue, but the Isle of Man can claim to be ahead of the United Kingdon and Europe in ridding its cattle of the disease. It is predicted that the Island will become a valuable reservoir for farmers elsewhere wanting to purchase tuberculosis-free cattle.

MEAT IMPORTS RESTRICTED
The importation of British and foreign meat has been made subject to strict controls by Tynwald. Local supplies will be given preference in a more secure market. Ever since de-rationing two years ago, when rows surfaced between producers and butchers over the quality of Manx fat stock and the threat of butchers to import better and less fatty cuts, it has been recognised that producers need to improve their marketing operations and provide some overall control. The Fat Stock Marketing Association has been given complete control over the wholesale marketing of meat on the Island. A commercial agent, the Fat Stock Marketing Corporation of England, has been appointed to buy all Manx fat stock for local sale and export. To avoid claims that a monopoly is being abused, the F.M.C.

RAMSEY DROWNING TRAGEDY
Six men were drowned when their rowing boat overturned and sank in Ramsey Bay as they were going out to a Fleetwood fishing trawler anchored offshore. Three were Ramsey men, the others were crewmen on the trawler. The six set off to make the 500 yard trip shortly before 11 p.m. in calm conditions. But the boat was overloaded, with only six inches of freeboard when it capsized.

MANX AIRLINES TAKEN OVER
Following the tragic loss of one of Manx Airlines' Dakotas last December, the airline is to be taken over by Silver City Airways, a subsidiary of British Air Services Ltd. In making the announcement in May, Manx Airlines' chairman, Captain George Drummond stated: ". . . In view of being unable to obtain suitable aircraft, the sale of the company is in the best interests of the Isle of Man, only large organisations being capable of coping with the ever-increasing traffic. Manx Airlines Ltd will continue to be domiciled and administered from the Island." Messrs Drummond, Vondy and Hankinson remained as directors and were joined by Mr Eoin C. Mekie, chairman of Silver City Airways. The remaining Dakota has been replaced by two 44-seat Bristol Wayfarers which will serve the Newcastle summer route and the busy all-year-round Glasgow route, which has nine returns weekly during the summer. Three Rapides have been retained for charter work and the summer Carlisle route.

LIFEBOATS NAMED
Thanks to the generosity of the late Mrs Ellen Cubbin two of the latest 'Watson' type lifeboats have been positioned on the Island. Both have been named after her son Mr Colby Cubbin who died in 1951. On the 25th July, Her Royal Highness the Duchess of Kent, President of the Royal National Lifeboat Institution, arrived on the Island for the Naming Ceremonies which were both gala occasions attended by locals and visitors alike. In the morning Port St. Mary harbour was a busy scene as the Duchess named its new lifeboat *Colby Cubbin No 2*. In the afternoon huge crowds gathered in Douglas to witness the launch of *Colby Cubbin No 1* following the naming ceremony. The lifeboat had been called out for the first time in June to take a sick man off a tanker off Douglas.

The scene in Douglas harbour on the occasion of the launching of the 'Colby Cubbin No 1' following the naming ceremony performed by H.R.H. the Duchess of Kent.

TEDDY BOY HOOLIGANS

Douglas was the scene this summer of unprecedented violent and drunken scenes involving young visitors, many of them Teddy Boys. Police were called out regularly to outbreaks of street fighting and disorderly behaviour in public houses. One establishment, the Texas Bar in the Douglas Bay Hotel, was prosecuted for permitting drunken scenes. Youths also caused trouble by indiscriminate firing of water pistols at innocent passers-by - sometimes loading their weapons with urine.

MANX T.T. RIDER KILLED

Castletown's Derek Ennett, arguably the best ever Manx motorcycle racer, was killed in August at the Ulster Grand Prix. He was 25. He was thrown off his machine at high speed when he hit a stone wall and died from head injuries. Ennett had a meteoric rise to fame after starting his racing career in 1951. In 1954 he won the Junior Manx Grand Prix and became a works rider for A.J.S. and Matchless in 1955. He came seventh in the Junior T.T. and finished on the Senior leaderboard in sixth place. This year he was runner-up to Ken Kavanagh (Moto Guzzi) in the Junior T.T. and gained another creditable sixth place in the Senior. He was about to sign up for the Moto Guzzi team following the Ulster races.

SUMMER CELEBRATIONS

An estimated 30,000 people atten-ded the popular open-air service at Kirk Braddan in August. It was the 100th anniversary of the service which was first held in the churchyard of Old Kirk Braddan. The service was led by Lord Bishop Benjamin Pollard who was joined by His Excellency Sir Ambrose Dundas. Also in August, the 80th anniversary of the Douglas horse tramway was celebrated in magnificent style with all 80 horses in the parade from Derby Castle to Victoria Pier. Pat Smythe, the famous international horsewoman, was the celebrity guest and she drove the official tram to Derby Castle. The entire promenade was lined three or four deep with waving and cheering people. Among the guests was the grand-daughter of Thomas Lightfoot, the founder of the Douglas Bay Tramway. During the peak period in early August, 30,000 passengers are carried each day by the horse trams which are now unique in Europe.

The Squadronaires have grown in popularity since 1953 and are now a great favourite with dancers in the Palace Ballroom.

NO JOE LOSS

There is no doubt that the summer has not been the same without Joe Loss and his orchestra performing at the Villa Marina. The orchestra has been in residence for the summer since 1947 and thousands of holidaymakers have been joined by locals to be put 'in the mood' for a night of dancing to the strains of one of Britain's top bands. And how they loved the vocalists such as Elizabeth Batey, Howard Jones and Rose Brennan, not to mention Tony Ventro for his more classical renditions. Saturday nights saw long queues stretching up Broadway waiting for the doors to open, and there is no doubt Joe Loss and his orchestra brought great fame to the Villa Marina as the result of regular broadcasts on B.B.C. radio. No official reason has been given for the absence of Joe Loss this year, but it is believed that the Corporation was not prepared to accede to the demands for an increase in his 60% share of the door takings. The employment of a band for this season was put out to tender. The beginning of the season saw Jack Parnell and his orchestra in residence, followed by Kenny Mac-kintosh as the star band. Ivy Benson and her popular all-girls orchestra were back at the Villa Marina playing for morning dances and entertaining in the Gardens in the afternoons. On Sunday nights she hosted the celebrity concerts which played to full houses.

At the Palace Ballroom Ronnie Aldrich and the Squadronaires have become established as the resident summer band. They appeared first in 1952. Ronnie has persuaded the management to drape curtains over all the windows on either side of the stage to get ride of irritating echoes in the vast ballroom. Everyone agrees there has been an improvement. The Squadronaires are now well supported by dancers who enjoy the slick music and rhythms of a fine orchestra. The annual Dance Festival held in the Palace attracts hundreds of the best

Bottom left: Famous international showjumper Pat Smythe, accompanied by His Worship the Mayor Councillor W. B. Kaneen, set out on the procession along the promenade as part of the 80th anniversary celebrations of the Douglas horse trams. (Town Hall Archives)

Below: Ronnie Aldrich, conductor of the Squadronaires.

Bottom: Derek Ennett, the Island's leading motorcycle racer who was tragically killed in Ulster.

Top: The factory in Hills Meadow occupied by the Douglas Carpet Manufacturing Co. Ltd. is the first to be built by Government as part of its drive to encourage light industries on the Island.

Above: The popular open-air service at Kirk Braddan, begun by Vicar John Drury, celebrated its centenary this year. Bishop Benjamin Pollard preached at a special service which was attended by about 30,000 people.

has been increased from one to two members. One seat has been taken from each of the sheadings of Ayre, Michael and Glenfaba. Country members have all along been against redistribution and it was no surprise that the representatives of the sheadings voted against the Bill. A last ditch attempt was made to save the seats by increasing the membership of the House of Keys from 24 to 27. It was only lost by the casting vote of the Speaker, Sir Joseph Qualtrough.

As a result of November's General Election, eight new members entered the House. The Keys now consist of 14 Independents, three Labour members, three representatives of the Manx People's Political Association and one Conservative. Sir Joseph Qualtrough has been re-elected Speaker of the House of Keys.

CHRISTMAS BLIZZARD
Finally, a sudden 72 mile an hour blizzard hit the Island on Christmas Day, causing drifts up to 12 feet deep and closing roads and railway lines. Electricity and telephone cables were brought down and Kirk Michael was cut off for four days.

The electricity black-out spoiled many people's Christmas dinners in what was the worst Christmas weather in living memory.

dancers in Britain. While sedate quick steps, waltzes and foxtrots are still enjoyed on the crowded dance floor, youngsters are turning to the new-fangled and boisterous jitter-bugging and jive.

PORT SODERICK PURCHASE
Port Soderick beach, hotel and glen, which were acquired on lease in the first instance, have now been bought by Douglas Corporation for £9,000. It intends to develop the area as a municipal enterprise. An expenditure of £95,000 is envisaged towards which the Government has made a small grant. It is hoped to restore the resort's pre-war popularity when it was served by electric railway running along the scenic Marine Drive. The railway is now derelict, as is the lift which linked the railway with the beach. The Corporation propose to provide a bus service when the restoration is complete.

REDISTRIBUTION, AT LAST!
During the year the Representation of the People Bill received Royal Assent. It provides for a redistribution of seats in the House of Keys, something which has long been advocated by political reformists. It is regarded as an historic event, no change in representation having been made since 1891. Douglas now has two more seats, making eight in total, divided between North, East, South and West Douglas. Ramsey's representation

The Calf of Man Crucifixion is an outstanding example of Celtic art which dates from the 8th century and was discovered a thousand years later among the ruins of an early Christian chapel on the Calf of Man. Carved from Manx slate, it is thought to have been an altar front. It has now been acquired by the Manx Museum and is an important addition to its collection of Celtic and Norse cross-slabs. (Manx National Heritage)

TYNWALD MATTERS: GOVERNMENT TO TAKE OVER M.E.R.

The decision by the directors of the Manx Electric Railway that they would be unable to maintain the service because of mounting maintenance costs exercised the minds of members of Tynwald throughout the year. On the table was the directors' offer to sell the entire system for £70,000. The Executive Council appointed a sub-committee, made up of Messrs J. B. Bolton, J. F. Crellin and H. K. Corlett, to look into the matter. They imported three railway specialists who produced an estimate of £674,000 for the complete renewal of cars, track and other equipment, to be spread over 16 years. It was suggested that it would be cheaper to use double-decker buses, which immediately aroused the interest of Isle of Man Road Services Ltd. Laxey Commissioners expressed alarm at the suggestion and Mr H. C. Kerruish, M.H.K., took 18 Keys members for a trip on the railway to the summit of Snaefell to consider what the loss of the railway would mean.

In June the Keys received the gloomy report from the sub-committee that there should be no support for the continuation of the railway. During the ensuing debate Mr J. B. Bolton strongly supported the idea of a road up Snaefell. However, it was decided to put the report aside and appoint a new committee to look at means of continuing the railway at a reasonable cost. The committee consisted of Deemster Sir Percy Cowley, C.B.E., Sir Ralph Stevenson, K.C.M.G., H. C. Kerruish, J. B. Bolton and G. Taggart. They sought the advice of tramway, rather than railway, specialists. They, in turn, agreed that the cost of reconstructing the line would be high, but its intrinsic value was incalculable. This was followed by a meeting of the Tynwald Committee with the M.E.R. directors. It was provisionally agreed that the sale price of the line to the Government would be £50,000, the directors making a sacrifice of £20,000 in the interest of preserving the railway for the benefit of the Island. The revised price was about the estimated scrap value of the railway, without the land value.

The committee's proposal to purchase the railway and to expend £25,000 a year for ten years on renewing the track from Douglas and Laxey, and from Laxey to Snaefell, came before Tynwald in December. Deemster Sir Percy Cowley made a strong plea for acquisition, his main opponents being Mr J. B. Bolton and Mr J. M. Cain, a director of the Isle of Man Railway and Road Services Companies. Points in favour of retaining the railway included the fact it was a popular visitor attraction, it was a help to Ramsey and that it employed over 30 permanent staff, many of whom had worked on the railway since leaving school. The take-over is to take effect from next June following Royal Assent being given to the necessary Bill.

1956
- Death of the author of *Winnie the Pooh*, A.A. Milne
- Republican Dwight Eisenhower re-elected President of US
- Hollywood film star Grace Kelly marries Prince Rainier II of Monaco

1956 NEWS IN BRIEF

JANUARY
1 - Weather report for 1955 showed that the year was the sunniest on record, with 1,897 hours of sunshine recorded.

FEBRUARY
14 - Douglas Licensing Bench approve 53 applications by residential hotels and boarding house keepers for 'unrestricted' short term liquor licences enabling them to sell spirits as well as beer and light wines as before.
17 - *Isle of Man Examiner* poll shows that 49% of the voters were in favour of a casino being established in the Island, with 49% against the idea. 67% were in favour of Sunday opening of public houses.
24 - The Calf of Man Crucifixion - an 8th century stone carving - bought for the Manx Museum for £750 through the National Art-Collections Fund and the Friends of the Museum.

MARCH
20 - Tynwald authorised the Water Board to prepare plans and submit tenders for the proposed £750,000 reservoir at Glen Rushen to supply the south and west of the Island.
27 - Ramsey and District Youth Committee decided to give up responsibility for the Northern Youth Centre following the Board of Education's refusal to re-appoint a full-time youth leader for the north of the Island.

MAY
4 - Mrs Mona Huke (mezzo-soprano) won both the Cleveland Medal and the F. M. Cubbon rose bowl for leider singing.
8 - Keys pass Bill to make licensing hours uniform throughout the Island. Summer hours were fixed at 10 am to 11 pm. Under existing regulations public houses other than towns closed at 10 pm.
21 - T.T. Course marathon won by former Olympic runner Tom Richards for the second time, beating four hours for the first time. He said it was the most gruelling course he has ever run. Manx runner Bill Kelly was second.
24 - David Ball, 16 years old Port Erin golfer won Manx Golf Championship when he beat Harold Cain.

JUNE
8 - Aerial prospecting over the Island began by Island Exploration Company. A Dakota aircraft towed a detecting instrument which recorded the presence of metal deposits in the ground.
12 - New Aristoc stocking factory at Ramsey opened.
13 - Official opening of the Corrin Memorial Home for old people in Peel by Lieutenant-Governor.

19 - Sir Ambrose Dundas presents his annual Budget. Tax relief given by increased personal allowances. Petrol rebate of 6d a gallon introduced last year is to continue. Budget proposed record expenditure of over £4,000,000, which was more than £900,000 above estimated receipts.
29 - Large number of 'homecomers' from overseas arrive.

JULY
6 - Douglas Corporation's plans to build an indoor swimming pool in the Villa Marina grounds, and likely to cost £500,000, received a set back when the Governor's Executive Council opposed the project. It would have meant the loss of much of the Villa Marina Gardens.
9 - Car parking allowed on both sides of the Loch Promenade, Douglas.
27 - Large shoals of herring around the Irish Sea resulted in record catches by boats based at Peel.

AUGUST
7 - During the Bank Holiday rush there were 34,000 arrivals of visitors, of which 5,000 came by air.

SEPTEMBER
13 - Battle of Britain Day at Jurby.
14 - An offer by the British Sugar Corporation to employ 100 men sugar beet harvesting and processing resulted in 104 men being given jobs.
18 - Reversal of Government decision to remove flour subsidy. Price of large loaf fixed at 9d.
21 - Provisional agreement made by Forestry Board to purchase Laxey Glen Gardens. Cost of £4,750 subsequently agreed by Tynwald.
27 - Deemster Sir Percy Cowley C.B.E. installed as Freeman of Douglas.

OCTOBER
1 - Final passenger figures for this season showed 542,305 arrivals, down on last year but better than 1953.
26 - Mr Anderson, Douglas Borough Electrical Engineer expressed opinion that the Island would have an atomic power station within 10 years.

DECEMBER
5 - Government announcement that petrol rationing would be introduced on 17th January as a result of the Middle East situation. This was followed by the Lieutenant-Governor announcing that a one shilling increase on petrol duty imposed in the U.K. would be offset in the I.O.M. by a rebate of a shilling a gallon to be met by Government.

1957

• Death of actor Humphrey Bogart due to throat cancer

• First edition of *The Sky at Night* shown on BBC TV

• Leonard Bernstein's musical *West Side Story* opens in New York

FREEDOM OF BOROUGH FOR SIR WINSTON

A Douglas Town Council deputation flew to London in a charter aircraft to present the Freedom of the Borough to Sir Winston Churchill at his home in Hyde Park Gate. The trip was organised because Sir Winston had had to refuse invitations to travel to Douglas, pleading political commitments and also his advancing years. But the occasion was overshadowed by a furious row that it caused in the Town Council.

The Council originally voted in 1947 to confer the Freedom of Douglas on Britain's inspirational leader in the Second World War, as did many other local authorities throughout the country. But in spite of repeated invitations to come to Douglas the great man could not be prevailed upon to make the trip. So, like many other councils, Douglas decided to take the Freedom to him, in July 1957. It was proposed that the full council should fly to London with the mahogany casket containing the Freedom Scroll and Charter but this idea led to opposition in the Town Council led by Alderman Alf Teare. He said that it would be nothing less than joy riding on the rates and that it had caused anger among ratepayers. Other councillors said Alderman Teare was casting a blemish on a unique, historic occasion - and they argued that the cost of the trip would work out at less than the cost involved in Sir Winston coming to the Isle of Man. As a result of the dispute, a number of councillors refused to go on the trip and in the end the Mayor, Councillor Bill Kaneen, led a party of 12 council members and Town Clerk Mr Douglas Blakey. In a 15-minute ceremony at Sir Winston's home the Freedom was formally conferred. Sir Winston was presented also with a parcel of Manx rock - and in return he presented the Mayor with one of his famous, trademark cigars - which Councillor Kaneen said he would never smoke!

PETROL RATIONING ENFORCED
Petrol rationing was imposed in the Island for the first four months of the year because of nationwide fuel shortages

caused by the Suez Crisis. Motorists were issued with ration cards entitling them to a maximum of 200 miles of motoring a month. Businesses were allowed extra supplies for their vehicles. The Anglo-French invasion of Suez led to a number of Army reservists in the Island being recalled to active service.

KEEPERS MAROONED AGAIN
For the second winter in succession severe gales delayed the relief of the lighthouse keepers manning the light on the Chicken Rock - preventing them spending Christmas with their families in Port St. Mary. In January last year the keepers were marooned there for 25 days beyond their normal six-week period of duty because the relief boat could not reach them. In January this year a similar situation made the men's relief 29 days overdue. Later in the year, in March, rough seas again delayed the relief of the Chicken Rock Lighthouse for a period of 24 days.

OIL DISCOVERY HOAX
Rumours flashed round London early this year that oil had been found in the Isle of Man. It turned out to be just a joke. Island Exploration Co Ltd was indeed drilling on the Island in search of minerals, not oil. Drilling, under a four year licence, is taking place at Shughlaig Quiggin, Sartfell, in a hunt for exploitable seams of lead. It is the result of an aerial survey carried out from a Dakota aircraft equipped with various systems to test rock structures. Company chairman, Arthur Kitto, says the company is optimistic of finding minerals.

THERMOSTAT FIRM STRIKES RICH
An incredible misunderstanding looks like triggering a major expansion for the small company in Castletown which manufactures thermostats. In the spring a company representative visited Morphy Richards in the U.K. in an effort

Prime Minister Sir Winston Churchill at his Hyde Park Gate residence, where he was presented with the scroll and casket of the Honorary Freedom of the Borough of Douglas by the Mayor, Councillor W. B. Kaneen. (Town Hall Archives)

to interest them in a new-style thermostat for electric blankets. Only six examples had been made and when someone in the buying department at Morphy Richards said they would have a few thousand to start with, the rep was naturally hesitant. Incredibly, the buyer suggested that perhaps a million would be more appropriate to get things going! The representative settled for half a million, in itself a major undertaking to fulfil. Castletown Thermostats has been expanding ever since.

TRIUMPH FOR BADMINTON TEAM
Victory at the Douglas Holiday Camp over Yorkshire in the All-England County Championships resulted in the Island badminton team becoming champions of the Division II Northern Zone for the first time. Previously, in the season they had defeated Lancashire, Cheshire and Westmoreland and their wins are a reflection of the high standard of badminton being played on the Island. It is also a credit to the Isle of Man Badminton Association who organise and finance the Island's participation in the championships. In the first of the knock-out rounds of the Division II Championship the Island met Northants at the Douglas Holiday Camp and were narrowly beaten 8-7. It is hoped that the Island will be strengthened next season by the return of the Island's triple-champion Donald Jones who is currently off the Island doing his National Service.

MANX ELECTRIC RAILWAY TRANSFER
On the morning of Saturday, 1st June, Lieutenant-Governor Sir Ambrose Flux Dundas drove flag-bedecked car No 32 from Derby Castle to Groudle to mark the transfer of the electric railway to Government control. On board were guests and the newly-appointed M.E.R. Board. Its chairman is Sir Ralph Stevenson K.C.M.G., M.L.C., with two Keys' members, R. C. Stephen and A. H. Simcocks. Two additional members are Mr T. W. Billington, an accountant, and Mr T. W. Kneale, M.Eng., retired executive engineer of the North Western Railway of India. Tynwald voted £40,000 to begin renewing the first two miles of track, and during October the Ben Ain delivered 3,000 sleepers at Ramsey, followed by 200 tons of rail. The season has been disappointing with a drop of 56,000 passengers but Tynwald, after considerable discussion, has voted a further £9,000 to offset losses and cover rising costs. The end of the year has seen the first cars painted in the new colour scheme of green and white; but railway enthusiasts have already expressed their strong disapproval.

MORE TEDDY BOY VIOLENCE
For the second summer season in succession Douglas was hit by Teddy Boy violence and drunkenness. There were repeated incidents of street fighting and disorderly behaviour on licensed premises in which flick knives and blackjacks were used. This led to a call by Garff M.H.K. Mr Charles Kerruish for the Manx courts to make more use of their powers to impose sentences of corporal punishment - birching. The Chief Constable had already appealed to licensees to help prevent drunkenness by not providing excess liquor to customers during the summer season.

CALL TO REDUCE INCOME TAX
A warning has been given that unless the Island's standard rate of income tax is reduced it will lose many of its so-called New Residents. In his annual report Mr J. R. Quayle, chairman of the Isle of Man Bank, said people were still moving into the Island from the U.K. and elsewhere to take advantage of its low tax. But even more were leaving because there was no sign of the Government reducing the current rate of four shillings and sixpence in the pound.

DOUGLAS HEAD THEATRE TO CLOSE
A long-standing feature of the Island's holiday season entertainment scene has come to an end. Douglas Corporation had decided that there will be no more pierrot shows in the open-air theatre the Corporation owns on Douglas Head, because of falling attendances. The Corporation has also decided that there should be a ban on motor traffic in Strand Street for the first time ever. It will apply for four hours a day during the holiday season in order to ease traffic congestion.

DENTAL DECAY INCREASING
Children in the Island are eating too many sweets and other sugary and starchy foods according to Principal School Dental Officer Mrs Kathleen Smith. In her annual report she said dental decay in young children was getting worse and there was a severe lack of dental hygiene. She said very young children were having to undergo multiple extractions. Mrs Smith said she believed the fluoridation of drinking water would ease the problem.

'DOUBLE' FOR ALAN HOLMES
After the excitement of the Golden Jubilee T.T. in June, in the September races Castletown rider Alan Holmes completed the 'double'. He became the first Manxman to win both the

The Island's victorious badminton team who won the Northern Zone of Division II of the All-England County Championships. Standing from left to right are Eve Johnson, Peter Kniveton, Charles Garrett, David Jepson and Lawrence Corlett. Seated are Vera Cottier, Mary Arrowsmith, Elaine Kewin and June Currie.

Alan Holmes of Castletown being congratulated by his mother and father after his magnificent win in the Senior Manx Grand Prix. Alan had already won the Junior race and he is the first Manxman to win both races in the same year.

1957

- USSR successfully tests inter-continental ballistic missile
- Racial tension increases in USA and first civil rights legislation enacted
- Six states sign the Treaty of Rome establishing the European Economic Community

Junior and Senior Manx Grand Prix in one year. He led the Junior race throughout and won at a record 90 m.p.h. He was chased hard by local riders Eddie Crooks, Colin Broughton and Bob Dowty, besides Ellis Boyce and Terry Shepherd. In the Senior, Ellis Boyce was leading until coming off at Glen Helen, allowing Holmes to win at record speed and setting up a new lap record of 94.06 m.p.h. This year's M.G.P. attracted a fantastic 380 riders and it was necessary to introduce a 'Newcomers' race which was won by Londoner Ned Minihan. Guest of honour was Group Captain Douglas Bader, the famous legless pilot of World War II.

DROP IN SUMMER ARRIVALS
The Island's visitor arrivals in the 1957 season were the lowest for 10 years. The number of arrivals from May to September inclusive was 506,000, a drop of 78,000 in two years. The loss was all on sea traffic. Ronaldsway Airport had a record year with nearly 100,000 summer arrivals and handled a total of quarter of a million passengers throughout the year - a figure which has doubled in six years.

TRAGIC RAILWAY ACCIDENT
Mr Frederick Norman Pugh was killed instantly when he was run over by a steam train at the Ballacrye crossing, Ballaugh. Fifty-three-year-old Mr Pugh, whose wife is gatekeeper at Ballacrye, was helping her to open the gates for the early morning train from Ramsey to Douglas. It happened on a dark December morning. Mr Pugh's body was found under the train's engine.

BETTER TV RECEPTION
The new B.B.C. television transmitter has been installed at last at Carnane on Douglas Head. It had been announced originally that the transmitter was to be on Snaefell. The new transmitter was switched on in time for Christmas and, in conjunction with the transmitters of Belfast and Carlisle is giving first class reception of B.B.C. programmes in 90% of the Island. Before this, the Island received programmes from the Holme Moss transmitter in the Midlands and reception was of variable quality. There are now calls for booster stations in the Island to improve reception of the new Independent Television programmes. Douglas made its live television debut in August when the first ever relay from the Island was televised to more than six million viewers by the A.B.C. network. The programme was in the series 'Holiday Town.'

1957 NEWS IN BRIEF

JANUARY
17 - Protest meeting held in Peel to oppose Commissioners' plans to construct £24,000 swimming pool at Marine Parade.
25 - Mr Sydney Kneale, O.B.E., appointed Second Deemster and Mr G. E. Moore appointed Attorney General.

FEBRUARY
15 - Free facilities for the inoculation of children from 3 to 10 years against polio were announced by the Health Services Board.

MARCH
1 - Eddie Crooks, best Manx performer in the 1956 Manx Grand Prix, voted 'Green Final' Sportsman of the Year. Second was his clubmate Alan Holmes and third, cyclist Millie Robinson.
15 - Two 120 feet chimney stacks of the former Ramsey Salt Works demolished by expert steeplejacks.

APRIL
1 - Following the withdrawal of the Government flour subsidy, price control was taken off bread and an additional 1½d added to the 9d large loaf.
16 - Estimates totalling £928,530 presented to Tynwald by seven Boards showing a £47,000 increase. Included was an £84,000 estimate by the Tourist Board which covered £21,500 for road racing events.
30 - House of Keys pass legislation to provide Government aid by loans to owners and tenants of boarding houses and hotels to improve accommodation.

MAY
1 - Arend-Roland comet photographed by Mr W. N. C. Salmond as it passed over the Island.
9 - For the first time the Cleveland Medal went off the Island when Mr Robert Kendrick of Birmingham won the competition.
10 - Manx artist Bryan Kneale had three paintings exhibited in the Royal Academy Exhibition in London.
16 - A badger was found dead on the Mountain Road. It had escaped from Glen Helen Zoo the previous summer.
21 - Tynwald approved a £14,000 scheme to reconstruct a section of the Marine Drive as an interim measure pending full consideration of its future.

JUNE
3-5-7 Golden Jubilee T.T. marked by special celebrations.
8 - First-ever Isle of Man Scooter Rally organised by the Tourist Board started by Sir Joseph Qualtrough, S.H.K.

JULY
5 - A Manx Wedding Pageant at Maughold Village attracted thousands of holidaymakers.
17 - A new concern - Manx Flux and Mica Ltd from Cheshire - began operating at Foxdale with an industrial plant for the production of china, stone, flux and mica.
18 - Duke of Gloucester was the reviewing officer for the passing out parade of officer cadets at R.A.F. Jurby.

AUGUST
2 - Headmistress of the Douglas High School for Girls, Miss M. G. Dickenson, announced her retirement.
14 - A party of Island Boy Scouts returned after taking part in the World Jamboree at Sutton Park, England.
21 - A Floodlit Tattoo drew 7,000 people to the King George VI Park Bowl. Highlight was a display by the 751st United States Air Force 'Jiving' Band.
29 - After last year's record herring catch, the Agriculture and Fisheries Board reported that to the end of July the herring season was "the worst in Great Britain in living memory."

SEPTEMBER
18 - Miss Geraldine Reid, daughter of the Rev R. H. Reid, was married to Australian World Championship motorcyclist Keith Campbell.

OCTOBER
15 - Peel swimming pool scheme approved by Tynwald when a grant of £15,000 towards the cost was approved.
15 - Chairman of the Civil Defence Commission, Mr T. A. Coole, M.H.K., reported that extensive tests made for possible radio-activity in the Island caused by a mishap at the atomic power station at Winscale, Cumberland, were negative.
22 - House of Keys decide that the new Tourist Bill should give power to the Tourist Board to introduce a compulsory system of registration, grading and inspection of boarding houses and hotels.
24 - Outstanding successes were achieved at the Blackpool Music Festival by Margaret Curphey, her father W. H. Curphey and her uncle Tom Gelling.
26 - A 16 year old boy was sent to prison with hard labour for a month by the Ramsey Magistrates for theft of £20.
30 - Postcard Censorship Committee reported that 34% of cards submitted to them in the past year had been rejected as unsuitable.

NOVEMBER
12 - Mr John Kneen of the Curraghs, Ballaugh, celebrated what is believed to be his 105th birthday.
21 - Official independent report recommends amalgamation of the Island's water authorities.
28 - Mr Geoffrey Rees-Jones appointed to succeed Mr S. E. Wilson as principal of King William's College upon his retirement.

NEWSPAPER RIVALRY COMES TO AN END

The *Isle of Man Times*, owned by members of the Brown family since 1861, was bought in August by a former Second World War French Resistance leader, Henri Leopold Dor. Just over a year earlier, on coming to the Island from the U.K. to establish a Manx-based marine insurance company, the eccentric former Lloyd's insurer bought the *Examiner*. So now, after decades of keen but friendly rivalry, the Island's two principal newspaper groups are controlled by the same man. He is reputed to be a wealthy entrepreneur, but his purchases owe nothing to his business acumen other than an opportunist streak. The newspaper companies remain owned by different companies but the two staffs and technical equipment are to be pooled to improve efficiency.

The *Examiner* came on the market because its owner, T. R. Radcliffe, one of the founders in the 1930s of the hire purchase company, Conister Trust, was ill and his surviving son, Jim, wanted to escape the Island's depressed economy by emigrating to Australia. There was little interest shown by Manx people in investing in the *Examiner*'s future and Mr Dor was able to negotiate a ridiculously cheap deal to acquire the newspaper. Shortly afterwards, 'T. R.' died, reputedly of a broken heart. A year later, a divided Brown family sold the *Times* to Mr Dor along with its extensive property buildings in Athol Street. Once again there was little interest shown by Manx businessmen and Mr Dor was the only prospective buyer. Now he is busy asset-stripping and is making a huge capital profit by selling off property and leasing it back. He dislikes assets and believes that unless Tynwald lowers income tax to attract new residents the long-term future of the Island is bleak. There are many critics who believe that too much power has passed into one man's hands. They suggest that the *Times* should be floated as a public company. The problem with that is very few trust Mr Dor or would be prepared to buy many of the shares.

This brings to an end the Brown dynasty which has influenced the political and commercial life of the Island. James Brown, the part-coloured founder of the *Times*, was imprisoned for his campaigning to make the House of Keys a publicly-elected body. His subsequent release, and the payment of compensation by the individual M.H.K.s for wrongful imprisonment, led to electoral reform. James Brown's son, Archibald Brown, was the founder and chairman of the Island's dance hall, theatre and cinema chain, the Palace and Derby Castle Co. His son, George, who died only several years ago, was the founder of the Manx Grand Prix. At the same time, the *Times* became an institution, and its associated jobbing printing works were bigger than all other printing firms put together. It is hard to grasp, therefore, that such a dynasty has crumbled so easily and that such institutions as the *Times* and *Examiner* have passed into the hands of a stranger who does not inspire trust.

T.T. GOLDEN JUBILEE CELEBRATED WITH FIRST 100 M.P.H. LAP

T.T. fans poured into the Island this year as the world's finest racing machines and their riders assembled to celebrate 50 years of the T.T. Races. The Senior race was extended to eight laps (302 miles) as the finale of the Golden Jubilee meeting. Favourites Geoff Duke and Bill Lomas were unable to take part as a result of injuries sustained in spills earlier in the season. Duke's 4-cylinder Gilera was taken over by Australian Bob Brown who joined Scotsman Bob McIntyre who, earlier in the week, was the record winner of the Junior Race. Dickie Dale took over the incredible 8-cylinder Moto Guzzi from Lomas, and was joined by Keith Campbell and John Clark riding the very potent single-cylinder Guzzis. John Surtees, last year's winner, was back for M.V. Agusta, though his partner, Terry Shepherd, was injured in a practice spill at the Nook. The Norton factory had withdrawn from racing, but last year's machines, with added streamlining, were made available to Jack Brett, John Hartle and Allan Trow. Matchless machines were provided for Derek Powell, Peter Murphy and Keith Bryen. German Walter Zeller was the lone B.M.W. entrant.

The early morning cloud of Friday soon cleared and the Island was bathed in sunshine as spectators flocked to their favourite vantage points. The anticipation of the first 100 m.p.h. lap added to the excitement. Hot favourite Bob McIntyre opened with a 99.9 m.p.h. lap, leaving Surtees in second place and Zeller third. McIntyre then proceeded to put in three magical 'ton' laps raising the lap record to 101.2 m.p.h. before stopping to refuel. Surtees was still second and Brown moved up to third place after Zeller had retired, with Brett moving into fourth place after putting up the fastest-ever lap by a Norton. However, a spill at Sulby Bridge was to put him out of the race after a valiant effort. With over a two minute lead, McIntyre eased off for the last two laps, allowing Surtees to catch him on the road for some exciting duelling which ended one of the greatest Senior races ever. Brown maintained third position and was followed by Dale and Keith Campbell on the Guzzis. This meant that Italian machines had filled the first five places. Best of the many Nortons entered was that of Allan Trow who finished sixth. Another Norton was ridden by local rider George Costain, who finished in a very creditable 17th place.

Bob McIntyre shows his grit and determination as he banks the Senior Gilera into Signpost Corner. During the eight-lap race he achieved the first 100m.p.h. lap setting a new record of 102.2m.p.h.

As with the Junior and Senior, all race and lap records were broken during Wednesday's racing on the Clypse Circuit. In the 250cc Lightweight race, Mondial riders Cecil Sandford and Sammy Miller set out to prevent the M.V. Agusta team from making a hat-trick of wins. It was Sandford who won after Miller slid off at Governor's Bridge. Second were the M.Vs of Taveri and Colombo, team-mate and last year's winner Ubbiali being forced to retire. The Czech team of Bartok and Kostir (C.Zs), and Statsny (Jawa) won the team prize. In the 125cc race, Tarquino Provini on a Mondial gained the lead at the end of the first lap and such was his determination to prevent Carlo Ubbiali win for the third successive time that he broke the lap record consistently for the little machines. Ubbiali had to be content with second place followed by his team-mate Taveri.

The highlight of the day was the massed-start of the sidecars, with 28 starters dominated by B.M.W. machines. First round Parkfield was F. Hillebrand who maintained his lead throughout the race. He was hotly pursued by W. Schneider as, one by one, the Nortons of Harris, Smith and Boddice dropped out. Third place was taken by B.M.W. rider F. Camathias. The day, and indeed the whole week, had been a great success. There were plenty of thrills and spills but, thankfully, no one was seriously hurt. Amongst the memories of the Jubilee was the return of the ever-popular ten-times T.T. winner Stanley Woods. No one can equal his record. During practices he rode one of the streamlined Moto Guzzis as 'A' reserve and lapped consistently at over 80 m.p.h.

ITALIANS TO QUIT

At the end of the racing season the news that Gilera, Moto Guzzi and Mondial were to withdraw from racing came as a shock to supporters of the T.T. A joint statement from the Italian manufacturers declared that speeds reached by road racing motorcycles "cause a problem as to whether it is right to expose the riders to the risks involved." This means that M.V. Agusta, who are not associated with the statement, are likely to dominate the solo classes for the foreseeable future.

Left: German sidecar ace Hillebrand and his passenger Grunwald slide the B.M.W. outfit round Willaston Corner, leading the race from start to finish.

Right: The dashing Italian rider Tarquino Provini rounds Parkfield Corner on the Mondial which he rode to victory in the Lightweight (125 cc) race at record speed.

Above: Adding excitement and glamour to the Senior race was the unique eight-cylinder Moto Guzzi seen here at the bottom of Bray Hill in the hands of Dickie Dale.
Below: Flag in hand, Lord Bishop Benjamin Pollard sets the Golden Jubilee T.T. in motion as G. T. Salt, on his streamlined Norton, is first away in the Junior race.

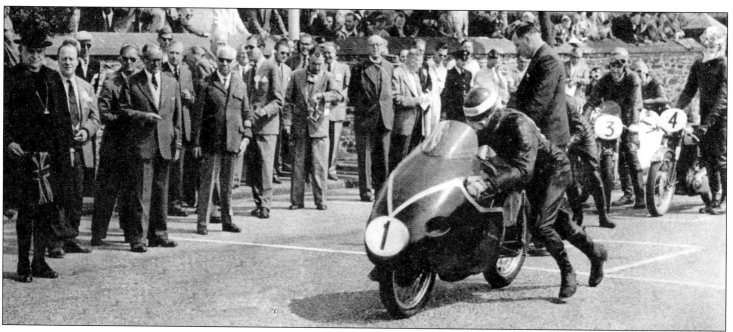

ISLAND IN SHOCK AFTER WORST-EVER AIR DISASTER

1958
- Hovercraft developed
- Scheduled transatlantic passenger jet services begin
- American Express credit cards launched

1958

Thirty-five local men died when a charter plane flying them from the Island to Manchester crashed into the upper slopes of Winter Hill in Lancashire. They were mainly motor traders, garage owners and coach proprietors going on a day trip to see the Exide battery factory. Only four passengers and the aircraft's crew of three survived what was the Island's worst ever air crash.

The flight was meant to be a social day out. It ended in a tragedy which had a profound impact on the life of the Island. Many people lost friends and relatives - and the crash left 27 widows and 33 fatherless children. The aircraft, a Silver City Airways Bristol Wayfarer, was making its final approach into Manchester Airport on a cold February morning when it crashed into the mist-shrouded Winter Hill. Tragically, the aircraft would have missed the 1,500ft summit if it had been 20 feet higher. In the terrible impact the fuselage broke into three pieces, scattering bodies over a wide area in six feet of snow. First Officer William Howarth, although injured, crawled 350 yards to the ITV transmitter station on top of Winter Hill to raise the alarm. Rescue teams set out immediately but had to struggle 2½ miles through the mist and the deep snowdrifts to reach the scene of devastation. There were seven survivors who were stretchered to waiting ambulances from Bolton Royal Infirmary. They had reached the scene with the help of snowploughs. Among the survivors were the three aircrew - Captain Michael C. Cairns, First Officer William Howarth and stewardess Jennifer Curtis. The four passenger survivors were Harold Williamson, James Crosbie, Frederick Kennish and Norman Ennett, brother of Derek Ennett who had been killed in the Ulster Grand Prix two years ago.

His Excellency Sir Ambrose Dundas immediately set up the Winter Hill Disaster Fund to help relieve the plight of widows and children. Donations poured in, and with the help of special events, the sum of £40,000 had been reached by the end of the year. The subsequent air accident report found that the aircraft was homed on the wrong radio beacon when its final flightpath instructions were issued by air traffic controllers at Manchester. The report blames the error on First Officer Howarth, and also Captain Cairns for failing to check the error.

DEATH OF SIR PERCY COWLEY

One of the greatest Manxmen of his time, Deemster Sir Percy Cowley, died suddenly at the age of 71. In January, he was taken ill with heart trouble while on a visit to London with Lady Cowley. Sir Percy had a brilliant career as a judge but his major contribution to the Island's welfare was in his role in the Manx Government. His exceptional foresight and ability helped to steer the Island through many difficult times, including the Second World War.

JOB LOSSES AT JURBY

Despite the growth of light industries, the Island's employment situation is still serious with over a thousand men and women out of work during the past winter. There have been more calls for the Government and Douglas Corporation to provide winter works schemes. Once again many men left for three of the winter months to work in the sugar beet harvest in East Anglia. The situation has been made worse by Jurby's C.O. giving notice to 40 civilian employees that they would be paid off at the end of March. The dismissals followed the decision to reduce the number of officer cadets passing through the station.

TYNWALD SAYS NO TO P.A.Y.E.

Tynwald has decided against the introduction of Pay As You Earn in the Island. This means taxpayers must go on paying their income tax annually. A report said there was no demand for weekly payments and the system would be too costly to administer anyway. The report added that out of the 19,000 employed persons in the Island only 6,000 earned enough money to have to pay tax. And two-thirds of these paid an average of £22-a-year or less.

MORE FREEDOM FROM WHITEHALL

A new milestone in the Island's progress towards more Home Rule has been reached following the Westminster Parliament passing legislation to free the Manx Exchequer

---

THOSE WHO PERISHED
27th February, 1958.

THOMAS ADAMS, garage proprietor, Ramsey.
JOHN C. BRIDSON, garage proprietor, Ballaugh.
NORMAN H. BROWN, motor engineer, Ballacain, Onchan.
WILLIAM (BILLY) CAIN, coach builder, Douglas.
WILLIAM R. CAINE, coach proprietor, Laxey.
THOMAS A. CALLOW, transport manager, Glen Vine.
THOMAS E. CHRISTIAN, director, Salisbury Garage, Douglas.
ERNEST R. CLAGUE, coach proprietor, Douglas.
ROBERT H. CORKILL, garage proprietor, Onchan.
DANIEL C. CORLETT, agricultural agent, The Lhen, Andreas.
WILLIAM N. CORLETT, son of the above.
GEORGE W. CORLETT, mechanic, Ramsey.
LOUIS A. COWIN, maintenance engineer, Tromode.
JOHN D. CRAINE, maintenance engineer, Douglas.
JAMES W. CRELLIN, storekeeper, Salisbury Garage, Douglas.
JOHN J. CRENNELL, of Crennell's Garage, Ramsey.
SGT JACK CRETNEY, Douglas Police.
JOHN W. FARGHER, coach proprietor, Peel.
THOMAS J. GILBERTSON, agricultural engineer, Santon.
ARTHUR L. GLEAVE, mechanic, Ramsey Motors.
BILL and DAVID HARDING, sons of Gilbert Harding, garage
    proprietor, Douglas.
DOUGLAS M. HOWARTH, garage mechanic, Onchan.
LESLIE S. KNEALE, garage proprietor, Port St. Mary.
GEORGE W. S. LACE, mechanic, Peel.
FRANK LEECE, garage proprietor, Douglas.
JAMES H. LINDSAY, garage proprietor, Ramsey.
VICTOR J. McMAHON, garage proprietor, Ballasalla.
WILLIAM R. MOORE, Civil Defence officer.
JOHN B. PARKES, agricultural storeman, Douglas.
EDWARD PARTINGTON, chief mechanic, I.O.M. Water Board.
CHARLES E. STALEY, carpenter and mechanic, Castletown.
WILLIAM A. TONKIN, managing director, Ramsey Motors.
THOMAS A. WATTS, electrical engineer, Foxdale.
THOMAS W. WILLIAMS, mechanic, Douglas.

The *Saint Ronan* was on her way to Runcorn, Cheshire, with a cargo from Sweden. She went on the rocks bow first but re-floated hours later on the rising tide. Since then, Commander Williams has given up his job of looking after the Calf for the National Trust, He is the third warden to leave in seven years and it is doubtful if a replacement can be found.

MAYOR BANNED FROM DRIVING
The Mayor of Douglas, Councillor Jack Killip, was fined £10 and banned from driving for 12 months after being found guilty of being drunk in charge of a car. He was arrested by police officers when he was trying to start the car after leaving a Douglas garage where he had been having a drink with other men after a visit to the Manx Automobile Club. Council-lor Killip said he had had only three gins but the High-Bailiff ruled that he was incapable of driving.

ISLAND IN COMMONWEALTH GAMES
The Manx flag was flown at Cardiff Arms Park when the Duke of Edinburgh opened the British Empire and Commonwealth Games in July. It was the first time the Island had taken part, and it was represented by a team of ten, six of them being cyclists. Hero of the team was Stuart Slack who won bronze for third place in the 120 miles cycling road race. Thirty-seven countries took part and the Island was one of 23 which won medals.

AUSTRALIAN RIDER KILLED
Australian T.T. rider Keith Campbell, who was married to the former Geraldine Reid, daughter of one of the best-known figures in motorcycle racing in the Island, the Reverend Bertie Reid, died in a race crash in France. His body was flown to the Isle of Man for burial at Douglas Borough Cemetery. He and Geraldine met in 1951 - at the Douglas wedding of her sister Pat to Geoff Duke. Mr and Mrs Duke this year bought the Arragon Hotel in Santon.

UPROAR OVER M.E.R. FUTURE
When M.E.R. chairman, Sir Ralph Stevenson presented his estimates in April for the coming year, he estimated that £45,000 would be required to cover renewal and operating costs, instead of the agreed £25,000. This resulted in a storm of protest and the Keys narrowly agreed that the railway should continue in business, but only as a scenic railway with no early or late cars, and a complete shut-down during the winter months. Renewal of the Douglas-Laxey track would continue with the aid of a loan of £20,000 raised by 5% guaranteed stock. Further sums could be raised in the future.

When the limited summer

A smiling Stuart Slack proudly displays the bronze medal he won in the 120 mile cycle race at Cardiff during the British Empire and Commonwealth Games. It is the first time the Island has competed in the Games.

from Whitehall control. However, it has its limitations. The Common Purse, under which the Island must keep its Customs duties in line with the U.K.'s, remains in operation. Also, the Lieutenant Governor continues in his dominant role as Manx Chancellor of the Exchequer.

GLASGOW STEAMER AGROUND
A Glasgow coastal steamer on her maiden voyage went aground on the Calf of Man in the early hours of the morning and, with her radio out of action, two crewmen had to scale 300 foot cliffs in mist and darkness to raise the alarm with Calf warden Commander Frank Williams.

(Opposite page) The Scottish coaster 'Saint Ronan' which went aground on the Calf of Man during her maiden voyage. Standing by is Port Erin lifeboat 'Matthew Simpson'. (Frank Cowin Library)

service began in June there was public uproar whereupon all members of the board, except Mr T. W. Kneale, resigned. A new board was formed with Mr H. H. Radcliffe, M.H.K., appointed chairman. They set out to manage the railway within the subsidy of £25,000 while maintaining a normal summer and winter time-table. The Snaefell Summit hotel was renovated and did good business in catering and the selling of postcards and souvenirs. The Bungalow hotel was demolished at the beginning of the year and replaced by a public shelter and conveniences.

CREMATORIUM FOR ISLAND

Cremation is coming to the Island for the first time. Douglas Corporation is to convert the existing chapel in the Borough Cemetery at a cost of an estimated £20,000. Councillors agreed to do this after Government agreed to fund the cost in order to meet a national need. The Corporation will operate and maintain the building which should be ready in 1961. Since the last war there have been increasing calls for cremation as an alternative to burial. Those who wish to cremate their dead are having to ship bodies to England. Last year there were 35 off-Island funerals.

FIRST MANX STAMPS

The Isle of Man has got its first postage stamp. It is deep lilac, has a face value of 3d and features a portrait of the Queen encompassed by a Celtic ring chain pattern. In common with U.K. practice, it does not refer to its country of origin but it does carry the distinctive Three Legs of Man in the top left hand corner. After being granted the Queen's approval, it was issued by the U.K. Post Office on 18th August as one of a regional set aimed at satisfying nationalist sentiments in the Isle of Man, Northern Ireland, Wales, Jersey and Guernsey.

For the Isle of Man the stamp is the result of more than 20 years of agitation, but campaigners regard it merely as a step towards the Island going postally independent and issuing its own stamps to promote the Island's heritage and scenic attractions. The Post Office has not allowed much flexibility in its ultra-conservative design policies. The incorporation of the Three Legs symbol and the Celtic ring pattern was the inspiration of the chairman of the Isle of Man Arts Society, and former photographic block maker for the *Isle of Man Times*, Victor Kneale, M.H.K.. He produced 18 of his own designs, but as a member of the Advisory Committee he was excluded from being commissioned as a designer. However, his influence was apparent in the designs submitted by three invited artists, the winning contender being 46-year-old John Nicholson, grandson of the famous Manx artist, John Miller Nicholson.

Men of the Forestry Board at work with a caterpillar tractor preparing rough hill ground in the west of the Island for afforestation. It is part of a scheme to plant an additional 2,000 acres of the Island with conifers. (Manx National Heritage)

The new Manx 3d postage stamp.

Exponents of the new Rock 'n' Roll display their skills in the Palace Ballroom. (R and L Kelly Collection)

1958

- Ordination of women begins in several Christian churches
- Death of British suffragette activist Dame Christabel Pankhurst
- Creation of National Aeronautics and Space Administration (NASA) in USA

A first day cover, showing the Island's first regional stamps, which was posted by Mr Victor Kneale, M.H.K. to his daughter. The cover is signed by Lieutenant-Governor Sir Ambrose Flux Dundas, Sir Joseph Qualtrough, S.H.K., the Head Postmaster, members of the Stamp Advisory Committee and stamp designer John Nicholson, who also drew the accompanying sketch of Castle Rushen. (The Mail of Mann - R. Kelly)

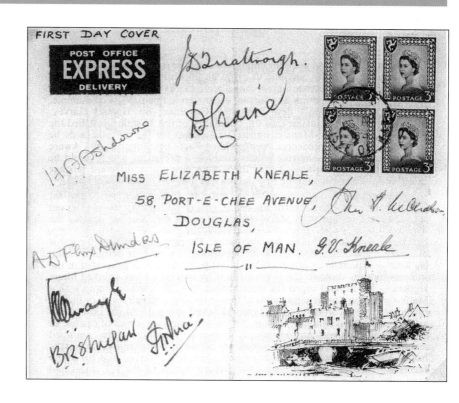

1958 NEWS IN BRIEF

JANUARY

2 - The Forestry Board in their annual report, stated that a five-year tree planting programme in an area of 2,000 acres of rough hill land was being carried out.

4 - Alan Holmes, last year's M.G.P. 'double' winner voted Green Final 'Sportsman of the Year'.

13 - Death of Sir William Percy Cowley, Kt, C.B.E., First Deemster and Clerk of the Rolls. He died suddenly in London at the age of 71.

25 - Sudden thaw of a snowfall caused serious flooding at Port St Mary Gas Works and the Rushen Fire Brigade was called to assist.

30 - Braddan Commissioners gave notice of a petition to Tynwald for leave to borrow £30,300 to enable them to purchase and modernise 42 cottages in Cronkbourne Village.

FEBRUARY

13 - Peel's new Town Hall, made possible by legacies from the Corrin family, was opened by the Lieutenant-Governor.

27 - WINTER HILL AIR DISASTER

MARCH

17 - His Honour Sydney J. Kneale, O.B.E., appointed as First Deemster and Clerk of the Rolls. His place as Second Deemster is taken by Mr Bruce Whyte Macpherson, a practising advocate.

19 - After a two day debate, Tynwald fails to approve the Marine Drive Planning Order. Objecting landlords pleaded it would seriously interfere with their rights.

26 - Well-known boxing enthusiast Alex O'Brien was granted the licence of Mount Murray Hotel by Castletown Licensing Court.

28 - The Ven Archdeacon C. V. Stockwood, M.A., died at his home, St. John's Parsonage, aged 72 years. Born in South Wales, he served at Ramsey and Douglas before becoming Archdeacon some 20 years ago.

APRIL

13 - With the return of badminton champion Donald Jones, the Island team was again triumphant in Division II Northern Zone of the All-England County Championships. After further victories over Northants and Durham, the Manx team reached the Division II finals for the first time. The final, against Surrey, was staged in a packed Villa Marina. The Island put up a great fight but were beaten 9-6.

17 - Ballaugh Curragh Methodist Church celebrated its centenary.

31 - Rev Canon E. H. Stenning, M.B.E., appointed the new Archdeacon of Mann.

MAY

6 - Mrs Ena Gelling won the Cleveland Medal at the 'Guild.'

10 - Integration with Britain was advocated by Liverpool M.P. Mrs Bessie Braddock when she spoke at a Labour meeting in Douglas.

21 - Tynwald agrees to Lieutenant-Governor's proposal to abolish entertainment tax for one year after a debate ' in which tempers were frayed a little.'

29 - A party of 129 homecomers from North America arrived at Douglas on the Cunarder *Carinthia*.

JUNE

3 - Visitors for the T.T. were down some 5,000 on arrivals for the Golden Jubilee. Both Gilera and Moto Guzzi withdrew, leaving John Surtees to win both Junior and Senior races for M.V. Agusta.

17 - Tynwald approved a no-change budget, the Governor saying "it is nothing to be proud of, but in the circumstances something to be thankful for."

JULY

9 - Veteran Douglas artist, 97-year-old Mr T. A. Bridson climbed Snaefell Mountain - his 17th ascent since reaching the age of 80.

22 - Chief Constable Beaty-Pownall rejected Laxey Glen Gardens application for a Bingo Licence for the second time.

31 - Mr H. L. Fletcher, O.B.E., M.A., resigned after 24 year's service as Director of Education. He is to be succeeded by Assistant Director, Mr H. C. Wilkinson, M.A.

AUGUST

3 - Prompt action by residents saved the Laxey Wheel from destruction by fire. An outbreak on the top platform caused damage to floor boards.

7 - A wage increase of 7/4d a week for some 5,000 workers announced by the T.G.W.U.

19 - The B.B.C. completed a series of four television programmes from the Island with 'Wish You Were Here.' The others were Kirk Braddan open-air service, 'Children's Caravan' and 'Six-Five Special.'

OCTOBER

1 - Preliminary 'drags' gave prospect of a good season when the escallop fishing season opened at Port St. Mary.

4 - Triplets were born at the Jane Crookall Maternity Home to Mrs Ruby Garrett, wife of Mr Glen Garrett, Glenfaba Road, Peel.

NOVEMBER

11 - Young Methodists at Crosby Guild Christian Citizenship meeting declared that they were teetotal and anti-gambling in their views, and would ban premium bonds, raffles and football pools.

DECEMBER

5 - Southern Methodists were urged at the annual meeting to vote against Sunday opening of public houses in the all-Island plebiscite recommended by the Licensing Commission.

SIR PERCY COWLEY – ONE OF THE GREATEST MANXMEN

On a bitterly cold January afternoon, St. George's Church, Douglas, was filled to capacity as people from all parts of the Island came to pay their respects to one of the greatest Manxmen of our times - His Honour Sir William Percy Cowley, Commander of the Order of the British Empire, First Deemster and Clerk of the Rolls. The service was conducted by the Vicar of St. George's, the Rev P. C. H. Matthews. The Lord Bishop, Dr. Benjamin Pollard gave the address to a hushed congregation. "A great Manxman had been called to higher service," said the Bishop. "A man who, all his life, typified the best in the Manx race. By his ability and energy and tireless service to his country, he rendered much of extreme value to the Island and its people in so many and diverse ways over a long and difficult period in its history."

As a schoolboy living in the north of the Island, his ambition was to be a farmer, but fortunately fate decreed otherwise, enabling his remarkable talents to probe and serve with distinction a far wider field of insular activity. The youngest son of the late Mr Robert Cowley, M.H.K., and member for Ayre in 1906, he was educated at Ramsey Grammar School and was articled to F. M. LaMothe, who rose to the same office as First Deemster and Clerk of the Rolls. Sir Percy was admitted to the Manx Bar in 1909 and his rise to the pinnacle of his professional and public life was accepted as a matter of course, while his warm and kindly disposition made him an endearing personality in the many social circles in which he moved.

During the First World War he served abroad as a paymaster-lieutenant in the Royal Navy and Sir Percy always had the interests of ex-Servicemen associations close to his heart. For many years he had been a trustee of the Isle of Man County of the British Legion. His many other interests included the Manx Blind Welfare Society, which he initiated. The T.T. Races also became more attractive when he became chairman of the Race Committee. Sir Percy was also a prominent Freemason and Oddfellow throughout his life and held the highest offices; at the age of 28 he became Provincial Grand Master of the Order of Oddfellows and at the time of his death was Provincial Grand Master in the Order of Freemasons. He had also been president of Douglas Rotary Club.

Returning to Ramsey after the war he was a member and chairman of the Town Commissioners. He was for many years chairman of the Ramsey Cottage Hospital, which commanded his whole-hearted attention. He served for a period as High-Bailiff of Ramsey and Peel and was a founder member of Ring, LaMothe, Farrant and Cowley. This led him to leave Ramsey and take up residence at Ballaughton. It was in 1934 that he was appointed Second Deemster in succession to Deemster R. D. Farrant, who was promoted First Deemster following the resignation of Deemster LaMothe on grounds of ill-health. Sir Percy came to the High Court with the reputation of being the ablest pleader at the Manx Bar, and during the years that followed he clearly stamped himself as being one of the Island's great judges.

In the Tynwald Court Deemster Cowley rivalled Attorney-General Ramsey Moore as the leading member of the Legislature - the most frequent speaker and the most influential. He was called upon to be chairman of a series of commissions such as the Public Works Commission and the Workmen's Compensation Commission. He was a member of the bodies investigating National Health and Unemployment Insurance, and was chairman of the Income Tax Commissioners and the Manx Museum and National Trust. Just before the outset of the Second World War 'an Emergency Committee of Tynwald' - in substance a War Cabinet - was formed, with Sir Percy as its chairman. Many hundreds of Orders were issued which guided the Island through the six years of war. It was said that Deemster Cowley was the real 'Governor' and, in recognition of his services was awarded the C.B.E. In 1952 His Honour was knighted in the Queen's first Birthday Honours List.

In the post-war era he devoted much of his attention to helping the tourist industry return to normal by the quick restoration of boarding houses; ex-Servicemen were helped by the provision of temporary housing. In July, 1947, Sir Percy was elevated to the highest role in the Manx Judiciary, as First Deemster and Clerk of the Rolls. One of his greatest achievements was negotiating with the Admiralty for the purchase of Ronaldsway Airport at the bargain price of £200,000. He received a hero's welcome on his return to Tynwald. In more recent times he led the fight for the continuance of the Manx Electric Railway - "It is not a question of whether we can afford it, but whether we can afford to do without it." Perhaps some day his fearless stand will be justified. It is still a contentious matter, and time alone will tell. Certainly, no other member of the Legislature could have carried an unwilling Tynwald to its historic decision. In 1956 the Honorary Freedom of the Borough of Douglas was conferred upon "the greatest living Manxman." As chairman of Tynwald's Works Committee for some 19 years, Douglas Town Council felt particularly indebted to him for his interest and support. The silver casket containing the Freedom scroll is decorated with views of his cherished Ballaughton.

Following the impressive service at St George's, the six-car cortege journeyed to Ramsey. People gathered on street corners in Waterloo Road and about 50 stood in Parliament Square to pay homage to the north's greatest son. The late Deemster was buried in Lezayre Churchyard and a special service of thanksgiving was held at St Paul's Church on the following Sunday.

Sir Percy proclaiming the laws during the Tynwald Ceremony of 1956. (Manx National Heritage)

REBELLION OF HOTELIERS AGAINST REGISTRATION

Some of the 800 hoteliers and boarding house keepers who crowded into the Villa Marina to voice their opposition to the threatened control of their industry.

Staying at the Nursery Hotel, Onchan, the arrival of the Japanese Honda team was not exactly welcome in some quarters. Here Taniguchi rounds Signpost Corner on one of the four Lightweight 125 c.c. machines which all finished and won the team prize for Japan.

A s the Island's visiting industry continues to show signs of failing, the Government and the hotel and boarding house industry clashed violently over the Government's plans to enforce improved standards of holiday accommodation. A meeting of 800 hoteliers at the Villa Marina decided to fight new regulations under which their premises will have to be registered with the Tourist Board and, eventually, graded according to standards. The confrontation ended with the Government deciding to delay the regulations.

Summer visitor arrivals have fallen to below half-a-million for the first time since the end of the Second World War. Last year the figure was 448,000 which was the lowest since 1926 when the holiday industry was hit badly by the General Strike which paralysed Britain. There has been a drop also in arrivals at Ronaldsway for the first time since the war. Three years ago, in 1956, a commission of inquiry set up by the Manx Government made one of its main recommendations an improvement in standards of holiday accommodation in the Island. Registration and grading was seen as the way to achieve this and this year the Tourist Board drafted the necessary regulations. This signalled a massive rebellion by the hoteliers who said they were having Government control forced on them and many of them would be put out of business. They rejected arguments that the move would be to the long-term benefit of the visiting industry and won at least a pause in the Government's campaign. Tynwald decided to shelve the regulations in order to have talks with the hoteliers and hear their objections. Meanwhile, the other recommendations of the Visiting Industry Commission also continue to hang fire. The proposed Continental-style gambling casino was dismissed out of hand immediately and no progress was made towards building a new indoor swimming pool in Douglas. Also, this year, the House of Keys rejected yet another attempt to get the Island's pubs opened on Sundays in summer.

BIRCH TO FIGHT HOOLIGANISM
In a bid to curb the wave of drunken hooliganism that has hit the Island and other resorts over the last two summers the Manx courts are to be given increased powers to use the birch. Judicial corporal punishment was abolished in the U.K. in 1948 but it remained on the Manx Statute Book. Its use was confined to under 15's but a new Bill expected to go through the Legislature next year will increase the age limit to 20 for crimes of violence. The maximum sentence will be 12 strokes of the birch.

SENIOR T.T. CHAOS
When Clerk of the Course Sam Hugget announced that the Senior T.T. had been postponed until Saturday because of the wet conditions and thick mist on the mountain section, it meant that thousands of day-trippers were stranded. The answer was to open the ballrooms of the Palace, Derby Castle and Villa Marina as dormitories. The Mayor of Douglas, Councillor J. D. Lewis, said that anyone stranded could stay at his boarding house free and other boarding house keepers made similar offers. The Steam Packet Company announced that day tickets would be extended another day without extra charge. Weekend schedules were re-organised to transport all the motorcycles and vehicles back to England after Saturday's race.

Fortunately, the weather on Saturday was fine enough for the race to start on time, but strong winds and heavy showers played havoc during the race resulting in many riders coming off. Riding the big M.V. Agusta, John Surtees' fourth lap speed dropped to below 80 m.p.h. but he finished the seven laps a clear winner. He had won the Junior race previously, thus completing the 'double' for the second year running. The Clypse Course saw Willi Schneider (B.M.W.) win the Sidecar event for the third time, and World Champion Tarquino Provini completed a brilliant double for M.V. Agusta in the 250cc and 125cc Lightweight races. In the latter event great interest was shown in the buzzing Honda machines ridden by Taniguchi, G. Suzuki, Tanaka

Peel's new swim pool at the Marine Parade opened this summer and was an immediate success. (Frank Cowin Library)

and J. Suzuki. They were no match for the MVs and East German M.Zs, but the newcomers all finished and won the Manufacturer's team prize.

THE HERRING SEASON

By the end of June fresh herring - scarcer than they had ever been before - were fetching an all-time record price at Peel, at £25 per cran. The minimum price per cran is £3.10s, and during the season rarely exceeds £5. However, the dearth of herring was compensated by a glut at the end of the summer. Herrings were being landed by the million daily, forcing prices down to their lowest level for 30 years. It was the biggest catch in living memory but it was too late for the Manx kipper industry. Most of the herring were exported to Europe and a large quantity went to the fish meal factory at Peel, though it eventually broke down under the strain of processing.

DRIEST AUGUST ON RECORD

Figures issued by Douglas Corporation revealed that August was the driest since records were started in 1868. It was followed by an Indian summer in October, causing the worst water shortage for years. In the south of the Island, where water reserves were down to ten days' duration, 12,000 people had their water rationed. Supplies were cut off from households and businesses during the night hours from 7p.m. to 7a.m. Rationing continued until rain returned in late October.

RECORD CONFERENCE SEASON

Douglas was chosen for some of the major conferences this year. The season began with the annual Easter conference of the National Union of Teachers at the Villa Marina, led by General Secretary Sir Ronald Gould. Over a thousand delegates travelled by sea and air. In September, Britain's most powerful trade union, the Transport and General Workers, held their conference. It was led by its all-powerful General Secretary Frank Cousins, who is in the forefront of the Union's campaign to oust the Conservative Government in Britain. Douglas also hosted the conference of Post Office Workers in May and the annual conference of Jehovah's Witnesses in October.

NEW GOVERNOR ARRIVES

The Island said farewell to Sir Ambrose Dundas and his wife at the beginning of September after their seven years in office. Shortly afterwards the new Lieutenant-Governor was sworn in at Castle Rushen. He is Sir Ronald Garvey, K.C.M.G., K.C.V.O., M.B.E. whose career has been in the Colonial Service, mainly in the Pacific area. He retired as Governor of Fiji in 1958 and, showed interest in the forthcoming vacancy in the Isle of Man. He was delighted, therefore, to receive the invitation from Home Secretary R. A. Butler to serve as Lieutenant-Governor of the Isle of Man. Aged 56, he is known to be a lively character and he brings with him a wealth of

His Honour Sydney J. Kneale, O.B.E., First Deemster, leads the procession into Castle Rushen where the new Lieutenant-Governor, Sir Ronald Garvey, K.C.M.G., K.C.V.O., M.B.E. was sworn in. (Frank Cowin Library)

The memorial to Sir Percy Cowley, founder member of the Manx National Trust, which has been erected overlooking the Sound and the Calf of Man.
(Manx National Heritage)

administrative and diplomatic experience. Residing with him at Government House is his wife, Patricia, and their four children. The two youngest, 13 year-old Lavinia and 12 year-old Julia, are to continue their education at the Buchan School.

PROTOTYPE JET IN SEA

People living in the north of the Island are becoming familiar with jet aircraft producing supersonic booms as aircraft break the sound barrier. There are fears that windows will be smashed but complaints receive polite apologies and assurances of compensation. It can be revealed that the jet aircraft in question are Lightnings being developed by English Electric at Warton. One of these came to grief in October when being tested at over 1,200 m.p.h. and flying at 40,000 ft. The Lightning was seen to plummet into the sea some 10 miles off the Point of Ayre. The test pilot ejected from his aircraft and survived 27 hours in the sea before coming ashore on the Scottish coast.

It is believed that this was the first time a pilot had been saved by an ejector seat at supersonic speed. The seat was designed by the Martin Baker company and is now in production for air forces around the world, including the American Air Force. The Ronaldsway Aircraft Company, often wrongly referred to as 'Martin Baker's,' now employs 160 engineers who produce many of the components of the seats which are assembled by the Martin Baker Aircraft Company at Denham. A chart on the Ronaldsway factory wall records that 330 lives have been saved by the seats to date.

ISLAND FOLLOWS E.F.T.A.

Tynwald has decided that the Isle of Man must abide by the regulations governing the new European Free Trade Area into which Britain has entered with six other countries. The Court was told that if the Manx Government did not fall into line with the Westminster Parliament decisions relating to E.F.T.A., it might be regarded as a foreign country. This would mean having Custom barriers erected against it. Members agreed that they had no option in the matter. Consequently, farmers are worried that free trade could lead to their monopoly marketing operations on the Island being stopped. However, they have been assured that, whilst imports will have to be permitted, they can continue with their own marketing societies.

1959 NEWS IN BRIEF

JANUARY

5 - First sitting of Tynwald's Licensing Commission appointed to investigate the set-up of the Island's drinking laws.

7 - Island in grip of 'Arctic' weather. Many vehicles stranded.

FEBRUARY

3 - Port Erin Commissioners offer Mr D. Ball, of the Rowany Golf Links, 100 four guinea subscriptions to keep the Links open.

3 - Laxey Commissioners announce plans to spend £2,000 on bathing cubicles and hot showers near to the beach.

6 - Little old lady of Baldrine - Miss Amelia Spencer Reddy - shook her neighbours by leaving £550,000 on her death, which was far beyond her apparent means.

17 - Tynwald pass controversial bye-laws which prohibit smoking and the playing of cards in taxis.

24 - Bid to hold a plebiscite in connection with Sunday Opening of public houses failed in the House of Keys by 11 votes to 10.

MARCH

15 - Death of the talented violinist and composer Haydn Wood who was brought up in Douglas where his brother, Harry, was musical director of the Palace and Derby Castle. Haydn became famous through his First World War classic 'Roses of Picardy'.

APRIL

7 - A Bill to permit opening of public houses on Sundays failed, the Speaker using his casting vote after voting had reached a deadlock of 11-all.

7 - Tragic death of 19-year-old student teacher Graham Norris Teare, who was found dying in his bedroom from a stab wound to his heart. He lived in Kensington Road and was a former pupil of King William's College. The inquest recorded an Open Verdict when there was insufficient evidence to show how the wound was inflicted.

14 - For the third successive year, the Island badminton team won the Northern Zone of the Division II County Championships, going on to repeat last year's achievement by reaching the finals. Once again, it was Surrey they met, this time at the Holiday Camp, the visitors winning by the narrowest of margins, 8-7.

24 - Prisoner in the Isle of Man Prison, Patrick Joseph Doherty of Belfast, was found hanging by a tea towel in his cell. He was serving an 11-month sentence for an offence against a woman patient at Ballamona Hospital where he was a nurse.

MAY

1 - Mass Radiography campaign opened as bid to eradicate Tuberculosis from the Island.

6 - Mezzo-soprano Miss Ethel Brookes of Douglas wins Cleveland Medal.

15 - Ramsey's reconstructed north breakwater was officially opened by the Lieutenant-Governor.

22 - Double fatality when two cars collided on the Whitebridge Hill, Onchan.

JUNE

9 - Pools Bill to legalise football pool betting failed to pass its third reading in the House of Keys.

16 - Keys agree to the Governor's Budget which raises level of duty on beer to same level as in England, less £1 per barrel for freightage. Bottled beer increased by 2d.

JULY

15 - Memorial to the late Sir Percy Cowley unveiled at the Sound by His Excellency Sir Ambrose Dundas. The memorial was erected by the Manx Museum and National Trust of which Sir Percy was a prominent member.

21 - Police raid on the Catholic Men's Club whilst a game of 'Housey-Housey' was in progress. The secretary was later fined £20 on a charge of permitting the premises to be used as a Common Gaming House.

SEPTEMBER

13 - St Mary's Roman Catholic Church centenary celebrations attended by the Archbishop of Liverpool, the Most Rev. Dr. John Heenan.

OCTOBER

15 - Former M.G.P. rider Harold Rowell covered over 1,000 miles of the T.T. Course in a non-stop 24-hour ride on a motor scooter.

20 - Seasonal visitor figures total 495,804, an increase of nearly 50,000 on last year's total.

20 - His Excellency the Lieutenant-Governor, Sir Ronald Garvey, was officially welcomed in Tynwald as President of the Court.

27 - Golden Jubilee celebrations of the 1st Douglas Boy Scouts troop.

NOVEMBER

1 - Arbory Parish Church celebrated its bi-centenary.

3 - Protest meeting at St. Jude's Reading Room on the proposed closure of St Jude's School.

19 - Freak tornado hit Belle Abbey Farm, Colby, in the early morning causing a great deal of damage.

DECEMBER

1 - After a demonstration of the Island's unemployed outside Government Office, a deputation of five from the House of Keys was appointed to meet His Excellency to discuss the Island's unemployment problem. Currently 585 men are on the official unemployed list.

THE LEGACY OF SIR AMBROSE FLUX DUNDAS

When Sir Ambrose Dundas was installed in September, 1952 he became the Lieutenant-Governor of an Island whose major concerns were that winter unemployment was likely to be over a thousand, that the visiting industry was seemingly moribund, and that the successive attempts to increase the control of the Island over its own affairs inevitably foundered in bureaucratic obduration. Furthermore, the Island's finances were in a parlous state and draconian cuts in expenditure, or increases in taxation, loomed ominously on the horizon. In this situation the task of making arrangements for the Coronation of Her Majesty Queen Elizabeth II must have come as a welcome relief.

To the Lieutenant-Governor the necessity of increasing revenue seemed of paramount importance and he embarked upon an initiative to attract new industries, both to provide more financial support and to absorb the pool of unemployed which characterised the Island's winters. Sir Ambrose personally made contacts with English industrialists and Tynwald played its part by assisting in the building of factories which are now found in various parts of the Island, one of the more recent ones being the new Aristoc nylon stocking factory in Ramsey. A Manx trademark was introduced and the first annual Manx Fair and Trades Exhibition was held in 1957 at the Palace Ballroom. While he admonished the Manx public for not giving more support to local industries, he would have been pleased to see the demonstration of a new Argosy freighter aircraft being loaded at Ronaldsway with goods produced by old and new Manx industries - aluminium ladders, coaloids, kippers, shaving brushes, model aero engines, beer and Manx tweeds.

Sir Ambrose's attempt to revitalise the visiting industry was the setting up of a Commission of Inquiry with authority to examine all aspects comprehensively. It acted with remarkable speed, no doubt spurred on by the Action Group, made up principally of Douglas businessmen involved in the holiday trade. In less than a year it reported to Tynwald and its recommendations were debated in February, 1956. Unfortunately, the debate with its numerous amendments and cross amendments, produced unparalleled confusion and Tynwald eventually voted only 'that the Report be received,' though the suggestion of a casino was deleted. However, the majority of the recommendations were accepted by the Tourist Board and in turn, with some alteration, by Tynwald itself. Matters were helped by the Redistribution Bill of 1956 which went some way to correct the population imbalance in the Keys' constituencies despite strong opposition from country members. Still unsettled is the thorny question of Sunday opening, vehemently opposed by Temperance organisations and the Church, and the registration of hotels and boarding houses.

More importantly, however, the major concern of these years was to bring to an end the seemingly interminable discussions with the Home Office on the matter of constitutional reform. Inevitably, this resolved itself into a consideration of the financial relations between the Island and the Imperial Government. It became the object of a Tynwald delegation to the Home Office to free the Island from the constraints imposed by the Acts of 1866 and 1867. Differences of opinion between the branches of Tynwald continued to prevent any rapid progress and it wasn't until 1956 that a draft agreement was produced. It was seen as a belated recognition that the Manx people were fit to manage their own affairs. In 1957 the formal agreement was signed, giving Tynwald the right to impose Custom duties and legislate on Customs matters, although Manx duties would be kept at the same level as those in the United Kingdom, thus enabling the Common Purse arrangement to continue. Tynwald agreed to make an annual contribution to the U.K. Exchequer for defence and other services and the way was cleared for Tynwald to decide spending on such matters as police, loans, civil service, harbours etc.

This was an immense advance and it led to a clamour by the elected members of Tynwald to gain complete authority over the government of the Island. Sir Ambrose already had in mind to appoint an independent commission to consider future constitutional developments. A row over the election of Board chairmen, when divisions between the Keys and Legislative Council were starkly revealed, made the matter more urgent resulting in the Keys forming their own Committee. By March, 1958, Sir Ambrose had been in consultation with the Home Office and it was decided to set up a Commission of five under the chairmanship of Lord MacDermott, and including former Home Secretary Chuter Ede. The Commission received the submission from the Keys' Committee seeking control of both the Legislative Council and the Executive Council, and in September held a public enquiry to hear further opinions. The Commission's recommendations were made known in March, and were favourably accepted by the majority of the Keys' members. Henceforth, there should be five members of the Legislative Council to be elected by the Keys, and the Second Deemster should be removed. Further, if a Bill was rejected twice by the Council it couldn't be rejected a third time. Also, a Finance Board with considerable power should be created to act as a Manx cabinet in a way the Executive Council never managed. The essence of the proposals was that they encouraged a marked shifting of power from the Lieutenant-Governor to a small body drawn from, and answerable to Tynwald.

While it remains to be seen when the Commission's recommendations will be implemented, the period of Sir Ambrose's governorship has paved the way for the Island to determine its destiny and a chance of weathering the storms that lie ahead. Besides his political foresight, Sir Ambrose will be remembered for his calmness and congeniality; he and Lady Mary, through their love of walking, became familiar figures in the Manx countryside and Sir Ambrose has taken steps to ensure that public footpaths are signposted and preserved for future generations.

1959
- Death of Buddy Holly in aircraft crash
- Singapore gains independence from Britain
- Fidel Castro becomes President of Cuba
- Mini Minor car, designed by Alec Issigonis, launched in UK

One of the many duties of Sir Ambrose was to greet public figures arriving on the Island. Here he welcomes H.R.H. the Duke of Gloucester at Jurby in 1956. Shaking hands with the Duke is Jurby C.O. Group Captain Burnett, D.S.O., D.F.C., prior to a Passing Out Parade of officer cadets. (Manx National Heritage)

HOUSE OF KEYS STRENGTHENS BIRCHING POWERS

The imposing new Library of the Manx Museum was officially opened in May. Built to the requirements of Museum Director Basil Megaw, the building provides ideal conditions for storing the priceless collection of books and records.
(Manx National Heritage)

The Isle of Man made headlines throughout Britain this year when the House of Keys decided to use judicial corporal punishment - the birch - as a weapon in the fight against the rising tide of holiday hooliganism. The House passed a Bill under which Manx courts will be empowered to impose sentences of up to 12 strokes of the birch on male offenders up to 20 years of age for crimes of violence. Meanwhile, in Britain judicial corporal punishment is outlawed.

When the Westminster Parliament voted in 1948 to abolish the birch, no similar action was taken in the Isle of Man. Birching remained on the Manx Statute Book but it was confined to juvenile offenders. Magistrates had campaigned for birching powers to be extended to the "older and bolder," but no action had been taken. After two summer seasons, however, in which the Island suffered drunken violence involving Teddy Boys, the Manx Government decided to strengthen its birching powers and also use them - to the envy of other British resorts who could take no such action. The move received overwhelming support in the Keys, although one Labour member, Mr Eddie Callister, spoke out against it strongly and controversially. He described the birch as a barbaric bauble for flogging children, a

symbol of sadism and thuggery, a move which showed the Manx people as giving way to primitive instincts of revenge. A birch was actually brought into the House by a police officer to be shown to members, some of whom swished it thoughtfully. The majority view was that the Island could use birching to clamp down on summer violence in a way that other resorts could not. The Bill was passed in February.

Attempts to block the granting of the Royal Assent were made in the House of Commons, but Home Secretary Mr R. A. Butler ruled that the Isle of Man was entitled to act independently of the U.K. This followed the passing of a resolution in March by the House of Keys which expressed its "grave concern" and displeasure over possible interference by the House of Commons. In June the first case of the birch being ordered under the new law involved a London youth charged with demanding money with menaces and possessing offensive weapons. This made more headlines. Now the threat of birching has become a powerful propaganda weapon to deter thuggery.

DEATH OF MR SPEAKER
In January the Island was saddened to learn of the death of another distinguished Manxman, Sir Joseph Qualtrough, C.B.E., J.P., Speaker of the House of Keys. He had not been well for some time and died in Noble's Hospital. Sir Joseph had represented Castletown since 1919 and during his 40 years in the House of Keys had served as Speaker for 22 years. A telegram of condolence was received from Britain's Home Secretary, Mr R. A. Butler. When the Keys met later in the month, Glenfaba member Mr H. K. Corlett, O.B.E., J.P., was unanimously elected as the new Speaker. He is only the sixth Speaker since 1867 when the House of Keys became an elected body.

TWO THEATRES LOST
Two live theatres were lost in February. First came news that the Derby Castle Opera House, built in 1895 and famous for its shows featuring music hall stars such as Marie Lloyd, Vesta Tilley and Florrie Forde, was to be turned into an amusement arcade. The news was followed quickly by the wooden Pavilion Theatre on Onchan Head being totally gutted by a spectacular night time blaze which lit up the surrounding neighbourhood. The Pavilion used to feature summer revues and, in recent times, shows by the hypnotist Josef Karma. He was a great attraction to locals on a Saturday night. At one time the fire threatened to take with it a number of other adjoining buildings in the White City Amusement Park. Firemen took from 10.30p.m. to 3a.m. to prevent sparks engulfing the entire complex.

The amusement park's owner, Barnett Myers, says he wants to rebuild the theatre but the likelihood is

John Surtees powers the mighty 500 c.c. MV Agusta out of Ramsey on his way to winning his sixth T.T., including a 'hat trick' of Senior wins. Surtees has announced that he is changing to Grand Prix car racing next season.

Far left: A view of the Highway and Transport Board's quarry at Poortown which has been equipped with the latest electronically controlled installations. The quarry will play a leading part in modernising the Island's roads.
(Frank Cowin Library)

Left: The bridge which takes the New Road through Laxey is to be widened in order to cope with the increasing amount of traffic.
(R. and L. Kelly Collection)

that the Pavilion has been lost for ever. Like the old Derby Castle, its day has passed. The cinema and television are reducing demand for live theatre. Meanwhile, whilst the authorities have tolerated the old-style wooden buildings which proliferated on the Island at one time, they are not likely to countenance similar replacements. Too many of them have been destroyed by fire.

BACKING FOR RADIO MANX
A Government-sponsored company called Radio Manx has been set up as a possible vehicle for launching commercial radio and television stations on the Isle of Man. Manx-based stations with power to broadcast across the British Isles would bring in substantial revenue to the Manx Exchequer. Investment finance has been offered by a number of backers based in Britain, including the Granada TV group in Manchester.

SUMMER OPENING AGREED
The House of Keys agreed, at long last, to the Sunday opening of public houses in the Island. This is for the first time in a hundred years, but it will be confined to the summer holiday season only. Repeated attempts to get Keys' approval for the move have failed over the last few years. But it has finally won a majority - in spite of a Methodist Church protest petition against it carrying 3,000 signatures.

PARISH WALK REVIVED
One of Britain's most gruelling sports events, the Isle of Man Parish Walk, has been revived - and won by a

Douglas postman who walks 16 miles a day on his rounds. Stan Cleator completed the 81-mile course in just under 20 hours, a record. The Parish Walk, so-called because walkers have to knock on the doors of all the Island's 17 parish churches, was last held in 1924. In the revived event there were 36 starters - including a Rushen young farmer, Noel Cringle - of which only four finished.

REGISTRATION COMPROMISE
Agreement has been reached between the Government and the Island's hotel industry on the registration and grading of hotels and boarding houses. Registration will be compulsory but submission to a grading process will be voluntary. Meanwhile, the Tourist Board has been given a £25,000 budget to advertise the Island for the 1960 season on television for the first time. The slogan is "Come abroad to the Isle of Man."

SURTAX ABOLISHED
The Island is to abolish surtax from April of next year in a bid to attract more new residents - wealthy people seeking to escape high taxation in the U.K. The move was put forward originally two years ago by East Douglas M.H.K. Mr Clifford Irving. Some M.H.K.s thought it was taking an unjustifiable gamble. They feared losing £85,000 a year that surtax has brought into the Manx Exchequer. However, it has been decided that it will actually increase the Island's overall revenue from

Far left: The 50-bed Princess Alexandra wing of Noble's Hospital which was officially opened by the princess in November.

Left: Princess Alexandra being welcomed by the newly-installed Mayor of Douglas, Alderman Tom Quirk and Mr H. C. Kerruish, M.H.K., Chairman of the Health Services Board.
(Manx National Heritage)

The late Sir Joseph Qualtrough, C.B.E., who served as Speaker of the House of Keys for a remarkable 22 years. (Manx National Heritage)

income tax. Sir Ronald Garvey has also announced that the Manx Government is to issue its own bank notes in the future.

CAR FERRY TO BE BUILT

The Steam Packet Company has recognised the increase in the number of holidaymakers' cars being brought to the Island by ordering its first purpose-built car ferry. She will be in service for the 1962 season and will carry 60 to 70 cars. For the first time ever cars will not be deck cargo and will not need craning on and off. The ferry will be the first Steam Packet vessel to have anti-roll stabilisers fitted to help make sea crossings more comfortable.

Meanwhile, Tynwald has decided that the Victoria Pier Arcade at Douglas harbour should be demolished and replaced with a new Terminal Building costing £400,000. This will provide much needed shelter from bad weather for travellers. The need to queue in the open-air to await departures has been a constant source of complaint.

The Chicken Rock Lighthouse which was badly damaged by fire just two days before Christmas.

SCALLOP FISHING BOOST

Manx fishermen have a new and profitable export trade - in scallops. A new company called Seaborn processes the scallops in Peel after which they are sent to Dublin to be quick-frozen and airlifted to the fish markets of Paris where they fetch high prices. Up to now scallop fishing has held little profit with only small quantities being sold to the London market at Billingsgate.

JET CRASHES AT CORNAA

A United States Air Force McDonnell F101 Voodoo jet fighter-bomber crashed on land at the Barony Farm, Maughold on 16th December. It was one of two aircraft taking part in a bombing exercise over the range off Jurby Head when it suffered loss of power. As the jet lost height the pilot ejected from the cockpit and the aircraft went on until crashing near the cliffs, causing a huge crater by the explosion and sending wreckage over a wide area. The pilot landed uninjured in a field at Rhenab, close to Cashtal yn Ard. Within an hour he was picked up by a helicopter and returned to his base in Suffolk. A party from Jurby were soon on the scene to clear up the wreckage.

NEWS FROM R.A.F. JURBY

The 100th Passing Out Parade for officer cadets in the Officer Cadet Training Unit at Jurby took place in December. It brings to 6,600 the number of R.A.F. officers who have been trained at the wartime station since December, 1953. A feature of every parade is the presentation of a Sword of Merit to the best trainee.

LIGHTHOUSE EVACUATED

Just two days before Christmas, the Chicken Rock Lighthouse was badly damaged by fire which swept through the structure. The blaze trapped the three keepers - Jack Ross, Andy Brown and Hugh Anderson - on the top of the lighthouse itself. Port St. Mary lifeboat, *Colby Cubbin No 2*, under Coxswain John Gawne, put to sea at 11.40a.m. in a dramatic rescue bid. With great difficulty, the *Colby Cubbin* managed to rescue one of the keepers, being unable to get closer than 100 yards from the lighthouse. Heavy seas were sweeping over the base of the lighthouse, and the Port Erin lifeboat *Matthew Simpson* stood by as the *Colby Cubbin* took the keeper, who was suffering from shock and exposure, back to Port St. Mary. The fire was raging throughout the lighthouse and there was the constant danger of an explosion from the fuel tanks. The *Colby Cubbin* returned in the afternoon and by 6.15p.m. the weather had moderated sufficiently for her to get alongside the landing jetty. The remaining keepers lowered themselves down the outside by rope and were returned safely to Port St. Mary. They had been stranded for eight hours and were suffering from minor burns and exhaustion.

SIR JOSEPH DAVIDSON QUALTROUGH, C.B.E., S.H.K., J.P.

In his long career of public service, lasting over 40 years, Sir Joseph Qualtrough, who has died, worked indefatigably for the good of the Island. He was a man of vision and ability. Eldest son of Mr James Qualtrough, Castletown timber merchant and once a member of the Keys and Legislative Council, Sir Joseph completed his formal education at King William's College. He had the unique distinction of being Head Boy while being a day-boy at the school. He was an ardent Methodist and became a local preacher at the age of 17. During the First World War he was commissioned in the Royal Army Ordnance Corps and the day after his release, in 1919, he stood successfully for election to the House of Keys. He was elected as member for Castletown on eight successive occasions.

During his time as a member of the House of Keys and its Speaker he did all he could to protect the dignity of the House, its rights and privileges, and to develop its power and authority. Within two months of becoming a member he was in the forefront of the fight for constitutional reform and was a member of the committee sent to the Home Office in 1920. Since 1943 he has been chairman of every committee on constitutional reform culminating in the recent McDermott Report.

His representation of the Island at the Home Office, at Commonwealth and Empire gatherings, Manx associations both home and abroad, and other notable gatherings, have been marked by dignity and distinction. During Sir Joseph's long service he has been in the forefront of the many social changes affecting the Island. He was chairman of the Electricity Board, the Advertising and Publicity Board, now the Tourist Board, the Council of Education and a member of Noble's Hospital Committee. He had been a member in his time, of the War Emergency Committee, the Executive Council, the Health Services Board, the Local Government Board and the Forestry Board. He was also a Trustee of the Manx Museum.

Affectionately known as 'J.D.' he will be remembered also for his wide interests in other walks of life. In his youth he helped to start the present Castletown Football Club and played at fullback for the club. He loved sailing and was Vice-Commodore of the Isle of Man Yacht Club. He also loved golf and was a member of the Castletown club. He contributed also to the musical and cultural life of the Island. For many years he was chairman of the Manx Music and Drama Festival and, being a fluent Manx speaker, was president of the Manx Language Society. He will be remembered always as a man of high principle and deep religious conviction. He was a great supporter of the Temperance movement and fought long and hard against the opening of public houses on the Sabbath.

Sir Joseph received the award of the C.B.E. in 1949 and, on the eve of his 69th birthday in 1954, was knighted by the Queen. The sympathy of all will go to Lady Qualtrough and their family of two daughters and son Ian, who is in the family business in Castletown. A large and representative gathering attended the funeral service in Arbory Street Methodist Chapel of which Sir Joseph had been a life-long member. During the service a moving tribute to his life and work was paid by the Rev Harry Maddrell, Chaplain of the House of Keys. Two lorries laden with floral tributes led the procession to Malew Churchyard for the final rites of one of the greatest Manxmen of our generation.

1960
- First descent to the bottom of the planet's deepest ocean, the Pacific Ocean
- Cyprus becomes an independent republic after 82 years of British rule
- European Free Trade Association (EFTA) comes into existence

1960 NEWS IN BRIEF

FEBRUARY

3 - After public inquiry, Board of Education disapproved proposal by the Education Authority to close St Jude's School.

25 - Plans announced for 63-bedroom extension to Castle Mona Hotel - the first big hotel building project on Douglas promenade for 50 years.

APRIL

29 - Opening of the 35th Annual Rotary Conference at Villa Marina attended by 3,000 delegates.

MAY

4 - Margaret Curphey won the Cleveland Medal at the Manx Music Festival. Earlier in the week she had won the Lieder and Oratorio finals.

11 - Geoff Duke, O.B.E., announced his retirement from motorcycle racing. The six-times T.T. winner last appeared on the T.T. Course last year when he came fourth on a 'lightweight' Norton in the Junior race.

JUNE

2 - The Lieutenant-Governor received a letter of thanks from H.R.H. Princess Margaret for the wedding present of a dinner service and Manx tweed sent to her as gifts from the people of the Isle of Man.

13 - Clypse course abandoned in favour of a return to the T.T. Course for the 125cc, 250cc and sidecar events. These were won, respectively, by Carlo Ubbiali (M.V.), Gary Hocking (M.V.) and Helmut Fath (B.M.W).

15 - Junior T.T. reduced to six laps, won by John Hartle (M.V.) at record speed.

17 - John Surtees makes up for disappointment in the Junior race by winning the six-lap Senior race and completing a hat-trick in this event. He raised the lap record to 104.08 mph. Race was notable for the first 100 mph laps by Nortons, the first by Derek Minter (101.05 mph) and then Mike Hailwood (100.37 m.p.h). Mike finished the race in third place behind John Hartle on the second M.V.

JULY

12 - The first 'Kermesse' continental type round-the-houses cycle race was held in Castletown.

15 - Shareholders of the Isle of Man Dairies Ltd unanimously rejected a take-over bid by the Milk Marketing Association for shares in the company.

SEPTEMBER

7 - Douglas was in the limelight again as the centre for the Trades Union Congress annual conference. Main issue debated was a ban-the-H-bomb policy.

OCTOBER

20 - Margaret Curphey (22) of Douglas climaxed her singing at the Blackpool Music Festival by winning the Rose Bowl, the festival's premier award.

NOVEMBER

9 - Princess Alexandra of Kent opened the £325,000 50-bed extension to Noble's Hospital. The princess was greeted on her arrival at the Town Hall in the morning by the out-going Mayor, Councillor T. D. Lewis. In the afternoon it was the newly-installed Mayor, Alderman Tom Quirk, who met her at Noble's Hospital!

15 - Both the Legislative Council and the House of Keys voted in favour of asking the Lieutenant-Governor to amend the Gaming and Betting Acts to enable a Casino to operate in the Isle of Man.

ROAD IMPROVEMENT PROGRAMME LAUNCHED

A major long-term improvement programme to widen and resurface the Island's roads has been launched. Work has started already on the main Douglas to Peel road. Another project, spectacular in concept, is the building of a new Marine Drive from Douglas Head to Port Soderick. Meanwhile, in anticipation of future improvements to the Douglas-Ramsey coast road, the narrow bridge in the centre of Laxey has been marked for demolition and replacement with a stronger, wider structure. The schemes will help to reduce further the number of men who are unemployed during the winter months; 855 men were in receipt of unemployment benefit last winter.

One of the original cars of the Southern Electric Railway being moved by Highway Board dumper trucks in 1951. The car is now preserved in the Transport Museum at Crich, Derbyshire.

The programme has been launched by the Highway and Transport Board following reorganisation during the past two years of its quarrying and stone-crushing facilities. Until recently stone for Manx roads was quarried at the Dhoon, Glen Duff and Poortown. New plant has been installed at the latter quarry and it will become the principal source of road-building materials in future. Poortown is well equipped to produce the quantities of tarmacadam which will be required, and last year the Board took delivery of a new Blaw Knox machine which can lay long stretches of completely smooth tarmacadam in one single process. The cost of the new programme is high and, for that reason, the Highway Board says it will take many years for the whole Island to benefit.

Construction of the Marine Drive is the biggest single scheme undertaken by the Highway Board since the war. It is likely to take two years to complete and the cost is estimated at £250,000. The former rail track of the Southern Electric Railway was acquired in 1946-47 and declared unsafe in 1949. In 1950 tramway enthusiast Mr F. K. Pearson suggested that one of the cars should be preserved for posterity and the Highway Board's Surveyor-General recommended that this should be done. It was agreed that car No. 1 should be removed from the shed at Little Ness

and Mr C. F. Wolsey, General Manager of Douglas Corporation Transport, loaned his horse tram road trailer which was converted to carry the 61/2 ton car. Two heavy dumper trucks of the Highway Board were used to haul the trailer along the tricky route as far as Keristal. The convoy then made its way slowly to the Board's depot at Quarter Bridge. It was not until 1955 that the car left the Island destined for the British Tramway Museum in London. The museum closed this year and the last car of the Southern Electric Railway was transferred to the Transport Museum at Crich, near Matlock, Derbyshire. The remaining five cars and trailers were scrapped in 1949.

The Marine Drive has been open to pedestrians and in 1956 initial work began on the roadway. The first step was the closure of the rickety bridges at Wallberry and Horse Leap, and the provision of a footpath for pedestrians at Wallberry. Subsequent work concentrated on either side of this problem area. A road between Oakhill and Keristal was built and then extended to Port Soderick with a car park overlooking the bay. At the Douglas end the culvert at Pigeon Stream was filled in and a road built as far as Wallberry. Now, what is being tackled is the trickiest section of all where the old railway had to use bridges. A ledge in the sheer cliff will have to be created to support the road which will require thousands of tons of rock to be removed by controlled explosions. When completed the Marine Drive will give motorists access to some of the most spectacular coastal scenery in the British Isles.

Completion of the Marine Drive may not be an end in itself if television dealer and member of the Tourist Board, Harold Colebourn, new M.H.K. for Castletown, has his way. He wants it to be incorporated into a grander plan which could reverse the decline in tourism. He envisages the creation at Port Soderick, with Tynwald support, of a giant theme park similar to the novel Disneyland in America. A novelty transport system should be established to operate along the Marine Drive, he says, and, to get people across Douglas Harbour, to the starting point, he envisages the erection by Tynwald of a chairlift similar in style to those used in the Alps. The old steam ferries across the harbour have served the purpose well, but something new and dramatic is considered necessary for modern travellers.

Two views of work being undertaken at the approach to Wallberry on the Marine Drive. Here, considerable blasting of the rock face has been necessary to provide a ledge for the new roadway. (R. and L. Kelly Collection)

THE MOTOR COACH TRADE : A REVIEW

The emergence at Easter time of the motor coaches, still referred to as charabancs, is a sure sign that another season is about to begin. The gaily coloured coaches have been a feature of Manx roads since the end of the First World War, operating under such charming names as Happy Days, Happy Wanderer, Highlander, Pride of Mona, Rambler, Sunny Hours, Queen of the Road, The Huntsman, Mona's Queen, Lily of the Valley and Mayflower. Although many have banded together as the Isle of Man Coach Owners Association in an attempt to impose some self-regulation of an industry which employs 400 in the summer, not all have done so. Consequently, they operate in a highly competitive fare-cutting environment. A Government inquiry into the industry's future was started last year. The result is likely to be the creation of an independent body to licence operators and fix their fares but that is not likely to occur for some time.

One of the arguments for an inquiry was the need to update Manx transport law which still refers to conditions which applied when the bulk of public transport relied on horse-power. Some restriction seems necessary also on the routes taken by coaches. Apart from a restriction that coaches wider than eight feet cannot use certain narrow secondary roads, drivers appear to be able to decide for themselves the routes they take. This can result in slow-moving convoys and congestion in certain areas. Already there is talk of popular destinations such as Peel promenade being placed off-limits in order to limit the scale of congestion.

The main concern of the industry's leaders, however, is its future viability. Many operators, with fleets of just two or three coaches, fear that fare-cutting in a limited working season will prevent them building up resources for modernisation. Before the war a new motor coach could be bought for £600. Now the cost is £4,000. Petrol has risen from 1s 2d a gallon to 4s 3d and the price of tyres, from £3.15 shillings to £12. Compared with that, the fare for a Round the Island trip from Douglas has risen from a pre-war five shillings to just seven shillings. In Ramsey, where there is less competition, the fare is 10 shillings - a significant guide to how severe the competition is in Douglas.

In 1957 a Bill to give the Highway and Transport Board powers to control coach operations was introduced into the House of Keys. It had the support of some coach owners who felt that stricter controls, including legally-fixed fares, were needed. It failed, however, because many people in the troubled tourist industry wanted to maintain a competitive low-fare coach industry as part of a low-cost tourist package.

Viability is related also to the number of vehicles licensed here, their type and the threatened use by U.K. tour firms of imported English coaches. Currently, licences for coach operators are issued by local authorities seemingly without restriction. The result is that the carrying capacity of coaches has risen steadily.

Towards the end of the immediate post-war tourist boom there were 164 licensed coaches, 76 of them pre-war models and many of the others second-hand imports. A wide variety of chassis was in use such as those built by BAT, Bedford, Commer, Dodge, Fordson, Guy, Star and Thorneycroft. Coach bodies were provided by a similar variety of builders. Today, the number of coaches in use has dropped to 133, of which 113 are at least ten years old, but numbers alone do not reflect the situation. At one time seating capacity was limited to 29 and some coaches had smaller capacities than that. Permitted seating capacity has risen in stages to 41, with Bedford-Duple coaches by far the most common. Now, with ten 41-seaters already in operation, 44-seaters are planned. Many people believe these are too big for Manx roads, despite long-term removal of awkward bends, widening of corners and resurfacing plans but the commercial pressures are such that they are likely to be introduced. Employing a driver to convey 44 passengers is a more attractive proposition than 26 (or, in rare cases, 22).

An array of motor coaches parked at Creg-ny-Baa after transporting thousands of T.T. race fans to the popular vantage point.

One long-term prognosis, despite future regulation, is a contraction in the number of operators and the emergence of a few large groups. They will have the resources to buy larger modern coaches which, in turn, will mean the ousting of the man who has kept going using an old vehicle and getting his business by offering cheap fares. Another sign of future developments is the basing here for the summer by Sheffield United Tours of one of its own coaches, driven by a local man. Manx coach men tried to stop it. They said they provided excursions for other U.K.-based inclusive tour operators. Sheffield United Tours, however, said its marketing of tours was based around the standard of its own coaches so, if its coach was banned, it would stop bringing tourists here. The Tourist Industry was unlikely to agree to that.

Above left: This Bedford-Duple 26-seater dates from 1938 and is still in service with Collisters of St. George's Street, Douglas, though it is due to be retired next year.

Above right: Most typical of post-war coaches is this 29-seater Bedford-Duple Vista of J. N. Clague of Douglas.

Right: This rare Austin-Plaxton 30-seater belongs to the 'Highlander' fleet which is due to be taken over by J.G. Downward next year.

Right: A list of independent coach operators and fleet details for 1960, compiled by Mr William Lambden of the Omnibus Society. Single-coach operators are not included.

Belmont Motors, Douglas, (The Huntsman) - 2 Bedfords, 1 Commer
E. D. Bryan, Hope Street, Douglas, (Tynwald Motors) - 2 Bedfords
A. and R. Caine, Laxey - 2 Bedfords
E. V. Clague, Esplanade Garage, Douglas - 5 Bedfords, 1 Commer
Harry B. Clague, Derby Square, Douglas - 2 Bedfords, 1 Commer
J. N. Clague, Linden Grove, Douglas - 1 Bedford, 1 Commer
Collister's Garage Ltd, Douglas - 2 Bedfords, 1 Albion
Corkill's Garage Ltd, Onchan - 4 Bedfords
A. R. Corlett, Peel Road, Douglas - 3 Bedfords
H. L. Cregeen, Port Erin - 1 Bedford and 1 Commer
J. R. Crellin, Castletown (Castle Rushen Coaches) - 3 Bedfords
Crennell's Garage Ltd, Ramsey - 3 Bedfords
E. A. Cretney, Hope Street, Douglas (The Burleigh) - 2 Bedfords
M. Duggan,, Port Erin - 1 Bedford and 1 Leyland
Fargher's Coaches, Peel - 3 Bedfords
Gales Western Coaches, Peel - 3 Bedfords
Fred Gash, Douglas (Empress Coaches) - 2 Bedfords
Hamill's Garage, Douglas - 9 Bedfords and 1 AEC
Q. Kneen, Douglas (Excelsior Motors) - 5 Bedfords
T. H. Kneen Ltd (Stanley Motors), - 6 Bedfords, 2 Leyland and 1 Commer

F. H. Magee, Douglas (Lily of the Valley) - 2 Bedfords
Mrs. S. Magee, (Conister Coaches) - 1 Bedford, Austin and Albion
A. McMullin, Douglas, (Queen of the Isle) - 2 Bedfords
J. McMullin and Son, (Mayflower) - 3 Bedfords
Millers Motors, Port St. Mary - 2 Albions and 1 Bedford
T. Moore, Douglas, (Moerzone) - 1 Bedford and 1 Commer
D. A. Price, Ramsey, (Glider Coaches) - 1 AEC, 1 Leyland and 2 Short
Ramsicabs, managed by Crennell's, Ramsey, - 3 Bedfords and 1 Commer
E. Ranson, Onchan, (Happy Ways) - 2 Bedfords and 1 Commer
R. Scott and Sons, Douglas (Scotts Tours) - 6 Bedfords
T. R. Sheard, Douglas, (Pride of Mona) - 2 Austins
W. H. Shimmin and Co., Douglas - 3 Seddons, 1 Bedford, Austin and Albion
W. C. Shimmin, Douglas, (The Silver Star) - 3 Bedfords
R. Stowell, Onchan, (Happy Go Lucky) - 2 Bedfords
J. Tasker, Douglas, (Waverley) - 3 Bedfords
J. W. A. Wightman, Onchan, (Sunny Hours) - 2 Bedfords
G. W. Wharton, Douglas, (Highlander) - 3 Albions, 2 Bedfords and 1 Austin, to be taken over by J. G. Downward.

CENSUS SHOWS ALARMING DROP IN POPULATION

April's census has revealed that in the last ten years the number of people domiciled on the Island has fallen from 54,499 to 48,150, a drop of 7,103, over 11%. Nearly all districts on the Island show a decrease in population with the total being the lowest recorded since 1841. Douglas now has 1,500 fewer people compared with ten years ago, falling below 20,000; Ramsey has 900 fewer, Peel, 150 fewer, Castletown, 200 fewer, Port Erin, 200 fewer, Port St. Mary, 140 fewer and Laxey, 200 fewer. The recent count reveals that there are 22,059 males compared with 26,091 females. It appears also that the proportion of older people in the population is now greater than ten years ago, and that the number of young people is considerably reduced.

Whilst alarming, the Census only confirms what has been expected, judging by the number of young people leaving the Island, and by the number of families who have either settled in Britain or emigrated to Commonwealth countries, such as Australia and New Zealand. For the majority the chronic winter unemployment situation has forced them to leave. Winter work schemes provided by the Government only go part way in reducing the dole queues. His Excellency Sir Ronald Garvey, in his budget speech to Tynwald, suggested that the Island would benefit from a five year development plan costing not less than £5,000,000. Traditional industries and new ones are offering job opportunities to the young, but many more are needed. With this in mind, an Industrial Officer has been appointed to attract new industries. The Government has also embraced a policy of attracting new residents to the Island, especially those from abroad who are seeking a place of retirement. This has caused some controversy in view of the imbalance which exists already between young and old. On the other hand, it is claimed the Island could accommodate 75,000 people without being overcrowded.

SIX DIE IN ANSON CRASH

In a tragic accident, reminiscent of wartime days, all six on board an Avro Anson C19 lost their lives when the aircraft crashed into the cloud-covered upper slopes of North Barrule. The Anson set off from its base in Berkshire on the morning of 20th February, destined for R.A.F. Jurby. Contact was made with Jurby when the aircraft was approaching Maughold Head and soon afterwards was heard passing over Hibernia. Then there was silence. One of the officers killed was Ft/Lt Humphrey David Furness whose parents live at Maughold.

I.O.M. BANK TAKE-OVER

The Isle of Man Bank, for the last 100 years an independent financial institution and a commercial symbol of Manx independence, has been taken over by one of Britain's Big Five clearing banks, the National Provincial. The offer of £1,320,000 for its shares was accepted by more than 90% of the shareholders in March. This followed the decision by Tynwald not to rescue the bank by nationalising it, after the Bank of England advised against such a move.

CASINO AND CRIME WARNING

Predictions by Archdeacon Stenning that Douglas will attract thugs, crooks and prostitutes if a casino is opened here were condemned in May as scaremongering. These sort of fears, however, along with predictions of suicides by gamblers who lose heavily and that the Island risks placing its economy in the hands of vested interests, gambling sharks and financiers, has led to a long delay in launching a casino. Now a final verdict will not be known until after the General Election for the House of Keys early next year.

The Island is divided between town and country as indicated by an *Isle of Man Examiner* survey. This shows that 88.5% of people in country districts are opposed to a casino but 63% of people in the towns, which depend on tourism, are in favour.

In May the Diocesan Conference denounced the casino plan after the Archdeacon said it would be a sin against God and the Church. The trouble it would cause would result in a doubling of the Manx police force. Churchmen circulated M.H.K.s with warnings about the moral issues. Even so, at the end of one of the latest sittings of the House - at 8.25 p.m. - members voted 15-9 in favour of the casino legislation. They may have been influenced by a painting produced on behalf of an anonymous group which

THE 1961 CENSUS		
Details of the recent Census of the resident population are given below, together with a percentage difference compared with the 1951 Census.		
TOWNS:		
DOUGLAS	18,837	(-7.2%)
RAMSEY	3,764	(-18.3%)
PEEL	2,487	(-3.6%)
CASTLETOWN	1,549	(-11.4%)
Port Erin	1,239	(-13.7%)
Port St. Mary	1,260	(-9.9%)
Laxey	1,125	(-16.1%)
Onchan	3,282	(-2.3%)
Michael	310	(-16.2%)
Andreas Parish	789	(-28.0%)
Arbory	711	(-9.0%)
Ballaugh	542	(-0.4%)
Braddan	1,834	(-13.5%)
Bride	345	(-14.6%)
German	721	(-33.3%)
Jurby (with R.A.F.)	796	
Lezayre	1,218	(-9.7%)
Lonan	902	(-15.5%)
Malew	1,949	(-16.0%)
Marown	863	(-6.1%)
Maughold	774	(-1.7%)
Michael	349	(-17.5%)
Onchan	339	(-80.0%)
Patrick	979	(-16.0%)
Rushen	825	(+1.2%)
Santon	360	(-5.5%)

TOTAL	48,150	(-11.6%)

This removal van was symbolic of the 1950s which saw many families leave the Island with their possessions as they opted to find work and a new life elsewhere.
(R. & L. Kelly Collection)

wishes to run a casino. This showed a 400 bedroomed hotel and casino at Pooilvaish.

Subsequently, a report in June by a five-man Keys committee led by Mr. Charles Kerruish recommended the licensing of two gaming establishments, one with an hotel and one without. The Legislative Council, however, succumbed in July to delaying tactics by the opposition. It deferred its consideration of the Bill for six months, until after the General Election for the Keys. Evidently Lieutenant-Governor Sir Ronald Garvey was disappointed. As a supporter of the casino, he had hoped to give his casting vote in the interests of the "good government" of the Island.

WOMEN M.L.C.S?

For the first time ever women are to be eligible for membership of the Legislative Council. Until now the Council has been a "men only" chamber. The new assertiveness for female equality, particularly identifiable since the last war, and the constant quest for reform of the Manx constitution, has led to a new law which will permit the House of Keys to elect a woman to the Council. Now all the Keys need is an abundance of women within its membership so it can choose one!

BAN ON ICE CREAM IMPORTS

In an act condemned as unfair discrimination and blatant protectionism, Tynwald approved a ban in June on the importation of ice cream. It means that local consumers will be denied the non-dairy products being launched nationally by firms such as Walls.

Recently it became known that Walls planned to establish a Manx distribution depot. Manx dairy farmers were worried about this as last year local ice cream manufacturers bought 122,000 gallons of Manx milk. Tynwald, of course, has a vested interest in protecting this market. After encouraging producers in 1956 to start marketing their own product, it introduced a guaranteed price the following year. A collapse in sales now, therefore, would cost Tynwald dearly.

Significantly, the ban came just six months after local producers, through their Milk Marketing Association, bought Isle of Man Dairies Ltd., the biggest Manx retail dairy, based in Spring Gardens, Douglas. Producers are anxious to develop added-value products for their surplus milk. Hence a marketing campaign for

fresh cream which has seen a 50% rise in sales this year as people have switched from imported tinned table creams. The production of Manx cheese from surplus milk since April has been extremely profitable too. Until now the milk was supplied to a private cheese manufacturer but the price received for it was poor. The private operator is expected to move to Ireland.

CURB ON SONIC BOOMS

An increasing number of complaints about the number of sonic booms being caused by jet fighters over the Irish Sea has led to an Air Ministry promise to Tynwald that they will be curbed. The Ministry says that a "new track" is planned for the test flights. It is believed that the booms are being caused by the new Lightning jet fighters being built for the R.A.F. at Warton, Lancashire. Fears that the booms could break windows have led to assurances that compensation will be paid for any proven damage.

PEEL'S VIKING FESTIVAL

Peel attracted the biggest crowds ever seen in the Western City for the staging of a spectacular pre-Tynwald pageant, which formed the centrepiece of the Viking Festival. Thousands lined the promenade and beach area for the occasion which was televised. Strong winds had hampered the preparations but Tuesday saw everything go without a hitch. The pipe band of the Irish Guards played as Celtic villagers, dressed in appropriate costume, went about their normal activities such as weaving, grinding corn and roasting sheep and pigs. Then the Vikings came! Smoke was seen rising from St. Patrick's Isle to signify its capture. Then four Viking longships appeared crossing Peel Bay and heading for the beach. The Celtic women and children rushed into hiding as the men took up positions in a stockade to defend their village. The Vikings swarmed up the beach armed with swords and axes and overcame the Celts after a fierce hand-to-hand battle. The Vikings carried off women and children, together with bags of loot. A group of Valkyries, girls dressed in white, then appeared and gathered round one of the ship leaders who had been killed in the battle. As the victory feasting and festivities got under way, there was a sword dance and dancing by a troop of children from Trondheim. Seagulls swooped round the area while the Vikings elected King Orry as their king. One of his first duties was to order the

Right: The prelude to the Viking Pageant sees the marauders landing on Peel beach intent on attacking the Celtic villagers. (Manx National Heritage)

Far right: Just part of the huge crowd which witnessed the enactment of the dramatic and highly successful Pageant. (Manx National Heritage)

1961
• Death of Carl Gustav Jung the Swiss analytical psychologist
• East Germany closes border with West Berlin; construction begins on the Berlin wall

burial of the dead warrior. Joined by a volunteer maiden he was set adrift in a ship which was duly set on fire by flaming arrows from the Viking archers. In the final episode King Orry declared he wanted Celt and Viking to live together peacefully and unite to form the Manx nation. The part of King Orry was played by Morris Kewley and the narrator was Wing Commander Roy MacDonald. All the hundreds who took part are to be congratulated on producing such a successful pageant which obviously has tremendous possibilities. Next year the Peel Vikings plan a raid on Kilkeel, Northern Ireland. Three ships are to be sent and captured Irish maidens will be offered free holidays in the Isle of Man.

THE NEW MANX NOTES

The Manx Government began issuing its own paper currency as from July 6th. Half a million ten shilling, £1 and £5 notes went into circulation despite predictions by critics, including former bank manager Edward Callister, M.H.K., that they would be revealed as a frivolous waste of money. The Manx Treasury, however, reckons that the currency will be an important interest-free loan for the Government. The issue of the notes ended a tradition whereby local branches of major banks were permitted to issue their own notes. Licences for the old notes were revoked as from July 31st. Most of the notes were withdrawn from circulation and destroyed but an estimated five to seven per cent were retained by collectors.

The issue of the new notes is being managed on behalf of the Government by the Isle of Man Bank. Unlike the notes issued by the commercial banks, the notes are undated. They carry also only a facsimile signature of the Lieutenant-Governor. This reflects a gradual conversion by banks to this practice.

The work-load involved in signing notes prior to their issue meant that there was a tendency by banks to keep dirty, creased or damaged notes in circulation. Now the hope is that Manx notes will always be pristine.

BORDER TV RECEPTION

Transmissions from the new ITV station opened by Border TV on 1st September have been welcomed in many quarters of the Island. Signals from the 1,000 feet high transmitter at Calbeck mean that improved reception can be enjoyed in many parts of the Island. Some homes, for the first time, can now receive such popular programmes as 'Sunday Night at the Palladium', 'Bootsie and Snudge', 'Emergency Ward 10', 'Wagon Train' and 'Coronation Street'. Border also intends to include the Island in news broadcasts.

FAREWELL TO FLEETWOOD

When the *Mona's Queen* took the last sailing from Fleetwood at the end of the season she signalled the end of the Steam Packet's association with the port which goes back to 1876. Since then millions of holidaymakers from Lancashire and Yorkshire towns have used the port. It was a favourite with day trippers.

The withdrawal from Fleetwood is the result of the British Transport Commission declaring that the berthage is in a bad state, and beyond repair. The Steam Packet's offer to pay substantially increased passenger tax at the port was rejected. Steam Packet officials have said that extra sailings are planned for next season from the traditional port of Liverpool. Arrival figures for this season show that over 500,000 visitors came to the Island this year, the best since 1957. Ronaldsway Airport had another record season, helped by B.E.A. employing Viscount aircraft on its Manx routes. However, the loss of Fleetwood is serious; how serious remains to be seen.

CASTLETOWN HIT BY STORMS

Unusually high seas and fierce storms tore away sections of Castletown's promenade at the end of October. In the House of Keys it was declared a 'national disaster' and emergency action was taken. Workers toiled for 48 hours to fill gaping gaps in the promenade wall with rubble and concrete. Houses on the promenade were evacuated as a complete collapse was feared, but the temporary repairs held.

NO NOVEMBER ELECTION

The life of the House of Keys has been extended for three months. This means the General Election will not take place until January. The main reason for this is to complete urgent legislation resulting from the recommendations of the MacDermott Commission. New Standing Orders, over 200 of them, have to be approved to allow for the administration and composition of the new Legislature.

Below: An example of one of the notes issued by commercial banks present on the Island, in this case a £1 note issued by the Isle of Man Bank Ltd. Issued with Tynwald approval, it was the custom for bank officials to sign each note individually.
(R. & L. Kelly Collection)

Bottom: An example of one of the new Government banknotes which will replace all others issued on the Island. They bear a facsimile signature of the Lieutenant-Governor.
(Frank Cowin Library)

Demolition of the Victoria Pier Arcade began in September to make way for the new Sea Terminal Building.
(Manx National Heritage)

GOING FOR A SONG

Water colours painted by the most celebrated of all Manx artists, Archibald Knox, are being sold off to the public by the Manx Museum - at £10 a time. Knox, who died 28 years ago, refused to sell his paintings in his lifetime. However, this year his family decided to give more than 100 of them to the museum to help set up an endowment fund. The paintings are being sold to all-comers and many people, recognising that Knox's work will appreciate in value in the future, are taking up the bargain offer.

1961 NEWS IN BRIEF

JANUARY

19 - Lieutenant-Governor, Sir Ronald Garvey, opened a Trades Fair and Exhibition at the Palace. He flew from Government House to the Palace grounds in an Army Air Corps' helicopter.

FEBRUARY

3 - After a public inquiry, Board of Education disapproved proposal by the Education Authority to close St Jude's School.

14 - Radio Manx Ltd applied to the Postmaster-General for a sound radio broadcasting licence.

MARCH

14 - A Bill, which aimed to legalise cash betting on horse racing in the Isle of Man, was defeated on its third reading in the House of Keys.

APRIL

19 - Four men and a woman from a Dutch ship, which sank after hitting rocks off the Calf of Man, were picked up from a rubber dinghy.

MAY

27 - 300 young enthusiasts took part in the 80 mile relay walking race around the Island's parishes, 65 teams from 35 organisations took part.

JUNE

7 - Mike Hailwood became the first rider ever to win three T.T. races in a week. Riding a Norton in the Senior, he completed the six laps at over 100 m.p.h. Favourite, Gary Hocking, on the M.V. Agusta, retired when leading. Riding for Honda, Hailwood had previously won the Lightweight 125 c.c. and 250 c.c. races, both at record race and lap speeds.

AUGUST

6 - The Women's World Track and Road Cycling championships opened at Onchan Stadium.

22 - A team of three divers, two local and one from Cumberland, undertook a hunt for a mermaid for which the Tourist Board offered a £20,000 prize during Angling Week. Messrs Irving and Colebourn of the Board put their motorboats at the divers' disposal. The search was made off the south of the Island, but the mermaid remained elusive!

SEPTEMBER

1 - Mr Frank Luckman, B.Sc., took over from Mr J. D. Boulton as headmaster of the Douglas High School for Boys.

20 - Demolition of the Victoria Pier Arcade began, and so did the erection of the new Sea Terminal.

21 - In celebrating his Silver Jubilee as Bishop, Dr. Benjamin Pollard announced that he planned to launch a world-wide appeal to restore St. German's Cathedral on St. Patrick's Isle.

22 - High-Bailiff Howard Lay collapsed and died as he presided over a court in Douglas. He was 62 and had been High-Bailiff since 1947. It has since been announced that he is to be succeeded by Mr Robert Kinley Eason, LL.B.

OCTOBER

1 - Stanley Cleator, the Onchan postman, won the first ever end-to-end walk from the Point of Ayre to the Sound in 7 hrs 19 mins and 18 secs.

11 - Douglas Corporation decided that all taxis operating in the town should have meters fitted.

17 - Tynwald passed resolution requesting the Queen to revoke the Order under the 1954 Television Act to enable an application to be made to operate a commercial television station.

NOVEMBER

20 - The Island's first Crematorium and Garden of Remembrance, in the Douglas Borough Cemetery, was dedicated by the Lord Bishop.

DECEMBER

8 - Radio Manx Ltd., a company formed to promote Island radio and television broadcasting, held its first meeting in London.

GOVERNOR PLUMPS FOR NEW RESIDENTS POLICY

In his first budget speech given to Tynwald last year the Lieutenant-Governor listed the attracting of new permanent residents to the Island as his number one priority. Development of the Tourist Industry and Light Industry came second and third respectively. His Excellency saw an influx of new residents as a means of boosting the Island's economy, while revitalising the building trades and providing increased employment in the service industries. The policy now has the backing of Government. Sir Ronald has in mind people like himself who have been in service abroad, perhaps as Civil Servants or Army Officers, and who are contemplating retirement. Sir Ronald has written the introduction to the attractive brochure, published by the Permanent Residents Committee of the Tourist Board, which details the attractions the Island has to offer and are already being enjoyed by those who have retired here.

TAXATION: To those who will retire on reduced incomes there is the attraction of significantly lower direct taxation than in the U.K. Here the standard rate of income tax is 4s. 6d. in the pound and there are liberal allowances covering earned income relief, marriage and single allowances, children's allowance and housekeeper and dependent relative allowances. Surtax has been abolished and the Manx Government does not impose death duties. The principal banks and insurance companies are well represented on the Island.

COST OF LIVING: Generally, cost of food and household goods compare with coastal regions of the United Kingdom. Tobacco and alcoholic drinks cost about the same as in the U.K. but petrol costs less. Local rates vary from 6s to 14s in the £. Agricultural land and buildings are exempt from rates.

COMMUNICATIONS: Probably no place on earth has benefited more from the introduction of air travel. Once, the only link with the mainland was by sea, but today the Island is linked by scheduled services to most parts of the British Isles. It is possible to have afternoon tea in the Island and dinner in London at any time of the year! There is, therefore, no feeling of being cut off from the world, or confined.

SOCIAL WELFARE: The National Insurance and pensions schemes are in the same form as in the U.K., and there is reciprocity between the two countries. The Health Service is on the United Kingdom pattern and the hospitals are included. Excellent medical, dental and ophthalmic treatment is available.

HOUSING: No problem exists, and there are numbers of properties available both to rent and to buy. The average three-bedroomed, semi-detached post-war house can be rented at from £100 to £200 a year. These can be purchased from £2,500 to £3,500 while detached residences of normal size begin at £3,000. Those who propose to build their own houses or bungalows will find no difficulty. The call for the development of light industries since the war has ensured that every town and village on the Island now has piped water, electricity and sanitation. Many also have gas.

TRANSPORT: Many Manx residents own cars, but there is an extensive public transport system which has been built up over the years for the seasonal visitor. This includes 47 miles of steam and electric railway and frequent bus services to all outlying districts. For those with their own cars, licences are low and, as already mentioned, petrol is cheaper than in the U.K. The Island has a network of 500 miles of roads which are rarely crowded and provide enjoyable motoring.

SCHOOLS: The Isle of Man operates a primary and comprehensive multi-lateral secondary education system through a Board of Education and the Education Authority. An education rate is levied throughout the Island. In addition, there are several private schools, principal of which are King William's College (boys) and the Buchan School for Girls. Both are found at Castletown and they cater for boarders and day pupils.

CHURCHES: The Diocese of Sodor and Man, headed by the Lord Bishop, is part of the Province of York of the Church of England. Each of the 17 ancient ecclesiastical parishes has a church and there are also town parishes. There are eight Roman Catholic Churches, and an Isle of Man Methodist District with five Circuits. There are also Presbyterian, Congregational, Baptist and Christian Scientist establishments.

ENTERTAINMENT: The Island is served by its own B.B.C., V.H.F. and T.V. transmitters, while I.T.V. signals are received direct from the Granada, Ulster and Border stations. British national newspapers are available on the morning of publication and there are six local newspapers. Cinemas are found throughout the Island and in the summer season there are magnificent ballrooms and theatres open. There are also several strongly-supported amateur operatic and drama companies which stage productions of a high standard. Choral societies and male voice choirs, among the most famous in Britain, are an all-year round activity.

RECREATION: The Island has an abundance of clubs and societies which cater for all interests such as golf, tennis, bowling, riding, sailing, fishing, old-time dancing and photography, to name but a few. Every district has its Women's Institute and there are busy Townswomen's Guilds. The social programme that goes with them is extensive and enjoyable. It can be said also that new members will receive a typically warm Manx welcome.

An example of one of the modern bungalows now being built, which will prove ideal for new residents who decide to retire to the Island.

GENERAL ELECTION GIVES NEW LOOK TO TYNWALD

The House of Keys General Election, delayed from last November, was completed on 3rd February and resulted in eight members (a third of the Keys) being elected for the first time. Sixteen former members were elected, while six were not returned. The eight new members elected are: Messrs. G.H.V. Kneale (West Douglas), Sir Henry Sugden (Ramsey), H.D.C. Macleod (Glenfaba), E.R. Moore (Garff), R.E.S. Kerruish (Ayre), J.R. Creer (Middle), F. Coupe (East Douglas) and C. Harcourt Matthews, who came in third place in the Rushen election. Labour and their left wing independents have secured their biggest ever representation in the Keys. They hold ten of the 24 seats, compared with three in the former House.

At the first sitting of the Keys, it was necessary to elect a new Speaker of the House after Mr. H. K. Corlett, who had been Speaker for the past two years, had failed to be returned in Glenfaba. As anticipated, his successor was likely to be chosen from senior members who had been in office since 1946 - Messrs. John Bolton (West Douglas), Charles Kerruish (Garff), Ffinlo Corkhill (Glenfaba), Spencer Kelly (Ramsey). Next in seniority is Mr Jack Nivison (Middle) who was returned in 1948. In the event, it was Mr Charles Kerruish who secured the confidence of the House. Aged 45, he is the youngest member ever to hold the Speakership.

Mr J. C. Nivison said farewell to the Keys when he was elected to the Legislative Council to fill the extra seat created by the constitutional reform legislation. This was followed by the Lieutenant-Governor appointing Mr J. B. Bolton as a member of the Council in place of Mr J. F. Crellin who had resigned earlier. He had been a member of the Legislature since 1924. These elevations caused two by-elections which saw the return of two brothers who had both lost their seats in the General Election. Mr J. M. Cain was returned in West Douglas and Mr H. S. Cain in Middle. Thus was completed the composition of the new Tynwald which is now in a stronger position to legislate for the Island's future.

NEW BOARDS OF TYNWALD
As the new House of Keys settled down to business the clash between Labour members and their left wing adherents on the one hand, and the independents on the other hand, soon became evident. This became evident from the start when the chairmanships of the several Boards were discussed. The most important was the new three-member Finance Board, charged with advising the Lieut-Governor on all finance matters. Its power is such that it now occupies a dominant role in Manx politics, rivalling the existing Executive Council. The eventual choice of Mr R. C. Stephen as Finance Board chairman reflects the maturity of the new Chamber. Mr. Stephen, a journalist by profession, is one of those dedicated politicians who has gained the respect of his colleagues. For many years he was the assistant editor of the Isle of

Man Examiner, a post he relinquished in 1950 in order to devote more time to politics. In 1956, standing as a Labour candidate, he was elected to represent South Douglas, and continues to do so. Another post to be filled for the first time is the chairmanship of the Commission responsible for the appointment of civil servants, previously the prerogative of the Lieut-Governor. Recent developments have also brought about the creation of a Police Board to administer the constabulary, though here the Lieut-Governor retains overall control on policy. These are heady times in Manx politics. The next five years will be full of interest as the new McDermott constitutional arrangements are put into practice.

BIDS FOR CASINO LICENCE
Applications by prospective concessionaires to run the new Isle of Man Casino are being considered by Tynwald's Gaming Board of Control. There are three - one from a Belgian group, another from the London gaming group of Crockfords and a third from an American syndicate which has its origins in Las Vegas. The final applications were lodged by mid-July. Since then it is believed the Board has been to Las Vegas.

Meanwhile, a School for Croupiers has been established on the ground floor of 57, Derby Square, Douglas. Romanian, Constantine Anghal (57), who has equipped it, says prospective croupiers must be under 30.

The General Election in February settled the casino issue. It was calculated that 30,000 votes were cast for candidates who supported the casino and just 19,000 against. Confronted by a new House of Keys with a membership overwhelmingly in favour of the casino, the Legislative Council passed the enabling legislation in late March, albeit with a ban on Sunday gaming. Although the legislation had been passed by the Keys before the General Election, it was ruled that the legislative process had to be started again by the new House. This time, however, the House hurried the process along. Whilst casino supporters disliked the Sunday gaming ban, they were unprepared to delay matters by arguing with the Legislative Council. In April, therefore, the Keys passed the Bill by 16 votes to 8.

Speed was considered essential because the opening of gaming clubs in the U.K. threatened to destroy the novelty value of a Manx casino. Because of this, Labour M.H.K. Edward Callister offered odds of 100-1 earlier this year on a casino ever being built. In fact, the situation is not that hopeless but U.K. developments could mean a contraction in the scale of what is launched here.

APPEAL FOR CATHEDRAL RESTORATION
St. German's Cathedral on St. Patrick's Isle, - the oldest cathedral foundation in the British Isles, dating from the 5th century, is to be restored, rebuilt, furnished for public worship and rehallowed. This is the ambition of the Lord

Bishop, the Rt. Rev. Dr. Benjamin Pollard who has launched the appeal aimed at Manx people throughout the world. At least £60,000 will be required. The Bishop says the Cathedral Advisory Com-mittee has "no hesitation in commending the proposal that this archaeologically important and most ancient cathedral should be restored to use and rehallowed." The money will be spent on restoring the existing ruins and rebuilding the south aisle. The money raised will also provide an endowment of £10,000 and at least £5,000 for the payment of the four canons for maintaining the work of the Cathedral. A high-powered executive committee has been set up to administer the scheme, including His Excellency the Lieutenant-Governor and Deemsters Kneale and Macpherson.

NEW AIR TERMINAL AND PASSENGER BUILDING OPENED

The Lieutenant-Governor, accompanied by Lady Garvey, officially opened the new airport and passenger building at the new Central Bus Station in Lord Street, on 17th May. It is the biggest post-war development in Douglas and is the result of co-operation between the Airports Board, Douglas Town Council and Isle of Man Road Services Ltd. The building is to the design of Borough architect Mr. J. C. Bregazzi, and it occupies the site of the town's first car park created by the clearances of the 1930s. The light and colourful modern building is set in the centre of the platform area of the new station and it gives the airline operators and the travelling public a pleasant amenity. The passenger hall contains offices for the airlines, I.O.M. Road Services, the Manx Electric Railway and Messrs. Hamill's who operate the airport coach service.

WELCOME FOR MANX MAID

Thousands lined the new Marine Drive and Douglas Head, the Breakwater and Victoria Pier to watch the arrival of the *Manx Maid II*, the Steam Packet's first car ferry. She arrived on the evening of Friday, 18th May to take on board guests, prior to her trials. She returned again to the Victoria Pier on Saturday evening, having exceeded the 21 knot contract speed with ease. Built by Cammell Laird at Birkenhead at a cost of £1,000,000, *Manx Maid* is also the first Steam Packet vessel to be equipped with stabilisers - good news for those wary of travelling by sea! With a tonnage of 2,724 she is slightly larger than her post-war contemporaries. Her car deck can accommodate up to 90 vehicles and the system of ramps near the stern means that access to the quayside is possible at any state of the tide, in any of the ports used by the company. This obviates the hitherto slow and irksome business of having to use a crane to transfer vehicles to and from the quay. This welcome addition to the Steam Packet means that its passenger fleet will remain at eight vessels, including the pre-war *Lady of Mann* and *Ben my Chree*. This total does not include the *Mona's Queen* of 1946 which is to be sold at the end of the season, as she has become redundant following the closure of Fleetwood. The Steam Packet also operates three cargo ships.

NO RADIO MANX

The Government's determination to set up the Island's own commercial station that could be received in the U.K. and Western Europe, and a television station to be received in parts of the U.K., has suffered a severe setback. In seeking Royal Assent to the Wireless Telegraphy (Isle of Man) Bill, which would empower the Lieutenant-Governor to license stations instead of the U.K's Postmaster-General, the Lieutenant-Governor has received a letter from the Home Office detailing its objections. It points out that such stations would be incompatible with the international obligations undertaken by Her Majesty's Government. Nor could broadcasting be considered a solely domestic affair to the Isle of Man when its effects on reception in the U.K. are taken into account. It has taken six months for the final response to be received from the Imperial Government following a deputation, led by the Speaker, Mr. H. C. Kerruish, visiting the Home Office. It sought the revokation of the Orders in Council which gave the Postmaster-General control of Manx broadcasting. The deputation received a cool reception. On its return a disappointed Mr. Kerruish said that the Home Office officials, led by Sir Charles Cunningham, "were singularly ill-informed about Manx affairs and possessing an attitude of mind towards our constitution that was outdated fifty years ago."

GERMAN DEAD EXHUMED

Some 25,000 internees, German and a few Turks, were held as prisoners in the Isle of Man during the Great War of 1914-1918, and over 200 were buried in the churchyard at Patrick. A dozen were buried in Douglas and one at Braddan. Earlier this year permission was given to the German War Graves Commission to exhume their dead and re-inter them at Cannock Chase, Staffordshire, now a huge German war cemetery for the dead of two world wars. In July permission was given for the removal of the Isle of Man remains and work started in August by the Commonwealth War Graves Commission. It was kept as quiet as possible. Screens were erected and sightseers discouraged. It took a month. The coffins were burned and the gravestones thrown into the graves before refilling. All that remains at Patrick are the graves of two German Jewish prisoners whose families did not want them to be buried alongside Nazis. The Turkish graves remain untouched.

1962
• Nelson Mandela arrested in South Africa
• Movie star Marilyn Monroe dies
• Britain and France agree to develop *Concorde* supersonic passenger jet

1962

A model of St German's Cathedral which shows the planned scheme of restoration for which the Lord Bishop has launched a world-wide appeal. It is also planned to rebuild the south aisle.
(R. & L. Kelly Collection)

The assembly hall of the new Castle Rushen High School which was officially opened in November.

NEW CASTLE RUSHEN HIGH SCHOOL
The long-awaited new building of Castle Rushen High School was officially opened in November by Sir Charles Cunningham, Permanent Under Secretary of the Home Department. The school hall was packed with invited guests, pupils, staff and parents. For the occasion the school orchestra played a 'Celebration Suite' specially composed by music master Mr. Harry Pickard. Not only was the new school being celebrated, but also the demolition of the obsolete wartime buildings which formed the old school and had been described as 'shanty town' and 'the dump'! Last winter there were over 100 burst pipes, the boiler frequently broke down and many of the roofs let in the rain. But the conditions were endured with a remarkably good spirit and the school has earned a high reputation for its success in C.S.E., 'O' and 'A' level results. The spirit of the school is shown also in its prowess at sport, holding its own against the bigger secondary schools in athletics, cross country running and football. The new school, of course, is a vast improvement - the foyer, assembly hall and dining hall are impressive and the classrooms and specialist rooms are pleasing. No doubt snags in the design will come to the fore as the school 'shakes down'. Built to accommodate 480 pupils, headmaster Mr. J. R. Smith is

Right: The Steam Packet's first car ferry which came into service in May. The Manx Maid has a system of ramps near the stern which will enable vehicles to be driven on and off the vessel at different states of the tide. (Stan Basnett)

Far right: Until this year, vehicles have had to be craned on and off ships - a slow and ponderous business. The photograph shows a trio of Manx Nortons arriving for last year's Manx Grand Prix. Cars and vans receive the same treatment on passenger and cargo vessels.

already forecasting extensions will be required, judging by the amount of house building going on in Castletown and the south of the Island.

PEEL'S WONDER CAR
The world's smallest car is being launched at this year's Cycle and Motorcycle Show at Earl's Court, London. It has been designed and built by Mr Cyril Cannell and Mr Henry Kissack of the Peel Engineering Company whose works are in Mill Road. Named the P50, the three-wheeler has a length of 4ft 2ins and a height of 3ft 10ins. It weighs just one hundredweight and can be parked easily. The P50 is powered by a 50 c.c. D.K.W. engine with three gears and is capable of speeds of up to 40 m.p.h. It is also capable of 100 miles to the gallon, and the car has conventional controls and fittings. Besides being the smallest car in the world, it is also the cheapest, being priced at £149. 10s, including tax. The makers feel that the P50 will meet the demand of thousands of buyers who require a car offering the economy and convenience of a scooter or small motorcycle, but with complete protection from the elements.

TYPHOID MYSTERY SOLVED
Two visitors from Cumbria who returned home from a camping holiday in the Isle of Man with typhoid fever set off an incredible act of medical detective work. When the Cumberland authorities contacted Noble's Hospital and asked if there was typhoid on the Island they were told: Most definitely not. Yet it was clear that the campers had contracted the disease here. The subsequent investigations, says consultant

patho-logist Guy Pantin, spanned almost 60 years.

In 1903 an epidemic of typhoid occurred in Kirk Michael and many died. Subsequent investigations revealed that it had been brought here by an African visitor. Once the source had been identified, the problem seemed to have been overcome. However, there were further, apparently inexplicable, outbreaks, a notable one being at Knockaloe Internment Camp during World War I. Doctors had their suspicions about their source but lacked proof to do anything about it. Now the experience of the Cumberland campers helped to unlock the mystery. When it was established that the campers had drunk water from a local river, pathologists went to its source. What they found was a cottage in which an old woman was living. When interviewed, she agreed that she had lived in Kirk Michael during the original typhoid epidemic. Since then she had been in the habit of emptying her chamber pot into the river.

Here was the answer to the mystery. Whilst the woman had never suffered typhoid, she had been a carrier. When conditions were right, she had infected others, perhaps through contaminating a river from which people were drinking.

The lesson for campers is not to drink river water. Even now there are traditional Manx Thie Vegs straddling rivers and discharging directly into them. There is a notable three-seater in Bride: one for father, a smaller one for mother and an even smaller one for a child!

Built by Peel Engineering Co., the P50 is seen at its launch at this year's Motorcycle Show at Earl's Court. The smallest car in the world, it offers the economy and convenience of a scooter or small motor-cycle, while giving protection from the weather. (H. D. N. Hanson)

1962
• James Howard Meredith becomes first black man to attend University of Mississippi

1962 NEWS IN BRIEF

JANUARY
9 - Manx Government banknote issue increased from £500,000 to £1,000,000.

FEBRUARY
23 - Mr Max Myers bought the White City fairground, Onchan Head, from his older brother for £50,000 and planned to spend a further £30,000 on improving and developing the site.

MARCH
6 - Storm caused £4,000 damage to Douglas promenade and sunken gardens.
22 - Formation of the Manx Democratic Party opposed to Socialist policies and adopting a middle-of-the-road policy with progressive outlook.

APRIL
20-27 Organised by Mr Harry Pickard, an International Festival of Music and Dancing was held with choirs, dancers and bands from several European countries. Castletown was the host to the Festival but groups performed in other towns and some villages.
28 - Henry Harvey, of Abbeylands, won the 85-mile Parish Walk for the second year in succession, in record time of 16hrs 25mins.

MAY
11 - Government Estimates for 1962-3 published providing for gross spending of £5,681,123, the biggest Budget ever in the Isle of Man.
11 - Cotton Mill operated at Union Mills for seven years closed down because of trade slump in Lancashire, caused by the importation of cheap foreign goods.

JUNE
4 - Mr J. R. Quayle, former chairman of Isle of Man Bank Ltd, awarded the O.B.E. in the Queen's Birthday Honours.
6 - Two Commonwealth riders killed in the Junior T.T., Tom Phillis (Australia) and Colin Meehan (New Zealand).
8 - A woman competed in a solo class of the T.T. for the first time. Mrs Beryl Swain of London, finished 22nd out of 34 entrants in the new 50 c.c. race.
10 - Gary Hocking (MV Agusta) won Senior Race after Mike Hailwood, on a similar machine, won the Junior Race.

19 - Budget proposals for a reduction in the standard rate of income tax by 3d to 4s 3d in the £, and for increased personal allowances approved.
21 - Sentence of six strokes of the birch on a 16 year-old Liverpool youth for assault.

JULY
11 - Douglas Town Council voted against the Sunday opening of the new Port Soderick amusement arcade.
25 - By 11 votes to 10 the Education Authority rejected a proposal to raise the school leaving age to 16, as in the United Kingdom.

AUGUST
13 - Celebrations for the 100th birthday of the Isle of Man's G.O.M., Mr Richard Cain, O.B.E., President of the World Manx Association, a member of the Legislature from 1919 to 1946 and head of the Castletown Brewery for over 40 years.
15 - Bob McIntyre, first man to lap the T.T. Course at 100 m.p.h., died from injuries received in a crash at Oulton Park, Cheshire.

SEPTEMBER
4-6 - Four riders killed in the Manx Grand Prix races.
13 - Surprise announcement that B.E.A. would be giving up their Isle of Man services in April next year. It was stated, however, that another company would take over and expand the services to meet increasing demand.

OCTOBER
6 - Commander Peter Scott, C.B.E., D.S.C., R.N.V.R., famous ornithologist and authority on wild life, installed at Peel in ancient office of Admiral of the Manx Herring Fleet.
16 - Retirement of Alderman Alfred Teare, M.B.E., J.P., from the Legislature after 43 years continuous membership - first in the House of Keys and then in the Legislative Council - and altogether 60 years active part in Manx public affairs, notably as a trade unionist.

NOVEMBER
6 - Manx team arrived in Perth, Western Australia, for the British Empire and Commonwealth Games.

1963
- Alcatraz, the island prison just off San Francisco, is closed
- Audio cassette tape marketed
- British Government minister John Profumo resigns after a sex scandal

LOSS OF O.C.T.U. IS BLOW TO RAMSEY AND THE NORTH

The final Passing Out Parade and the ceremony of Beating the Retreat marked the departure of the Officer Cadet Training Unit which has been stationed at R.A.F. Jurby for the past ten years. It was a windy October day and the conditions meant that the ceremonies had to be held in the main hangars rather than the parade ground.

Lieut-Governor, Sir Ronald Garvey, in full ceremonial dress, was the reviewing officer in front of Group Captain A. P. Dart, D.S.O., D.F.C., the station commander. He relinquishes his position as the O.C.T.U. transfers to R.A.F. Feltwell in Norfolk, where the unit will be housed in more permanent buildings. The occasion also included a service which was attended by invited guests and parents of the cadets. During the service the Lord Bishop, Dr Benjamin Pollard, spoke of the "great loss to the cultural, social and sporting life of the Island . . . and also the great economic blow which was estimated at a quarter of a million pounds." Two hundred civilians who are employed at the station have been made redundant. About 60 R.A.F. personnel will remain on the station until its future is decided.

The shock news of the closure was announced by the Air Ministry in January. It prompted His Excellency to hold talks with Home Secretary Mr. Henry Brooke in an attempt to reverse the decision. Ramsey Commissioners held an emergency meeting to consider the effect the closure would have on the town. It was estimated that the loss to Ramsey would amount to £150,000 a year. The Commissioners put forward suggestions for the possible future use of the site, including the establishment of an industrial area, development of a holiday camp and the creation of a new civil airport to serve the north of the Island. Commenting on this, the Airports Board said in a statement that the airfield should remain available as a diversionary air strip, and "developed to accommodate the largest type of aircraft now using Ronaldsway".

TYNWALD'S DEVELOPMENT PLAN

Tynwald has approved in principle the Development Plan sponsored by its Executive Council. Costing in the region of £4,500,000, the Plan is designed mainly to broaden the approach to the tourist industry and help maintain the Island as a leading resort. The Plan embodies ideas put forward by Boards of Tynwald and local authorities. Included are schemes for a new indoor swimming pool, a winter garden and ice rink, a creche and children's playground in Douglas. A new swimming pool, hotel and flats is planned for Ramsey and a hotel and chalets at Laxey. Other ideas include a Field Study Centre and a Wild Life Fowl Trust development at Ballaugh Curraghs. Money will be available for building new and modernising old hotels; the renovation of Port Erin swimming pool, and the building of new Government Offices, Police Headquarters and Law Courts. The Development Plan includes the building of a new sea passenger terminal in Douglas. Also accepted is the novel idea, put forward by Mr. Colebourn, M.H.K., to construct a chairlift across Douglas Harbour to connect with the Marine Drive, the big attraction being a miniature Disneyland at Port Soderick. Each part of the Plan will be presented separately for Tynwald's approval when details and costs are finalised.

THAT WAS HIS WEEK, THAT WAS!

Charged with leaving his car without lights in a lane behind his house late at night, a resident of 11, York Road, Douglas, was fined £1 in the Magistrates Court. The culprit told a police constable, "I was watching television and forgot to put the lights on." A member of the bench enquired with a grin, "Was he watching 'Z Cars'?" Inspector Clague, prosecuting, replied, "Not on Saturday, sir, the day of the offence. I think it would more likely be 'That Was The Week That Was', at 11.20 p.m.!"

BLIZZARD PARALYSES ISLAND

What has become known as 'The Great White-Out' has paralysed the Island. In February it lay buried under the worst snow drifts of this century. Although some roads were opened after five days it took weeks for struggling Highway Board crews to break through in the Kirk Michael area.

The 100 m.p.h. blizzard struck in early February after exceptional snowfalls in January. A family of four at Druidale Farm, who had been cut off for 22 days, had been forced to make a break-out through drifts when paraffin stocks were exhausted and bottled gas supplies were getting low.

The new blizzard, with temperatures so cold that a barrel of beer at the Keppel Gate Hotel froze solid, lasted for several days and disrupted Island life. Cottages were buried. Drifts of up to 25 feet were common. On Glencrutchery Road, Douglas, they towered above all who walked to Douglas from Onchan.

Highlight of the year was the four-day visit of Her Majesty the Queen Mother. She is seen here on her way to presiding over the Tynwald Ceremony.
(R. & L. Kelly Collection)

At the height of the blizzard there was a night-time drama at the Marine Drive when the 350 ton Dutch coaster *Grietje* was driven on to rocks three miles south of Douglas. Three lifeboats could not get close enough to rescue the crew of eight and, although six of the crew reached a small beach by liferaft, they were unable to climb the 200 foot cliff. Douglas Rocket Brigade had to establish a cliff ladder, despite the snow, and bring everyone up it at first light. The *Grietje* was left to break up.

CURRAGHS SCHEME UNDER FIRE
Despite a vigorous defence of the 300 acre Wild Fowl Reserve scheme by Mr. H. H. Radcliffe, one of the members for Ayre and chairman of the Board of Agriculture and Fisheries, a resolution passed at a meeting at Sulby roundly condemned the £45,000 scheme. Over 200 people from the farming community crowded into the tiny Sulby Hall to express their views. It was a resolution by Mrs. Ruth McKibbin that gained everyone's approval. The farmers' 'concentration camp' was how she described the Curraghs plan as the mood of the meeting turned quickly from laughing to the stamping of feet, applause, then booing. Mr. Edward Callister, M.H.K., well known for his opposition to Tynwald's Development Plan, condemned the scheme as a waste of money. He claimed the Curraghs should be irrigated and drained so it would produce agricultural wealth. The meeting lasted for over two hours, but Mr. Radcliffe and his fellow member for Ayre, Mr. R. E. S. Kerruish, remained unbowed, claiming it was vital that the scheme should go ahead and provide another attraction for visitors. Mr. Percy Radcliffe, who chaired the meeting, said he had contacted Mr. Peter Scott, the well-known ornithologist, and he had been assured that by extracting certain wing feathers the birds would be confined to the Reserve and would not damage crops in the surrounding area.

RAMSEY'S NEW SHIPYARD
After a year of preparations, Ramsey's new shipyard was officially opened by the Lieut-Governor, Sir Ronald Garvey, when he cut a wire stretched across the new slipway and unveiled a special plaque. The new crane and lifting gear has become a familiar feature of the harbour already and of particular interest is the new fishing boat taking shape on the stocks. She is called *Peep O'Dawn*. The shipyard is also geared to undertake repair work. In opening the shipyard, Sir Ronald congratulated the Industrial Advisory Council in the efforts to introduce new industries. In addition to the new yard at Ramsey there was, he said, an extension at the Aristoc factory which was providing further employment in the area.

MARINE DRIVE OPENED
The new Marine Drive between Douglas Head and Port Soderick, built by Tynwald at a cost of £240,000, was opened on May 9th by Lieutenant-Governor, Sir Ronald Garvey. He said the project illustrated the Island's bright prospects.

Work on the Drive started in November, 1955 but it was only in the last two years that the most difficult sections were completed. These were where railway bridges had spanned gorges in the old drive which was used by the Southern Electric Railway. A new roadway had to be blasted out of the cliff face. Approximately 360,000 cubic tons of rock had to be excavated. It was dangerous work but there were only 11 minor accidents.

Douglas television dealer Harold Colebourn still wants to develop a miniature Disneyland at Port Soderick with a chairlift across Douglas harbour to feed it but, although Tynwald agreed originally to build the lift, the finance for it has been axed from Treasury spending plans. It looks now as if neither it nor Disneyland will be built.

CHAIRLIFT PLAN AXED
Sir Ronald Garvey, who remains the Chancellor of the Exchequer, balanced the 1963-64 Budget by lopping £300,000 off the £4,142,487 estimates submitted earlier by Boards and Departments. The biggest saving was the ending of the 6d a gallon rebate on petrol. But the first casualty of the cuts was the £125,000 Douglas Head chairlift scheme. It was thrown out of the Budget after a further debate in Tynwald. Earlier in the year the chairlift, the dream of Mr. T. H. Colebourn, member for Castletown, had gained the overwhelming support of Tynwald, by 21 votes to 7, after a heated debate. The chairlift was seen as a way of revitalising Douglas Head and connecting with the newly-completed Marine Drive. This magnificent scenic road has been opened to pedestrians and motorists and it leads to Port Soderick which has been refurbished and developed by Douglas Corporation at a cost of £100,000. Mr. Colebourn expected that be-tween 150,000 and 200,000 people would make use of the spectacular chairlift annually and, at 2/- a ride, would show a profit of £6,000 a year. Critics thought otherwise.

CASINO OPENS, AT LAST!
Britain's film industry's sex symbol, Diana Dors, set the roulette wheels spinning on Monday, May 27th, when the Island's first American-style casino opened in the Castle Mona Hotel, Douglas.

Among the 500 guests was Alex Moore who, as a Douglas Town Councillor, first proposed the idea to the Visiting Industry Commission in September, 1955. He

The opening of the Marine Drive to traffic complements the efforts of Douglas Corporation to restore and develop Port Soderick as a popular resort. For the convenience of visitors, there is a bus service from Douglas using the scenic route.
(Frank Cowin Library)

On the afternoon of Tynwald Day, the Queen Mother visited the Villa Marina Gardens where she was greeted by thousands of schoolchildren who gave her a rousing three cheers. (Town Hall Archives)

Before departing on the Sunday, the Queen Mother travelled to Kirk Braddan to attend the Open-Air Service. She is seen here being introduced to the driver of the Royal Train at the Kirk Braddan halt. (Manx Press)

thought then that he had committed political suicide because of the outrage it caused among church leaders.

Now, after one of the most heated political struggles this century, Mr Moore saw his dream come true, at least in part. It was not exactly what he had imagined. He had visualised the world's super rich coming to the Island in their private yachts. In fact, the casino is more down-market, geared for the masses with a heavy emphasis on late night drinking, slot machines and low-stake gaming. The minimum roulette stake is just £1.

Anyone who wants to take advantage of drinking into the early hours must be a registered member of the casino club but membership can be obtained on demand and the charge is only £1 a year or 10 shillings for 28 days.

The Castle Mona is only a temporary casino, adapted hurriedly by the concessionaires after they were awarded the concession on March 20th by Tynwald's Gaming Board of Control. An unnamed Belgium group had been the preferred concessionaires but they withdrew on learning that the hotel associated with the permanent casino had to be a new one, not an existing one.

American property developer and bingo parlour operator, Mrs Helen McGarvey Saul from Maryland, has put up a £100,000 deposit with the Gaming Board as a security pledge that the American group will build a new hotel and casino within two years. The favoured site is at Baldromma, just north of Groudle Glen, but other sites have been mentioned. The 64-year-old widow joined her partners,

Buddy Albury and John Hickey, to bid for the casino concession when they approached her in Las Vegas. Her interest in the Isle of Man existed already because she had "inherited" a black Manx cat called George from a tenant of a farm she owned near Washington D.C.

VISIT OF THE QUEEN MOTHER

Fine and sunny weather blessed the four-day visit of Her Majesty the Queen Mother beginning on Thursday, 4th July. Arriving on board the Royal Yacht Britannia in Ramsey Bay, her Majesty landed on the Queen's Pier and was received by the Lieut-Governor, Sir Ronald Garvey, Lady Garvey and the Reception Party. Highlight of her visit to Ramsey was meeting the children of the town assembled in Parliament Square. She then visited the Town Hall and partook of afternoon tea with the Commissioners. Her Majesty then travelled to Laxey Glen Gardens where she met local officials before proceeding, via Creg ny Baa and Brandywell, to Peel for an official welcome. In the evening she witnessed a performance of the Viking Festival. She then returned to Britannia from the breakwater.

Tynwald Day began with Her Majesty arriving at the Victoria Pier, Douglas, and she travelled by car to St. John's where she presided over the Tynwald Ceremony. On Tynwald Hill His Honour the First Deemster and Clerk of the Rolls, Sydney Kneale, O.B.E. was invested by the Queen Mother with the C.B.E. Lunch was taken at Government House and Onchan children lined the driveway as she left for a ride by horsetram to the Villa Marina Gardens. Here she was greeted by thousands of schoolchildren who gave her a rousing three cheers. This was followed by a Garden Party at Government House. At night she attended the Tynwald Banquet at the Castletown Golf Links Hotel.

On Saturday morning Her Majesty paid visits to Port Erin and Port St. Mary, returning via Castletown where she stopped in the Market Square and visited Castle Rushen. In the evening she attended the Charity Ball in the Villa Marina and switched on the illuminations. On Sunday morning she travelled by steam train to Braddan where she attended the Open-Air Service and then returned to Victoria Pier for the final farewell. The Queen Mother had completed a hectic round of visits, with

The Grand Island Hotel, formerly the Ramsey Hydro, has been extensively refurbished and extended with considerable Government financial support. It was officially opened in April by His Excellency Sir Ronald Garvey. (Frank Cowin Library)

everybody having a chance to see her and to demonstrate their loyalty.

SWIM POOL FOR THE VILLA MARINA GARDENS

The £500,000 swimming pool project for the Villa Marina grounds, part of the Development Plan for the Island, was given the all-clear by Douglas Town Council at its August meeting. Approval was given by 16 votes to 6 on the proviso "that the carrying out of the proposed scheme be subject to satisfactory financial arrangements with Government". There was a long and heated debate in which many expressed the desire to see a swimming pool worthy of the resort built in the Villa Marina grounds, probably using the site of the Pavilion. Alderman Teare, led the opposition, however, in an impassioned speech against the "mutilation of the Villa Marina Gardens". It will be remembered that Sir Ambrose Dundas, refused Tynwald support for the same reason for a similar scheme some years ago, but apparently that bar has now been removed.

BISHOP IN TROUBLE OVER CATHEDRAL RESTORATION

The world-wide Cathedral Restoration Appeal, launched by the Lord Bishop, Dr. Benjamin Pollard, early last year has run into difficulties. Initially there was quiet acquiescence by clergy and laity to the ambitious £60,000 scheme which seeks to restore the ruined St. German's Cathedral on St. Patrick's Isle to its former glory. The plan gained the support of the Cathedral Advisory Committee of the Church of England. But now opposition to the scheme has been sparked off as a result of comments by the Lord Bishop in the November issue of the Church Magazine. He claimed that his enthronement in St. George's Church, Douglas, in 1954, was the result of being put under pressure by the then Archdeacon, The Ven. C. V. Stockwood, and the Vicar-General, Mr. F. B. Johnson. He believes his enthronement should have taken place in "the lovely ancient Cathedral on Peel Island".

The Vicar-General has denied that neither he, nor any other person, caused pressure to be applied, as he can prove by the bulky file of correspondence with the Lord Bishop. But more serious is the response of three senior clergy of the Diocese who are Canons of the Cathedral - Canons C. A. Cannan, John Duffield and H. Maddrell. In an open letter to the Lord Bishop they deplore his remarks concerning the late Archdeacon Stockwood which they consider an "unworthy slur on his memory". Concerning the restoration itself, they say the bishop told them it was no concern of ours as we were only Canons of the pro-Cathedral at Bishops-court. "You brushed aside our objections to the scheme - inaccessibility, impossible winter conditions and the unlikelihood of such a restored building becoming the centre of Diocesan life". We suggested the alternative of some large parish church. After this we could only give a very reluctant agreement not to oppose your plans. But we stipulated that priority should be given to the rebuilding of All Saints Church in Douglas, and that the parishes should never be asked to contribute to the maintenance of the cathedral. That was two years ago and we now find that there is growing unease and increasing opposition amongst clergy and laity. The letter concludes with the canons saying that, with regret, they withdraw the reluctant consent given in 1961. The Lord Bishop, as yet, has not replied, though he has said a final decision will be made at the Diocesan Conference next May.

SOUTH RAMSEY PLAN APPROVED

The South Ramsey Development Plan gained almost unanimous support at Tynwald's November sitting. Almost £2,000,000 Government money was made available to advance the scheme. In moving the resolution, Speaker of the House of Keys and chairman of Executive Council, Mr H. C. Kerruish said that a positive approach by Government would encourage private developers to become involved. Before the run-down area could be cleared there would have to be 250 new houses built elsewhere on land owned by the Government or by Ramsey Commissioners. The cost of the housing was estimated at £750,000, some of which would be borne by Ramsey Commissioners. The swimming pool included in the scheme was to cost £80,000 of which a quarter would be covered by the Commissioners. Government envisaged a £250,000 hotel, housing units costing £300,000 and a shopping area costing £30,000. Providing services and roads would cost £150,000 and the Government's responsibility would amount to £55,000 a year on loan charges. Mr Kerruish gave an assurance that the building of flats and houses would attract private developers. Of the four who were not prepared to back the scheme, Mr T. H. Colebourn (Castletown), a member of the Tourist Board, wished the matter to be deferred and the money spent on helping the tourist industry. Mr R. E. S. Kerruish (Ayre) said he did not feel the scheme was right and it was "one of the biggest gambles the Island has ever endorsed".

Work has begun on demolishing the Church of All Saints which was built in 1898 to serve the growing upper part of Douglas. Built mainly of corrugated iron, it is known affectionately as the 'Tin Tab'. It is to be replaced by a church of modern design.
(Frank Cowin Library)

TYNWALD MATTERS:
INTEREST RATES UNCHANGED : LOANS FOR HOME BUYERS

Recent attempts to free interest rates on the Island from statutory control resulted in the introduction of a Usury Bill in the House of Keys to do just that. It failed, but its supporters, and there are many, argue that the restriction of interest rates here to 6% - a rate appropriate for gilt securities - represents an artificial control that can only lead to the disadvantage of the Island. U.K. building societies cannot operate here, private investment from elsewhere is inhibited, development is stifled, and so on. Its opponents simply state that removal of control would send interest rates rocketing and prevent local authorities from borrowing the monies necessary for their schemes. The Bill produced a furious debate, but it failed by 12 votes to 10 at the second reading. Shrewd observers judge, however, that a rise in interest rates is inevitable; it is just a question of when and by how much.

Fears that new residents could buy up the Island and Manx people, unable to raise capital, could be reduced to being second class citizens have been answered by Tynwald. Low interest mortgages, some with outright grants, were introduced in October to help Manx couples buy or build their own homes. Grants and loans for the modernisation of pre-war homes are likely to come later. The move follows the failure of a Commission set up by Tynwald to investigate ways of establishing a U.K. building society on the Island, or to finance its own building society. Instead, Government are to provide mortgages direct, as it did in the immediate post-war years. Applicants must have lived on the Island for 15 years at any one time, five consecutive years since 1947, or be a widow of someone who could have satisfied the latter requirements. Two new schemes have been introduced: one principally for the purchase of existing properties and for which buyers can get almost the full amount of the purchase cost repayable over 30 years, the other for the building of new ones. The cost of the latter, bearing in mind rising wage and material costs, is restricted to a maximum of £5,000 - the cost of a well-appointed family-sized bungalow. Government will provide a 10% grant, a further 10% free of interest and a further 20% at just 4%, the capital repayable over 30 years. Applicants are required to provide 10% themselves and fund the remainder by obtaining a traditional mortgage from private sources, secured as a first charge on the property.

1963 NEWS IN BRIEF

FEBRUARY
7 - St. George's Woollen Mills, Laxey announced that they were replacing their power looms with old hand-operated looms.

MARCH
5 - A National Insurance Order, increasing pensions and allowances on the same scale as England, passed by Tynwald.
26 - Local Government Board enabled to grant larger loans for tourist accommodation premises.

APRIL
24 - A charter plane took three tons of prime Manx spring lamb on the first leg of its journey to Paris. This was the second consignment, the first being a trial consisting of 55 carcasses.
25 - Plans announced for rebuilding of All Saints Church, Douglas.

MAY
13 - The Mayor of Douglas, Councillor T. A. Corkish, opened the conference of the Union of Post Office Workers at the Palace Ballroom.
26 - First Manx Trophy Car Rally held.

JUNE
3 - 3,000 delegates began Co-operative Conference in the Palace.
10 - T.T. rider Tony Godfrey seriously injured after crashing at Milntown when leading the 250 Lightweight Race. He was flown by helicopter ambulance to Ramsey Cottage Hospital. It was the first time the newly-introduced helicopter had been used.
11 - The Manx Hospitals Lotteries Bill given final reading in the House of Keys.
14 - Mike Hailwood (M.V. Agusta) won Senior T.T. and raised lap record to 106.31 m.p.h.
19 - Second Deemster remained in the Legislative Council after Bill designed to remove him fails in the Council by seven votes to four.
30 - The Grand Island Hotel, formerly known as the Ramsey Hydro, officially opened by Lieut-Governor after reconstruction and modernisation.

JULY
18 - H.R.H. The Duchess of Gloucester landed at R.A.F. Jurby to review the passing out parade of R.A.F. and W.R.A.F. cadets.
19 - The Erskine Clothing factory at Laxey, for 35 years one of the largest employers in Laxey, closed down. Cheap foreign imports were given as the reason.
25 - A 16-year-old Douglas boy was ordered six strokes of the birch at Castletown Juvenile Court for assault.

30 - A Radar Speed Detection meter, allocated for use by the Manx police, was demonstrated in Douglas.

AUGUST
9 - A Whitehaven trawler skipper was fined £15 for illegal fishing in Manx territorial waters.
21 - A 14-year-old boy was ordered four strokes of the birch by Douglas Juvenile Court for his part in thefts.
23 - The local 'Phantoms' rhythm group won the top prize at the new Manx Festival of Modern Music.

SEPTEMBER
6 - David Williams raised lap record for the Senior Manx Grand Prix to 98.18 m.p.h. One rider was killed in the race.
9 - Planning approval in principle was given by the L.G.B. for redevelopment of the Douglas Holiday Camp.
15 - Junior House at King William's College badly damaged by fire.
19 - A 16-feet, two-ton basking shark was caught in a net at Peel.
25 - A practice bomb from an aircraft using the bombing range off Jurby Head was dropped on a hillside farm near Kirk Michael.

OCTOBER
6 - Mr George Moore, Attorney-General, appointed Second Deemster in succession to Deemster Bruce Macpherson. Mr David D. Lay appointed Attorney-General.
17 - Season visitor arrival figures fell to 435,289 which was 11,330 fewer than 1962.
17 - Compromise decision reached on the Northern Lighthouse Board's plan to supply electricity to the proposed new lighthouse by overhead cable from Cregneash to the Calf of Man. The lines will take a revised route but will not be permitted overhead from that point to the Calf.
30 - Tourist Board refuse to continue financial assistance for the International Festival of Music and Dancing held for the second time at Easter this year. Later, the decision was made by the Festival Appeals Committee to abandon the Festival for next year.

NOVEMBER
5 - Legislative Council passed the Curraghs Acquisition Bill which empowers the Government to take over part of the Ballaugh Curraghs to set up a Wild Fowl Trust.
20 - Tynwald approved a £20,000 development at Onchan Park which will include a boating lake.
25 - The Manx Democratic party failed to win their first seat when its candidate was defeated by Mr Percy Radcliffe (Independent) at a bye-election in Ayre, following the elevation of Mr H. H. Radcliffe to the Legislative Council.

WELSH COMPANY TO RUN MANX AIR SERVICES

In a joint statement issued at the beginning of the year by British European Airways and the Isle of Man Airports Board, it was announced that Cambrian Air Services, based at Roose, Cardiff, had been chosen to take over B.E.A.'s former routes. The name of Cambrian meant little to the Manx public and added to the feeling that B.E.A. was deserting the Isle of Man. However, assurances were given that the Liverpool, Manchester, London and Belfast routes would continue to be served by the popular Viscount aircraft. This was made possible by B.E.A., which has a financial interest in Cambrian Airways, transferring four of their older Viscounts to the Welsh company. Indeed these aircraft are already familiar at Ronaldsway. They first appeared in Cambrian's bright red colour scheme from 1st April.

Following the removal of B.E.A.'s monopoly by the 1960 Civil Aviation Licensing Act, the favourite to take over its Manx routes had been British United, the largest independent airline which, under Mr Freddie Laker, took over Silver City Airways last year. British United (Manx) operate the summer services which continue to bring in the largest number of seasonal visitors, with Blackpool being the busiest of all. Mr Laker made a strong plea, emphasising that the Isle of Man should have its own 'national' airline under which all Manx routes, summer and winter, should be served. However, the Airports Board said: "We do not think

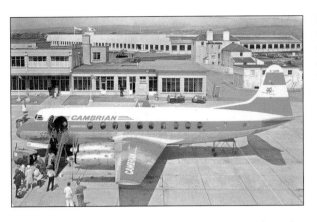

One of B.E.A's former Viscounts which has been transferred to Cambrian Airways, the Welsh airline which has been entrusted with serving the Manx all-year-round routes.

it prudent to place air services which are vital to the economy of the Island in the hands of a single operator."

The number of passengers handled at Ronaldsway continues to rise. The 300,000 mark was passed last year for the first time. Mr J. H. Nicholls, chairman of the Airports Board, has announced that the airport will remain open all night this summer, with the last scheduled flight arriving at 3.30 a.m. He has appealed to hoteliers and boarding house keepers to be prepared to welcome the late arrivals. This summer British United will be celebrating the fact that over one million passengers have been carried on the Blackpool route since schedules began in 1948.

CAR RALLYING HITS MANX ROADS

Headlights flashing across the night sky, cars speeding through timed sections of rough roads and tracks, unclosed to the public, heralded the arrival of car rallying on the Island in a dramatic way. The survivors of the 75 starters, including 26 local entrants, reassembled on the morning of Saturday, 25th May, this time to tackle eight sections of tarmac roads which were officially closed and marshalled in true Manx tradition. To most, previously restricted to forest tracks, this was a unique experience and added to the flavour of a highly successful event. Locals came out in their hundreds and, as expected by the experts, it was one of the Ford Anglia Allardettes, powered by a 1500 c.c. Cortina engine, which won the event. The winner was Reg McBride assisted by Don Barrow as navigator. Behind the Allardettes was a string of Minis and Mini Coopers.

How did it all start? It was during the Veteran Car Club Run last year that rally enthusiast John Hopwood got into conversation with Tourist Board chief, Leonard Bond. It was Mr Hopwood who pointed out that the Island's roads were ideal for rallying. "But we haven't got an organiser," replied Mr Bond, "and we don't know much about the subject." It was then that John Hopwood found himself volunteering and, with every assistance from the Tourist Board, set about planning what was to be called the Manx Trophy Rally. Back home in Cheshire, he press-ganged his club friends of Ecurie Cod Fillet, of which top rally driver Roy Fidler, a fishmonger, was a prominent member. The June Effort Committee agreed to assist with ferry costs and the *Daily Mail*

covered printing costs. The organisers were not disappointed in the entries received from the 'rally circus'. Entries included such well-known names as Vic Elford, Brian Culcheth, Reg McBride, Rodney Goodchild, Roger Clark and ex-T.T. rider Philip Simister.

The prizes were presented on the Saturday night in the newly-opened Casino in the Castle Mona. Mayor of Douglas, Councillor T. A. Corkish, gave a stirring speech and, to loud cheers, promised that more roads could be closed next year. The week-end concluded on the Sunday morning with exciting driving tests on the walkway of Harris Promenade. Huge crowds turned out to watch the spectacle with the eventual winner, Rodney Goodchild, receiving the magnificent *Daily Mail* Silver Rosebowl. As the crowds dispersed, it could be felt that four-wheeled motor sport on the Island, last experienced when car racing ceased in 1950, was back with a vengeance in the form of rallying.

Below: Reg McBride at the controls of the winning Allardette - a Cortina-engined Anglia. They are seen here at the top of Injebreck during the day stages of the inaugural Manx Trophy Rally.

Bottom: Triumph works driver Vic Elford on the unclosed Glen Roy night section. Pressed into service was local enthusiast Ken Harding. (Daily Mail photographs)

1964
- Home kidney dialysis introduced
- "Pirate radio" ship *Radio Caroline* begins broadcasting near Britain
- 135 people die in riot at football match between Peru and Argentina
- Nelson Mandela sentenced to life imprisonment in South Africa

WELSH COMPANY TO RUN MANX AIR SERVICES

The Island's fledgling Manx Radio took to the air for the first time when it broadcast the T.T. Round the Course commentaries which have for many years been heard through the loud speakers of the public address system. This year radio listeners were able to tune into the commentaries transmitted on the 91.2 megacycles V.H.F. waveband. The reception of the V.H.F. signal was of high quality, especially in the Douglas area, and listeners heard the voices of lawyer Peter Kneale from the Grandstand, Dollan Kelly and Jack Quayle from Sulby Bridge, and Ian Cannell from Keppel Gate. To begin with they were unaware that their commentaries were being broadcast! History was also made with the broadcast of the first 'commercial' when it was announced that the race broadcasts were "by kind permission of T. H. Colebourn Ltd." It was announced also that the transmissions through the Pye installations, which had been set up in a caravan near Signpost Corner, Onchan, were being treated as a test. "It will not be possible for a regular service to be provided until a medium wavelength licence has been issued by the Postmaster-General," said the announcer.

Despite last year's refusal by the Home Office and the Postmaster General, to entertain the idea of the Isle of Man having its own high power radio and television transmitter stations, the Manx Government has persisted with its demands. Pye Ltd. were appointed technical consultants earlier this year and have been working in close co-operation with Mr T. H. Colebourn, M.H.K. Amid news that the 'pop' pirate Radio Caroline was to move from the English Channel to Manx territorial waters, Pye was awarded a secret concession to establish Manx Radio on the Island. This was in partnership with R. M. A. Ltd., which is associated with a number of foreign radio and T.V. stations. Everybody was left to think that Manx Radio was the Government venture originally known as Radio Manx Ltd. The end of May saw the arrival by air of Pye equipment from Dublin and the specially designed caravan arrived at Douglas on board the Peveril. The caravan was hauled by tractor to Signpost Corner.

The secret concessionaires were unwilling at first to launch a station on the sort of V.H.F. and Medium wave licence the U.K. was prepared to grant. The power was no more than a light bulb and the medium wave, 188,

extremely poor. For the T.T., the concessionaires transmitted on V.H.F. only and then shut down in the hope of negotiating a better deal. When more was forthcoming, they were persuaded by Tynwald to launch Manx Radio and then bid for a better licence. Manx Radio was eventually launched in July when Lieut-Governor Sir Ronald Garvey spoke over the air from Fort Anne. He described the radio station as the 'youngest born legitimate commercial radio station in the British Isles.' He announced that Tynwald had approved unanimously the appointment of the Isle of Man Broadcasting Company to operate Manx Radio and to provide the Island with its own local service. His Excellency spoke of the long battle to overcome the restrictive practices they had encountered, and the problems still to be overcome. The low-powered medium wavelength - 188 metres - is most unsatisfactory for Island reception, and a more easily tuned wavelength has been requested. In conclusion, His Excellency said that the object of Manx Radio was to provide listeners with a 'full programme of entertainment and to keep you fully informed of all the activities in the life of our Island . . . Happy listening to you all'. Mr Colebourn was heard to comment that all we now have is 'the remnants of a pipe dream'.

RADIO CAROLINE

On Tynwald Day, of all days, the pirate radio ship *Caroline* steamed into Manx waters and anchored four miles off Ramsey, after a journey from Harwich. Radio Caroline immediately blared out pop music across the north of Britain for 18 hours a day. The commercial radio works in conjunction with Radio Atlanta based off the Essex coast. Approaches had been made by the bosses of Radio Caroline to work with Radio Manx. The response was a call on the Prime Minister and the Postmaster-General to take action in the commercial radio situation which was likely to steal Manx Radio's listening audience. At the end of July, the Postmaster-General, Mr. Bevins, announced to the House of Commons that no action was proposed against the pirate broadcasting ships, adding that they were not interfering with B.B.C. transmissions. Pirate bosses say their object is to legitimise commercial radio stations in the future. In August, the Tourist Board made use of the pirate ship to advertise late season events.

ONCHAN TAKE-OVER?

The report of the Local Government Districts (Administrative) Commis-sion was debated in the Keys and Council in February. Among the suggestions were the amalgamation of Douglas and Onchan, and the formation of a new district combining Port Erin, Port St. Mary and the south of Rushen Parish. An attempt to remove the Douglas-Onchan issue from the report succeeded in the Keys by 11-10 but was lost in the Council 4-5. As the two houses were not in agreement the amendment fell, and the report was 'received'. Douglas Town Councillors sought to pursue the matter, pointing out that many people in Onchan found

Manx Radio made its first broadcast from this caravan which is sited near to Signpost Corner in Onchan. Transmissions of the T.T. Race commentaries were made possible by the use of Pye equipment.
(R. & L. Kelly Collection)

1964

employment within Douglas, and enjoyed the amenities of the town. However, letters between the two parties were less than cordial. Mr J. C. Binns, Clerk to Onchan Commissioners, wrote to the Council: "My Commissioners would say now in the strongest possible terms that they do not accept your reasoning, and they will oppose by every means at their disposal any attempt to 'take over' Onchan".

DEATH OF ARCHDEACON STENNING

The Island lost one of its leading personalities when the Ven. Archdeacon E. H. Stenning, M.B.E., T.D., M.A. died in Noble's Hospital in February, at the age of 79. Born in Sussex, he was "Manx by adoption" having come to the Island in 1909 after leaving Cambridge, where he studied medicine and took his degree in natural sciences. He obtained a post at King William's College and intended to stay originally for two years. In fact, he stayed there for 44 years, becoming vice principal in 1942. Many thousands of boys were taught by him and he was renowned for his love of sport, especially soccer, cricket and swimming. An outstanding feature of the 'Stenning era' at college were the songs he sang at end of term concerts. His wife, who died some years ago, was a great support to him and was 'mother' to hundreds of pupils. He had a distinguished career as a clergyman which began when he was ordained as chaplain at K.W.C. in 1911. He became a Canon in 1944, and was appointed Archdeacon in 1958. His love and knowledge of the Island resulted in him being commissioned to write a book about the Isle of Man for the famous County series. First published in 1950, it is one of the most popular books about the Island and is illustrated in the main by his own photographs. Photography was one of his favourite pastimes and the Archdeacon was the first President of the Isle of Man Photographic Club. A Freemason since 1914, he was latterly Provincial Grand Master for the Isle of Man.

Another of his great loves was motorcycling. In 1912 he started his career as an official of the T.T. Races - marshalling at Ballacraine. He was a founder member of the M.M.C.C., promoters of the Manx Grand Prix, and was a race steward at every race meeting. In 1956 he was awarded the M.B.E. for services to motorcycling. He will be remembered for his jovial presence on the Palace stage for the M.G.P. presentations. All looked forward to his well-chosen jokes which were a prelude to calling the riders for their awards. Everything about Ernest Henry Stenning was giant-size - his achievements, his stature, and the esteem in which he was held by all who knew him. He became a legend in his own time and that legend will live on.

BISHOP HUMILIATED

The Lord Bishop's ambitious £68,000 plan for the restoration of St. German's Cathedral was rejected overwhelmingly at the Diocesan Confer-ence held in May. A motion that the restoration should not go ahead was presented by Mr. H. H. Radcliffe, M.L.C., supported by Canon Duffield and His Honour Ramsey Johnson. The resolution was agreed almost unanimously by a show of hands from the clergy and laity. The Lord Bishop, Dr Benjamin Pollard, took part in the debate from the chair and declared that "the whole trouble really

The Ven. Archdeacon E. H. Stenning, M.B.E., T.D., M.A. He was a much-loved personality throughout the Island and was awarded the M.B.E. for his services to motorcycling. (Frank Cowin Library)

behind this opposition is that some of you are thinking you will have to put your hands in your pockets". This was greeted by cries of dissent from the packed hall. Dr Pollard then attacked the Canons who he said had "ratted on me and made a scandal all over England, through their extraordinary behaviour, producing a dreadful atmosphere about the Church in the Isle of Man among my fellow bishops." Before the vote was taken, Mr Charles Kerruish, S.H.K., deplored the bishop's unwarranted attack on the people of the Island, and on the clergy who had the courage to stand up to the bishop's proposals which, said Mr. Kerruish, had been handled in a 'completely harebrained manner'.

DEATH OF A WITCH

The death of Dr. Gerald Brosseau Gardner, who presided over the Witches Mill in Castletown, brings to an end the life of one of the most bizarre characters of recent times. He was a self-professed witch and was once the assistant professor of Egyptology at University College, London. The Witches Mill opened in 1951 and has attracted coach loads of fascinated tourists, though locals regard much of what is said about the place as pure marketing nonsense. 'Devil's bite sausages' and 'bewitched eggs' are on the menu of the Folklore Restaurant, and the Museum of the Occult contains a medieval sorcerer's temple, a witch's kitchen for the working of magic, an alchemist's den and an African witch doctor's hut. Dozens of artefacts from broomsticks to exhibits relating to spells, charms, omens and curses give a mystic atmosphere to the old mill building. One of the more sinister features is the circle with its altar, candlesticks and symbols, sealed off behind a glass screen; there have been repeated reports that rituals are held here and that the circle has been given supernatural power by the visit of a mysterious sect which deals with the occult. The museum

Dr Gerald Gardner poses in the magic circle of the magician's room with its altar, candlesticks and symbols.
(R. & L. Kelly Collection)

has become a focus of those who profess to being priestesses and high priests of covens. It is understood that the Mill is to be taken over by a Mr. Worrall.

CORPORATION TO BUY DERBY CASTLE SITE

Alderman J. C. Fargher, Chairman of Douglas Town Council's Finance Committee, announced plans in April for a £1,000,000 facelift to the Derby Castle site. It is planned to build a sports and social centre, provided negotiations with a Manchester development company and the Manx Government will result in substantial financial support. Prefacing his remarks, Alderman Fargher said that plans for an indoor swimming pool in the Villa Marina Gardens had been abandoned following "forthright opposition". The purchase price of the site from the Palace and Derby Castle Company is likely to be £80,000. Main feature of the Sports and Social Centre will be the swimming pool and fronting the building will be a glass-fronted area for sunbathers. Other indoor activities and amusements will provide an all-weather facility which Douglas lacks. There is a possibility that work on the site will start in October and the handsome new building will be completed for next season.

CLEAN GAS FOR DOUGLAS

Production of gas from coal, a messy process which cast smells and smoke across lower Douglas for generations, ended early this year. Douglas gasworks installed new German equipment which converts liquid butane into gas. It became operational in May. The butane is imported by small tanker by Kosangas of Denmark and unloaded by pipeline from a berth at The Tongue.

One of the consequences of the new process is the loss of coke and tar as by-products. Schools and offices used to burn the coke in their central heating furnaces. New mains have had to be provided for the gas and all appliances have had to be adapted. Now, it is claimed, the Douglas gas supply area is capable of adapting more easily to a natural gas supply if any is found near the Island.

VISIT OF ROLLING STONES

There were fantastic scenes at the Palace Ballroom in

August when the famous pop group, The Rolling Stones, made a one-night appearance. At first, admission was to be limited to 5,000 ticket holders. But because of the demand this plan was abandoned. It was estimated that upwards of a record 12,000 people were crammed into the Ballroom. People had claimed that the Manx police would need outside help to keep order because of the peculiar effect the group had on their fans. In the end, while there was plenty of screaming, there was no riot or mayhem, and there was no rock 'n' roll - nobody could move!

JURBY RUNWAY EXTENSION

Early in the year Tynwald approved the purchase of the vacated R.A.F. station at Jurby for the sum of £133,000. The property involved consists of 379 acres on which are 81 dwellings and 300 structures. It was thought that Mr Billy Butlin, who has already visited the Island in search of a site for one of his holiday camps, might have been interested. However, he has not responded to the situation. While the future use of the station has not been decided, Tynwald has approved a scheme to repair and extend the main runway by 400 yards in order to permit Viscount aircraft to land at Jurby when Ronaldsway is 'blacked out'. Chairman of the Airports Board, Mr Nicholls, said that while he was aware of demands for an airport in the north, there was no intention to provide one because Ronaldsway was well capable of meeting existing demand. The runway is to be extended across the Sandygate road at a cost of over £100,000.

MATTER OF PUBLIC CONCERN

The case of a five-year-old girl has caused considerable concern throughout the Island. It followed the girl's death in Ramsey Cottage Hospital after being admitted with a broken wrist, ribs and bruises. She had lived with her foster parents at Ballamoar Cottages, Jurby. At the inquest in Ramsey, the jury returned an open verdict. Following enquiries by Local Government Board officials, the parents were charged with ill treatment of the little girl in a manner likely to cause unnecessary suffering or injury. The case was heard in October and the foster father was sentenced to one month's imprisonment, and the foster mother to two months. The girl's treatment so horrified the Island and there have been demands to bring in legislation to amend existing child welfare laws.

Creation of a new petrol brand for Britain known as IMP - short for Isle of Man Petroleums - lies behind a controversial American plan to build an oil refinery on the Ayres. Allied industries which manufacture oil-based products are expected to be established nearby. The San Francisco-based oil company of Natomas plans to bring the oil here from the Middle East by super tanker and discharge it by pipeline into land-based holding tanks spread over 275 acres on the Ayres. Petroleum products will be fed to tankers also by pipeline. Natomas expects to process 10,000 barrels of oil a day. Under a further concession from Tynwald, it plans also to hunt for oil and natural gas in Manx territorial waters.

Horrified conservationists have warned about the risk of sea and air pollution and spoilation of the Ayres but Tynwald, which has been locked in secret negotiations with Natomas for more than a year, seems committed to

letting the project proceed. It has been described as "one of the most wonderful developments the Island could ever have." In addition to creating job opportunities, a Manx refinery is expected to bring local fuel costs down.

News about the refinery broke in the autumn after a General Development Bill was passed to enable Tynwald to cut through all the usual red tape necessary for a major project. No one would say at first what it concerned and this led to much speculation, particularly last year. There was concern, too, over the extent to which Tynwald seemed prepared to go to accommodate the wishes of secret developers.

CROCKFORDS OF LONDON SAVE CASINO

Amid allegations of immorality, fraud and a shortage of funds, the Island's Las Vegas-connection came to a dramatic end this year. The casino was saved by a British take-over but not before there were fears that it could be shut down permanently.

When the casino concession hung in the balance, casino supporters feared that if it was withdrawn or surrendered, the church-led opposition lobby to the casino might be able to prevent a new concession being awarded.

The problems for the casino began when police raided the casino in late December last year just as the concessionaires were preparing plans for a new £500,000 casino on the White City Amusement Park site on Onchan Head. Officers entered the gaming room at 5 a.m. as staff were shutting down. Financial checks led to five American staff being charged with financial offences which introduced new expressions to the Island, principally "a cut off the top" and "top money."

Two of the concessionaires subsequently attracted critical comment but no action was taken against them. John Hickey had just gone to America for a holiday. William Albury did so in January and neither returned. In May they withdrew

from the concession, leaving Mrs Helen Saul as the sole concessionaire. As the trial of the American staff went ahead in the Tynwald Court Chamber, the staff were convicted in July and then had their convictions quashed on appeal in October. New plans for the casino indicated Mrs Saul's preference for a site at Baldromma but it became apparent that she was having difficulties raising sufficient working capital. Worries about the concession led to speculation in Tynwald that either it or Douglas Corporation should take over the casino and run it as a summer-season-only enterprise.

This did not proceed but, as a two-year time limit for building a new hotel and casino began to narrow and Mrs Saul's £100,000 deposit looked like being threatened, she opened negotiations with Crockfords, the other group originally interested in the concession. A six month extension of time for building the hotel was granted and in September Crockfords took over Mrs Saul's liabilities. A new Manx company was established led by Mr Tim Holland and Sir Dudley Cunliffe-Owen of Crockfords and the latter embarked on plans to build a new casino and hotel on the site of the Palace Coliseum on Central Promenade, Douglas. A successful take-over bid followed for the Coliseum's owners, the Palace and Derby Castle Company.

Top: Rally favourite, Sir Peter Moon, with John Davenport as navigator, is first away from the ramp outside the Sefton Hotel to start the night sections of this year's rally. Whilst in the lead, Sir Peter rolled the immaculate Mini-Cooper (centre) on the infamous 'jumps' of Druidale during the penultimate section.

Bottom: The once peaceful farmstead of Little London has become a place of notoriety for competitors and spectators alike. Here the badly damaged M.G.A. of C. Cuthbert is being examined after an 'off'.

TYNWALD MATTERS:
HOUSE OF KEYS VERSUS LEGISLATIVE COUNCIL

It would appear that the end of the long-running saga over the composition of the Legislative Council is now in sight. Reformists, backed recently by the MacDermott Commission, have long argued that the Legislative Council should have a majority of elected representatives of the people at the expense of appointed members. To this, supporters of the status quo argued that the existing system had served the Island well and should not give way to spurious arguments about democracy and independence.

The present battle began early last year when the Keys passed a Bill to remove the Second Deemster from the Legislative Council. As expected, the Bill received short shrift when presented before the Legislative Council. Later in the year, the Keys re-introduced the Bill and added a further one reducing the power of the Council to delay legislation passed by the Keys. By January of this year the battle lines were clearly drawn. The Council, after vigorous debate, amended the Keys' Bill in that, while agreeing to the removal of the Second Deemster, they proposed to increase the Lieutenant-Governor's appointments from two to three, one of whom could be the Second Deemster. The Keys rejected the Council's amendments outright and they reacted just as furiously at the Council's rejection of their other Bill. The conflict raged on, the Council expressing their horror at the 'cavalier' manner in which the Keys had treated their amendments. A proposal for a conference on constitutional reform was dismissed summarily by the Keys as cynical delaying tactics.

In October this year, the Keys forced the issue to its end. Existing rules stated that if a Bill was passed by the Keys on two successive occasions, rejected by the Council on those occasions, then passed again by the Keys in the third session, if not agreed to by the Council within two months, the Bill was deemed to have been passed. Thus, at the end of October the Keys introduced a new Bill to remove the Second Deemster, though at the same time conceding the additional appointed member. The Bill passed its three readings within minutes, and a further Bill reducing the delaying power of the Council from three to two sessions was also passed. That the Council threw out both these Bills can be seen only as a small and rather petty last act of defiance. Perhaps the members of the Council feel that it is necessary for them to be seen fighting for their position and that they see themselves as laying down a marker for the future. The Keys may have won the battle, but the war to transform the Legislative Council into a popularly elected body continues.

1964 NEWS IN BRIEF

JANUARY

1 - Speaker of the House of Keys, Mr Charles Kerruish, C.P., is awarded the O.B.E. in the New Year Honours List.

9 - Harbour Board workmen moved into South Ramsey to start clearance work for the development plan.

27 - It was revealed in the Great Train Robbery case that the Isle of Man Bank lost £151,250 in the hold-up.

31 - Death of Mr R. C. Stephen, M.H.K. after an operation in Liverpool. A former assistant editor of the *Isle of Man Examiner,* he turned to politics and was elected for South Douglas in 1956. He was held in high esteem, and was chosen as the first chairman of the powerful Finance Board, and was a member of the Executive Council at the time of his death. He was 62.

FEBRUARY

13 - Number on the unemployed register stands at 521 men and women. This compared with a figure of 627 this time last year.

15 - The *Mona's Isle,* leaving Peel to collect passengers at Douglas for Liverpool, went aground on rocks below Peel Castle. Two fishing boats freed her.

17 - Mr Norman Crowe, M.H.K., elected chairman of the Finance Board.

MARCH

18 - Mr John Bell, President of the Manx Labour Party, became the second youngest M.H.K. after winning the South Douglas by-election.

19 - Heavy seas breach 50 yards of sea wall at Laxey. The harbourmaster's office was demolished.

26 - Fort Anne Hotel re-opened after extensive alterations by the new owners, Heddon Hotels.

27 - A plan to put a 'roof' on Strand Street was revealed by architect Mr W. E. Quayle. The plan had the backing of Douglas business interests.

MAY

11 - Budget proposals announced by Lieutenant-Governor included a shock rise of 3d a pint for beer. But income tax remained at 4/3 in the £, and there were increases in National Assistance. Pensions will rise by 5s 6d for married couples and by 3s 6d for single persons.

13 - Damage estimated at £400 was caused by vandals to the centuries old church at Ballure, Ramsey.

19 - Second Manx Trophy Rally, organised this time by the experienced John Brown of the British Tourist Authority. 79 entries, including Geoff Duke, were received and all sections, night and day, were on closed roads. Winner was David Friswell with Keith Binns in a 1275 Mini Cooper S.

JUNE

2 - Record entry of 450 for this year's T.T. Races. Three wins for Honda machines - Redman (Junior and 250 c.c.) and Taveri (125 c.c.). After being ill all week, Mike Hailwood (M.V. Agusta) won his third Senior T.T. Two sidecar passengers were killed - one at Braddan Bridge and one at Ballaugh Bridge. A one-way traffic system on the Mountain Road was introduced for 'Mad Sunday'.

5 - Lieutenant-Governor opened the first phase of a Government-assisted half million pound development scheme of the Douglas Holiday Camp, now renamed the Isle of Man Holiday Centre. Luxury chalets had been built together with a large indoor swimming pool.

25 - Announced that M.H.K.s and M.L.C.s were to get an extra £100 on their £400 basic wage.

AUGUST

27 - Announced that the Island's fishing limits are to be extended to 12 miles in October under an Act of Parliament.

31 - Discovered that a research vessel, *Hamburg,* which had been a regular visitor to Douglas for the past five months, was looking for oil off the Manx coast.

OCTOBER

7 - For nearly two hours in a force 8 gale, eight members of the crew of the *Manxman* risked their lives to rescue a passenger who fell overboard. But it ended in tragedy - the man drowned before he could be recovered.

15 - Season arrival figure of 460,643 showed an increase of over 25,000 on last year. The total was the best since Fleetwood closed two years ago.

NOVEMBER

5 - Announced that the lease of the Grand Island Hotel had been granted by the Government - who had now taken the lease over - to Island Caterers Ltd., a subsidiary of a Northern Ireland catering firm. The refurbished hotel was opened last year after £150,000 of Government money had been granted. Government Treasurer Mr K. W. Carney admitted that the Government was cutting its losses.

OIL REFINERY FOR THE AYRES?

Creation of a new petrol brand for Britain known as IMP - short for Isle of Man Petroleums - lies behind a controversial American plan to build an oil refinery on the Ayres. Allied industries which manufacture oil- based products are expected to be established nearby. The San Francisco-based oil company of Natomas plans to bring the oil here from the Middle East by super tanker and discharge it by pipeline into land-based holding tanks spread over 275 acres on the Ayres. Petroleum products will be fed to tankers also by pipeline. Natomas expects to process 10,000 barrels of oil a day. Under a further concession from Tynwald, it plans also to hunt for oil and natural gas in Manx territorial waters.

Horrified conservationists have warned about the risk of sea and air pollution and spoilation of the Ayres but Tynwald, which has been locked in secret negotiations with Natomas for more than a year, seems committed to letting the project proceed. It has been described as "one of the most wonderful developments the Island could ever have." In addition to creating job opportunities, a Manx refinery is expected to bring local fuel costs down.

News about the refinery broke in the autumn after a General Development Bill was passed to enable Tynwald to cut through all the usual red tape necessary for a major project. No one would say at first what it concerned and this led to much speculation, particularly last year. There was concern, too, over the extent to which Tynwald seemed prepared to go to accommodate the wishes of secret developers.

CHIEF CONSTABLE IN HOT WATER

At the April meeting of Tynwald Mr. G. C. Gale, M.L.C. informed members that they had been referred to as 'bloody fools' by the Chief Constable, Mr. C. C. Beaty-Pownall. It happened during a speech at a Police Sports Club hot-pot supper and social at which members of the public were present. Mr. Gale wanted to know what disciplinary action was to be taken and asked should the Home Office, who appointed the Chief Constable, be involved. The Lieut-Governor said he had been informed of what the Chief Constable had said and only last night he had summoned Mr. Beaty-Pownall to Government House to explain certain matters that had been brought to his attention. As a result of the conversation the question had arisen as to whether or not there had been a breach of privilege. Therefore he would investigate the matter thoroughly, but he thought it was in his own competence to deal with the matter rather than involve the Home Office. At a later meeting of Tynwald, His Excellency told the members that the Chief Constable had apologised for his remarks, and there had been no breach of privilege.

T.T. BROADCASTS

In April the Tourist Board Race Committee announced that the B.B.C. and the A-C.U. had reached an agreement whereby continuous running race commentaries would be transmitted from the V.H.F. stations at Carnane on Douglas Head, and from Cumberland and Northern Ireland. The commentary team was headed by Murray Walker, son of former T.T. rider Graham Walker who presented B.B.C. commentaries in the 1930s. The short commentaries on medium and long wave also continue. As a result of this new arrangement, the public address loud speakers placed at 14 vantage points around the course were abandoned. However, they were resumed for the Manx Grand Prix after strong protests. This successful system was introduced for the Manx Grand Prix some years ago and was adopted and developed for the T.T. Races. As yet, few portable transistor sets are fitted to receive the V.H.F. signals so the crowds largely depended on the decision of enclosure owners to install amplification equipment. The B.B.C. agreed that this could be done. However, vantage points such as Parliament Square, Ramsey and Keppel Gate, were not privately owned and fans had to rely on their radios.

Responding to this new arrangement, Mr. John Grierson of Manx Radio announced that during the race periods they would give a full news service, interrupting programmes with the latest information. A commentary box, connected by telephone to Manx Radio's studio, will be set up behind the time-keepers hut at the Grandstand. In charge of the service will be Peter Kneale who joined Manx Radio as a part-time sports reporter last year, and is now a full-time announcer. He will be assisted by news reports 'phoned in by Jack Cretney at Ballacraine, Ken Leece at Ballaugh and Ian Cannell at the Bungalow. The broadcasts will be transmitted from Manx Radio's new studio in the ground floor premises of the Masonic Buildings on Loch Promenade.

AIR RALLY IS A HIT

The Jurby airfield came alive again when it made a splendid setting for the revived Isle of Man International

An impressive view of the new Sea Terminal which was opened in July by Princess Margaret. (Frank Cowin Library)

The Island's latest tourist attraction is the Wild Life Park, created out of the Curraghs and opened by Sir Ronald Garvey in July.

as Crown Welding Ltd., it produced components for the wartime aircraft industry. After the war the works continued to flourish under the name of R. D. Engineering Ltd., and in 1963 it became part of the Cheltenham Dowty Group founded by Mr Robert Dowty's brother, now Sir George Dowty. As part of the Group the local works became known as Iloman Engineering Ltd. Sir George was also present and spoke of his long interest in the Isle of Man. What his brother had started, he said, proved that Manx labour was perfectly capable of being trained to operate machines to produce high quality precision engineering work. Here was an opportunity for more young men to find local employment and support the Island's economy. Sir George explained that the factory covered 2,500 square feet with room to double that area. He announced that 14 apprentices, 40 semi-skilled engineers and 10 skilled engineers would be added to the workforce by the end of the year, bringing the total to 187. He also called upon the Board of Education to provide training courses for apprentices. A canteen is provided for the staff whose basic wage is £15 a week with plenty of opportunity for overtime. The factory will specialise in the manufacture of hydraulic equipment and the fabrication of components for modern jet aircraft now in production.

Air Rally and Manx Air Derby on Saturday, 29th May. Many of the aircraft on view were vintage pre-war machines including the famous Mew Gull in which Alex Henshaw won the last Manx Air Derby in 1939.

The Air Derby itself was run over two laps of a course which took in Peel, Douglas Head and the Point of Ayre, via Maughold Head. Aircraft were handicapped according to power and performance and the early starters of the 26 entries were into their second lap before the 'scratch' machine took off. It was the special Piper Commanche flown by the famous Miss Sheila Scott who had recently set up records from Northolt to different European capitals. All looked northwards to get the first glimpse of the leaders as they made a final dash to Jurby in the early evening sun. First across the airfield was Flt. Lt. Turely in a Proctor who completed the course at a speed of 143.5 m.p.h. Miss Scott finished in sixth place averaging 207 m.p.h. The race over, the crowds were treated to one of the first displays by the newly-formed Red Arrows. Flying in one of the seven Gnats was Manx pilot Flt. Lt. Gerry Ranscombe who is a brother of Bob Ranscombe, well-known photographer and instructor to the Isle of Man Flying Club.

At night there was a Presentation Dinner at the Castle Mona Hotel hosted by Airports Board chairman Mr J. H. Nicholls. Guest of Honour for the occasion was Sir Alan Cobham who presented the awards and recalled his visit in 1929 as part of his campaign to popularise flying and for the building of municipal airports. Officials of the Royal Aero club said the Air Rally had been a great success and looked forward to returning next year.

WILD LIFE PARK OPENED

The Lieutenant-Governor officially declared open the Curraghs Wild Life Park on Saturday, 3rd July. Hundreds of invited guests admired the transformation carried out and Sir Ronald described the development as a co-operative effort by many branches of Government. Conceding that the Park was a 'speculative venture' he said he was sure that it would become a worthwhile amenity for visitors and locals alike. There was much praise for Curator Mr. Tom Kind and his staff who had worked overtime to get the Park ready. Mr. Kind has worked on similar projects in various parts of the world and is a believer in the modern way of giving birds and animals as much freedom as possible, rather than being in cages and behind bars. Already in residence are monkeys, cranes, pelicans, Japanese deer, llamas, tropical birds, two lion cubs, bear cubs, tapirs, red and fallow deer and flamingoes. One of the great attractions is a baby elephant which was flown into Ronaldsway from Burma. Many more birds and animals are due to arrive by steamer.

PRINCESS MARGARET 'CAPTURES' THE ISLAND

Huge crowds turned out to greet Princess Margaret and her husband, Lord Snowdon, on their two-day visit during which they visited most parts of the Island. They flew into Ronaldsway on the evening of Sunday, 4th July, for a visit which bristled with unscheduled items. These enabled the royal couple to escape the normal protocol and join in the holiday fun. After dinner at Government House they were whisked up to the Bungalow for an unofficial ride on the Snaefell Summit railway. On the Monday, Manannan's mist cloaked St.

NEW ENGINEERING FACTORY IN ONCHAN

Sir Ronald Garvey declared open for business the new factory for Iloman Engineering Ltd. at Ballachrink, Onchan at the end of May. Sir Ronald recalled the work of the late Mr Robert Dowty who set up an engineering works at Castle Hill, Douglas during the last war. Known

1965
- Hindi becomes official language of India
- BASIC computer language developed
- Militant US black civil rights leader Malcolm X assassinated

John's for the Tynwald Ceremony over which the Princess presided, wearing a sprig of bollan vane. The ceremony followed the traditional form with Deemster Sydney J. Kneale reading this year's 26 Acts of Tynwald and 'Yn Llaidher', Mr. Charles Craine, reading them in Manx. A moment of light relief was when the name of the Public Lavatories (Turnstiles) Act was read out. A ripple of laughter and cheers among the crowd greeted the Act which removes all turnstiles from public toilets, mainly to help women who have to cope with shopping and young children. In the afternoon the royal couple undertook a 60 mile tour of the south of the Island visiting Castletown, Port St. Mary and Port Erin. They then travelled northwards to Glen Maye, Peel and then on the T.T. Course as far as Sulby. Here they left the course for Tholt-y-Will to visit Lord Strange whose title comes down from the Dukes of Atholl. At night they drove to Ramsey where they signed the visitors' book in the Town Hall to mark the centenary of the town.

LORD SNOWDON LAPS THE T.T. COURSE!

Undoubted highlight of the visit was Lord Snowdon's unscheduled excursion round the T.T. Course. It was the result of a chance remark by Lord Snowdon, a keen motorcyclist, at the Tynwald dinner held at the Grand Island Hotel, Ramsey. It prompted Lt. Col. Brian Mylchreest, A.D.C. to the Lieutenant-Governor, to contact Manx Grand Prix rider Dennis Craine to organise the trip after breakfast the following morning. With police motorcyclist Constable W. E. Prescott leading the way on a glorious sunny morning, Lord Snowdon followed, dressed in full motorcycling gear, riding a borrowed Triumph 650 c.c. twin. Dennis Craine kept in close company indicating the tricky sections ahead. Back at Government House, Lord Snowdon said how much he had enjoyed the lap which had taken about 45 minutes. His ride brought the whole visit alive and news of it was broadcast widely by newspapers, radio and television services.

SEA TERMINAL OPENED

Princess Margaret's final duty was to open the new Sea Terminal on Tuesday morning. With Lord Snowdon, she drove along the promenade lined with thousands of holidaymakers, joined by waitresses in their black and white uniforms. After the presentations were made, Mr.

A. S. Kelly, chairman of the Harbour Board, spoke of the fulfilment of a promise of many years' standing that this gateway to the Island should be a fitting symbol of our progressive and modern outlook. Princess Margaret was then called upon to unveil the commemorative plaque in the main passenger hall and, on appearing on the promenade outside, a 'fanfare' was sounded by the sirens of all the vessels in the harbour. This was followed by an official luncheon in the Crow's Nest Restaurant.

The Sea Terminal has taken five years to complete and has received considerable praise for its design and construction already. Mr C. J. Kneen, of architects Davidson and Marsh, is credited with the design which takes the form of three curved arms, likened to the Three Legs of Man. Main contractors were Messrs McCormack and Davies with many other local firms being involved. The ground floor is given over entirely to the reception of passengers, with a main hall capable of seating 1,000 people. Adjacent are amenities such as shops, a buffet and left luggage office. The first floor gives space for promenading and the Harbour Board offices are in the south arm. The north arm houses the main kitchens. The

Lord Snowdon made headline news when he had the opportunity of lapping the T.T. Course. Here he is negotiating Creg ny Baa on a borrowed Triumph 650 twin. (R. & L. Kelly Collection)

Built in 1926, and after a long and distinguished career in peace and war, the *Ben My Chree* made her final departure from Douglas on the night of 11th September. Many hundreds of admirers turned out to witness her farewell sailing. (Stan Basnett)

central feature contains a lift shaft and staircase giving access to the restaurant at third floor level. The circular restaurant has seating for 120 persons. The central feature is surmounted by a slender 140 feet concrete spire. In all, this most modern sea terminal can be described as 'harmony in concrete' and is sure to attract wide architectural interest.

ISLAND STRIKES OIL - IN A FASHION!

Years of political negotiation between the Island and the U.K. have given the Island a slice of the action in Britain's promised oil bonanza.

Ever since research vessels started detonating explosive charges on the sea bed around the Island in the late 1950s, it has been suspected that there could be oil and natural gas beneath the Irish Sea. Researchers said they were simply undertaking seismological tests for a university study but, in fact, they were hunting for evidence of oil and natural gas.

Until the late 1950s the suspected deposits were in international waters and no one country could claim ownership. Then an international conference on the Law of the Sea in 1957 divided the "Continental Shelf" between countries bordering the sea. In August 1958 the U.K. asked Tynwald to ratify the agreement to which it had bound the Island. That led to a Manx claim to ownership of a large part of the Continental Shelf in the Irish Sea. The U.K. claimed that oil and gas was unlikely to be found beneath the Irish Sea but Tynwald persisted in its claim. Finally, in July, when under pressure from Executive Council led by Mr Charles Kerruish, the Home Office conceded a Manx entitlement. Rather than yield it, however, the U.K. offered a deal. In return for Manx acceptance of U.K. administration of that part of the Irish Sea Continental Shelf claimable by the Island, it said it would share oil and gas royalties with the Island on a population basis from the entire British Continental Shelf. This was accepted and is expected now to yield many millions of pounds for the Manx Treasury as the North Sea Continental Shelf starts to yield considerable quantities of oil and gas.

The Isle of Man, meanwhile, retains absolute control over its territorial waters and these could be extended in future from three to 12 or 20 miles.

THE GREAT CASINO INQUIRY

A high-powered Commission of Inquiry set up by Tynwald has dismissed allegations of wrong-doing and corruption in high places in the Manx Government in relation to the Casino Trial of last year. In a 16,000 word report the commission said there was not the slightest suspicion falling on anybody in a position of authority. It said that Mr J. M. Cain, M.H.K., chairman of the Gaming Board of Control, acted with integrity throughout. Also, Attorney-General Mr David Lay was not guilty of delaying the Casino Trial to keep the casino going by finding new concessionaires. The commission said there was no corruption through improper actions although "certain things might have been done which were not done". The commission was headed by Sir Benjamin Ormerod, a former Lord Justice of Appeal. It was set up by the Lieutenant-Governor following sensational allegations against the persons named in the report, made in Tynwald by West Douglas M.H.K. Mr Victor Kneale, after the completion of the Casino Trial and the subsequent successful appeal by the American defendants.

The inquiry's public hearings lasted for three weeks in March, with Mr Kneale taking on the role of a prosecution counsel. He alleged that irregularities were allowed by the Attorney-General,

the Board of Control shut its eyes to what had happened under American direction, and senior Government officials conspired to see that the casino concession was kept alive. The allegations were strongly refuted and, in particular, Attorney-General Lay said it took a long time to bring the Americans to trial because of the complexity of the case. He also said the reason why American concessionaires William 'Buddy' Albury and John D. Hickey were not charged with the 'cut off the top' racket was that there was insufficient evidence against them. The hearings took place against the background of the new concessionaires, Crockford's of London, going through the planning procedures to enable the new Palace Hotel and Casino to be built on Douglas seafront.

In spite of the commission's findings, Mr Kneale said there was much in them which was of serious concern to the Government and they should not be shelved or forgotten. But that is what is happening. The report has been presented to Tynwald, but is not to be debated. The feelings are that the Island has had enough bad publicity over the casino and it is time to consign it to the past. The cost of the inquiry falls entirely on the Manx Government. The commission recommended that Mr Kneale be allowed the sum of £40 to meet his expenses.

Gone is the magnificent Palace Coliseum which has been demolished to make way for the Casino and 100-bedroom Palace Hotel, now under construction for Crockfords. (R. & L. Kelly Collection)

Right: Demolition of the Derby Castle Theatre and Ballroom has been completed, but withdrawal of the Manchester firm of developers involved has meant further delays in the Corporation's plans for an indoor swimming pool and leisure centre. (R. & L. Kelly Collection)

1965 NEWS IN BRIEF

JANUARY

8 - Demolition of All Saints Church began. The 'Tin Tabernacle' was built as a temporary structure in 1898 and is being replaced with a new building.

19 - Lieutenant-Governor sought assurance from NATO that aircraft engaged in bombing practice off the west coast would avoid flying over Peel.

25 - Legislative Council and Keys meetings at which tribute was paid to Sir Winston Churchill, the great statesman and wartime leader, who had died.

FEBRUARY

11 - Steam Packet's new cargo vessel *Ramsey* entered service. She replaced the *Conister*.

11 - Manx Radio said it was to build a new transmitting station at Foxdale, so as to extend Island coverage.

28 - Blizzards swept the Island, with sub-zero temperatures. Roads were closed and more snow was forecast.

MARCH

3 - A 60 m.p.h. blizzard swept the Island bringing chaos to air, sea and road services. A party of school children were marooned for a time in their school bus at Kirk Michael.

11 - First restaurant liquor licences granted in respect of the Anne Hathaway Café, Victoria Street, and the new Sea Terminal.

14 - Ramsey Steamship Company took delivery of the *Ben Veg*.

26 - Border Television began almost total coverage to the Island by opening their new transmitter on Richmond Hill. Lord Hill, head of I.T.A., was guest at a dinner at Fort Anne Hotel.

APRIL

8 - Deemster Moore ordered two Foxdale men to each receive six strokes of the birch followed by imprisonment, for attempted rape of an 18-year-old girl.

8 - The Manx Government purchased the Laxey Wheel for £5,000 from building contractor Mr Edwin Kneale, who had charge of it for 27 years. It is planned to fully restore the wheel.

14 - A ballot by members of the Licensed Victuallers Association revealed that a big majority were against Sunday opening during the winter.

26 - Four-day hearing of a tribunal to decide on 'needle time' of British records broadcast by Manx Radio, resulted in permission for the commercial station to broadcast such records for up to half its air time. Phonographic Performances Ltd., the B.B.C. and the Musician's Union had 'ganged up' to prevent this.

MAY

18 - Government agreed to buy eleven acres of land belonging to the Isle of Man Children's Home on Glencrutchery Road for £42,000.

19 - Government to take over the Peel Gas Company, the first step in dealing with an emergency situation in much of the Island's run-down gas industry.

22-23 Third successful Manx Rally, this time organised entirely by Manx enthusiasts with John Stott as Clerk of the Course. Event won by Tony Fall in a 1275 Mini Cooper S. Sensation was Ramsey driver Don Lindsay who took third place in a Minivan! But it was a unique Minivan, having the front end of a 1275 Mini Cooper S.

25 - Bill to allow cash betting shops on the Island failed in the House of Keys.

30 - First ever car hill-climb event, organised by the Lancashire Automobile Club at Tholt-y-Will, voted a 'hit'.

JUNE

16 - Record entry of 476 received for the T.T. Rhodesian world champion Jim Redman on Hondas won his third successive Junior and Lightweight 250 c.c. Races. Mike Hailwood (M.V.) won his third successive Senior Race despite coming off at Sarah's Cottage in the damp and dismal conditions.

21 - Record 1,500 cyclists arrived for International Cycling Week.

28 - The popular Manx Scooter Rally received a record entry of 384, 167 more than last year.

JULY

2 - Agreed that members of the Legislature receive £575 salary, an increase of £75.

5 - Gold coins issued by Government to mark the 200th anniversary of the Revestment Act. They were not legal tender.

19 - Four Scottish youths each ordered to receive nine strokes of the birch after injuring three visitors on Douglas Promenade during a disturbance.

AUGUST

12 - Dr. William Roy Costain appointed new Psychiatrist and Medical Superintendent of Ballamona Hospital.

31 - Old Time Dance Festival attracted 3,500 dancers to the Palace.

SEPTEMBER

7-9 - Dennis Craine, riding a Greaves machine won Lightweight M.G.P. Nigel Warren on an A.J.S. made a brave bid to win the Junior, finishing just six seconds behind Malcolm Uphill. Uphill scored a 'double' by winning the Senior in poor conditions.

16 - Home Secretary Sir Frank Soskice opened the new £48,000 extensions to the Ramsey Cottage Hospital. He was on the Island for talks with the Manx Government.

20 - The International Six Day Trials began. Held in the Isle of Man for the first time, it proved to be the toughest yet. 300 riders from 17 nations took part, the East Germans won the top awards. Four Manx riders took part, Dennis Craine and Roger Kelly gained bronze awards.

OCTOBER

8 - Civil engineers surveyed land at Ballaghennie on the Ayres as first steps towards constructing the oil refinery for the American firm Natomas Ltd.

22 - Season's arrival figures totalled 462,124, an increase of 1,481 on 1964.

29 - Health Services Board decided there would be no more free private wards in Noble's Hospital for members of the Legislature.

29 - The Isle of Man won the prestigious British Travel Association 'Come to Britain' trophy for the Sea Terminal.

NOVEMBER

1 - Second Deemster was removed from the Legislative Council.

9 - Repairs and extension to main runway at Jurby completed at cost of £130,000. Three Dakota aircraft of British United flown in for winter storage.

TYNWALD MATTERS:
SIR RONALD GARVEY REVIEWS ISLAND'S ECONOMY

In an upbeat Budget Speech to Tynwald the Lieutenant-Governor, who is also the Island's Chancellor of the Exchequer, reported a surplus of £568,578 on the year 1964/65 against an estimate of £67,134. Common Purse receipts were over £3½ million, mostly from spirits, wines and beer, tobacco, petrol and oil, and purchase tax. Contribution to the U.K. Government has now been fixed at 5% of Common Purse receipts. Receipts from income tax amounted to £1,270,000. Main expenses to Government in the ensuing year will be in connection with Social and Health Services, Education, Agriculture, Highways and Transport, Airports, Harbours, the Tourist Board, Local Government and Executive Government. His Excellency said that the standard rate of income tax would remain at 4s 3d in the pound, with small increases in income relief designed to help young families and the elderly. The tax on owner-occupied properties was to be abolished and there were to be increases in child and pension allowances.

INDUSTRY: In his speech Sir Ronald set out to show what Government had achieved in the past three or four years. He spoke of an 'industrial revolution' which had been aided by Government grants and loans. In the last three years the number of industrial establishments had more than doubled to 35, employing 1,026 males and 390 females - a total of 1,416 employees. This had resulted in a considerable drop in unemployment. Principal exports from the Island were engineering products, textiles and agriculture and fishery products.

TOURIST INDUSTRY: Sir Ronald said that it should be made known that during the past three years £850,000 had been made available to assist the industry in projects and modernisation. Much of the money was by way of direct loans to hoteliers and boarding house keepers to help bring their properties up to modern standards. He paid tribute to the Tourist Board for introducing the Voluntary Registration Scheme and the extensions of the Inclusive Holiday Scheme, introduced last year. The M.E.R. stations at Ramsey and Laxey had been improved impressively and he was sure the opening of the Curraghs Wild Life Park would prove a major tourist attraction.

AGRICULTURE: Sir Ronald likened the changes in agriculture to an 'agrarian revolution' which was linked to the industrial revolution mentioned previously. Not surprisingly, the hard work and low pay of farm workers had seen a movement away from the land to the factories with better pay and conditions. It was this movement that had forced the farmer to resort to increased mechanisation which had, to some extent, revolutionised the industry. The Board of Agriculture and Fisheries had been working diligently to improve and strengthen the industry and could be proud of the animal health record; recent years had seen the eradication of both brucellosis and the warble fly. The Government had spent an enormous amount of money on support schemes and guaranteeing prices. While appreciating that agriculture affected all our lives, there were often complaints about the high costs. It was something that had to be kept within bounds.

NEW RESIDENTS: Sir Ronald believed that the policy of attracting new residents was proving successful, though he admitted that it was difficult to convince many people that this was so. There were no official statistics available, but enquiries made by the Treasurer indicated that over a thousand bank accounts had been opened by newcomers and the three estate agents between them had sold 208 properties to new residents since 1960. His Excellency found these figures encouraging when one remembered these newcomers spent a high proportion of their income on the Island. He added that elderly new residents were not a burden on our social services as their retirement pensions were no liability to the Island.

NEW VENTURES: Turning to the proposed oil refinery, Sir Ronald was convinced that the project had untold economic possibilities, which would become evident one day to those who currently opposed such a project. The protracted negotiations had finally paid off with Natomas deciding to establish the oil refinery on the Island rather than elsewhere. Already there were regular visits from various technical officers and Sir Ronald hoped to announce soon when the foundation stone would be laid.

Finally, Sir Ronald referred to capital spending and the burden of loan charges which had to be judged carefully. He then recommended the creation of a Development Fund to be used for future schemes. One scheme he had in mind was the building of new Central Government Offices which he felt were both necessary and desirable.

Onchan's new Iloman Engineering factory was opened officially in May by Sir Ronald Garvey, in the presence of Sir George Dowty, chairman of the Dowty Engineering Group based in Cheltenham. The factory is part of the Government supported 'industrial revolution' Sir Ronald referred to and will have a workforce of nearly 200 by the end of the year.

ISLAND STRANGLED BY SEAMEN'S STRIKE

After 48 days of unprecedented isolation by sea, unable to import anything by British shipping other than emergency supplies, the Island is recovering slowly from a paralysing seamens' strike. The discovery that local stock levels were inadequate for the emergency, meanwhile, has led to Tynwald planning to increase the Island's store of essential supplies.

The national strike over working hours and pay began in mid-May. It decimated the tourist industry and led to the postponement of the T.T. until August.

Tynwald tried several times to persuade the National Union of Seamen to exempt the Island because the Island could not influence U.K. events but it refused to do so. All it would accept was the operation of occasional cargo vessels as "Mercy Ships," the crews of which donated their wages to the Union's strike fund. Indeed, after a flying visit here by N.U.S. Assistant Secretary, Tom Sutton, during the strike, the Union made things worse by refusing to allow certain essential raw materials for industry to be carried by the "Mercy Ships."

Airlifts brought in some goods and visitors but there was a limit to what they could do. Fishing boats were used also, notably on runs from Ireland into Peel.

Feelings ran high as the tourist industry faced disaster and workers elsewhere anticipated lay-offs. The situation looked like becoming ugly when victims planned a protest outside the Douglas offices of the National Union of Seamen. Tynwald's Strike Emergency Committee got it called off but hostility to Manx seamen remains.

The ending of the strike on 2nd July by the arrival of the Steam Packet's Manxman at Douglas was marked by celebrations at the pierhead led by Majorettes and Douglas Town Band. Tynwald, meanwhile, launched a late season extension drive. This included free morning and afternoon entertainment for visitors on wet days. Legislation was rushed through to permit T.T. races on a Sunday for the first time. This was necessary because the T.T. would have clashed otherwise with races at Oulton Park on August Bank Holiday Monday. Emergency loans at four per cent interest and repayable over three years were made available by Tynwald to hoteliers and guest house keepers who were hardest hit.

SUPER SPY OPENS CASINO
Britain's fictional super spy - 007 'licensed to kill' agent James Bond - opened the Island's new casino on 6th May with the first spin of a roulette wheel.

Bond, alias the film star Sean Connery, flew to the Island in between film engagements. As Bond he drives some of the most exotic cars imaginable. On the Isle of Man, however, he travelled from the Sea Terminal to the casino in leisurely style - aboard a horse tram! An accompanying tram was packed with V.I.P.s.

Work on building the casino hotel will not be completed until early next year. The casino, however, has been built as a separate building which will be tacked on

to the hotel when that is ready. Gambling at the Castle Mona Hotel finished at 5 a.m. on Friday, 6th May, the last day of the casino's lease of the hotel. Staff had 12 hours to shift gaming equipment to the new casino.

RAIL DISMAY
Thousands of letters were received from railway enthusiasts all over Britain and beyond following the announcement by Isle of Man Railway Company chairman Mr J. M. Cain, O.B.E., M.H.K., that the system was to close forthwith. He reported heavy losses last year and a fall in passengers from 133,838 in 1954 to 71,093, whilst wages and material costs were rising steeply. As an economy measure, refurbished diesel railcars were used on the Peel line since 1962 but even these were halted in November. Mr Cain said the number of passengers using buses operated by Isle of Man Road Services were also in decline. Had it not been for the railway taking over the bus companies in 1925 the railway would not have survived beyond the 1930s. The railway played a vital part during the war and enjoyed a post-war boom. Now, however, many Manx people and tourists have their own transport.

Considerable goodwill exists towards the railway

James Bond, alias Sean Connery, performs the opening ceremony of the new Casino in May. Next to him is Mayor of Douglas, Alderman Alex Moore who, as a Councillor, had first suggested the idea of the Island having a casino. Just a week after the Casino opening, the Island was hit by the seamen's strike.
(Manx National Heritage)

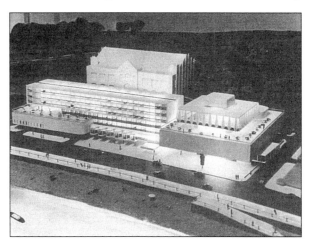

An architect's model of the Casino with the adjoining Palace Hotel due to be completed next year. Behind is the Palace Ballroom.
(Frank Cowin Library)

1966
• Laker Airways formed
• US and USSR both land probes on the moon
• Measles vaccination developed
• England wins football World Cup

now that diesel and electric-powered engines have replaced the great steam engines of the past elsewhere. The Isle of Man Railway is regarded by many as the finest steam railway still operating. A Railway Supporters Association has been formed and a report by Tynwald's Transport Commission recommends the railway's preservation as a tourist attraction but it doesn't say how. No doubt fingers will be pointed at the Manx Electric Railway where more Government money is being invested. The reappearance of the suggestion that a road should be built to the summit of Snaefell, now with a 'Crow's Nest' restaurant at the top, found little favour. Instead, £145,000 was voted to relay the rail track. In respect of the steam railway, however, it may be a case of 'once bitten, twice shy.'

TRAFFIC COMMISSIONERS

The long-awaited Road Traffic Commission came into being this year. It can regulate and licence bus and coach routes, fix fares and the siting of bus stops and coach stands. Already, the use of minor roads has been banned, including the popular Injebreck route. Coach operators who applied to the Commission for their first licences in March, had to list up to 50 separate tours. Many coach owners have wanted this for a long time, to replace the fierce competition which has led to the demise of some.

BEN-MY-CHREE ARRIVES

The Steam Packet's second car ferry made her maiden voyage to Douglas on 12th May - just three days before the seamen's strike. The fifth vessel to be named Ben-my-Chree, she is virtually identical to the Manx Maid which entered service in 1962. Since then there has been a big rise in the number of cars shipped here. Last year over 25,000 vehicles were carried on Steam Packet vessels.

TROUBLE AT MILL

Local youths were banned from Castletown's Witches Mill, after vandalism. The trouble began soon after the new proprietors, Mr Campbell Wilson, and his wife, Monique, self-styled "Queen of the Witches," moved in. Most of the damage was in the dance hall. The juke box

and record player were damaged, windows broken, benches and a table wrenched out of the walls, seat covers ripped and one of the lavatories was flooded by an electric light bulb being jammed in the floats. Mr Wilson said the trouble was due almost entirely to local teenagers and it was impossible for his staff to provide constant supervision. Young people who came with coach parties would still be admitted. One local youth, who denied that local boys were solely responsible, said the ban was unfair.

MANX GOLD

Hundreds of people jammed Ronaldsway Airport building in August to welcome home from Jamaica the Island's Empire Games team. In their scarlet red blazers, the 12-man team was led through an archway of cycle wheels by gold-medallist, Peter Buckley. Peter had won the cycle road race in a record time. Team members were taken to a reception attended by the Deputy Governor, Deemster Sydney Kneale O.B.E., Sir Ralph Stevenson, the Rev. Fred Cubbon (team commandant) and the Rev. Bert Reid, chairman of the Manx Empire Games Association. Peter Buckley was presented with a silver tray to mark the occasion. Nigel Dean, who narrowly missed winning a medal in the 10-mile track race, thanked team manager Curwen Clague and his assistant, Ron Killey, for their help. Four years ago the Island competed in the Games at Perth, Western Australia.

LIEUTENANT-GOVERNOR SWORN IN

The Island's new Lieutenant-Governor was sworn in according to custom in Castle Rushen on 7th September. Sir Peter Hyla Gawne Stallard, K.C.M.G., C.V.O., M.B.E., and Lady Stallard arrived in Castletown Square to a royal salute by the band of the 1st Battalion the Lancashire Fusiliers. Sir Peter was escorted then by First Deemster and Clerk of the Rolls, the Honourable Sydney Kneale, into the castle. The ceremony in the court house was broadcast to the public in the square. Sir Peter is of Manx descent. His mother, Eleanor, belongs to the long-established Gawne family. Sir Peter completed his education at Corpus Christi, Oxford, and entered the

Below left: Feature of the new Casino is the high-class cabaret which is performed nightly in the "King's Club".
(Photos: Frank Cowin Library)

Below right: What's it all about? Punters get down to business at one of the new roulette tables.

Colonial Service in 1937. He was posted to Nigeria and by 1958 was secretary to the Nigerian prime minister. In 1961 he moved to British Honduras as Governor and was knighted. He and Lady Stallard are joined at Government House, which he occupies rent-free, by their daughter Sarah and son Robert. He will benefit from salary rises awarded to Crown officials. His salary is £4,000 with an allowance of £2,000 for expenses (both tax free).

SHORT SKIRTS

Women's skirts are getting shorter. Evidently, young women have been getting bolder ever since the appearance of topless dresses two years ago. They went to Barbara Wood's clothing shop in Ramsey to try one on "to see what they would look like" but didn't dare wear one in public. Mini skirts, though, seem to be a different matter - despite what they can reveal when women stoop over!

FUN FESTIVAL

The Tourist Board marketed a September "Festival of Fun" to compensate for the lost June attractions. All events were advertised heavily by Radio Caroline at no cost. During the first week there was a £3,000 treasure hunt. The Palace Ballroom was given a clubland atmosphere with drinks served by waiters. One of the postponed events was the Manx Trophy Rally. This was held after the Manx Grand Prix on 16th and 17th September. There was a reduced entry of 62 of which 16 were from up-and-coming Manx drivers. They made the most of their opportunity and filled the top six places. The winner was Dennis Easthope, with Dennis Craine as co-driver, in a

FAREWELL SALUTE FOR SIR RONALD GARVEY

ONE of the Island's most charismatic and personally popular Lieutenant-Governors, Sir Ronald Garvey, ended his seven-year term of office and left the Island aboard the Royal Navy fishery protection vessel, H.M.S. Brereton on 9th August. As the ship left Douglas, Lady Garvey cast a wreath of flowers into the sea as a sign that they would return. A salute of 17 rockets was fired by H.M. Coastguard and the sirens of ships in the harbour sounded a farewell chorus. The presence of a huge crowd to see the couple off indicated the high regard in which Sir Ronald and Lady Garvey were held by Manx people. Earlier, in July, when Sir Ronald took his leave of Tynwald, politicians broke the normal solemnity of the Court chamber by singing "For He's a Jolly Good Fellow."

Socially, Sir Ronald and Lady Garvey gave of their time freely to participate in local events where Sir Ronald's easy geniality quickly banished formality. Officially, say politicians, Sir Ronald was the inspiration for the Island to throw off the lethargy of 50 years. A man of fertile imagination and ideas, he worked strenuously to improve economic and social conditions. It was he who accepted that the international promotion of low income tax on the Island and the absence of death duties would attract wealthy new residents in greater numbers than before and stimulate Manx business and commercial life. He recognised also that endemic winter unemployment had led to the disastrous drop in the Manx population in the 1950s because thousands of young people had emigrated to find better opportunities. Sir Ronald continued to foster Tynwald's drive to attract light industry and it was he who sponsored the idea of a five-year Development Plan. In fact, during his time, and in what has become known as 'the swinging sixties,' the word 'development' became the Island's watchword.

Sir Ronald's love of exciting ideas to promote the Island characterised his time in office. He was a tireless publicist who recognised the value of getting the Island a high profile in the news media. To this end he made himself more accessible to journalists than any Lieutenant-Governor before him. Some may say that this was an era of gimmickry and failed ideas but low taxation, the Island's own currency and its own radio station flowed from it. Sir Ronald supported strongly the plan for a casino in Douglas and saw this achieved in 1963. Despite its disastrous start under the American syndicate, it was still the first public casino in the British Isles. One of his 'pet' schemes was, and remains, the establishment of an oil refinery on the Ayres. When he initiated it, he believed it would bring great economic value to the Island despite many local people fearing that the environment would suffer. Whilst all seems to be in place for the building of the refinery, which could be seen as a 'monument' to Sir Ronald's Governorship, there are still no signs of it starting. Perhaps environmentalists have nothing to fear.

Sir Ronald wore his ceremonial dress at every opportunity. He is seen here greeting Her Majesty The Queen Mother at the Victoria Pier for her visit in July, 1963.

The Island's new Lieutenant-Governor, Sir Peter Stallard, and Lady Mary Stallard. They are seen here with their son, Robert and daughter, Sarah. (R. & L. Kelly Collection)

Ford Cortina GT. The hectic month of events boosted the season's arrival figures to 408,694. This was still 59,000 less than last year but it could have been worse. Ronaldsway airport handled a record number of passengers.

STRIKE LESSONS

Tynwald should raise at once with the T.U.C. the possibility of isolating the Isle of Man from future U.K. trade disputes, says a report by Tynwald's Strike Emergency Committee. Never again, it says, should a situation occur where there is not a single Steam Packet vessel available to meet the needs of an emergency. The committee, chaired by Mr Charles Kerruish, S.H.K., calls for more independence so that the Island can be

regarded as a separate self-supportive entity. The report wants more transmission power for Manx Radio, too. It says it was only through Radio Caroline that the Island's plight could be heard in the U.K. The committee recommends the maintenance here of a three month supply of petroleum products and increased reserves of flour, sugar, salt, fats, medical goods and essential industrial gases.

HOVERCRAFT ADVENTURE

A hovercraft, attempting to cross the Irish Sea in October, was diverted to Douglas because of gales but stopped on Peel shore instead. After refuelling, the 38-seater SR.N6 took V.I.P.s for trips in the sheltered bay. Next morning, she left Peel at 40 knots and negotiated the Sound despite a dangerous swell. Heading to Douglas, the hovercraft was forced to turn back to Peel by waves. On doing so, she electrified Port Erin by heaving up on the shore for a coffee break! On board were newspaper photographers Bill Peters and John Gaggs. Mr Peters said the ride was like being on a bumpy bus. They were thrown around when they hit waves. After another day's delay, the hovercraft reached Douglas.

Earlier this year, Steam Packet chairman, Mr J. B. Garside, told shareholders that the company had told the Air Transport Board that it planned to apply for licences to operate hovercraft. What effect the recent experience will have on this remains to be seen.

GENERAL ELECTION

Nine new members were elected to the House of Keys in the General Election. Miss Jean Thornton-Duesbery (Garff) became only the third woman member. The

Part of September's 'Festival of Fun', designed to make up for the loss of summer visitors, was the Dance Festival Week held in the Palace Ballroom. Annually, the Festival attracts up to 3,500 dancers from all parts of the British Isles.

election was held over three days, beginning 30th November. There were 54 candidates for 24 seats and the supposed threat to the Island's independence posed by the Common Market was to the forefront. At the first meeting of the new House, Mr Charles Kerruish was re-elected Speaker.

WAR ON RATS

The Island's war on rats has started to rely on poison used by government extermination teams. It reflects the rising affluence on the Island. Fewer people are prepared to become part-time rat-catchers, cutting off tails to claim the rat bounty of 4d each. That's double what it used to be yet the annual claims for bounties have dropped from 23,000 20 years ago to just 6,000. The use of poison, meanwhile, is worrying ornithologists. They fear that birds of prey, particularly owls, who catch and eat the poisoned rats will be poisoned themselves.

REFINERY HITCH

A financial hitch is delaying the building of the oil refinery on the Ayres. Financial restrictions imposed by the U.S. Treasury and the U.K. Chancellor of the Exchequer - in part, possibly, because of the Vietnam war - are preventing Natomas from progressing with the project. Detailed planning is at an advanced stage, however, and the company is investigating alternative sources of finance. The Lieutenant-Governor says that Natomas wishes to start the project as soon as possible.

Postponed from May until September, the Manx Trophy Rally suffered from a reduced entry. Local drivers took their chance and gained the top five places! Shown here are the first three drivers who are, from left to right, Doug Baird (2nd), Denis Easthope (1st) and John Dodsworth (3rd). Ken Leece was fourth and Horace Saville fifth.

1966 NEWS IN BRIEF

JANUARY
1 - Mr J. H. Nicholls, M.L.C., chairman of the Airports Board, awarded the O.B.E.
12 - Death, at the Mannin Infirmary, of the Island's oldest resident, Mr Thomas Arthur Bridson. It happened only weeks after celebrating his 105th birthday. Until several years ago he celebrated his birthdays by climbing Snaefell.
28 - Agrimark began operations at the Island's first major food ' factory' at Castle Hill, Douglas for packaging and canning.

MARCH
9 - Conversion of old Douglas Market Hall into a new amusement arcade by the Palace Company approved.
18 - Manx lottery ticket sales slump after Lieutenant-Governor says that a committee has been set up to examine lottery legislation and regulations.

APRIL
8 - Plan to hold a wedding in Peel Cathedral as part of the Viking Festival called off when clergy refused to officiate.

MAY
15 - Start of National Union of Seamen's national strike.

JULY
2 - Official end of seamen's seven week strike.
5 - Tynwald ceremony, attended by representatives from various other parliaments including the Speaker of the House of Commons, marks the centenary of the popularly-elected House of Keys.
28 - Swoops by police on local 'bookies' who were using their premises as illegal cash betting shops.

AUGUST
12 - News of retirement, after an eventful 27 years, of Mr William Shimmin, the Island's first driving examiner.
19 - Mr Godfrey Cretney, former headmaster of Castle Rushen High School and now of Regis School, Tettenall, knighted at Buckingam Palace in recognition of his pioneering work in comprehensive education.

22 - Start of T.T. practices and a month of action on the T.T. course, including the Manx Grand Prix.
28 - Being Mad Sunday, public houses were permitted for the first time to stay open on a Sunday for weekday hours.
28 - First T.T. race on a Sunday. The Swiss rider, Fritz Scheideger, won the Sidecar T.T. by four-fifths of a second from German, Max Deubel.
30 - Mike Hailwood won Lightweight T.T. for Honda in record time. Bill Ivy on a Yamaha won the 125 c.c. Lightweight, setting new records.

SEPTEMBER
1 - Giacomo Agostini won Junior T.T. for M.V. Agusta after Hailwood's Honda stopped at Bishopscourt on the first lap. Ralph Bryans won the 50 c.c. event for Honda.
3 - Mike Hailwood won his ninth T.T., establishing a new record lap in the Senior race of 107.07 m.p.h.

OCTOBER
10 - First stage completed of paving the way for the automatic telephone exchange to be introduced next spring. So far, 2,300 subscribers have had their numbers changed.
20 - Following an inspection of the T.T. course by an R.A.C. official, it was announced that there was little hope of the car T.T. races returning to the Island.
28 - The Very Reverend Eric Gordon enthroned in St George's church, Douglas, as the Island's new Lord Bishop.
28 - Opening of the luxurious casino restaurant and grill room.

NOVEMBER
9 - Part of South Ramsey flooded by the sea. Shops and houses in Old Cross and Church Street flooded to a depth of two or three feet.
27 - Huge gap in road at Horse Leap on the Marine Drive reduced traffic to one way at a time. The fall was much bigger than one which appeared in May. Erosion at the base of the cliff has resulted in movement of the rubble on which half the roadway is built.

THE MANX HOSPITALS LOTTERY: AN UNHAPPY ENDING

Bitter rows surround the ending of a Manx public lottery. The *Isle of Man Examiner* even faced a possible action against it by Tynwald for breach of parliamentary privilege. However, in November the Lieutenant-Governor decided that the dignity of the chamber might suffer far less than if an action was pursued officially.

The idea of a Manx lottery is nothing new. During the 1950s and early sixties the United Football Society raised enough money to fund many improvements to soccer pitches on the Island. Draws in the wholly-charitable shilling-a-week lottery were drawn at Castletown stadium every Wednesday evening. The promoter was Mr C. Peach of Ellerslie Nurseries, Castletown. Ramsey A.F.C. owes its purchase of Ballacloan and development of its stadium principally to lottery receipts. Attempts to stage a lottery on a large scale, however, never came to fruition until 1964 when the idea of a lottery based on the Senior T.T. race found favour in the Legislature. It was decided that the draw would take place after the race, thus avoiding the unease felt in many quarters about a pre-race draw. The object of the lottery was to raise money for Manx hospitals and this was embodied in the Manx Hospitals Lottery Bill which received overwhelming support in the House of Keys. A Manx Hospital Society was established with a committee of seven appointed by the Lieutenant-Governor, the lottery to be conducted by a manager. Although concern remained about the T.T. being used as a promotional feature of the scheme, this was assuaged when it became known that the A-C.U. had no objection. Consequently, the Royal Assent was given to the Manx Hospitals Lottery Act in July, 1964. The Society was formed and thousands of leaflets which gave details of the draw, to be made after the 1965 T.T., were distributed. By now the lottery was being compared favourably with the Irish Sweep Stake.

When it came to finalising the Hospital Lottery Regulations, however, doubts were expressed in both the Keys and Council about the financial credibility and morality of the venture. It was not until December that the final regulations were agreed. These provided that 25% of the proceeds had to go to a hospital fund while the rest of the money, after deducting "authorised expenditure," had to go as prizes. Money received in excess of the advertised prizes should be added to the prize fund, whereas, if there was a shortage of receipts the prizes should be cut proportionately. The delay meant that time was running out to organise the lottery in time for the 1965 T.T. A manager was appointed and an office established at the grandstand but it became apparent that the best that could be achieved was the use of the Manx Grand Prix as the lottery's main feature. As the summer progressed, ticket sales went sufficiently well for the manager to say that a second lottery would be based on the 1966 T.T. and a third on the 1967 F.A. Cup Final.

By September lottery supporters were euphoric. The first draw took place on the Thursday of M.G.P. week in a packed Palace ballroom. Prize money totalled £79,025, composed of a main prize of £25,000 and 44 lesser prizes. Authorised expenses were covered and the hospital fund received its 25% of gross receipts. The following week the winners received their cheques at the Arragon Hotel. Tickets were on sale already for the 1966 draw and, to sustain interest, an interim draw was planned on 20th December with £2,000 in prizes.

LOTTERY CRITICISMS

Towards the end of the year, however, criticism of the lottery and its employment strategy began to gain momentum. In Tynwald vague and allegedly scurrilous suggestions came thick and fast. These included a claim that the hospital fund had received less than its due. Both the chairman and manager of the lottery made a spirited, indeed, vehement, defence and insisted that there had been a scrupulous adherence to the Act and lottery regulations. They conceded, however, that the vociferous attacks on the lottery had damaged its reputation, perhaps irreparably. An analysis of the finances seemed to reveal that, in order to provide prizes and a donation to the hospital fund, £30,000 had had to be borrowed against future receipts. This, taken with plans for lottery money to be used to develop a British world-beating racing motorcycle, added to unease.

Even so, it became apparent that interest in the second lottery was booming. The interim draw at the Villa Marina on 20th December was a big success. The organisers were so confident that they held a further interim draw in March with £2,000 in prizes. Then the inquiry committee's report was published. This recommended that the lottery should be suspended until amendments to the regulations had been completed. The Lieutenant-Governor accepted this view so, whilst the 1966 T.T. draw was allowed to proceed, the third lottery was stopped until the amending legislation was in place. Hospital money had to be adjusted so there was no deficit and, among other things, a Steering Committee was appointed to supervise the Society.

RESIGNATIONS

Naturally, lottery supporters were appalled by what they considered to be draconian and unnecessary measures. Arguments became increasingly bitter and personal. Then in May the Seamen's Strike led to the T.T.'s postponement and a delay for the second draw. This was too much for the promoters. On the eve of the Senior T.T. in September, the chairman and entire committee of the Manx Hospital Society resigned. Bitterly disillusioned, they expressed their regret that "a scheme of so much promise had been strangled." The Lieutenant-Governor refused to accept their resignations until the draw was completed, this time in the Douglas Holiday Camp ballroom. A new chairman and committee were appointed, seemingly to tidy up details of the last lottery. They said there would be no further lottery until legislation had been amended and clarified. The last nail in the lottery coffin, however, was truly hammered in when £6,500 of public money was requested to pay off an existing deficit.

It was a sad end to a scheme which had promised so much. With hindsight, it can be said that the lottery was not properly funded in the first place and that the regulations were conflicting. Should the hospital contribution have been taken first and what was left go to the prize fund, or should it have been the other way round? The vagueness seems inexcusable. It certainly put the Manx Hospital Society in a difficult position. Lottery opponents, meanwhile, feel that their misgivings have been justified. Now it seems unlikely that there will be another attempt to stage a Manx lottery, unless memories fade and attitudes change.

CRISIS OVER U.K'S MARINE BROADCASTING BILL

1967
- Breath tests to detect drunk drivers introduced in Britain
- Coronary bypass surgical operation developed
- Electronic quartz wristwatches developed

FRIDAY, 1st September was named "Black Friday" by Speaker of the House of Keys, Mr Charles Kerruish. That was when relations between the Island and the U.K. collapsed to an all-time low. The occasion was the forcible extension to the Island of U.K. law aimed at starving out the 'pop pirate' Radio Caroline in Ramsey Bay and others like her elsewhere. The U.K.'s action was legal but Mr Kerruish condemned it as morally indefensible.

Four days later Minister of State at the Home Office, Lord Stonham, flew here by private jet in an effort to mend the breach. He proposed talks on the Island's constitution. These were agreed but he was left with no illusions as to how tough they will be. Protestors lined his route from Ronaldsway and Mec Vannin members carried a coffin through Douglas and outside Government House, purporting to contain "Manx Freedom."

What happened in September was the climax to failed attempts by Tynwald to barter its co-operation in legislating against Radio Caroline in return for higher transmission power for Manx Radio which would have given it coverage of the U.K. When this failed, the House of Keys rejected in March the Manx version of the U.K.'s Marine Broadcasting Offences Bill. When the U.K. said it would extend its own Act to the Island, the Keys decided to petition the Queen not to sign the necessary Order. This was described as a moment "unique in Manx history." At issue by now was the constitutional right of one state to legislate for another and the fear that the U.K. might try to control other domestic issues in the Island such as taxation. Whilst the U.K. conceded that, in most cases, the Island had a right to determine its own domestic laws, the Island was obliged to act against Radio Caroline because of international treaty obligations and, if it would not do so, the U.K. would have to force it to do so because it was responsible for the Island's international relations.

The petition to the Queen led to talks in London in May between a Manx team and her Privy Council, which was composed of the very politicians against whom the Island was protesting. When the latter told Her Majesty that it could not support the Manx petition, Tynwald was summoned from summer recess in July and asked to petition the United Nations to prevent the imposition of U.K. domestic policies on the Island. The world's press descended on the Island, packing the public gallery.

What followed was a bitter, nationalistic debate based on the principle of 'no legislation without representation.' Divisions between the Keys and the Legislative Council over embarrassing the U.K. internationally, led to the Keys keeping the dispute within the British family of nations by it petitioning the Commonwealth Secretariat instead but the petition never got there. The Island's relationship with the U.K. meant that the petition had to be given to the Home Office to pass on and it didn't do so.

The U.K.'s Marine Broadcasting Offences Act came into force on 14th August and shut down most of Britain's pirate radio stations. The Order in Council to extend the Act to the Island did not take effect until 1st September because the Queen was unavailable earlier to sign it. At midnight on the night the Order took effect, Radio Caroline played the Manx National Anthem to emphasise Manx independence which was being challenged. She still continues in Ramsey Bay, drawing supplies from Ireland and advertising from companies outside the British Isles. It is uncertain how long she can operate like this. What is certain, however, is that the Island's relationship with the U.K. will never be the same again. Manx nationalism has been roused to the point where virtually no one will be satisfied until the Island has extracted an understanding from the U.K. that it is entitled to total independence if it should ever wish it.

BACK IN STEAM!

Victorian costumes and pageantry brought Douglas Railway Station alive again on the morning of Saturday, 3rd June. Guests for the re-opening of the railway included His Excellency Sir Peter Stallard, dressed in top hat and morning coat. A large crowd saw engine No.15, Caledonia, break a tape while five other locos were in steam nearby. Guests departed on the first train to Peel followed by four more. Peel station had never seen such activity. In the afternoon there were more visits to Peel and the line from St John's to Ramsey was also in action. Two engines returning from Peel were coupled immediately to carriages waiting on the Castletown line, beyond which it was not possible to travel due to gas mains being laid.

The re-opening of the railway was made possible by a group of wealthy enthusiasts led by the Marquess of Ailsa, of the Ailsa Shipbuilding Company. The railway's revival was announced earlier by Lord Strange who lives

Tynwald's opposition to the United Kingdom's determination to remove the illegal Radio Caroline from Manx waters received considerable public support. Here, members of the nationalist Mec Vannin assemble to mount a protest march led by a coffin representing the death of Manx freedom.
(R. & L. Kelly Collection)

Back in steam, engine No 8 'Kissack', passes through Union Mills on the day of the re-opening of the steam railway. It is resplendent in the fresh green of the Ailsa livery, the coaches being finished in maroon and primrose.

at Tholt-y-Will and is the Island's only resident baronet. Sir Philip Wombwell, who has taken up residence at Baldwin, will manage the operation. In a highly technical arrangement with the Isle of Man Railway Company, the object is to operate the railway as a tourist attraction, making use of former railway employees. The project has the backing of the Manx Railway Preservation Society.

MANX AIR DERBY
Jurby airfield came alive again when the Manx Air Derby was held at the end of May. Guest of Honour was Group Captain Douglas Bader, the legless wartime flying ace. Visiting aircraft included the Piper Commanche in which Sheila Scott became the first woman pilot to fly around the world. In the afternoon the crowds were treated to a flying display by a Spitfire, Mosquito, Mustang, a Hunter jet fighter and the Red Arrows display team. Because of weather conditions, the race was delayed until early evening. The winner was W. H. Todd in a Bolkow.

REVOLUTION DEFERRED?
Plans to change local government outside of Douglas look set to trigger rows that could go on for years. Tynwald's Local Government Board wants to scrap all existing local authorities, other than Douglas Corporation, and replace them with four regional

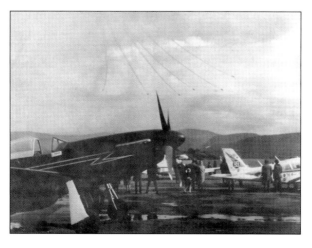

The scene at Jurby after the end of the Manx Air Derby. Overhead, the Red Arrows present their second display in Manx skies while, on the ground, the Mustang is seen in company with Sheila Scott's Piper Commanche, in which she became the first British woman pilot to fly around the world.

boards. Most parish and village authorities oppose it. Whilst it might encourage a few parish and village authorities such as Laxey Village and Lonan Parish Commissioners, Kirk Michael Village and Michael Parish Commissioners and Onchan Village and Onchan Parish Commissioners to merge, the majority of the authorities seem set to fight for their independence.

T.T.'S DIAMOND JUBILEE
A colourful ceremony at the grandstand on T.T. Saturday started the celebrations to mark 60 years of T.T. motorcycle racing. Douglas Town Band led a parade of riders and representatives of the competing nations. Past winners present included 10-times winner Stanley Woods. After the parade, a special three lap race for production models was held. John Hartle (Triumph) won the 750 c.c. event, Manxman Neil Kelly (Velocette), the 500 c.c. class and Bill Smith (Bultaco) the 250 c.c. one.

In race week Mike Hailwood (Honda) won three races for the second time, bringing his tally of wins to a record 12. He set up race and lap records in the Lightweight 250, Junior and Senior races. The Senior race was the most electrifying. Giacomo Agostini (M.V. Agusta) broke the lap record from a standing start. This led to an epic duel with Hailwood who set a new record of 108.77 m.p.h. on the next lap, despite problems with a loose twist grip. Agostini kept a slender lead until Lap 5 when his M.V.'s chain broke at Windy Corner. He coasted home in tears but to a great reception. Hailwood, meanwhile, is everyone's hero but he is said to be turning to car racing next year.

BULGHAM BREACH
Normal services of the Manx Electric Railway between Laxey and Ramsey resumed on Monday morning, 10th July. This followed completion of work at Bulgham where the track was breached after the collapse of part of the embankment, made up of shale used to fill a deep cleft in the 600 feet high cliff. This occurred in January. Until July 66,000 tram passengers transferred by foot on the road from trams on either side of the breach. Road traffic was diverted via Ballaragh. Engineering consultants advised on repairs to the embankment and track. Work started in May and wire mesh was embedded in the shale. A lattice of over 100 piles positioned on the rock face was filled with rubble and concrete. Pre-cast concrete was used to form the base for the tram track.

MAN AND WIFE GAOLED
The man who acted as Island agent for Crockfords in their take-over of the casino, Albert William Kerruish (52), was gaoled for two years by Deemster Moore at a Court of General Gaol. Twelve charges of fraud involved more than £1,000. He asked for 54 other charges of fraud to be taken into consideration. His wife, Evelyn Rosalind Kerruish (49) was sentenced to three months imprisonment on five charges involving £363. All the offences arose out of allegations of gross

mismanagement in the conduct of the affairs of the company Industrial Holdings (Isle of Man) of which Mr Kerruish was chairman and his wife a director. Mr Kerruish has been adjudicated a bankrupt and has resigned his directorship of Palace Hotel and Casino Ltd.

DISEASE SCARE

Pre-Christmas life on the Island was disrupted badly. Public meetings were cancelled and no fresh fruit and vegetables were allowed into the Island from England, Scotland or Wales - only by fishing boat from Ireland.

The cause was the introduction in November of controls to prevent the spread to the Island from Shropshire and Cheshire of a deadly outbreak of foot and mouth disease. They included a ban on the importation of all vehicles and implements other than cars which could be shown as having come direct from a factory. Even they had to have their wheels and underparts sprayed with disinfectant. Arrivals by air and sea had to walk over coconut matting soaked in disinfectant. Even then, farmers who had visited the U.K. were told to stay at home for 48 hours. Visitors from England, meanwhile, were told not to visit farms. One farmer said he had a shotgun ready for unwelcome visitors. There was speculation, meanwhile, that a ban on the movement of all people in and out of the Island might become necessary.

These precautions might seem draconian but the disease could cause havoc on the Island's 600 farms. Between them, they have 27,500 cattle, 50,000 sheep and 5,500 pigs.

SHIPYARD FOR SALE

Ramsey shipyard is for sale. Started in 1962 by the Ramsey Shipbuild-ing and Engineering Company, it is in financial difficulties despite Government support estimated at £250,000. Since July the company has been run by a Receiver. Now Mr John Bolton, chairman of Tynwald's Finance Board, says the yard is to be sold as 'a going concern.' A buyer will get a slipway which can take 400-ton vessels, a fitting-out berth, fabricating shop, joinery department and blacksmith's shop. Currently under construction for the University of Wales at a cost of £120,000, is the research vessel, Prince Madoc.

AIR OF PROSPERITY

The tearing down of old terraced properties in the Chester Street development area of Douglas, which started in mid-January, marks a determined commitment by Tynwald to stimulate development in lower Douglas. Included in the Local Government Board scheme is a new hotel - if an operator can be found.

Even though visitor arrival figures are holding up well, there seems to be a growing pessimism over the viability of the new tourist venture.

Some planners want to tear down much of Loch Promenade, Strand Street and Castle Street, too, and build a new frontage and shopping centre. The economic argument is that if new residents continue to

arrive at the present rate the resident population by 2,000 A.D. will be 75,000. That will make the economy equivalent to a good summer season all year round. Figures released by the Local Government Board show that 681 houses were built in the last five years and the rate of building is accelerating, notably in Ayre, Rushen and Middle sheadings. Birch Hill farm has just been acquired for a major housing development and a shortage of bricks has led to them being imported.

The Island is enjoying a wave of new prosperity. In the last five years the number of taxpayers has risen from 6,579 to 15,163, 3,000 of them in the last year alone. As this exceeds the growth in the resident population, the figures indicate that new industries and the attraction of new residents are creating wealth creation opportunities among the established Manx.

The Island's new bishop, the Rt Rev. Eric Gordon (above) consecrated the new Church of All Saints, Douglas, in April. (Frank Cowin Library)

The collapse of the embankment at Bulgham halted normal M.E.R. traffic from January to July.

TYNWALD MATTERS:
PROSPECT OF THE EUROPEAN COMMON MARKET

The new House of Keys has a mammoth problem confronting it - what will the Isle of Man's position be in relation to the Common Market in Europe? Its potential is enormous and it will change the face of Europe. As it seems likely that the United Kingdom will join, will this mean that the Island has to follow with the same terms and conditions? This raises once more the whole constitutional relationship with the United Kingdom - a relationship already under close scrutiny, and from the Manx point of view, highly critical. To be fair, the U.K. Government recognises that the Island has special concerns. Our agriculture could be seriously affected; mobility of labour might be introduced while control of taxation matters could be taken out of the hands of the Manx Government. In some ways Tynwald would be simply a local authority.

The U.K. Government has said that the choice is ours. The Common Market has an item known as the Special Treatment Protocol which enables the small dependencies of Common Market countries to stay out of the Market but to continue to trade freely with their mother countries. This possibility merits the most thorough and urgent examination to discover the most advantageous position for the Isle of Man. It is in this Protocol that our salvation may well lie.

1967 NEWS IN BRIEF

JANUARY

1 - Steam Packet abolished 1st and 2nd class fares. A new fare structure was introduced. The return fare on the Liverpool route was fixed at 67/6d.

12 - Demolition work started in the Chester Street development area of Douglas.

17 - Tynwald committee formed to study possible 'nationalisation' of Island's transport services.

FEBRUARY

3 - Palace and Derby Castle Company take over running of the Mooragh Park from Ramsey Commissioners.

3 - Resignation called for of Mr A. W. Kerruish, chairman of Peveril Hotel Ltd.

17 - Committee of Inspection appointed to investigate affairs of Industrial Holdings (I.O.M.) Ltd of which Mr A. W. Kerruish is chairman. Creditors claimed £31,000.

22 - Nicki Clothing Ltd of Union Mills received $100,000 order for their buoyant sailing jackets.

25 - Tynwald rejected proposal that senior positions in the Civil Service should be given only to Manxmen.

MARCH

3 - Peveril Hotel offered for sale by auctioneers acting on behalf of Receiver.

7 - Douglas rates rose from 11/3d to 12/3d in the £ because of a much heavier charge for Derby Castle project. Education rate rise brought combined rate to 20s in the £ for Douglas and Castletown.

20 - Palace Hotel and Casino Ltd awarded permanent licence by Gaming Board of Control. It is an exclusive concession for the next 20 years.

28 - Lack of organiser halted revival of International Music Festival held in 1962 and 1963. Mr Harry Pickard had withdrawn for health reasons.

APRIL

20 - New All Saints Church in Douglas, consecrated by Lord Bishop.

MAY

15 - Mr Howard Simcocks assured Tynwald that the proposed £12 million oil refinery would be built.

15 - Rating and Taxation Committee report suggested abolition of existing local authorities and the creation of a new single authority of 50 members.

16 - Lieutenant-Governor inaugurated STD telephone system with a call to London.

19-21 Manx Trophy Rally organised by a committee on behalf of Manx Auto Sport. Winner was Norman Harvey in a 1275 Mini Cooper S. The Manx crew of Ken and Evelyn Leece came second in a similar car.

JUNE

5 - Tynwald approved sale of Peveril Hotel to Island Caterers Ltd for £50,000.

27 - French trawler skipper fined and had equipment confiscated for fishing inside Manx territorial waters with illegal gear.

JULY

16 - Archbishop of York, Dr Donald Coggan, took part in Braddan open-air service.

AUGUST

10 - Two 19-year-olds from Douglas were given six strokes of the birch each and three months imprisonment for an attack on the police dog handler.

29 - Alex Jackson (15) from Onchan and the Buchan School was chosen to swim internationals for Great Britain. She shares the national record for 110 yards freestyle with Diana Wilkinson.

SEPTEMBER

1 - New Murray's Road School, Douglas, ready to receive infants and juniors from the old school which will be demolished. Parents expressed concern that the new school would not be big enough to accommodate all the children.

5-7 - Nigel Warren repeated his performance of 1965 in the Manx Grand Prix by coming 2nd in the Junior race and 6th in the Senior.

22 - Opening of the first all-Island abbatoir forecast for Christmas. It is sited at Cronkbourne and has been built by English specialists at a cost of £190,000.

24 - Earl of Derby handed over 'in perpetuity' priceless documents relating to his ancestors' Lordship of the Isle of Man between 1406 and 1736.

25 - Record herring catches. Landings last week of 3,113 crans were the best for 10 years. Dozens of Manx, Scottish and Irish boats made a rare spectacle in Douglas. Big consignments of barrelled salted herring were shipped by Dutch vessels.

OCTOBER

4 - Dock strike in Liverpool hit Isle of Man for third week. Steam Packet's cargo vessels, *Peveril*, *Ramsey* and *Fenella,* were held up.

9 - Business methods of Agrimark Ltd and the various Agricultural Marketing Associations which sponsored the company were alleged to be "unethical and unfair" at an inquiry held by a Tynwald committee.

18 - Tynwald decided not to take over the Post Office on the Island. Telephone engineering staff were opposed. Tynwald, meanwhile, feared an unknown cost to operate the telephone service. The U.K. would not sell the postal side alone. This was Tynwald's principal interest because it wanted the Island to issue its own postage stamps.

30 - Mersey dock strike ends after six weeks. Many shortages were caused by delays in freight deliveries.

31 - Last scheduled Dakota flight on Manx services. The aircraft flies from Ronaldsway to Blackpool. British United are to introduce Handley Page Dart Heralds on Manx routes.

NOVEMBER

23 - Planning Committee lay down conditions for building of Derby Castle solarium following objections about its height from residents who will overlook it in Strathallan Road.

RADIO CAROLINE TOWED AWAY

1968
- Oil discovered in Alaska
- *Apollo* 8 becomes the first piloted spacecraft to orbit the moon
- Epidural anaesthetic developed

The rusting and thickly barnacled 'pop' pirate Radio Caroline was towed away from Ramsey Bay by tug boat on Saturday evening, 2nd March. Several days later she was in dry dock in Holland. So ended an incredible era which started in 1964 and brought the U.K. and Manx Governments into heated conflict last year.

It appears that the Offshore Tender and Supply Company - a subsidiary of the Dutch Wijsmuller Group which serviced Caroline - wanted to withdraw from its arrangement yet could not abandon the vessel where she was. The 'pirates', meanwhile, would not come ashore of their own volition.

'Operation Caroline' happened after the arrival in Ramsey Bay, without explanation, of an ocean-going tug. After lying alongside Caroline for some time, a line was put aboard and the pirate was taken in tow. One of the three D.J.s aboard Caroline, Don Allen, said later that no one knew what was happening. There was no explanation from the tug crew. "All they would say was that we were being towed away for our own safety. Some of us thought we were going to be taken to Southern Ireland but we were just guessing. A few asked if they could be dropped off at Ramsey but they were refused. We had to just go along with the tugmen and that was it."

It was claimed later that the pirates had been taken off air to allow repairs to be undertaken and would be back on station within a short time. Few Manx people believed then, or since, however, that the Island would see Caroline again.

The pirate's departure marked a new era at Manx Radio. In January Tynwald agreed to nationalise the station, buying out joint owners, Pye Ltd and Richard Meyer, for £50,000. The take-over took effect nine days after Caroline's departure. Appar-ently Tynwald members believed that a state-owned and operated radio station could function outside the U.K.'s licensing restrictions and, therefore, could increase its transmission power to whatever level it wished. They discovered soon, however, that it couldn't. The U.K.'s Postmaster-General, Mr John Stonehouse, helped enlighten them with a contemptuous dismissal of new plans for Manx Radio to cover the U.K.

Now Tynwald is left with a purely local station, pressure to increase its public service transmissions and costly demands by staff for better deals on pay. The station's losses are expected to soar.

USURY LAW RELAXED

With bewildering haste and a certain degree of secrecy, both bodies of Tynwald, in February, swept away the Usury Act which, for 277 years had protected borrowers from unscrupulous lenders. Persistent attempts, beginning in 1960, had failed to remove the existing maximum borrowing rate of 6%. But objectors were confronted with the high bank rate in the United Kingdom, the effects of devaluation and the financial policies of the British Government. It became apparent that there was little investment on the Island; investors were taking their money elsewhere, such as the Channel Islands where Jersey had repealed its Usury Act some years ago. On the afternoon of 8th February the matter was speedily dealt with and the Privy Council granted Royal Assent later in the month. This introduced a new interest limit of 8% and almost immediately the Lieutenant-Governor laid before the Court an Order increasing the rate to 7%. The expense of the Sea Terminal, aid for tourist attractions and hotel support were all cited as reasons for the crisis. The effect on rents and mortgages, the increased expense of Government and Local Authority borrowings were voiced with concern, but to no avail. However, the Island will now compete in the money market on equal terms with others - such is the march of progress.

NO ROOF FOR SHOPPERS

Weather-proofing plans for the Douglas shopping areas of Strand Street and Duke Street were rejected in May by Douglas Town Councillors. The Tourist Board idea was that a plastic roof should be laid over the area. Apart from the technical problems of establishing a roof over buildings of varying heights, Island Chief Fire Officer, Mr C. Pearson, warned about fire dangers, particularly the inability of firemen to use a turntable ladder system in such an arcade. "An entire block of buildings could be lost in a fire," he said.

AIR DERBY

Over 40 aircraft came to Jurby for this year's Manx Air Derby. Guest of honour was Miss Sheila Scott O.B.E. The afternoon began with a display by Royal Navy Gannets and R.A.F. Lightnings. The course for the race was shortened so that aircraft were in sight for most of the

Radio Caroline, which had been a familiar feature of Ramsey Bay for the past four years, was towed away in March, following the U.K.'s new law making all pirate radio stations illegal. (R. & L. Kelly Collection)

Ramsey's new indoor swimming pool leads the way in plans to develop South Ramsey. Parts of the area have been demolished already in anticipation of the arrival of developers who will transform the land behind the South Promenade. (R. & L. Kelly Collection)

building of the new pool by Parkinsons Ltd started last June. The entrance foyer gives access to the changing rooms and a cafe, from which there is an opening to the spectator gallery overlooking the pool hall which contains the main pool and teaching pool. The main pool has six lanes and is large enough for county and district championships. A filtration and purification plant supplies the water, which can be maintained at a temperature of 78 degrees Fahrenheit.

'BAN THE BOOM' CAMPAIGN

Britain's Noise Abatement Society is distributing "Ban the Boom" stickers on the Island. It follows increasing Manx concern about sonic booms from the new supersonic airliner, Concorde. Not only is she to be tested near the Island but, when she enters service, commercial flights are expected to pass either over or near the Island.

The Ministry of Technology said a route plan for the testing of Concorde passed over the Isle of Man. In January, amid reports that compensation claims for damage caused by sonic booms were being rejected because of a lack of evidence, the Lieutenant-Governor said he had raised the matter with the Home Office.

HOVER POWER SOON?

Ramsey Commissioners have suggested to Tynwald's Local Government Board that provision should be made in a new South Ramsey for either a hoverport or a hydrofoil terminal. In July it was confirmed that a company, North West Hovercraft Ltd, planned to operate hovercraft services between Fleetwood, Morecambe and Barrow-in-Furness. If the 30 knot 90-seater Denny Sidewell proved satisfactory, the company said it might extend its services to the Isle of Man. In the meantime, it launched an excursion service between Fleetwood and Douglas using the 1,339-ton diesel-powered Stella Marina, chartered from a Norwegian company.

It is three years since the Steam Packet formed a subsidiary company, Manx Sea Transport Ltd., to investigate new fast craft and operate them if and when they became economic. In April, 1966, representatives of the British Hovercraft Corporation and Westland, came to the Island to promote their proposed new 160 ton SRN4 as being suitable for Manx routes. This is a hovercraft capable of carrying 500 people, or 250 people and 32 cars, and is to be introduced on cross-channel services. Steam Packet chairman, Mr J. B. Garside, said its reliability had still to be proved and the economic issue of acquiring such a craft for seasonal operation had still to be resolved.

time. Race winner was W. H. Jones, who was accompanied by his dog in a Condor. Manx pilot, the photographer Bob Ranscombe, came fourth and earned enough points to clinch the British Air Race Championship. The fastest speed award went to Charles Masefield who flew his Mustang.

NEW RAMSEY POOL

Ramsey's new £135,000 swimming pool was opened officially on 26th June by Mr Maurice Strickett, chairman of Ramsey Commissioners. It forms the first part of the South Ramsey Development Scheme. A large part of the remaining area has been cleared and the lease of the land is being offered to developers at one shilling a square yard.

Designed by Davidson, Marsh and Co., architects and surveyors of Douglas and Ramsey, and commissioned by the Local Government Board for Ramsey Commissioners,

Douglas Town Councillors admire the architect's model of the imaginative swimming pool and leisure complex which is seen as the answer to maintaining the town as a major holiday resort. Work on the swimming pool began last year and is expected to be completed next year. (R. & L. Kelly Collection)

TYNWALD MATTERS: SPEAKER OUSTED FROM EXECUTIVE COUNCIL

On Tuesday, 9th April, the Speaker of the House of Keys signed the certificate upon the announcement of Royal Assent to an Isle of Man Constitution Act. With that signature he also signed away his membership of the Executive Council and brought to an end the rancorous, indeed raucous, controversy that had raged for months. After the last General Election, when member for Garff, Mr Charles Kerruish, was re-elected Speaker, he was omitted from any consideration for Board chairmanships on the grounds that he must not only be impartial, but must be seen to be so. This status, however, was affected immediately by his nomination to the Executive Council by the Lieutenant-Governor. The Speaker had, of course, not only been a member of the Council for the past five years, but also its chairman. The acceptance of the nomination by the Speaker provoked an outburst of criticism and complaint, conducted, it might be argued, in unnecessarily personal terms. Fourteen Keys' members wrote to complain about the appointment to the Lieutenant-Governor, but he declined to cancel his nomination. As a result, the Keys passed, in an unprecedented move, a vote of censure on their Speaker who then refused to resign. The outcome was the introduction of a Constitution Amendment Bill which proposed that the Speaker could not be a member any longer of the Executive Council or participate in Board administration. This Bill received its expected fairly easy passage in the Keys and a more reluctant one in the Legislative Council. The Speaker's revised position should remove the acrimony that has been evident recently among our legislators and, although the Speaker has expressed his deep disappointment, there is no doubt that he will continue to be a powerful influence on the political scene for years to come.

AIRLIFT FOR LIGHTHOUSE

A helicopter airlift was responsible for the building by the Northern Lighthouse Board of the new lighthouse on the Calf of Man. Because of difficulties of access, the 870 tons of building materials were flown there from Port St Mary and Cregneish. Operating sometimes five trips an hour last year, mostly from Port St Mary quayside, the Bell 47G, carried up to 5 cwt of freight at a time in crates slung in netting beneath the aircraft. The helicopter averaged five trips an hour, simply lowering its cargo to the ground and then departing. It landed on the Calf only once in every five trips to collect the discarded nets. The noise made some breeding birds abandon their nests.

The new light, close to two ruined towers of former lights, was opened by Lieutenant-Governor, Sir Peter Stallard, on 24th July. He accompanied lighthouse officials there aboard the Lighthouse Commissioners' tender, the M.V. Pharos. Had there been bad weather arrangements had been made to perform an official switching on by remote control from The Sound.

The two million candle power light is visible for 23 miles. It is powered by diesel generators, the fuel for which will be landed on the Calf once a year and pumped, as required, from its store at South Harbour. Five years ago, when the Lighthouse Board planned the new light -

the first to be erected here in more than 50 years - it wanted to erect overhead electricity cables across the Sound. The planning committee insisted, however, that any cables would have to be laid underground to protect the view. Because of the cost, the Board decided on diesel generation. The light can operate on just one of the three generators that are available.

RAMSEY AND PEEL LINES TO CLOSE

The last train from Ramsey ran on 6th September and the following day saw the last trains on the Peel line. Railway enthusiast the Marquis of Ailsa said that his attempts to maintain the steam railway system had met with disappointing results. It had been a mistake to provide summer services on all three lines. The Port Erin line had shown the most promise but the Marquis made it clear that unless he was given financial assistance there would be no more trains on that line. It is hoped that the offer from the Tourist Board, of a grant of £7,500 a year, will be approved by Tynwald in the new year so that at least part of the historic railway system can be kept alive.

LIFE-SAVER

The first artificial kidney machine to be installed at the Intensive Care Unit at Noble's Hospital was provided in

Far left: The new Calf of Man lighthouse seen in company with one of the original twin lighthouses built in 1818. (R. & L. Kelly Collection)

Left: The new and the old, with Chicken Rock lighthouse in the background. It was abandoned as a result of a fire in 1960. (R. & L. Kelly Collection)

This year's Manx Rally winner, northern farmer John Huyton, with Bob Corrin, powers the Cortina GT through one of the day sections. He is the second Manxman to win this rally which has now been granted national status.

August. It was a life-saving measure for a Manx resident who had kidney failure. It transpired later that two others needed it also. Until now anyone who had to use a machine on a regular basis had to be sent to a U.K. clinic. The Manx machine, financed in part by Douglas Round Table, was ordered in May when it became apparent that pressure of demand for the machines in the U.K. meant that Manx users could not rely any longer on their availability there. Noble's Hospital is believed to be the first British hospital to be equipped with a machine. Kidney machines are installed in clinics in the U.K.

SCARE ENDED

After several terrible false alarms, the Island managed to prevent the spread here earlier this year of the U.K.'s outbreak of foot and mouth disease. Controls were severe as the Government vet monitored the situation. Marts were stopped and non-Manx boarding pupils who returned to King William's College and the Buchan School after the Christmas holidays were isolated from Manx day pupils for 48 hours in case they spread the infection.

Easing of restrictions began in January when commercial growers were allowed to import seeds and bulbs under licence and fresh fruit, tomatoes and vegetables were allowed in provided they were brought here in a container which was sealed for 48 hours and had not passed through a U.K. market. Marts resumed in late January.

One result of the controls emerged later this year. Farmers reported a plague of blue hares despite a reduction last year in the close season for shooting them. During the scare people were stopped from walking across farmland. That halted hunting and left hare and rabbit populations to grow uncontrolled. Rabbit numbers had been rising for years ever since some had developed a resistance to myxamatosis. The large blue hare, however, which was introduced some years ago for sport, is causing the worst crop damage because of its voracious appetite.

1968 NEWS IN BRIEF

JANUARY

18 - Tynwald decided to keep the death penalty despite the unprecedented intervention by the Lieutenant-Governor in the debate.

20 - Dalby and immediate area without electricity for three days as a result of ice bringing down power lines.

FEBRUARY

2 - Island's first two policewomen, Margaret Corkill and Patricia Moss, take up their duties.

16 - First application for a theatre licence at the Gaiety Theatre to serve patrons during the interval was refused by the Licensing Bench.

20 - On occupying the old Palais de Danse, the Maypole Supermarket was refused a retail liquor off-licence. Local grocers opposed the request.

MARCH

10 - Most of the restrictions, in force for months due to the foot-and-mouth epidemic in the British Isles, were lifted. Importation of uncooked meat was still banned.

APRIL

16 - After fierce criticism in Tynwald over financial losses, the Curraghs Wild Life Park started the year well with a gate of 2,000 during the Easter period.

MAY

4 - Board of Education's mobile library began weekly visits to all parts of the Island under the direction of librarian, Mrs Sheila Cowin.

7 - Mr Allan Wilcocks (bass) became the first person in the Manx Music Festival's history to win the Cleveland Medal four times. He had won the coveted award previously in 1961, 1963 and 1964.

19 - Manx Trophy Rally was granted national status and attracted top British rallyists. Bride farmer John Huyton, with Bob Corrin, won in a Cortina GT. The consistently highly placed John Dodsworth, with Adrian Hundleby, came second in a 1275 Mini Cooper S.

JUNE

14 - Bill Ivy, winner of the Lightweight 250 race, became the first to lap at over 100 m.p.h. in the Lightweight 125 race. The engine slowed, however, to let Yamaha teammate Phil Read win. Giacomo Agostini completed a comfortable Junior and Senior 'double' for M.V. Agusta.

19 - Manxman Brian Roche won the 25-mile Scratch Time Trial in Cycling Week.

23 - Peter Lawson (B.R.M.) won the Tholt-y-Will Hill Climb at 114.8 m.p.h. This might have been the last Hill Climb in the series because of rising costs of competing.

JULY

5 - First Manx passports issued.

18 - Divers discovered the wreck of *H.M.S. Racehorse* - a brig which founded on Langness rocks in 1822.

25 - A hard-pad and distemper epidemic reached terrifying proportions on the Island.

AUGUST

14 - Alex Jackson chosen for British swimming team in the Mexico Olympics.

18 - Agrimark, the commercial arm of the Island's producer-owned agricultural marketing societies, cleared of having unfair trading advantage by Select Committee.

SEPTEMBER

3 - John Findlay (Norton) won the Junior Manx Grand Prix. By the last lap, Manx rider Nigel Warren, was lying second but came off his A.J.S. at Doran's Bend. Injuries included a fractured leg. Findlay completed the 'double' by winning the Senior.

OCTOBER

8 - Representatives of the I.O.M. Fishermen's Association met the Harbour Board in a bid to resolve differences between the two sides which threatened to close-down the Island's £250,000-a-year escallop industry.

8 - Lieutenant-Governor Sir Peter Stallard warned that there was a feeling of unrest on the Island because legislative decisions were not explained to the public.

11 - Messrs Booth W. Kelly, ship repairers and engineers of Ramsey, re-located from their premises on Bowring Road and Derby Road to Ramsey Shipyard. The Government-financed shipyard had still not been sold.

12 - Miss Margaret Curphey returned to the Island to sing in a recital of sacred music at Arbory Church, accompanied by the Country Singers and Miss Emily Christian, L.R.A.M. Miss Curphey had gained an international reputation as an opera singer and is currently with the Sadler's Wells Opera Company.

17 - Bumper year for tourists - over 494,600 visited the Island during the season. This was helped by the re-starting of a Fleetwood service. For the second year in succession, however, there was a slight decline in air passengers handled at Ronaldsway because of rising costs.

29 - The principle of giving security of tenure to Manx tenant farmers was approved for the first time by the House of Keys.

DECEMBER

26 - The Island's package holiday trade was reported to be booming with at least 60 British travel firms offering all-in tours to the Island.

DERBY CASTLE POOL COMPLETED - AT LAST!

1969

1969

• Australian media magnate Rupert Murdoch buys the *Sun* newspaper

• *Concorde* makes its maiden flight in France

• Post offices bombed by Republican terrorists in Ireland

Douglas Corporation's long-awaited new swimming pool, the Aquadrome, was opened at the end of July. Engineering difficulties had caused long delays.

The main pool, housed in a large, light and airy hall, is just short of 110 feet. Three lengths equal 100 metres. At the diving end the water is 12 ft 6 inches deep and the diving boards include the type used in the Tokyo Olympic Games. There is also a beginners' pool and the area is surrounded by heated benches. It is reckoned that 650 swimmers can be accommodated along with 900 spectators on two balconies. A dominating feature of the hall is its construction against the natural rock of the cliff face. It is planned to produce a display of tropical and other plants to which the hall's heating and ventilation are suited. Elsewhere, other forms of bathing are provided by sauna baths, Turkish baths, Russian baths and an aerotone health bath.

The Aquadrome has taken over two and a half years to build. Work is progressing now on the adjoining solarium and leisure centre, due for completion by the end of next year. The total cost is £1,787,023, considerably more than originally expected. Prices have been affected by the devaluation of the pound. Government has contributed a grant of £600,000 towards the cost.

RACE COURSE TEST

A 5.75 mile car race circuit at Jurby, proposed by Geoff Duke of the Tourist Board's Race Committee, was tested one early spring morning by four of motorsport's top drivers - Stirling Moss, Tony Brooks, Maurice Trintingnant and four-times winner of Le Mans, Olivier Gendebien. FordSport airlifted four Formula Fords to Jurby airfield by British Air Ferries Carvair and the cars were set off at 7 a.m. by Lieutenant-Governor, Sir Peter Stallard. They averaged 67 m.p.h. despite a startled milkman joining them for a time. The drivers liked the course but the cost of R.A.C. safety requirements are expected to be prohibitive. That is the history of repeated efforts to get car racing back to the Island, either on the T.T. course or elsewhere. A 4.35 mile course devised by Mr Duke in 1965 was based around the Round Table with a grandstand at the Round Table cross roads. The circuit followed a clock-wise direction to Cronk-ny-Irrey Laa, turned right near Cronk Fedjag on to a rough track which needed resurfacing, went on the inside of Eairy Cushlin, along the perimeter of Kerrowdhoo and Kella plantations. The £400,000 cost for road works and safety measures ruled it out. Mr Duke may return to the idea if the Jurby course is abandoned but cost will always be a stumbling block.

MEAL BREAK STOPS AIRCRAFT LANDING

The necessity for an aircraft to circle over Ronaldsway Airport whilst control tower staff had a meal break, has led to a row. It happened on 24th August when Ronaldsway Airport was shut down for most of the day because of fog. Some of the air traffic controllers were sent north to open Jurby as a diversionary airport. That night, Cambrian's evening Viscount flight from London, via Liverpool, had to

Interior of the Derby Castle Aquadrome which has taken over 2½ years to build. The inclusion of the cliff face as one of the sides is a unique feature, though it presented major engineering difficulties. (Frank Cowin Library)

1969
- Neil Armstrong becomes the first man on the moon
- Woodstock music festival begins in USA
- Death of North Vietnam President Ho Chi Minh

circle Ronaldsway for 20 minutes before contact could be made with air traffic control. Someone who was waiting was told by Cambrian staff that there was no Airports Board staff in the control tower. An official who confirmed this said the controllers had to have their meals and the aircraft would have to wait until they were ready. Later, Airport Commandant, Mr Eric Cheshire, said the problem arose from having to operate two airports with one staff. The controllers had been on duty since early morning and somehow they had to have a meal as air traffic regulations stipulated. So many had to be on duty at any one time and it was impossible to spread mealtimes. The problem arose because the Cambrian flight arrived sooner than expected. Mr Cheshire added that, had it not been for Jurby, passengers would not have been able to land at all on the Isle of Man.

RADIO TALKS

Talks between the Manx and U.K. Governments on Manx Radio's transmission strength took place throughout the year. Requests for more power, however, were refused. Suggestions that the station should 'turn up the wick' unilaterally led to Broadcasting Commission chairman, Major Geoff Crellin M.H.K., warning that this could lead to the station's closure and prosecutions against the directors and staff. The problem is that Manx Radio wants to be heard in the U.K. but the U.K. Government insists that the station must be confined to the Island.

THREE CURRENCIES

The Isle of Man is to have the coinage of three nations in circulation despite bank hostility. There will be English and Irish as before and now Manx. Local coinage, the first for about 130 years, is to be introduced in October 1971 following the decimalisation of British and Irish currency in February that year. The coins will be produced on Tynwald's behalf by the Royal Mint in London. As a precursor, it will strike a Manx crown featuring a Manx cat for release in November next year.

The banks are opposed to the new coinage because of

the labour cost of sorting it. Other critics think that holidaymakers will be irritated by having to sort through their loose change before leaving the Island to get rid of coinage which is not accepted in the U.K. Tynwald, however, likes the idea because of tradition, convenience and the wish to extend the image of Manx independence.

The majority of existing coinage in circulation comes from the U.K. Irish coinage isn't legal tender but so much is imported by Irish visitors and workers that it is accepted. In April the Speaker of the House of Keys ruled in the Keys that Irish coinage wasn't legal tender but advocate, Mr Howard Simcocks, said it had been in circulation for so long it would be difficult to establish that it was illegal. Later, the Select Committee of Tynwald, which recommended the minting of distinctive Manx coins, said it was best not to interfere with the "tacit acceptance" of Irish coinage.

FACELIFT FOR LADY

Progress is being made in a facelift for the 115-year-old Laxey Wheel, 'Lady Isabella.' Work began four years ago when the Government bought her. Supervising the refurbishment is the Water Board's chief engineer, Mr J. Peacock, advised by the previous owner, Mr Edwin Kneale. When work started many of the timbers showed signs of rot but no main component had reached a state of collapse. It has been possible, therefore, to renew each part piece by piece. The original pine of the 48 spokes has been replaced by boxed-in steel girders while new timber has been used to renew the 168 buckets. The most difficult part has been replacing the oak blocks of the main bearings which support the axle. The 75 ton wheel had to be lifted so that the blocks could be removed. Twenty-five-ton jacks lifted the wheel one-eighth of an inch. The oak was cut away and replaced by reinforced concrete which is to be faced with oak to preserve the original appearance. The 10 ton forged iron axle was found to be virtually as good as new. This coming winter the crank arms and balance buckets will be checked, then the facelift will be completed with fresh coats of paint.

TAX RELIEF

Manx Post Office staff in both the postal and telecommunication departments became liable for Manx income tax for the first time as from October. Until now the Post Office was a U.K. state-run department. Consequently, all Manx employees received their pay from the U.K. with the much higher U.K. tax deducted at source. Conversion of the Post Office on 1st October into a public corporation freed Manx staff from the tax.

OFFICE PLAN

Agreement was reached in October that new centralised Government Offices should be built on the existing site. It will mean the demolition of an old terrace of houses which has been used as offices and the red-bricked St Mary's R.C. junior school at their rear. The houses have suffered from dry rot and collapsing ceilings for the last 10 years. The hope is that the development will end the tendency for Government departments to be scattered throughout

An earlier view of the Aquadrome as it nears completion. (R. & L. Kelly Collection)

TYNWALD MATTERS: LORD STONHAM'S WORKING PARTY

The news towards the end of last year that a Royal Commission was to be established with the task, among other things, of examining the constitutional relationship of the Isle of Man and the United Kingdom was greeted with dismay by our politicians. The U.K's unilateral imposition of a commission halted existing constitutional negotiations. In 1967 Lord Stonham was appointed chairman of a Joint Working Party following the forcible extension of the Marine Broadcasting Offences Act by Order in Council, despite the fierce opposition of the House of Keys. Their position was that this was not just a little trouble over a pirate radio station, or an attempt to gain more power for the legal local radio, but an attempt by the British Government to deny the Isle of Man what little self-government it saw itself as possessing. It was seen as part of the continual struggle to increase the Island's right for more independence.

By the autumn of 1966 meetings with Tynwald representatives began in London and continued throughout last year. The appointment of a Royal Commission created an entirely different political landscape. Solutions, if any, agreed by both sides of the Working Party had to be set aside, the only recourse being to give evidence to the Commission. The whole matter is being complicated by the impending decision about the United Kingdom's entry into the Common Market. This remains a major worry and this has not been eased by the publication in May this year of the Working Party's report. The 100,000-word document, is seen as nothing more than a very damp squib. A few points produced some sort of agreement; the rest are to be put to the Royal Commission. There is no mention of the Isle of Man being granted greater independence and claims that the Island has a right to negotiate for itself on an international basis seem not to have been pursued. Perhaps such claims are seen as ploys to justify separate Manx negotiations regarding the Common Market issue instead of being involved with the U.K. While the Royal Commission has undoubtedly put an end to the Working Party, the agitation not only to preserve what hard-gained measures of independence the Island already enjoys, but to increase it, must continue in accordance with the opinion probably of the majority of the Manx people.

MORE POWER FOR THE KEYS

While the slow and painful negotiations with the U.K. Government have occupied considerable time over the past two years, here at home the Keys have shown determination to increase their influence in the law-making process. The position of the Speaker has been resolved in a climate of excitement, even crisis, and a revision of the composition of the Legislative Council is nearing its climax. The current Isle of Man Constitution (No.2) Bill is aimed at removing the power of the Lieutenant-Governor to nominate two members of the Legislative Council and empowering the Keys to elect the two members instead. This is seen by most as another step in the march of democracy, while others see it as unnecessary and ill-advised. Not surprisingly, the Bill passed through the three Keys' readings without trouble. The reasons put forward by the Constitutional Development Committee were that elected members were just as capable of providing stable and informed authority as those benefiting from the existing system of nomination. In the Legislative Council, no doubt, there will be strong opposition. It does appear, however, that the only likely amendment to the Keys' Bill will be to enable the Attorney-General to retain his vote and, with that exception, it is anticipated that the passage of the Bill will be completed by both houses later this year. This will mean that the Legislative Council will consist of the eight members elected by the Keys together with the First Deemster, the Attorney-General and the Lord Bishop.

Douglas but many in Government doubt this. They don't believe there is sufficient space for long-term expansion on the existing site.

Speaker Charles Kerruish wanted to re-locate Government Buildings to the land in front of the Isle of Man Childrens' Home buildings in Glencrutchery Road, Douglas, once used for vegetable growing. The various large buildings used by the Home and the land was bought by Government several years ago when it became apparent that in these more affluent and healthier days, the long-established charity did not need the accommodation it once did. The number of children in residence has fallen steadily, to 19 in 1966 and now a dozen. The Home rented a small property on the site from Tynwald until it could find an alternative base. This proved to be Knottfield in Woodbourne Road, Douglas.

NEW RAMSEY HOTEL
A million pound scheme to provide Ramsey with an

hotel, holiday apartments, flats, shops and parking facilities, has been announced. The plans have been prepared by the Malcolm Milton Partnership, parent company of Post and Beam Developments Ltd, the Manx company which will carry out the building. The main building, adjacent to St Paul's Church, will be known as an 'apart-hotel.' A Government grant of £100,000 has been approved. Demolition of seafront property is ready to start but the final clearance of South Ramsey is being delayed by house owners who refuse to accept Local Government Board valuations. Compulsory purchase orders are to be issued.

CLASSROOM CRISIS
Board of Education chairman, Mr Victor Kneale, has warned that, despite extensions to existing schools and the building of new ones, pressure on accommodation is mounting. He attributes this to the fact that many new residents are families with children of school age. Many

The last moments of an American Super Sabre F100 jet caught by an amateur cameraman. The pilot ejected safely over the Jurby bombing range and was picked up by a fishing boat and brought into Peel. (R. & L. Kelly Collection)

others want to come here and are only being held back by a lack of job prospects. Mr Kneale has given Onchan, where 1,500 new homes are planned, as an example of the problems caused by growth. Onchan School has had two extensions in the past 15 years and now has almost 400 pupils compared with 265 in 1958. Land at Ashley Hill is to be bought to provide a second school. All Douglas schools are filled to capacity, even the new Murray's Road School, which means that a new school will have to be built in this area. Willaston Infants School has been extended, yet is full.

The extension to Braddan School is filled too. Mr Kneale has hinted that a 'breathing space' could be gained by converting the Tromode Drill Hall into a school. However, despite bitter Corporation opposition, Tynwald has earmarked the site for a new Fire Station.

BABY BOOM

The number of births is rising steadily. Last year's 650 births were 16% up on 1967. Now this year's total has topped 700. Although the death rate still exceeds births and is set to do so for a long time to come because of the older structure of the population, the birth trend is seen to be the result of the Government's plan to retain Manx families on the Island and reverse the population drain of the 1950s. The Jane Crookall Maternity Home is to be equipped to the standards of a full maternity hospital. This means that caesarian sections, which hitherto have had to be done at Noble's Hospital, will be capable of being undertaken at 'The Jane.' Mr A. S. Townsend has been appointed consultant obstetrician.

ANTI-BIRCH CAMPAIGN

The birching in November of a 15-year-old for the theft of a handbag, just two days after he tried to kill himself, has breathed fresh life into a new anti-birching movement. The Manx Penal Reform Group is led by the Belgian, Angèle Kneale, the journalist Valerie Roach and the former W.P.C. Mrs Millicent Faragher, wife of Rushen M.H.K. Mr Tom Faragher who actually supports the birch.

The group has launched a petition for an inquiry into birching but it can expect a hostile response from most Manx people who believe that birching deters serious crime. Already a rival pro-birching petition has been launched.

1969 NEWS IN BRIEF

JANUARY
1 - Lieutenant Colonel J. B. Mylchreest, A.D.C. to the Lieutenant-Governor since 1956, awarded the O.B.E. in the New Year Honours list.
7 - Announced that the Kursaal gaming rooms would be in the old Opera House of the Palace Ballroom.
8 - Children and Young Persons Bill passed. It included a clause which forbids parents from leaving children under seven without supervision for an unreasonable time.
21 - Tynwald agreed a tax cut on petrol by 2d a gallon.
23 - Lord Bishop Eric Gordon made history by becoming the first Anglican Bishop to preach in a Manx R. C. church - St Mary's, Douglas.
28 - Bill to give hotels with room for more than 50 guests, and providing live entertainment, an extra hour's drinking, approved by Keys.
28 - Keys pass Bill to legalise cash betting but betting shops were not licensed to take cash bets this summer. Illegal cash betting has been endemic in Douglas for generations but bookies were warned that they could expect a hard time if they were caught this summer.

FEBRUARY
2 - Public inquiry into South Ramsey called for at a public meeting in Ramsey held by Sir Henry Sugden M.H.K.
4 - New Isle of Man Children's Home in Douglas christened 'Knottfield.'
18 - Isle of Man Railway given three year reprieve by Government grant of £7,500 a year.

MARCH
6 - Highway and Transport Board plan to test all imported vehicles welcomed by local garage owners.
11 - Ceiling on interest rates lifted 1% to 8%, the second rise in a year.
11 - Legislation to end property owner's right to vote wherever they have property approved in principle.
18 - Government said it had had no return on the £50,000 it spent to 'nationalise' Manx Radio.

APRIL
9 - Housing developers obtained an option to buy the Howstrake estate in Onchan, including the golf course.
28 - Coach operators failed to break Douglas Corporation bus department's monopoly on the Marine Drive route to Port Soderick.

MAY
1 - Mrs Eleanor Shimmin (contralto) won the Cleveland Medal for the third time. She won it last year and in 1965.
19 - Record entry of 125 for Manx Trophy Rally. Winner was Colin Malkin and John

Davenport in a Hillman Imp. The best Manx result was third place for John Huyton and Margaret Kennish in a Lotus Cortina.
24 - Increased tax allowances in Budget removed 600 from income tax bracket. A record surplus of £1,600,000 reported for the last financial year.

JUNE
5 - Giacomo Agostini completed another 'double' for M.V. Agusta with little opposition from single cylinder machines. Australian, Kel Carruthers (Benelli) won the Lightweight 250 race.
5 - Stock car racing at Onchan Park Stadium forced the abandonment of the annual international cycle track meeting because of alterations that had to be made.
8 - World premiere at the Regal Cinema of British film comedy 'Carry on Camping' attended by stars, Sid James, Kenneth Williams and Hattie Jacques.

JULY
15 - Two French trawler skippers were each fined £80 and had catches worth £1,900 confiscated for fishing in Manx territorial waters.
24 - American pilot of a Super Sabre F100, which crashed into the sea over Jurby Head bombing range, was rescued by fishing boat.
30 - Holidaymakers poured into the Island although there were no vacancies in hotels.

SEPTEMBER
2 - Deemster George Moore made First Deemster and Clerk of the Rolls on the retirement of Deemster Sydney Kneale, O.B.E. High-Bailiff Roy Eason became Second Deemster.
7 - Record catches of herring created fish export boom.
15 - Mr Neil Hamilton-Meikle, former R.A.F. pilot and head brewer for Okell's, died as a result of his gyrocopter crashing on Black Mountain, Ballaugh.
17 - Island's worst-ever road tragedy when three men were killed on the Whitebridge Hill, Onchan in a head-on crash between a van and a Daimler car.

OCTOBER
21 - Tynwald agreed to vote £6,000 to enable a new plan to be drawn for Government Offices.
28 - Maximum rate of interest allowed on the Island raised by 2% to 10% A Tynwald Order only will be necessary for new rates to take effect.

NOVEMBER
14 - Rowany Golf Course to be bought by Port Erin Commissioners for £12,000.

CONCORDE SONIC BOOM JUST A 'DULL THUD'

'Operation Trafalgar' - the first testing of the new supersonic airliner, Con-corde, on a route near the Island and using Ronaldsway Airport as one of its 10 tracking stations - proved to be an anti-climax on 1st September. After fears about the noise from its sonic boom, people reported hearing no more than "a dull thud". It was enough to start seagulls crying but that was all. Concorde was at an altitude of eight miles.

Earlier concern about Concorde led to Tynwald being asked in January to object to Concorde's testing on an 800 mile south to north flight path 20 miles off the Island's west coast. Speaker of the House of Keys, Mr Charles Kerruish, wanted a Select Committee to ask the U.K. Government for a change of plan. He was worried not only about damage to property but also to humans and animals. Most members expressed support for British involvement in a project which could bring future benefits. Nevertheless, the U.K.'s Ministry of Technology undertook in April to tell Government Office in Douglas one day in advance of any likelihood of booms. The latter is now broadcasting warnings on Manx Radio.

In August a U.K. compensation scheme for anyone who suffers damage from sonic booms was extended here but now it seems unlikely there will be many calls upon it in respect of Concorde. Two farmers at Kirk Michael, however, have lodged claims after a low-flying N.A.T.O. bomber caused a dramatic drop in egg production by their hens. Mr George Metcalfe of Beach House, Kirk Michael, says he is installing loudspeakers in his hen houses so his 6,000 egg-layers can be accustomised to sudden noise.

RABIES SCARE
The quarantining of local dogs in England until a rabies scare there passed led to protests. An estimated 25 dogs owned by Manx residents were trapped in England in October last year when the ban on the movement of dogs and cats to the Island was introduced. Dog owners thought their pets should be allowed in on humanitarian grounds.

LANDMARK GOES
Douglas quayside lost one of its famous landmarks in January. The Imperial Buildings, formerly a Victorian hotel and latterly the offices of the Steam Packet Co., were demolished. The clearance was to make space on the crowded quayside for the unloading and loading of containers by the cargo vessels which berth nearby.

BID TO STOP BOMBING
Two crashes by American Super Sabre F100 jets led to a public petition in February to close N.A.T.O.'s bombing range at Jurby. Residents of Michael, Ballaugh, Jurby and German parishes were concerned that there could be a serious accident over land. Already bombs had been dropped on farmland. In the first crash last summer the pilot ejected safely but in the second, at the end of January, the pilot died. Peel lifeboat and the Essex Girl assisted naval vessels in the recovery of the body and wreckage. The petition to the Lieutenant-Governor said that as an alternative to closure of the range, the bombing target, currently two miles off the Michael coastline, should be moved further out to sea.

LIDO POPULAR
In its first year (ended April last) as a gaming kursaal, the former Palace Ballroom, now known as the Palace Lido, attracted 250,000 people. Replying to claims that teenagers are visiting the Lido, the Gaming Board of Control says that the gaming rooms in the former Palace Opera House are off-limits to under-21s. Some people have been required to produce birth certificates.

BETTING SHOPS
The first Manx cash betting shops were licensed by the Gaming Board of Control in early May and began operating as from 24th May. Although 10 were permitted, the Board licensed only seven of the 15 applicants - seven in Douglas and one each in Ramsey and Peel.

JET SERVICE
Cambrian Airways, now part of British Air Services, replaced its Viscounts with B.A.C. 1-11 jets on its London Heathrow scheduled services in May. There was an inaugural visit of a jet at the end of March when Airports Board members and officials were given a flight. On their return to Ronaldsway, a sherry party was held to celebrate the event and the christening of the main runway, now brought up to standard to receive jet aircraft. Later, Airports Board chairman, Mr C. L. P. Vereker, M.H.K. announced a £100,000 modernisation programme. This includes the linking of the Terminal Building with the Control Tower by a covered pier which will give passengers closer access to aircraft and provide waiting rooms. There will be new Customs accommodation and the old Customs hall will be equipped

The introduction of Cambrian's B.A.C. 1-11 passenger jet on the London route may have been a milestone for Manx aviation, but its early morning departure has brought a stream of complaints from the residents of Castletown.

The Wheel Turning Ceremony attracted thousands of people to Laxey reminiscent of the 1854 christening of 'Lady Isabella'. The occasion marked the completion of the restoration of the famous wheel.

with a conveyor system to receive passengers' baggage.

Footnote: Residents of Castle-town are not so impressed with the arrival of Cambrian's B.A.C.1-11. The jet's early morning departure to London is an unwelcome alarm clock. They say the noise is unbearable and Tynwald should provide grant aid for the sound-proofing of homes.

T.T. PROTESTS

The deaths of six riders in the T.T. race period led to more protests from those who want to stop racing on the T.T. course. They received some support from Italian star Giacomo Agostini who said the T.T. was too dangerous to be included in the world championships. Agostini is still the main attraction for T.T. fans. With only privateers to contend with this year, he completed his third, and comfortable, race 'double' on an M.V. Agusta.

This year's Manx Trophy Rally was marred also by a death. A Twin Cam Escort went out of control on the notorious bumps of the Switchback road and rolled over. Spectators risked their lives to rescue the driver, Mark Rideout, from the blazing wreck but were unable to save co-driver Richard Colley when the petrol tank exploded. As a mark of respect, Saturday night's prizegiving was postponed until Sunday morning. Winner was Chris Slater and John Davenport in an Escort T.C. Locals, John Huyton and Bob Corrin came fourth in a Lotus Cortina.

BONNETS FOR LADY ISABELLA

Thousands of Manx people, joined by tourists, flocked to Laxey to see the Wheel Turning Ceremony of the refurbished Lady Isabella. Held by the Tourist Board on the afternoon of 5th July, it re-enacted the scene when the Wheel was christened in September, 1854. A short service in Laxey church, broadcast by loudspeakers, began the proceedings, during which those in Victorian dress assembled in the grounds of the M.E.R. station. Laxey school children, many dressed as miners with candles in their hats, were joined by parents and villagers in Victorian attire. Free rides on the electric railway for those who dressed for the occasion attracted 2,000! Men wore top hats but bonnets worn by the ladies stole the show. Laxey

Brass Band led a procession to the Wheel. Even surrounding fields were filled with people. Speaker of the House of Keys, Mr Charles Kerruish, and his wife, Mrs Margaret Kerruish, unveiled a plaque and turned on the water to start the Wheel in motion again. A mighty roar was heard over the valley as the buckets filled and the Wheel began to turn, her great crank moving the rods on the viaduct which once operated the pumps. Unnoticed by many was the water splashing from the buckets on to the platform party below! There was much praise for Water Board engineer, Mr Jack Peacock, who supervised the work, Mr Edwin Kneale who had cared for the Wheel for many years, and for the contractors.

HORSE POWER ENDS

The last horse-drawn open-top float for the delivery of fresh milk in Douglas was withdrawn from service in August. It was operated by Tommy Brew, his wife Daphne and the horse 'Ramsey'. Motorised vans, some electrically-powered, have replaced the floats. Veteran roundsmen say they miss the ability of experienced horses who could follow roundsmen as they walked from door to door and could stop and start on their own initiative.

A more long-term change already being planned is the phasing-out of metal churns for the transfer of milk from farms. Within five years it is proposed to start the introduction of milk tankers for the bulk collection of milk. This will require dairy farmers to equip themselves with refrigerated storage tanks. Hence the need for long-term planning. Even so, it could be 10 or 15 years before churns are declared totally redundant.

Further long-term plans include a new Creamery at Tromode. Its construction should start in 1972 and it should become operational in 1974. This will be financed in part by Government and the rest by a subscription of shares by producers.

END OF TIPS?

Open tipping will be a thing of the past soon, according to Tynwald's Local Government Board. There is talk even of making it an offence. The predictions have come following the go-ahead in May for a new Tynwald-financed refuse pulverisation plant at Richmond Hill. It follows arguments and expensive delays on the composting of rubbish which span 15 years. All local authorities will send their rubbish to the plant. Some are worried about the travelling time but they have been told to buy larger refuse vehicles to reduce the number of trips.

DOUBTS ABOUT YACHT VILLAGE

Creation of a yachting village in Ramsey's inner harbour hangs in the balance. The scheme, with its 140 split-level marine houses with balconies overlooking the harbour and private moorings for yachts, has excited a lot of interest but there are problems.

The artist-developer Leslie Salts, announced his £1.5 million plan in August last year. He said the village would be the first of its kind in Britain. It involved sealing off the inner harbour's mud banks, retaining between seven and

1970
- Typhoon and tidal wave kill more than 150,000 in East Pakistan
- 27 year-old Guitarist Jimi Hendrix is found dead
- Edward Heath becomes Prime Minister of Britain

nine feet of water there for moored yachts, and providing loch gates in a barrage bridge to enable yachts to come and go as required.

Planning approval in principle was given in April but it has been plagued by set-backs ever since. Revised plans were produced in September with the support of Ramsey Commissioners. Mr Salts said then that the scheme could be completed within 18 months but pessimists question whether work will ever start. Tynwald's Harbour Board is opposed to it. Board chairman, Ramsey M.H.K., Mr Spencer Kelly, says the project is not a genuine yachting marina. It is a housing estate with a lake. The Board believes it would be wrong for the Board to part with a large proportion of the tidal area of Ramsey harbour for private gain, especially when the ship repair yard needs some of the space for the berthing of vessels. Another obstacle is a fear of what could happen to Ramsey harbour if work stops mid-way. Not everyone believes Mr Salts has the resources to see it through.

Meanwhile, at least development of South Ramsey is underway. The Malcolm-Milton Partnership opened a show flat in April. Now work has started on what is to be known as St Paul's Square. By 1972 an Apart-Hotel should be operational. The entire scheme, with 135 flats and 18 shops, is expected to take about four years to complete.

REPORT ATTACKED

Constant fear that the Isle of Man is in decline as a major holiday resort because of the growing popularity of low-cost package holidays to the Mediterranean has resulted in another Inquiry: this time by the Tourist Industry Development Commission. When debated by Tynwald, its report was criticised for being "obvious," ridiculous and impossible to implement. Recommendations included establishing duty-free facilities for the sale of drinks and cigarettes, more provision of bedrooms, chalets and

Work which began last year in removing the eyesore of the Foxdale 'deads' continues, the material being used as hard core for building sites and road works. The photograph shows the forlorn Foxdale railway station from where thousands of tons of the lead ore were once carried by rail northwards to Ramsey for export. (R. & L. Kelly Collection)

camping sites, the introduction of a compulsory grading scheme for existing tourist accommodation, and better use of the Island's natural amenities such as its glens. The report recommended also increased spending by the Tourist Board on marketing, long-term training of executive staff but a reduction in other staff. Despite this, the Board was praised for what it does. Last year over 500,000 visitors came here. During the past decade annual season arrivals by air and sea averaged 474,000 compared with 522,000 in the 1950s. That's considered not too bad in the circumstances but a pointer to the future is a decision by the Douglas Hotel and Guest House Association to abandon as from this year the traditional Douglas Holiday Guide. It's not financially viable.

END OF THE LINE?

The dismantling of the Groudle Glen Railway has been completed. It closed in 1963 after being plagued by technical troubles dating back to wartime neglect. Three years ago the locomotive Polar Bear was taken for preservation by the Brockham Museum Association. The semi-derelict remains of the other loco, Sea Lion, were transferred later to the Steam Centre run by John Walton at Kirk Michael. Most of the carriages were destroyed by vandals. Now much of the old line has been removed and the engine shed and station has been demolished.

END OF THE SAGA OF THE FOXDALE 'DEADS'

Work continues on the removal of the waste heaps - the 'deads' - which have been a blot on the landscape ever since the lead mining operations ceased in the Foxdale area in 1910. As with Laxey, huge quantities of the waste were removed during the war for use in the construction of the Jurby, Andreas and Ronaldsway airfields. Prior to this, some of the Laxey waste had been used by a Liverpool company as aggregate for the making of lintels and cills. These were used in the building of the Ballakermeen High Schools. During the 1950s there was renewed interest in the Island's mining prospects and the Island Exploration Company undertook geophysical and geochemical prospecting as well as a small amount of drilling. The results were poor and the activity ceased.

Also during the 1950s, Metaliferrous Holdings Ltd installed an extracting plant at the Snaefell mine, above Laxey, to work its waste heaps. When these were exhausted, material was trucked from Foxdale until the plant could be relocated at Kionslieu. Then the plant closed suddenly and stood idle for years until its removal to South Africa. A legacy of the cyanide extracting process was the heavy pollution of rivers into which the tailings were discharged. In 1963 Tynwald engaged a firm of consultant geologists and mining engineers. Its report ruled out any

profitable mining in the foreseeable future.

Another product of Foxdale's mining area, commonly used in new buildings, was the crushed quartz spar dash. This was supplied by the Foxdale Flux and Mica Company as a sideline in its production of china clay flux for the pottery industry. In conjunction with another company, it also produced 'catsilva' Manx granite bricks to meet demand during the 1960s building boom. The making of bricks was taken over by the Foxdale Brick Company for a time but then ceased.

In 1968 Lieutenant-Governor Sir Peter Stallard, accompanied by Government officials, toured the remaining Foxdale 'deads' and met the directors of the brick company which owned the land involved. It was agreed that when brick production ceased the land would pass into Government ownership. This was the prelude to clearing away the last of the 'deads' and removing what had long been an eyesore. Work began in the spring of last year, the waste material being dispersed throughout the Island as hard core on building sites and in road construction.

Soon, only the mine buildings and shafts will remain as the last vestige of the mining which prospered during the 19th century. Local stories, meanwhile, suggest that the shafts have become host for large quantities of old, unwanted, government records.

Ramsey Commissioners have expressed their anger at the Harbour Board's decision to close the Queen's Pier to shipping. Throughout the century the pier has received thousands of visitors to the northern resort. The photograph, from the 1950s, shows the Steam Packet's 'Victoria' leaving for Douglas after calling in from Belfast. Now such scenes are likely to be a thing of the past. (R. & L. Kelly Collection)

1970 NEWS IN BRIEF

JANUARY

18 - Alderman Alex Moore accused the Water Board's five members of defying the expressed wish of Tynwald in its attempted 'snatch' of Douglas Corporation water undertaking.

FEBRUARY

2 - Compulsory purchase of houses in South Ramsey Development Area given the 'go-ahead' by House of Keys.

3 - House of Keys approved Bill which will give 18-year-olds the vote in elections.

10 - Usury Bill passed by Legislative Council. It raised the ceiling on interest rates to 10%.

11 - Douglas Corporation said they would fight a plan to build a new fire station at Tromode to "the bitter end."

25 - Civil Defence Commission proposed a scheme to keep Emergency Services for a further 10 years.

25 - Steam Packet shareholders attacked plans to instal gaming machines on their vessels. The rival *Stella Marina* had operated gaming tables already outside Manx territorial waters.

MARCH

13 - Seven motorists caught in a radar trap on Bray Hill, Douglas, fined by the High-Bailiff.

APRIL

8 - A Court of General Gaol Delivery told that facilities at Ballamona Hospital are not adequate for the care of criminal lunatics.

MAY

5 - Opposition to the proposed siting by doctors of a group practice surgery at Ramsey Cottage Hospital.

6 - Youth leader proposed the instruction at Manx schools on the use and danger of drugs like marijuana.

11 - The 45-year-old June Effort and Season Extension Committee wound up because of lack of support.

19 - Mr Howard Simcocks M.H.K. called for a modified Pay As You Earn tax system to be introduced. Tax arrears of £930,000 was revealed.

JUNE

7 - Near riot on Douglas promenade during T.T. week.

24 - Legal action by Corporation over the Local Government Board's plan to convert Tromode Drill Hall into the main Douglas fire station.

27 - Over 110 members of the North American Manx Association arrive at Ronaldsway after flying to Ringway. They were joined by others for the N.A.M.A. Conference at the Majestic Hotel, Onchan.

JULY

8 - Corporation defied Government's proposed 25% rise in council house rents.

22 - Inquest on Ramsey hotelier Stanley Lance Waring (42) of the Antrim Hotel,

Mooragh Promenade, who shot himself at West Kimmeragh gravel pit, Bride. His wife said he had a fixation with death after a fortune-teller told him he would die at 42.

30 - Bishop's Youth Chaplain, the Rev. Brian Partington, refused a grant from the Board of Education for a recent visit to Russia. One member said his visit might contribute to the spread of Communism.

AUGUST

3 - Island's first-ever drugs case in court. Manchester student gaoled for six months.

12 - Councillor John Bell said the Villa Marina was "rampant with dry rot."

22 - 14th Olde-Time Dance Festival at the Palace Lido.

SEPTEMBER

4 - Mr Peter Gelling, lecturer at Birmingham University, discovered Viking-style house with corn and drying mill, when excavating about 700 feet up at Dalby.

OCTOBER

9 - Mr and Mrs Wilfred Costain died as fire swept through their Colby farmhouse.

9 - A tree dragged Mr William Ridgeway to his death by drowning at Agneash.

10 - Palace Company sold the Royalty Cinema, Walpole Avenue, Douglas to Island Gift Shops.

20 - Tynwald rescinded a 1961 decision to keep Queen's Pier, Ramsey open for passenger traffic.

21 - Ramsey Commissioners expressed their "disgust" at the Harbour Board's decision to close Queen's Pier. Approaches made to the Lieutenant-Governor.

24 - Local banks told clients who received interest of over £15 that details would be given to the Income Tax Department.

27 - Mr J. B. Bolton lost his seat on the Legislative Council when the House of Keys decided that he and Sir Ralph Stevenson should be replaced by Messrs Bill Quayle and Norman Crowe.

29 - Mrs Eleanor Shimmin won the Rose Bowl, Blackpool Music Festival's premier award.

NOVEMBER

3 - An all-British wind speed record of 150 m.p.h. recorded by Air Ministry men on Snaefell summit.

28 - Death of Speaker's wife, Mrs Margaret Kerruish, J.P.

DECEMBER

17 - Two fishermen saved by helicopter after being in the sea for 15 hours.

ISLAND CHANGES TO DECIMAL COINAGE

D Day was February 15th. That was Decimal Day - the day when the Island, along with Britain, abandoned the old L.s.d. It was the beginning of the end of a tradition of 20 shillings to the pound, 12 pence to the shilling, half crowns, sixpenny bits and threepenny dodgers.

The new system of 100 pence to the £ meant so much confusion for most people, despite years of preparation, that some huge percentage price rises were imposed by businesses without the general public being conscious of them. One Manx item, for example, which had been priced at a 1d was repriced at a penny halfpenny in the new currency. It seemed a relatively small rise. In fact, it represented a 400% increase. At first many shop prices had to be displayed in both currencies - 89p-17/9d - but inflationary prices were imposed even so.

For a time both currencies were acceptable, apart from cheques which had to be in the new currency from the start. Comprehensive guidelines were issued on how to cope with the novel situation. For example, if one patronised an L.s.d. shop and wanted to buy some sweets costing 1/2d, one could either give one shilling and two pence in old currency or, in decimal coinage, 5p, 2p and a halfpence, making 7.5p. As this equalled 1/6d old money (one shilling and six pence), change of 4d was due. How long such a transaction could take was not explained.

In the week prior to "D-Day" the British Bankers Association operated a chartered light aircraft to and from the Island to freight sackfuls of cheques written in the old currency. Bankers were anxious to clear all L.s.d. cheques as fast as possible.

PINTA CHANGE

The daily pinta started to arrive on doorsteps in pyramid-shaped plastic containers as from Wednesday, February 3rd. That was when the Isle of Man Milk Marketing Association abandoned the sale of bottled milk. The Colby-based Belle Abbey dairy, run by Walker Bros Ltd, also introduced the containers for some supplies though it is still providing bottled milk too. The Tetrapack cartons were said by the Association to be light to carry, more hygienic than bottles and healthier because vitamins in milk were protected from the effects of sunlight. There was resistance from some consumers, however. They switched from Association rounds to supplies from dairy farmers who still supply bottled milk. They said they found the packets difficult to stack in fridges, they disliked being unable to see the cream and they were accustomed to leaving notes for milkmen in empty bottles.

REFINERY BATTLE

Indications that the long-promised oil refinery on the Ayres might go ahead at last has erupted into a major conservation battle. Tynwald seems tied to an old agreement whereby it is committed to ensuring that the refinery will be built but even in Government there is

pressure to stop it. The Harbour Board has indicated its hostility because of pollution fears. Until now it seemed that the venture had foundered because the American oil company, Natomas, was unable to raise the necessary funds because of U.S. and U.K. financial controls. Now it has obtained the funds internationally and wants to proceed.

MAJESTIC FACELIFT

Extensive improvements were completed in the spring at the Island's largest residential hotel, the Majestic at Onchan. It is now one of the best equipped conference hotels. Mr C. B. Bellamy, its owner and managing director, intends to keep the hotel open in the winter for functions and bar trade. Hotel manager is Mr Bernard Hamer. The dining room can sit 450 at one sitting and there is a well-equipped kitchen. The ballroom has been given a new look with carpeting and upholstered chairs, a new bar, new lighting and a redecorated stage for cabaret shows. All first floor guest rooms have hot and cold water, some with showers, and a third have been fitted recently with an enclosed bath and toilet. There is a spacious residential lounge with sea views on this floor and a television room overlooking the main entrance. Throughout, the hotel has been given an air of quality by rich carpeting. Bookings for the summer were good.

RISING POPULATION

The result of April's census shows the Island's resident population has made a remarkable recovery since the dramatic fall recorded in 1961. During the past ten years the population has increased from 48,150 to 54,581, the highest this century. Just about every part of the Island has shown an increase. This is attributed largely to the policy of attracting new residents. Most of these are of retirement age, which has created in imbalance in the age structure of the community, though some families have been attracted here, too, by new light industries and the current building boom. Government policy is to attract more. The newly-issued Island Plan is based on a population of 75,000. The Local Government Board's Planning Committee says that only 5% of the Island is developed. There is plenty of in-fill areas that can be built on before any significant spread into new areas. Despite this, there are calls for population controls so that the Manx identity can be preserved. In the past, small numbers of new residents have been assimilated with ease. The problem now is that there are too many too

1971 CENSUS FIGURES		
Results of the recent census are given below with a percentage comparison with the 1961 census.		
DOUGLAS	19,847	(+5.4%)
RAMSEY	4,909	(+30.0%)
PEEL	2,958	(+19.0%)
CASTLETOWN	2,724	(+75.8%)
Port Erin	1,620	(+30.7%)
Port St Mary	1,451	(+15.1%)
Laxey	1,140	(+1.3%)
Onchan Village	4,625	(+40.9%)
Michael Village	491	(+58.4%)
Andreas Parish	814	(+3.1%)
Arbory	862	(+21.2%)
Ballaugh	514	(-5.1%)
Braddan	2,008	(+9.5%)
Bride	322	(-6.6%)
German	737	(+2.2%)
Jurby	537	(-32.5%)
Lezayre	1,128	(-7.4%)
Lonan	971	(+7.6%)
Malew	1,920	(+1.5%)
Marown	979	(+13.4%)
Maughold	700	(-9.6%)
Michael	391	(+12.0%)
Onchan	386	(+13.9%)
Patrick	991	(+1.2%)
Rushen	1,186	(+43.8%)
Santon	370	(+2.8%)
TOTAL	54,581	(+13.4%)

Part of the huge crowd which thronged the Valley Gardens for the revival of the traditional Laxey Fair. Dozens of stalls in the upper part of the Gardens did brisk business. (Frank Cowin Library)

container base. A Commissioner felt the tail-race should have been filled in and a new bridge built at the head of the harbour. In Douglas the development of container traffic led to the demolition by the Steam Packet of the former Imperial Hotel, which had been the company's head office since 1887. The new head office, opposite the Peveril Hotel, was opened in 1969. The Imperial Hotel site is occupied now by a huge crane which handles the containers. The former Royal Hotel is being used as an office for the goods and catering departments.

FAIR REVIVAL

Dancing until midnight in Laxey Glen Gardens ended a revival in July of the original Feailley Laxa which survived until well into the 19th century. In those days, stalls for farm produce were set up on the meadows where the harbour is now and men traded horses and cattle. This time, gaily decorated stalls were set up by local organisations in the Valley Gardens and did brisk business. The area was packed with people. There were tug-of-war, wrestling and judo competitions, Manx folk dancing, music by Laxey Brass Band and singing by Aeglagh Vannin and the village choir. The evening began with guests arriving in the M.E.R.'s royal car. The Lieutenant-Governor and Lady Stallard came in a vintage Daimler. At 7.15 p.m. Laxey Band led a parade from Mines Road, down Church Hill to the Valley Gardens. Hundreds of children and adults dressed in period costume added a Victorian atmosphere. His Excellency and Lady Stallard were welcomed by Mr J. W. Kneale, chairman of Laxey Commissioners, Mr H. C. Kerruish S.H.K., his fellow member for Garff, Miss Jean Thornton Duesbery, and Mr Hugh Condra, chairman of the Laxey Fair Committee. After a formal opening by His Excellency, crowds watched Laxey schoolchildren perform their 'Pageant of the Mines'. The evening went with a swing and village licensees did such a roaring trade that fair committee secretary, Mr Maurice Faragher, said he hoped it would become an annual event.

quickly. Also, many are middle-class retired people who tend to move into neat centrally-heated bungalows on estates and keep to themselves. Others, who move into large old houses or build new ones, remain aloof from the day-to-day life of the Island. Critics of Tynwald's policy fear a repeat of what happened in the Channel Islands. The local population was swamped by wealthy new residents who sent property prices soaring. This is beginning to happen here. Now Tynwald is being urged to provide low cost housing to meet the needs of young Manx people who are necessary to preserve a balanced society.

NEW TOWN BRIDGE

Castletown Commissioners accepted an offer in May by Tynwald to build a new fixed road bridge over the harbour in place of the swing bridge. It should be completed by next year. The bridge was deemed necessary because of traffic problems caused by freight containers being craned on to the quayside. The town's M.H.K., Mr C. L. P. Vereker, however, said the answer to the rise in container traffic was a properly organised

GAIETY THEATRE SAVED

The Gaiety Theatre was saved from threatened demolition in February. Tynwald agreed to buy it from the Palace Group for £41,000 rather than see it replaced by a shopping arcade, flats and offices. Speaker of the House of Keys, Mr Charles Kerruish, said the theatre would provide a home for the Island's amateur societies which provided an element of culture.

Tynwald had no intention of running the theatre, however. Nor did it propose a Government-financed renovation programme, apart from some urgent repairs and decoration. Mannin Entertainments Ltd, owned by local businessmen John Marsland and Ken Daly, leased the theatre for 20 years. Part of the agreement was that it would undertake repairs and redecoration during the next ten years and in consultation with the Arts Council. This could be a formidable commitment as the Gaiety's structure and technical system has been in decline for years. The roof leaks so badly that water drips on to seats in the stalls. Chilling draughts, mainly from backstage, mean that winter audiences in the stalls bring blankets to wrap around their

knees and flasks of hot tea or coffee, sometimes laced with whisky! Performers have been forced to wear thick underwear. The theatre's stage lights are believed to date back to the earliest days of electricity. One operator says they are kept going "on a wing and a prayer."

Mannin Entertainments' main interest is summer entertainment. The running of the Gaiety during the winter, therefore, has been passed, at the instigation of the Arts Council, to a consortium composed of Douglas Choral Union, the Manx Operatic Society, the Legion and Service Players. The consortium's chairman is Director of Education and Arts Council chairman, Mr H. C. Wilkinson. The consortium has paid Mannin Entertainments £1,250 for a sub-lease of the theatre between November 1st and May 12th. This includes the use of the manager's services. The amount represents double the usual hire charges paid by the societies for their respective productions at the Gaiety. However, they have a full winter to fill with entertainment and can recoup some of the cost by hiring the Gaiety to other societies.

NEW SCHOOLS

More new schools and extensions are either being built or planned. It is in response to increased numbers of children. In April Ballaquayle Infants school was opened in Douglas and work started on building a new primary school at Ashley Hill, Onchan. A desperate need for a new school in Ramsey was identified. Director of Education, Mr Frank Bickerstaff, has warned the Education Authority also that at least 675 new places in secondary schools will be needed soon, sufficient for a new half million pound school. Extensions to the Ballakermeen sections of the Douglas High Schools are being mentioned and an extension to Castle Rushen High School has been approved. A new Onchan secondary school is being considered; also one in Peel, which has been demanding one for years.

The present accommodation crisis will mean delays in the raising of the school leaving age to 16, to bring the Island into line with the U.K. Even so, the teachers' unions support it and Board of Education chairman, Mr Victor Kneale, has given notice that he is to propose it in the House of Keys. He has given notice also that it is the Board's intention to build a College of Further Education in the Douglas area to replace the old Technical College.

POSTAL TAKE-OVER

The principle of a Tynwald take-over of Manx postal services was agreed in the autumn - but it could be nearly two years before it happens. Abandoned in the 1960s because of fears over losses and opposition by Post Office staff, campaigners, led by Mr Victor Kneale M.H.K., got the go-ahead after overcoming, in part, two of the principle obstacles. Originally, the U.K. had said that if the Island took over the postal services it must acquire also the telephone system. That was where the big costs lay and Tynwald did not want them. The attraction of the postal services was that the Island could issue its own postage stamps to promote itself internationally and, hopefully, make a lot of money. Negotiators achieved a break-through in that the U.K. agreed to separate the postal and telecommunication sectors of the Manx Post Office and defer a Manx take-over of the latter for up to ten years, during which time the telephone service would be modernised. Staff who were concerned about the loss of promotion prospects in the U.K. Post Office and about pay and working conditions in a future Manx-controlled operation, received assurances, meanwhile, that they could retain transfer rights to the U.K. Post Office for five years. Now negotiations on the detail of a Manx take-over of postal services and the designing of the first Manx stamps are proceeding. The capital cost, including all Post Office property, is put at £127,000.

CASINO LOSSES

Shareholders in the Palace Hotel and Casino reacted angrily in June to losses of £162,000, sustained by organised junket trips to the casino of gamblers from Canada. The gamblers left unpaid gambling debts and hotel accommodation bills which could not be recovered.

At the same time, U.K. newspapers reported that London businessman, Mr Judah Binstock, was behind a £250,000 deal to buy a one-third stake in the casino company. He was reported also to be investing in Manx property.

T.T. ATTACKED

World champion and T.T. hero, Giacomo Agostini, made an astonishing attack on the T.T. in June. He said in Milan that course safety measures were insufficient. It was "crazy" to compete in such conditions. He thought the course should be banned and threatened to ask the M.V. Agusta factory not to compete in the event again. The attack angered people connected with the T.T., especially those who had implemented recommendations on course safety. After the deaths last year of six riders, racing stars Peter Williams and Tommy Robb were asked to inspect the course and suggest improvements. The result was the improvement of two miles of road surfaces, repositioning of flagmen and an increase in the number of straw bales from 1,500 to 2,000. A-C.U. secretary, Mr Ken Shierson, said he was surprised at Agostini's attitude. There had been no complaints from other riders. In fact, others had been complimentary about the improvements.

Prior to his attack, Agostini brought his tally of T.T. wins to eight with another comfortable Senior win. In the Junior race he stopped with engine trouble at Ramsey on the first lap. This allowed some close racing for honours by the privateers. Tony Jefferies won on a Yamsel and Phil Read set the fastest lap on his Yamaha.

SUMMERLAND OPENS

Summerland opened for business on July 9th, though it wasn't strictly ready. Although proclaimed fire-proof, the Island's fire chief wanted an extra emergency escape from the upper terraces in the form of a bridge well away

1971
- Britain adopts Decimal currency
- USSR launches the *Salyut I* space station
- Disney World opens in Florida, USA

Summerland opened in July as a unique all-weather entertainment centre. The main hall shown here is surrounded by plastic Oroglas tinted in bronze to give natural light the effect of golden sunrays.
(R. & L. Kelly Collection)

The Lady of Mann, pride of the Steam Packet fleet for 41 years, was bade an emotional farewell by the crowds who turned out to witness her final departure from Douglas. (Stan Basnett)

centre, the management could be held responsible. The provision of artificial sunshine, therefore, had to be confined to a sun dome where bathers could be restricted to half an hour.

Despite this, the sensation of being outdoors whilst undercover captured imaginations. Part of the effect was achieved by the incorporation of the cliff face in the structure and the provision of a waterfall cascading down it. Several real palm trees added to the atmosphere. Blackpool Town Council sent representatives to inspect the place immediately it opened.

FINAL DEPARTURE

The Steam Packet's flag ship, the Lady of Mann, made her last departure from Douglas on the sunny night of August 20th. Built to the highest standards of craftsmanship in 1930, the Steam Packet's Centenary Year, she had served the Island for 41 years and had played an heroic role in World War Two. Few Manx people have not sailed on her. Thousands stretched from Onchan Head to Douglas Head in an emotional tribute to the 'Lady.' She blew them long farewells on her siren as she set off for Birkenhead. She was towed later to Glasgow for breaking up. Hundreds of enthusiasts are reported to have applied for mementoes.

from the transparent acrylic Oroglas cladding of the exterior walls. The bridge was a condition of a Douglas Licensing Bench licence but when the complex opened, the lessees - Trust Houses Forte Leisure Ltd - were still building it. Work on it continued for several weeks when business was quiet, usually between 9 p.m. and 11.30 p.m. As a temporary measure, in case of an emergency, a builder's ladder was propped against the bridge.

Built by Douglas Corporation on the former Derby Castle site, the Summerland structure cost about £1.5 million, including £645,000 of Government assistance. The lessees spent a further £500,000 on equipping it.

What opened, however, was not quite what people had expected. There was no artificial beach and man-made sunshine wasn't everywhere. It had been discovered that if anyone suffered sunburn in the

NUNNERY FOR SALE

The future of the Nunnery mansion house and its estate, which covers most of Douglas Head, is uncertain. The house and grounds have been put on the market, priced at £110,000, by the owner, Mr Robert Bacchus-Goldie-Taubman. Hopes that Tynwald might buy the property were dashed when it rejected the idea. A public petition, however, is calling for it to reconsider. The Nunnery estate was inherited by its present owner in 1970 following the death of his 88-year-old mother. To inherit, he had to add the names Goldie-Taubman to his own.

COPING WITH THE U.K. POSTAL STRIKE

The first postal strike in the history of the U.K.'s Post Office ended on March 7th after more than six weeks of disruption. It started on January 20th. During it, the Isle of Man gained its own privately-run postal service with matchbox labels as postage stamps! Post Manninagh was run by 45-year-old Douglas manufacturer and wholesaler of tourist novelties, Mr Gordon Quirk.

Mr Quirk's Island Distribution Company, of Duke Street, Douglas, launched the service when a national strike over pay halted normal postal services. He did so at first without official approval. When it became clear that the dispute would be a long one, however, the U.K. Post Office waived its monopoly rights and agreed to authorise private collection and delivery services in Britain by approved operators. Mr Quirk applied for authorisation as one and received it via Douglas Head Postmaster, Mr George Christian, on January 27th. It lasted until the Post Office letter service was restored.

Everything happened so quickly that Mr Quirk had no time to produce suitable postage stamps. He used instead the paper covers for souvenir matchboxes which he was printing in readiness for the summer season. These depicted an outline of the Isle of Man in two

colours. The brand name of the matches - "Ad Match" and other wording such as "Foreign - Average Contents 30" - was guillotined from the outer edges of the design. Other souvenir matchbox covers depicting the Three Legs of Man were used as demand for deliveries soared beyond Mr Quirk's expectations.

His delivery charge in the Isle of Man for all mail weighing less than five pounds was 1s 6d. Delivery was guaranteed either the same day or within 24 hours.

Stamps were cancelled by a numbering machine which had been used previously for invoices. Eventually, Mr Quirk printed pictorial stamps with decimal values of 25p, 50p and £1. These depicted the T.T. and Douglas harbour. Post Manninagh also launched an overseas delivery service, using couriers, and issued a few commemorative covers. Printing stamps and making deliveries became a seven day a week job between 7 a.m. and 10 p.m. When it ended, philatelists feared that the market might be flooded with mint stamps. In fact, Mr Quirk had been so busy providing a legitimate postal service he had not had time to mass produce items for collectors.

BLACKPOOL FESTIVAL

History was made at the Blackpool Music Festival when, for the first time, all four finalists in the Oratorio Solo class were Manx. The winners of the sections were soprano Alison Deakin of Colby, bass singer Wally Curphey of Braddan, tenor Jim Mitchell of Douglas and contralto, Joyce Gilrea of Port Erin. In the final Wally Curphey repeated his success of last year. Prior to this, Jim Mitchell won the Light Operatic solo class and Muriel Curphey was second. Mr Mitchell also won the Vocal Solo (British Composers) class and Muriel Curphey won the Vocal Challenge class. Cleveland Medal winner, Margaret Murray, won the Negro Spiritual class and, with Tom Gelling of Braddan, won the Open Duet class. Peter Cringle (tenor) also won high praise when he competed in the final of the Operatic solo.

TERRORIST ATTACK

The Ramsey Steamship company vessel, Ben Vooar, had more than £2,000 of damage caused to her in October by a terrorist attack whilst berthed at the Irish port of Cork. An explosion occurred two hours after her arrival but none of her crew of seven was injured. Police said five pounds of gelignite wrecked the bridge and the main mast. If the I.R.A. had targeted a Manx vessel, it was thought the attack must have been a mistake.

ARRIVALS SLUMP

The number of passengers who arrived by sea and air this season dropped by 29,560 to 465,297, the lowest total since 1966, the year of the seamen's strike. The figure included a drop in day trippers - 93,989 - as none came from Fleetwood or Llandudno. The overall reason for the drop was blamed on increased travel costs. Hopes for the future lie in Steam Packet plans to provide a mid-week service from Fleetwood next year now that improved berthage is available. A new car ferry is also being built. This will open new areas. Another breakthrough is that major package holiday firms such as Cosmos plan to include the Island in their 1972 brochures.

Mr Gordon Quirk who hastily set up his Post Manninagh to provide a postal service during the strike by U.K. postal workers.

1971 NEWS IN BRIEF

JANUARY
14 - Three people died after an accident involving two cars near Marown church on the Douglas to Peel road.
15 - Total ban on the import of live and dead poultry due to fowl pest epidemic in England.
22 - Tynwald approved plan to establish a Consumer Council.
26 - Keys pass final reading of Bill to lower the age of majority - the right to marry and vote in elections - from 21 to 18.
29 - Traffic lights installed at St Ninian's crossing, Glencrutchery Road, Douglas.

FEBRUARY
4 - Appeals Committee upheld Health Services Board decision to site a group practice surgery at Ramsey Cottage Hospital. Ramsey and northern residents opposed the plan because of a lack of transport to the site.
5 - By a 6-2 vote, Onchan Village Commissioners rejected a plan to seek town status.
10 - Douglas Town Council appointed an expert to advise on the feasibility of the decades-old plan to amalgamate Douglas with Onchan Village. The Commissioners reacted vehemently to the idea.
12 - Commemorative stone unveiled on the wall of Ramsey Court House in recognition of the public service of Ambrose Spencer Kelly M.H.K., J.P., member for Ramsey from 1946 to 1969.
15 - Day of change-over to decimal currency.

MARCH
5 - Port Erin decided to seek talks on possible union with Port St Mary.
19 - Ballaugh Wild Life Park lost £16,000 in a year.
19 - Ramsey Commissioners criticised the new Lezayre Road estate, alleging that houses were not weatherproof.
26 - Manx Electric Railway deficit of £66,000 estimated for the coming year.

APRIL
1 - Improved facilities at Ronaldsway Airport came into use. A covered pier connected the terminal and air traffic control buildings and provided a waiting room for passengers and new customs accommodation. The old Customs hall was used for a conveyor system for arriving baggage.
2 - Ramsey rates increased by 25%.
9 - Use of the Ayres as a gun range by the Army was seen as a threat to the area.
23 - Grenades found by children at Ballamoar, Foxdale.

MAY
21 - Trustees of Isle of Man Children's Home spent £10,750 on an extension to the Children's Home at Knottfield, Woodbourne Road, Douglas.
25 - British rally star Roger Clark won the Manx Trophy Rally in an Escort RS 1600. John Huyton and Horace Saville finished fourth in a Lotus Cortina.
28 - Lifeboat and helicopter used in cliff top tragedy at Port Erin.

JUNE
4 - Record Ramsey Yacht Week - 100 craft in the harbour.
4 - Row over early morning explosions on the Ayres during army exercises.
12 - Ray Ellington and his band broadcast live on B.B.C. Light Programme from the Isle of Man Holiday Centre.
15 - Government to support bus operators, I.O.M. Road Services and Douglas Corporation, by rebate on fuel taxes and grants towards maintenance.
18 - Bid by M.H.K. for southern swimming pool defeated in Tynwald.
23 - First Manx £10 notes issued.
25 - Souvenir hunters blamed for the disappearance of Manx flags from poles on the processional way to Tynwald Hill.

JULY
9 - Go-ahead for £800,000 new Government offices.

SEPTEMBER
17 - Ramsey Commissioners buy Plaza cinema for £10,500.

OCTOBER
26 - Protests about plan to build new observation tower at Jurby Head in connection with the bombing range.

NOVEMBER
5 - Boy saved from drowning in Mooragh Lake, Ramsey.
17/18 General Election. Shock result in Castletown. Mrs Elspeth Quayle ousted Mr C. P. Vereker. In East Douglas Miss Katherine Cowin took seat from Mr Charles Burke.
24 - Mr Charles Kerruish, Speaker of the House of Keys for 10 years, re-elected.

DECEMBER
3 - Douglas was said to have a drug problem. The smoking of 'hash' was "quite prevalent."
10 - New law on accidents to passengers. Drivers must insure.
24 - New car ferry, Mona's Queen, launched.

The *Lady of Mann* leaves Liverpool for the last time in August 1971.